A

CW00689838

ries

RUDOLF STEINER'S CURRICULUM FOR WALDORF SCHOOLS

An attempt to summarise his indications

A collection of quotations for the benefit of the different Waldorf Schools

Karl Stockmeyer

"Today it is not enough merely to think about the world. One needs to think about the world in such a way that one's thinking gradually becomes imbued with a sensitive feeling for the world. For from out of such a feeling there grow the impulses for reform, for working at greater depth. Anthroposophy wants us to reach an understanding of the world which will not remain in the abstract but which will evoke a sense of what needs to be done and in this way become a foundation for pedagogy and for the art of teaching."

Rudolf Steiner (27)

Steiner Schools Fellowship Publications

Alice Lanagh-Davies

Issued by the Steiner Schools Fellowship 1969
by permission of the Rudolf Steiner Verlag, Dornach, Switzerland
and of the Verlag Freies Geistesleben, Stuttgart, Germany

Translated by Roland Everett-Zade from the Second German Edition of 1965
by kind permission of Frau Anna Stockmeyer

First edition	1969
Second edition	1985
Third edition	1991

This edition, with extensive revisions and corrections,
produced in the present format and
edited by Stephen Cradock
April 2001
Reprinted October 2001
Reprinted February 2005
Reprinted January 2007
Reprinted March 2011

ISBN 1 900169 10 X

All rights for the text are held by
(German) Rudolf Steiner Verlag, Dornach, Switzerland
(English) Steiner Schools Fellowship Publications

Steiner Waldorf Schools Fellowship
Kidbrooke Park, Forest Row, East Sussex RH18 5JA
Telephone (01342) 822115 • Facsimile (01342) 826004
E-mail: office@steinerwaldorf.org
Registered Charity Number 295104   Company Number 519230

Typeset in Times 10 point
Produced by Imprint • Crawley Down • Sussex RH10 4LQ

Contents

SECTION 1: SCHOOL AND LESSONS IN GENERAL

SECTION 2: THE CURRICULUM ARRANGED ACCORDING TO SUBJECTS

SECTION 3: OTHER ASPECTS

Preface

The content of this book was given to the teachers of the Steiner Schools (*10), to enable them to work from a "living" curriculum given by Dr. Rudolf Steiner. Although the following volume was not written by him it contains many indications, admonitions, advice on education and classroom work, etc., which can be found scattered over his extensive works. This compilation of his principles of education was made so that they may live ever more deeply among the teachers working in the Steiner Schools.

It is not my intention to preserve as a dogma what was built up between the years from 1919 to 1924. Nor would it be right to alter the original "Lehrplan" (the first curriculum published in 1919) because "the children of to-day have undergone great changes".

People incarnating at the present time are bound to have a different world outlook from those born around 1919. Nevertheless, one would greatly underestimate Steiner's teaching if one believed that the pedagogical impulse which he called the educational task of the fifth post-Atlantean epoch in the first lecture of his course "Study of Man" was already out of date one generation after its inception.

Considering the fact that Steiner never intended to form a dogma, but that for him the respect for the freedom of the individual was of paramount importance, the attitude of a Steiner School teacher could only be one of reverence for the pedagogical bequest of a great personality, and together with like-minded colleagues one would wish to put into practice an ideal of human striving. One can only hope that such an attitude will bring forth truth and blessing and that it will work livingly into man's future development. May history show that Steiner's art of education has made an impact on man's development and that it has worked towards the salvation of Mankind. However, this will only happen if those who feel called upon to nurture this impulse also show a certain loyalty towards its ideas until in time they may recognise by the results their rightness and effectiveness.

This loyalty is quite easily broken unconsciously, with the result that one may believe Steiner's aims to be quite impracticable, whereas in reality one had not struggled sufficiently to fulfil his demands.

The teacher of Steiner's methods has to face a twofold riddle: on the one side there is the riddle of man himself and on the other there are the problems arising from Steiner's various indications about the actual teaching. Both will have to be experienced by the teacher, the former awakening in him the desire to understand the child's soul–life and the latter making him wish to find the proper soul nourishment for the child in the fifth post-Atlantean epoch.

This then leads us to a twofold task: to a most careful meditative study of Man and to the working out of countless indications. One can only encourage people again and again to persist in their efforts regarding the former, and much could be achieved if in the different Colleges (*12) just this task could be pursued with relentless vigour. Towards the second task the author of this work wishes to make a contribution by having compiled the many different remarks and indications of Steiner so that the reader may experience directly the problem arising from the apparent contrasts and even contradictions of the different suggestions.

The way in which Steiner has expressed his ideas on education immediately calls upon the teacher to act out of his own inner freedom, an approach which is inseparably bound up with work in Steiner Schools. Steiner's indications are never dogmatic – they always allow free scope for the teacher's initiative and they encourage him to find his own answer to the various problems.

I owe a debt of gratitude to my friends of the first College of Teachers (*12), who have augmented this book by making available advice given to them personally by Steiner, and also to those colleagues who have given me the results of their own attempts to create their lessons and courses. Special thanks are due to Dr. Erich Gabert and to Dr. Karl Schubert whose notes of the Teachers' Meetings (Conferences) (*4) with Rudolf Steiner have really made this work possible.

Furthermore, I thankfully acknowledge the full support of the Pedagogical Research Centre of the Rudolf Steiner Schools Fellowship (die Pädagogische Forschungsstelle beim Bund der Freien Waldorfschulen) for this publication.

The reproduction of Steiner's quotations in this publication has been approved by the executors of Rudolf Steiner's literary works in Dornach (Rudolf Steiner Verlag Dornach).

E. A. Karl Stockmeyer
Malsch, October 1955

Notes on the Use of This Book

Data in brackets after quotations or in the text refer to the Bibliography, e.g., (23) or (23 lecture 4) or when asterisked, e.g., (*4) to the Glossary.

Figures and letters put in brackets e.g. (2.6.22) refer to the "Conferences" (*4) which were compiled by Dr. Erich Gabert and Dr. Kart Schubert and published for work in Steiner Schools. They indicate the date of the meetings.

Brackets found within a quotation of Rudolf Steiner suggest amendments or corrections of otherwise unintelligible passages in the shorthand notes.

Explanatory Note regarding the English translation

Quotations from Rudolf Steiner's lectures already translated into English have been used in this book.

Indications for Mathematics Teaching has been translated by R A Jarman; and Eurythmy and Gymnastics by A W Mann.

German terms which have no parallel in English expressions are explained in the Glossary.

Any additions or explanations, which are suggestive and not authoritive, have been inserted in brackets.

Finally the reader is reminded that the word "German" in the curriculum refers to the mother tongue and not to a foreign language.

Roland Everett–Zade
Heidelberg, December 1966

Glossary

Numbered asterisks in brackets, e.g., (*3) found in the text refer to this Glossary.

*1	Abitur	Secondary school leaving examination consisting of a set of some ten subjects taken after nine years at a secondary school. Only this examination qualifies for entry into a University (translated: school leaving exam).
*2	Einheitsschule	A school which was to put Rudolf Steiner's pedagogy into practice (translated: Comprehensive Steiner School) – see *9.
*3	Gymnasium	A secondary school leading to university entrance, based on the humanities with Greek and Latin as compulsory main subjects.
*3A	Oberrealschule	A secondary school leading to university entrance, with emphasis on the sciences. These schools have become modified since World War 2.
*4	Conferences	Teacher Meetings. The "Conferences" quoted in this book took place in the early years of the Waldorf School (*10) under the guidance of Rudolf Steiner. Shorthand notes of these meetings are published under the title "Conferences". (41)
*5	Kulturrat	A group of people, chosen by Steiner, who aimed at influencing the cultural life in Germany towards a more spiritual outlook.
*6	Lebenskunde	A study of all kinds of activities in life, such as agriculture, industry, commerce, transportation, etc, whose aim is to lead towards a social consciousness of the world. Translated: Lessons Preparing for Life.
*7	Sachunterricht	Lessons given to the children from six to nine years old. In this subject the teacher is to interpret the child's surroundings in an imaginative way. Farming, housebuilding and stories about plants and animals belong to this subject. Translated: Home Surroundings.
*8	Seminar	A course of practical training for teachers which was initiated by Rudolf Steiner in August 1919. Translated: Discussions with Teachers. (13)
*9	Volkspädagogik	Rudolf Steiner's education programme, free from compromise and catering for all types of pupils up to the eighteenth, nineteenth year. Translated: Comprehensive Steiner Education. (*2).
*10	Waldorf Schule	The original Steiner School, opened in 1919. Translated as Steiner Schools when sister schools opened later are referred to.
*11	Weltanschauungsunterricht	A study of subjects which will help the student towards a philosophy of life, towards a world outlook. History, geography and the sciences form the core of this study.
*12	College of Teachers	The name given to the body of teachers in a Steiner School. It was intended that the teachers should work together without a headmaster.

Bibliography

Works of Rudolf Steiner are quoted without the author's name.

Writings and lectures of Rudolf Steiner which are important for the understanding of his art of education and his curriculum. The works given below are in the text with a number and shortened title. Where a translation is readily available the English title is given.

1   Einleitungen zu Goethes Naturwissenschaftlichen Schriften.
Goethe the Scientist.

2   Grundlinien einer Erkenntnistheorie der Goetheschen Weltanschauung.
A Theory of Knowledge Implicit in Goethe's World Conception.

3   Wahrheit und Wissenschaft. Truth and Science.

4   Philosophie der Freiheit. Philosophy of Freedom.

5   Veröffentlichungen aus dem literarischen Frühwerk.

6   Die Erziehung des Kindes vom Gesichtspunkte der Geisteswissenschaft.
The Education of the Child.

6a   Von Seelenrätseln. The case for Anthroposophy.

7   Die Kernpunkte der sozialen Frage. Towards Social Renewal.

8   Ansprache vom 24 April 1919.

9   Drei Vorträge über Volkspädagogik, Stuttgart 11, 18 May, 1 June 1919.
A Social Basis of Primary and Secondary Education.

10   Die Aufgaben der Schulen und der dreigliedrige soziale Organismus. Stuttgart 19 June 1919.

11   Allgemeine Menschenkunde als Grundlage der Pädagogik. 14 lectures Stuttgart August- September 1919. Study of Man.

12   Erziehungskunst – Methodisch – Didaktisches. 14 lectures Stuttgart August-September 1919. Practical Course for Teachers.

13   Pädagogisches Seminar. 14 discussions August – September 1919. Discussions with teachers.

13a   Die Erziehungsfrage als Sociale Frage. 6 lectures Dornach 9 – 17 August 1919. Education as a social problem.

14/15 Die Waldorfschule und ihr Geist. 2 lectures Stuttgart 24 and 31 August 1919.

16   Drei Lehrplan-Vorträge, Stuttgart 6 September 1919, Three Lectures on the Curriculum*.

17   Ansprache bei der Eröffnung der Waldorfschule. Stuttgart 7 September 1919.

18   Übersinnliche Erkenntnis und sozialpädagogische Lebenskraft. Stuttgart 24 September 1919.

19   Die pädagogische Grundlage der Waldorfschule.

20   Erster naturwissenschaftlicher Kurs – Lichtlehre. 10 lectures Stuttgart 23 December 1919 – 3 January 1920. The First Scientific Course (The Light Course)*.

21   Zweiter naturwissenschaftlicher Kurs – Wärmelehre. 14 lectures Stuttgart 1 – 14 March 1920. Heat Course.

* Steiner Schools Fellowship Publications.

Quotations on Education and Anthroposophy

"Discriminating people nowadays demand a type of education which does not aim merely at dispensing knowledge, but which tries to call forth capacities; an education which does not merely sharpen the intellect, but which works towards a strengthening of the will life. The rightness of this attitude can hardly be doubted. However, one cannot train the will and its underlying soul life unless one develops an understanding of what it is that awakens impulses in the soul and in the sphere of will. A mistake which is frequently made nowadays is not that too much knowledge is given to young people, but that one gives them knowledge which does not stimulate and develop real initiative in life. Whoever believes himself able to train the will without giving it the proper nourishment in education is under an illusion."

"To be clear on this point is the task of an up to date pedagogy. This clear insight can only be the result of a living understanding of the whole human being." (19)

"In a way Spiritual Science makes one tend at every moment to forget the spiritual content of what has been absorbed previously through Spiritual Science, so that one needs to absorb and recreate it ever anew. One does not possess Spiritual Science as something which can be remembered... In this way I have also tried to prepare the teachers of the Waldorf School so that they should enter their classrooms with a kind of virgin soul, in order to face a completely new situation, completely new riddles every time. To be able to forget – and this after all is only the other side of inwardly digesting – is what Spiritual Science trains one to do: it is a result of self-discipline gained through Spiritual Science." (23)

"Mankind had a different task in the first post-Atlantean epoch, a different one again in the second, and so on right into our fifth post-Atlantean epoch. And it is a fact that mankind recognises what has to be achieved within such an epoch only a certain time after the actual beginning of the epoch. Our present epoch began in the middle of the fifteenth century. Only today does the recognition of what needs to be developed in the pedagogical sphere in our own epoch emerge to a certain extent from the spiritual background. Until now educators have worked in the old way, out of the aims of the fourth post-Atlantean epoch, however full of good will they may have been. A great deal will depend on our attitude towards our new task, on our being able to understand that we have to give education quite a definite, new direction, not because it will be valid for all times, but because it is right for our time." (11)

The question arising from these words is further illumined by the following words of the Ilkley Course, given in the year 1923. There, in the lecture of August 7th, a survey of the development of education is given and the problems are elucidated which arise from the development of the social life from Ancient Greece, via the Middle Ages right into our own time. A number of clarifying sentences have been chosen from this lecture:

"The thoughts of the Greek towards a child's education ran approximately as follows: I bring up the child in the best possible way if, through my attitude, I keep the growing forces, which the child has developed up to his seventh year, as fresh and healthy as possible; if I educate him in such a way that these forces which are there up to the seventh year, remain with him throughout his life right until death. This was the great and mighty principle of Greek education, this significant maxim: to ensure that the child in man should not become lost until death." (35)

"We can but admire Greek education. However, it was based on three conditions, on ancient slavery, on the position of womanhood in ancient times and on the attitude towards spiritual truth and spiritual life of those days. None of these conditions prevail today, nor would they be considered worthy of the human race." (ibid.)

"Mankind then developed a new consciousness which would not tolerate slavery, and which brought about the respect for the rights of women. At the same time, within the development of the individual, the growing child between the seventh and fourteenth year – that is during a stage when there is not only a physical development but when the soul is becoming emancipated from the body – the growing child would no longer accept the continued preservation of childhood forces, as it had been practised previously." (ibid.)

"And so, during the Middle Ages, education was tossed about like a ship which could not keep its proper course in a storm, for it is extremely difficult to grasp the human soul. One can get at the body, one can exchange ideas about the spirit, but man's soul is so deeply hidden within the individual that it is most difficult to fathom it. But it was entirely a matter of the human soul whether man could find his own inner way to those authorities, which safeguarded traditions for him, whether reverence could grow in such a way that the word of the medieval priest-teacher was strong enough to anchor tradition within humanity... And it needs tact of soul to foster the memory in others without violating their inner freedom by inculcating what one would like them to absorb." (ibid.)

"For a long time within man's development these difficulties prevented him from finding clear aims in education and they made the period in which tradition and memory had to be developed appear an extremely difficult one for educational ideas. Today we have reached a point in history when man demands certainty in his aims, when he is no longer satisfied with unsure fundamentals as was the case in the Middle Ages. This searching for a new foundation has resulted in the numerous endeavours for educational reform, and out of the recognition of this fact Waldorf School pedagogy has arisen. It rests on the question: How can we educate if the pupil's soul between the seventh and fourteenth year continues to rebel against the attempts to preserve the childhood in him? But how can we educate if, apart from this question, man has lost the old medieval relationship to tradition and memory, as is the case today? Outwardly man has lost his trust in tradition, inwardly he wants to become a free agent who, at every moment, faces life without prejudice." (ibid.)

1

This is the concrete question of the pedagogy of the fifth post-Atlantean epoch which Rudolf Steiner wanted to answer with a deed through the Waldorf School.

Introduction

The final Steiner School curriculum, at least for the first eight classes of the then existing middle school, was given to the Waldorf School in the three so-called "Curriculum Lectures", held on 6th September 1919. These lectures conclude the pedagogical training course given to the first group of teachers, which contains the "Study of Man", the "Practical Course for Teachers" and "Discussions with Teachers" (*8) (see 11, 12, 13).

It was elucidated and supplemented in numerous teacher meetings (*4). When in Autumn 1920 a ninth class was to be added Steiner gave it a new curriculum which was extended year by year. (41)

In the Spring 1923 (meanwhile the opening of a new school year had been put forward to Easter) a twelfth Class was opened for the first time. This class was the equivalent of the top class in a Gymnasium (*3) ("Oberprima"). The parents took it for granted that their sons and daughters would take their final school-leaving examinations (Abitur *1) at the same time as they would have done in a State school. Steiner wanted to oblige them although he was forced to make some grave compromises because of the demands of the official examination authorities. He did not feel at all happy about the situation and looked upon the necessary compromise as a very unsatisfactory makeshift.

In Spring 1924 he therefore decided to make a drastic change in the arrangements by authorising a new curriculum for Class 12 which was based entirely on his pedagogical principles and which would give the pupils the proper conclusion to their education, irrespective of whether they wished to take the final school-leaving examination or not. Furthermore he planned to prepare those pupils who had passed through Class 12 and who were suitable candidates for the examination, in an "Exam-Prep-class" (Vorbereitungsklasse) as he wished it to be called. In this class they were to be taught whatever the existing examination authorities demanded beyond what the Waldorf School curriculum had offered. This "Exam-Prep-class" was instituted for the first time only after Rudolf Steiner's death on March 30th 1925. Meanwhile the school-leaving examinations had been put back one year also in the other German State schools in accordance with the School Laws of the Weimar Constitution.

Steiner intended to work out systematically in writing the curriculum which so far had only been given orally, but he was unable to carry out his intentions. Much of what he had planned for the Waldorf School has remained a challenge. However, the curriculum with its full details does exist and its author expressed how he wanted it interpreted.

> "We ought to approach this curriculum in such a way that we could recreate it ourselves at any moment; we must learn to read in the children how they should be taught in their 7th, 8th, 9th, 10th year etc." (12 14th lecture)

Soon after Steiner's death Dr. Caroline von Heydebrand, with the help of several colleagues, undertook to formulate and to publish the curriculum according to Steiner's indications. In autumn 1925 this valuable effort was published.

A whole generation has passed since the first edition of Heydebrand's publication. Meanwhile many lectures and lecture courses which Steiner had given during the last years of his life have become generally available. Furthermore Dr. Erich Gabert and Dr. Karl Schubert have collected all shorthand notes and notes of the teachers' meetings (Conferences *4) at which Steiner was present. These notes have become a most valuable mine of information which was only partly available to Caroline von Heydebrand when she compiled her version of the curriculum. It therefore appears justified to revise and to enlarge Steiner's indications for the curriculum.

It would not be in keeping with Rudolf Steiner's art of education to fix its underlying principles into a tight scheme. His educational work remains half-way between two poles, one of which concerns the child's physical, mental and spiritual development. And through the ages this changes only very gradually. The other polarity consists of the social and cultural background in which the children will have to live, and this second pole is liable to change more rapidly. Both poles must be fully appreciated by the educator. However, apart from this polarity there are the actual children with their different characters and their quite individual aims, and among them there stands the teacher with his own personality, temperament, previous training and life experience, with his knowledge, ability and world outlook; and finally, between all these there is the curriculum. When dealing with younger pupils the curriculum must tend more towards the first pole, towards the observation of the typical stages of development, and more towards the second pole when teaching adolescents; for the adolescent must make his link with the cultural situation of his time in order to be able to play an active part in life. However, all this must remain fluid in order to remain alive. A fixed educational system would never answer the problems of such a living process. Thus a real curriculum should lead the consciousness of the educator towards certain necessities, but it nevertheless must allow full scope for the teacher's inventive interpretation. For it is the enthusiasm which will come about by really meeting the child, the creative stimulus born out of this meeting with the child, which can produce perhaps quite unique inspirations just at the right moment, so that they will work as a blessing upon the child because they were born out of the teacher's full participation, out of complete spiritual freedom and out of love for each pupil.

Therefore the proper curriculum should only be a collection of all the pupils' needs in their different stages of development, which the teacher of the various age groups should fully bear in mind. The curriculum could answer these needs in two ways: it could indicate subject matter to be covered and it could give pedagogical hints. Anything further could only be examples of the conditions in which the pupils live, enlivened by the teacher's gifts. The world makes its claims and the teacher meets these consciously, considering them in his pedagogical work just as carefully and deliberately as an engineer has to consider the laws of stability in his constructions. However much these claims may restrict the teacher, there ought to be the freedom for him to choose the content, his examples and his practical teaching methods,

Steiner looked upon his curriculum as meeting such outer demands. But he also made many suggestions, partly because of the particular situation of a teacher but also because he wished to illustrate by examples how some of these demands could be met in practice, for sometimes it is simpler to illustrate a point by a concrete example than to explain it by a general definition.

This, however, does not mean that the teacher in a Rudolf Steiner School can do as he pleases. Steiner looked upon the curriculum's fundamentals as strictly binding. Just because he had been able to recognise the particular needs of each stage in the child's development and then base his principles upon them, he had to insist on his instructions being carried out faithfully. A few very critical remarks of his prove this. Thus on 10th May 1922 he said, after hearing a language teacher declare that he could not fulfil the curriculum's demands:

"The compromise has already been made in the curriculum (this refers to what was already added to the curriculum in order to enable pupils to change over to State schools). If we fulfil the tasks of the curriculum we will also reach the necessary level for our pupils to pass examinations. But not every effort is being made to put our curriculum into practice." (10. 5.22)

The following sentences, spoken shortly before the above quotation in connection with the curriculum of class XI, are to be understood in a similar way:

"We shall have to discuss the curriculum in detail, especially with regard to this eleventh Class. For here the difficulties of achieving a practical classroom technique (i.e. for the pedagogical ideas to have become experience and habit) really become apparent. With this technique we simply must get them far enough to pass examinations." (10.5.22)

Furthermore, on 21st June 1922:

"Something which does not belong here has arisen namely, real slovenliness. Slovenliness has crept into the school because one has allowed oneself to take the easy way." (21.6.22)

Steiner was convinced that pupils in Waldorf schools could pass exams if the curriculum given by him were strictly applied by the teachers. Nevertheless there is a tendency to neglect the curriculum because of examination work, whereas in reality this is an excuse for not truly fulfilling its pedagogical demands. Steiner, however, reckoned with the entire human and pedagogical dedication for this curriculum. In this way we must also understand the following sentences, spoken on 28th April 1922, in answer to a complaint of a language teacher that the pupils would not be able to enter a class of the same age group in a State school:

"This problem can only be solved if we work through our curriculum from the bottom upwards. One cannot solve the problem with pupils entering Class 4 or 5. We must solve it with the pupils who have been with us from Class 1 onwards... In this case it would be our failure if we did not succeed. In the essential subjects we must get our children far enough to pass examinations." (28.4.22)

The above-mentioned thoughts are expressed very clearly in Steiner's answer on 9th December 1922 to a request by a shorthand teacher to make shorthand lessons optional:

"This is a pity. When do we begin to teach this subject? In Class 10. I cannot understand why they (the pupils) should not like it. Many things are being judged by us without our being aware of the fact that we have a different approach and a different curriculum from other schools. Since I have been in classes more frequently I can say that compared with other schools we obtain good results if we apply what is generally called Waldorf School pedagogy. If the necessary results have not been achieved we should ask ourselves whether somewhere, quite unconsciously, we have failed to apply our methods. I do not wish to be hard, there is no need for a thunderstorm every time, but the Waldorf School methods are not being carried out in every class. Sometimes there is a falling back to a lazy routine – wherever our methods are applied results are being obtained... Even though the standards of the language classes vary, really good work is being done there. There are good results in the lower classes in what is usually called calligraphy. In arithmetic lessons I have the feeling that often the Waldorf School methods are not being carried out." (9.12.22)

After these words Steiner proceeded to clarify his remarks about shortcomings, as can be read at the appropriate place.

It is not my intention to give a complete summary of Rudolf Steiner's art of education, as such an attempt would go far beyond the scope of this study. Nevertheless it seemed expedient to include hints which may be of practical value by refreshing the memory of those already familiar with Steiner's art of education, and by stimulating the new reader to further thought while at the same time drawing his attention to Steiner's numerous lecture–courses, especially to the fundamental Stuttgart courses of 1919 (11, 12, 13). A close study of these courses is essential for a deeper understanding of Rudolf Steiner's pedagogy.

The plan of this study of the curriculum could either be based on the different subjects which are being taught simultaneously in each class, or on one subject at a time throughout the different classes. In the first instance one is concentrating on only one stage of the child's development and one can see how each subject brings a contribution towards the entire education at one particular stage. In the second case one follows through the entire development of the child with each subject anew, and one can experience how the child is being led by the particular discipline of each subject. Both ways have advantages and every teacher has his own way of working. It therefore appears helpful to follow both courses, first the one according to subjects in detail, and then the one following the different age groups in a more condensed form.

SECTION 1 – SCHOOL AND LESSONS IN GENERAL

1 Different Phases in the Development of the Curriculum

The following lines, written by Rudolf Steiner before the opening of the first Waldorf School, show how his picture of the school gradually took form, how it developed and even changed, in order to suit outer circumstances.

In 1898, in an essay entitled "Secondary Education and Public Life" (not yet translated) in "Magazine for Literature" (5) he sketched a plan for future education:

"Primary schools have the enviable task of making the young people into real people in the truest sense of the word. There the teachers must ask themselves what natural talents are hidden in every person and what they must bring out in each child so that the pupil may finally realise his own humanity in balanced integration. Whether the child will one day be a doctor or a ship-builder need not concern the pedagogue who teaches him at the age of six. His task is to make him into a full human being."

About the task of secondary schools he wrote:

*"The teacher of a 'Gymnasium' (*3) cannot possibly arrange his work following a similar line of pedagogy... A real 'Grammar School' pedagogy would have to answer above all the problem of what needed to be developed in the pupil between his twelfth and eighteenth year."*

He continued:

"One has to weigh up the needs of the individual man with those of practical life."

About the "Abiturium" (* 1) he wrote:

*"Usually the young people entering further education or a university are eighteen years old. At that age anyone who will later be able to produce good work as a chemist is able to understand a fundamental text book on chemistry. If one were to make the examination syllabus of a 'Gymnasium' (*1) serve a useful purpose one should bring the candidate up to a level where he could comprehend and methodically progress with any scientific textbook which starts at the beginning."*

After referring again to the complete picture of Man which should be the aim of the teacher in primary education, he continued:

"Colleges and universities do not have to consider such a picture of man's nature. This is not at all their function, for they are an institution and their task is to make such an institution a true reflection of the cultural background of the times. How the student fits himself into his college or university as far as choice of profession or his social needs are concerned, is his own affair."

He concluded:

"One can see how I visualise a college or university. Like a microcosm it should mirror perfectly the cultural conditions of its time and at the same time it should offer the highest degree of individual freedom. The student should be given the opportunity to absorb as much as possible of the civilisation and culture of his time, but no restrictive regulations should accompany his progress. (5)"

This picture of a future education allows full scope for further expansion which its author has made later in life. With regard to the question whether a Steiner school should be an ideological school, i.e., a school in which anthroposophy should be taught directly, Steiner answered in a meeting of representatives of the "Bund für die Dreigliederung des sozialen Organismus" (Movement for the Institution of the Threefold Social Order) on 24th April 1919:

"Above all we should never open anthroposophical schools. Anthroposophists ought to transform the methods and organisation of the school, but never teach Anthroposophy directly. We ought to be the first one to realise the importance of spiritual freedom. Above all we must avoid the founding of ideological schools."

In answer to a further question as to whether feelings of insecurity and disunity would affect the children if they experienced that their teachers were teaching them from entirely different and even opposing ideological backgrounds, he said:

"Here a pedagogical factor enters. If we educated the children up to their fourteenth year all in exactly the same mould and then let them loose into today's struggle for existence, we should turn them all into neurotics. However, with the spiritual freedom (of the teachers) truth will reign in the school instead of hypocrisy and this will be the compensation. In education it is far less important which religion lessons a child has attended than that one meets the child with an inner truth." (8)

After Emil Molt's decision to open the Waldorf School, Steiner outlined its first curriculum on 25th April 1919 in the presence of Emil Molt, Herbert Hahn and myself. He recommended that the pattern of an Austrian "Unterrealschule" (comparable with our Secondary Modern Schools) should be followed, taking pupils up to the age of sixteen. In German (the Mother tongue) the curriculum should lead up to business correspondence; in History, the history of home surroundings should be studied after a course of general history, and geography should be approached in a similar way. Languages, above all English, were to be taught, and mathematics and physics, the latter with special emphasis on mechanics; also natural history, drawing and especially painting; singing and gymnastics were to be included. He made a list of the number of lessons per subject per week, without however mentioning main lesson periods, which were introduced later. He then pointed out that the teaching of Latin was merely a tradition left over from Monastery schools of the Middle Ages and that Greek was of more value. He said that the Gymnasium (*3) was producing a mummified education which would without doubt disappear in the future, and that the teaching of mechanics was of greater importance than that of Latin.

Such a school was to become the generally accepted school of the future. The two years which were missing from the secondary education (of his time, which consisted of three years of preparatory school and twelve years of secondary education) would be allocated to the university courses which would use them for general education before passing on to a specialised training. Internal university examinations would also become simplified so that only the final examinations leading to degrees and full qualification would remain. Degrees however would not secure privileges, as only quality of work and ability would count in the free competition of life.

My notes, written from memory immediately after the conversation end here. I should like to add that these indications of the education of the future were made under the assumption that the impulse for a threefold society would have become a reality by the time the Waldorf School (*10) was instituted.

On 25th May of the same year Steiner gave me a draft of the curriculum worked out in greater detail, based on the condition that there should not be more than 150 pupils in the school grouped into eight classes. This was known already on 25th April and on that date Steiner had advised us to put together two classes at a time. On 25th May he worked out the curriculum which is given below on the basis of combined classes, because it offers an insight into the gradual development of the final curriculum. The following notes were written at that time:

> "Before the 12th year all subjects to be taught by the Class teacher.
>
> **Class l and 2:** Reading – analysierend, i.e. ...from the whole word to the letters (Cp. "Look and Say Method" in England) – writing – drawing – first steps in arithmetic – singing – music – eurythmy – languages 'ad libitum':
>
> 1 English, 2 French. (ad lib according to ability of teacher and pupils?)
>
> **Class 3 and 4:** Reading – the children becoming conscious of the grammar in the language ("Betrachtung der Sprachform") appreciation of colour ("etwas Farbenbehandlung") – singing, music and eurythmy to be continued – adding and subtracting (up to 100 in Class 1), arithmetic tables from memory – free choice of animals and plants.
>
> **Class 5 and 6:** Mechanical concepts derived from the study of a cart – subjects of the previous year to be continued – animals and plants – basic concepts of meteorology and climatology (rain and sunshine, rising and setting of stars, seasons) – quite general concepts of geography – in arithmetic: proportions.
>
> **Class 7 and 8:** Resume previous work – study of the mother tongue leading to the structure of poems, meter of verses, art forms in poetry – continue everything else.
>
> **Class 7:** The complete process from the grain of wheat in the field to the finished product, bread.
>
> **Class 8:** Different trades – matters concerning plants (Pflanzen Betreffendes) some meteorology – some

> geography – historical concepts; pre-Christian, post-Christian, Indian, Persian, Egypto-Chaldean, Graeco-Roman culture – geometrical drawing leading to concepts in geometry – commercial arithmetic, first introduction to book-keeping – perspective drawing – a simple introduction to algebra – astronomy leading to the Copernican system.
>
> Later: Compare languages (e.g., testa – tête) – technical drawing, plans, maps – mathematics up to equations – conic sections, applied geometry, levelling – architecture – concepts of technical chemistry – commercial style – elements of book-keeping – Weltanschauungsunterricht (* 11) – Man: body, soul and spirit – descriptive geometry – first aid."

Much of the above is reminiscent of the lectures on Volkspädagogik (*9), e.g., the theme of the cycle of a grain of wheat, the study of trades, commercial arithmetic, commercial language, and the lessons about world philosophies.

Other points already contain later features, such as the "Look and Say Method" of reading in Classes 1 and 2, the art forms in poetry, geometry developed from drawing, perspective drawing, technical drawing, plans, maps, applied geometry, levelling, architecture, technical chemistry, descriptive geometry, first aid.

It is of particular interest to find that proportions for Class 5 and 6 are only mentioned in this place, thus remaining the only indication as to when proportions should be introduced.

About 10th June 1919 Steiner spoke to me about the structure of the curriculum and about the new plan in which some subjects were to be rearranged. During three to four days of the week – so he said – there was to be singing during the first lesson, and on the remaining days, drawing instead. (There were six school days a week). This was to be followed by, say, arithmetic, a subject taught in periods, and then religion. Lessons were not to begin before 8.00 am and were to end at 12 noon. Classes above the first class were to have fewer lessons. The afternoons were to be given over to practical activities.

In the third lecture of the Volkspädagogik (*9), given on 1st June 1919, main lesson periods are mentioned for the first time. In the above-mentioned conversation of 10th June Steiner included them in the daily lessons for the first time, but they were not yet placed at the beginning of the morning sessions, as artistic activities were to be taken first.

On 15th July 1919 Steiner gave me a list of subjects which were to be taught in main lesson periods: German, including reading and writing – English – French – mathematics – geography – nature study history. Singing and gymnastics, so he thought at that time, might have to be dropped after the fourteenth year in order to make time for other activities.

Here the two living languages are included in the main lesson periods, whereas later they were to be given in single lessons.

About the 4th July 1919, Steiner stated in a conversation that since it had not been possible to institute the Movement of the Threefold Social Order the possibilities of reforming eduction should now be made use of.

A decisive change of outer circumstances thus became evident. No longer could the Waldorf School (*10) be looked upon as part of the threefold social order which was intended to support and to carry it. It became clear that the school, as a seed of a free spiritual life, would have to fight for its own existence and recognition within the general social background of the post-war years. This fact should be borne in mind when the development of Waldorf Education is studied. And it was in this situation that the Free Waldorf School (*10), based on Steiner's curriculum, was finally opened in autumn 1919. (Compare 12 lecture 13)

Steiner gave a cross-section of the "ideal" curriculum (i.e., a curriculum free from compromise) in the 10th lecture of the Practical Course for Teachers (12) which deals with the three smaller phases of the child's development between the change of teeth and puberty. This lecture is particularly instructive because it throws light on fundamental principles and is therefore a good introduction to the fundamentals and aims of the curriculum.

In the 13th lecture of the same course Steiner speaks about the compromise which has to be made to bring the pupils in the lower classes to a level acceptable to the State authorities.

Finally, on 6th September 1919 and following the pedagogical courses given to the chosen teachers of the new school, Steiner gave the three Curriculum Lectures (16). In these lectures, which in their short but concentrated form are a most important contribution, Steiner more or less finalised his pedagogical aims for the first eight years, and these were supplemented only in two ways: (a) through particular examples given by him in the teachers' meetings, and (b) through the extended syllabus for the new classes of the upper school.

When the Waldorf School was opened Rudolf Steiner sent a memorandum to the Minister of Education in Würtemberg, in which he stated to what degree the Waldorf School was prepared to adjust its own curriculum in order to enable its pupils to change over to another school. Here is a copy of its text:

"Re: Curriculum

The College of Teachers of the Waldorf School asks for permission to use the available lesson time during the first three years according to its own educational principles only; on the other hand it will aim at bringing its pupils to a level entirely corresponding with that of a public primary school by the end of the first three years. This intention is to be carried out in such a way that a pupil of the third class wishing to change over from the Waldorf School is able to enter a fourth class of another primary school without difficulties. In the fourth, fifth and sixth school years the arrangement of lessons and approach to subjects is again to be left entirely free to the teachers of the Waldorf School. At the completion of the sixth year the pupils are to have reached the level of the sixth class in a primary school, or that of a class in a secondary school which corresponds to the age of twelve. The same arrangement is to be made again up to the completion of the eighth year. The pupils are to reach the standards of secondary education,

so that they are able to change over to classes of the same age in any other school of secondary education. The College of Teachers asks for a free hand in teaching its pupils only during the periods ending with the three age limits mentioned above:

1 From the beginning of school until the completion of the ninth year.

2 From the ninth year until completion of the twelfth.

3 From the twelfth year until completion of the third age limit.

At the end of these periods the Waldorf School is to reach the same standards of achievement as any State schools."

Steiner has spoken about this memorandum in several of his lectures, and in greatest detail in the Easter Conference 1923 in Dornach:

"And so, since our at aims are not founded on fanaticism, but always on objective reality, something bad had to be done right from the start, namely a kind of compromise had to be made. From the very beginning a memorandum had to be drafted in which I had to lay down the following points: In the first three classes the children are to be taught, if possible, from stage to stage according to the needs of the growing child. At the same time, during those first three years, the teacher must bear in mind what is generally demanded of the children in other schools, so that after the third class a child could change over to an ordinary primary school. This must be for the teacher – I have to use this tautology – a "leaning-over-backwards-compromise". It is inevitable. A realistic person has to act like this, for discretion is essential. A fanatic would act differently. Many difficulties will of course result from such a compromise and many a teacher would find it much easier to steer a straight course towards his aims. A great deal needs to be discussed in detail so that one can find the right way between the two aims. Furthermore my original memorandum stipulates that when the children have completed their twelfth year i.e., when they have completed Class 6, they again can enter the appropriate class of their age group in any other school. The reason for my choosing this particular year is based on the fact that man, as he has been described here in the last few days, stands at a special point in his development at this particular age. Again, pupils must be able to change to another school of their choice after the fourteenth year. Well, all this works fairly smoothly in the first three classes. At this first stage you can achieve something in this manner. It can also be attempted with a great deal of trouble up to the twelfth year. The real difficulties only begin with the later years. For, although this happens almost unconsciously, out of a dim feeling of man's true development which has been preserved from ancient times, the time of the change of teeth is still considered the right moment for the child to enter school proper." (34)

In his Basle Course for Teachers (23 lecture 5) Steiner also spoke about his so-called compromise; likewise in one of the Stuttgart teachers' meetings. After having dealt with the content of his memorandum and after pointing out that the same principle could be extended to the eighteenth year he said in this teachers' meeting:

"We must now see to it that we not only talk about this aim (of achieving standards of the State schools) but that by using the greatest possible economy of time in teaching we really do reach this aim. One really can get the pupils far enough to reach this required level. Examine a pupil in the "Obersekunda" (7th year in a German Gymnasium (*3), the equivalent of Class 11 in a Steiner School) and make allowance for all he has forgotten, examine what he knows in history. You will find that our pupils of the same age could have the same knowledge of history. Naturally we don't always cover our subject matter because sometimes the teachers are not in a position to prepare their lessons adequately. The lessons ought to be worked out still more carefully, then we could write the report (which had been discussed) with a good conscience." (28.4.22)

In the Oxford Course the memorandum of 1919 is also mentioned. There Steiner concluded, after calling the end of primary education a third stage:

" The same will happen when the children, well – the young ladies and gentlemen – leave school in order to continue their education at a college or university. There should be complete freedom from the time of puberty till the beginning of further education. But then the pupils should be able to gain entry to any college or university – for the Dornach "Hochschule" (High School or University) won't be recognised for a long time as an institution which students can enter in order to gain generally recognised qualifications." (29)

2 Aims and Problems

An outline of Steiner's hopes and plans for the future, which were to be put into practice in the Waldorf School, is to follow this last section on the development of the curriculum which was mainly dealing with the past.

First of all he wanted to plan anew the syllabus of modern languages; and secondly he wished to introduce a partial streaming in the last classes of the school with special regard to the teaching of trades and apprenticeships. These two problems led him to redraft the curriculum, which was to be an organic continuation of all that the main lesson periods had already introduced. Other problems we also discussed, but they were left in abeyance to be tackled at some future date. Nevertheless these problems did affect the considerations of the day. Here are some of Steiner's views regarding the replanning of the foreign language lessons and streaming in the upper school.

Replanning the Foreign Language Lessons. Streaming in the Upper School

During the last teachers' meeting of the first school year

Steiner said, somewhat unexpectedly:

"It is easier to cope in language lessons because here matters are not fixed quite so much according to classes (presumably he referred to the subject matter to be covered in each class). We should not adhere too strictly to division into classes in the language lessons. This system has simply evolved, but on the whole there is no need to arrange language lessons strictly according to classes." (24.7.20)

After a remark about something quite different Steiner continued:

"In general we can say that in the language lessons it is feasible to mix older and younger pupils, because the younger ones will learn from the older ones and the older ones will progress by having to pull along the younger ones. It is possible to mix the ages." (ibid.)

A year later, towards the end of the Waldorf School's second year, Steiner said after hearing a report of a language teacher:

"One can try to achieve something by dividing pupils into groups. We could form groups of pupils of similar knowledge and ability." (26.5.21)

And, after a few other remarks, as if to confirm and conclude his ideas on the subject, he continued.

"We shall have to replan the language lessons." (ibid.)

Then general remarks about language teaching followed which need not be repeated here. However, it became clear that language lessons had to be replanned.

Some six months later, when asked what he thought about extra coaching in foreign languages, Steiner answered:

"We must investigate whether it would be feasible to give language lessons to selected groups of pupils rather than to the usual classes." (16.11.21)

Again a year later Steiner stated that the pupil's shortcomings in the language lessons would not be improved by an increased number of lessons:

"The maximum number of language lessons has been reached... because of it the children are unable to concentrate properly. It would be necessary to allow them to decide which languages to take. This means that pupils wishing to pass their "Abitur" (*1) should be limited to Latin and Greek lessons. They would have to drop other subjects. They ought to cut down on modern languages and should be given more scope for Latin and Greek." (15.10.22)

"The trouble is that pupils of similar calibre are not put into one group. Would it really be impossible to regroup the children?... Teaching languages in classes has become an established custom. This is a dreadful waste of our energy. Would it really be impossible to give language lessons to ability groups and not in the usual classes?... I do believe that this would work. I think it would. I believe that it would be possible to group pupils according to ability, that one could teach in this way and nevertheless cover the ground of the curriculum. I think one could manage with the same number of lessons. I can't imagine that it would be impracticable to have certain lessons of the week

earmarked for languages to be taught in ability groups. In this way it would work." (ibid.)

On 28th October 1922 the difficulties of the time-table, which had to remain fixed after the main lessons, were discussed in detail. Steiner's attempts at grouping pupils in language lessons according to ability played into these deliberations; so did his wish to partly stream the upper classes, beginning with Class 7, to enable the more academic minded pupils to take their examinations and to free from Latin and Greek those who would not need these subjects for their vocational training. An attempt was made to fit these requests into the time table. When the Latin teacher asked that the ancient language lessons should be taught in double periods immediately after the main lessons Steiner answered:

"This is a good idea, especially if one adds a little colour to the lessons by teaching more formal work in the first period and using the second period for readers. In that case it is better to have a double period. With regard to Greek and Latin it is only possible to keep languages going if one lets the pupils decide from a certain class upwards whether they wish to choose French and English or Greek and Latin... We must work towards getting the children to pass examinations (Abitur *1). This can only be achieved if we allow them to choose – in full co-operation with the parents – Greek and Latin, or French and English. Since we teach French and English from the first class onwards we can no doubt do something about going over old ground again in these languages for the older pupils who are taking Greek and Latin, if they so wish. But we must accept this rearrangement of lessons." (28.10.22)

After a question on a different subject he continued:

"But since we begin teaching foreign languages from Class 1 upwards it would be hopeless if we were not able to continue with these languages in the upper classes with a minimum time for revision because they need Latin and Greek. We must manage somehow to spare time for this. We cannot keep going as matters stand now." (ibid.)

Finally it was decided to give pupils in the upper classes who wanted to take examinations in Greek and Latin (which were compulsory subjects of the Abitur (*1) only a few revision lessons in French to enable them to concentrate on Greek and Latin, but they would have to give up English. This arrangement was to begin in class 7.

A timetable was made for the lessons following the main lessons, which was to make it possible for language lessons (ancient and modern languages) to be given during the first two periods after the main lesson, so that groups of pupils could be made according to ability and knowledge. Details of such a timetable will be given in the section dealing with the timetable.

When the above plan was being worked out Steiner remarked:

"Now we can interchange pupils. But we must see to it that we retain the same number of language lessons as previously. Such a surgical operation can't

be considered pedantically. We shall have to carry some two to three weak pupils who are unable to keep up with their group." (ibid.)

However, this "surgical operation" was not carried out immediately at all. Steiner only wanted it put into practice *"when he could be present for a few days."* (ibid.)

Steiner looked upon this new arrangement of modern language lessons and the streaming in the upper classes as an important step in the history of the school and greeted this event with the following words:

"This will cause a big change if we are aware of the present situation. We must be clear about the implications. This great change will spread its effect right into the main lesson subjects, even into the soul of the children. The children will realise that at least some matters are being tackled in earnest." (ibid.)

He added in conclusion:

" We shan't be able to alter the present grouping into classes in language lessons until the new timetable is fixed. Perhaps it would be a good thing if all of you would show an interest in the new timetable."

The "Big Change" was not the new timetable. It was the decision to reorganise the modern language lessons and consequently the relinquishing of the established division into language classes, taught by the same teacher; also the decision to stream the upper classes according to ancient and modern languages.

In the next teachers' meeting of 24th November 1922 the new timetable, based on the discussions of 28th October, was checked. Steiner once more clarified the aims of grouping according to ability in modern language lessons after an objection that it was "irrational" to have so many language groups:

"This attitude is the result of wishing to keep to the old arrangement of teaching languages in classes. From a pedagogical point of view, this old arrangement need not be continued after Class 4. I admit that up to Class 4 the Class teacher should give the language lessons to his class. To stick to this practice after Class 4 is not necessary." (24.11.22)

The way for the regrouping of modern language lessons was now definitely open. Meanwhile a questionnaire given to the pupils of the upper classes had shown that only four to five pupils wanted the humanistic "Abitur" (*1) (which included Greek and Latin) if they had to give up English. Steiner nevertheless insisted that even such a small group should be given the opportunity to take the "Abitur" (*1). He even declared:

"I would even go so far as to say that we could use the first lessons of the day for Latin and Greek for those pupils who wish to take the examination in classics. We would look upon these lessons as main lessons and could postpone science lessons to late in the day." (ibid.)

Shortly afterwards he said:

"Now and again it does happen that one teacher is needed for only a few pupils." (ibid.)

Then after many doubts among the teachers:

"Those pupils who demand a humanistic examination (i.e. Latin and Greek) must give up English. If they are not prepared to do so they must give up their examination. There only remain four or five pupils from all classes who would take this examination. If we continue teaching Greek then we must see to it that those four or five can take their examinations." (ibid.)

A further sentence followed which is not quite clear:

"Two things are involved: whether we should deprive our pupils of the possibility of learning Greek? I don't mind so much about Latin. Should we deprive the pupils of the possibility of learning Greek?" (ibid.)

Its implication however is quite clear: Steiner believed it to be of the utmost importance for the Waldorf School to offer its pupils the opportunity of taking the Abitur (*1) and also to learn and study the Greek language.

The streaming in the upper classes was arranged in the following way:

"Let us tackle it as follows: up to Class 8 inclusive – Greek. In the 5th, 6th, 7th and 8th Classes Latin and Greek will be compulsory subjects of the Waldorf School curriculum, but we will nevertheless allow certain pupils whose parents do not want these languages to be freed from these two subjects... Streaming could begin with Class 9: either Greek or English. At this point we have to separate the Greek and Latin lessons. I think that we shall come back to the Waldorf School principles of teaching Greek and Latin in Classes 5, 6, 7 and 8 as well as the modern languages, and begin streaming only in the last classes. In this way we ought to get the children to examination level." (ibid.)

This settled the streaming in the upper classes. Later on in other Steiner schools it was adapted to examination demands by offering the choice of either French or Greek instead of English or Greek.

The other point, that of the reorganisation of the modern language lessons, was left in abeyance and was not discussed again during the following months. Only in 1923 Steiner spoke about it again after a complaint by a language teacher about the difficulties of covering enough ground because of the presence of particularly weak pupils:

"It would perhaps be desirable to settle the whole language business separately, and to put new pupils, who have not yet been taught these languages, together with the younger ones. We should put such pupils into lower classes. The new arrivals would simply have to join the next lower class for languages." (3.5.23)

The reorganisation of the modern language lessons was not put into practice after all. However, Steiner continued to favour it, but it was no longer discussed. As a teacher of other subjects, who was not directly involved in the problem and who had followed the talks with Steiner more as an observer, I gained the impression that not only objective arguments, such as the difficulties of recasting the timetable, were held against his proposals. I felt that personal aspects also played their part, such as attachments to pupils whom teachers would have lost under the new arrangements – attachments which were looked upon as

karmic connections. All this finally led to a complete silencing of the plan to regroup language lessons when, in the summer of 1924, a new timetable was made for English and French.

At the reopening of the Steiner Schools after the collapse of Nazi Germany new attempts were made to overcome the resistance to the remoulding of language groups, the resistance of indolent hearts, but still without success. Nevertheless we should not simply drop Steiner's earnest proposals which he persistently reiterated.

Steiner's views about language teaching are most clearly illustrated in the previously quoted sentences of 24.7.20 and of 24.11.22. These show that up to Class 4 languages should be taught by the Class teacher if possible, and that after Class 4 they should be taught separately from the usual class system. These views correspond to Steiner's curriculum indications of 2.6.24 where it is suggested that Classes 5 and 6 should be taken together, as also Classes 7 and 8. Class 9 should be taught as a single unit, while Class 10 should be grouped together with Classes 11 and 12.

It would not be too difficult to make a timetable in which Classes 5 and 6, and again Classes 7 and 8, would share language lessons. One must realise that by this arrangement each class would be linked for one year with the class above and in the following year with the class below. Following this arrangement, the same two groups composed of younger and older pupils would be reunited as a class every two years, and this would enable each group to compare its own progress with that of the other group. The other consequence of such a plan, which also has a pedagogical aspect, would be the fact that there would be approximately twice the number of pupils in language lessons as in the main lessons. If lack of classroom space made this impracticable, one would have to halve these large groups again, which, after all, would only necessitate the same number of teachers as the conventional way of teaching each class as a unit.

The margin between the weaker and the intelligent pupils which, on 24th July 1920 Steiner called a makeshift arrangement, would hardly become wider by putting classes together, but the working together of older and younger pupils which Steiner thought to be beneficial could come into full play, especially in Classes 5 to 8. So Classes 1 to 4 would be taught language lessons in classes, Classes 5 to 8 would be joined with an adjacent class, upwards or downwards; Class 9, with its special task of grammar, could concentrate on its work as a single unit; and in the upper classes, where a contact with the folk soul and the art of the other nation is striven for, the emphasis on the more pedagogical side of teaching would be of less importance anyhow.

Considering that Steiner made such efforts to free the language teaching from the fixed age groups – and the various passages of the published notes on the meetings (the Conferences (*4)) bear witness to this fact – and that he later dropped this question altogether and did not even mention it when the curriculum for modern languages was being discussed on 2nd June 1924 makes one strongly suggest that this problem should be taken up again anew. It is for this reason that the above suggestions were made.

Further Education and Training for Apprenticeship. School Leavers at Fourteen

In his lecture about "Comprehensive Steiner Education" (*9) given in the summer of 1919 Steiner spoke about teaching more mature adolescents:

*"Only from the age of fourteen can pupils be trained in forming judgements. At that age one can introduce what appeals to the powers of judgement. One can bring, for instance, matters relating to a logical understanding of realities. You will see that if, in future places of education, a joiner or an apprentice of mechanical engineering is sharing the lessons with a person who is going to become a teacher, then something will evolve which, though being a form of specialised education, still remains a kind of comprehensive school (Einheitsschule (*2)). In such a school everything will be offered which is needed for life – and if it were not included we should become involved in the social upheaval of our times even more than we already are. All teaching must contribute towards a more thorough knowledge of life. One will have to teach people aged 15 to 20, in a reasonable and economical way, everything connected with farming, trades, industry and commerce. Nobody should be allowed to pass through these years without having at least an idea of farming, trade, industry, and business. These subjects will have to be planned as disciplines which are far more essential than a lot of trash which is being taught nowadays. Furthermore at this age everything pertaining to what I should like to call matters concerning a world outlook (Weltanschauungssache *11) should now be introduced. This includes above all some knowledge of history and geography, everything which is connected with the understanding of nature, so that man will learn to know the human being in his relation to the whole universe. Among people trained in this way there will be some who, urged on by the social conditions to become workers of the Spirit ('Geistesarbeiter'), will be trained in special schools of spiritual science in all kinds of realms." (9 lecture 1)*

This passage characterises the aim which was to be realised by the Waldorf School Movement, namely the creation of one school catering for pupils right up to college or university level (Einheitsschule (*2)). In the early years after 1919 when the Waldorf School was going through its first stages the achievement of such aims was not yet possible. But one had experienced the importance of the unifying principle of the entire education and one had learned to look at pedagogical questions within the context of the whole social background. The teachers found it hard to accept that nothing could as yet be done for the further education of the young people who had to earn a living or who had to start a vocational training at the age of fourteen. Therefore time and again the request was made to Steiner to incorporate into the Waldorf School a centre of further education, in order to enable the school leavers of fourteen who had to go into an apprenticeship, to remain within the Waldorf School education. Steiner answered such a request in the following way:

"We should make the absurd mistake of putting the

children into specialised branches of training. We cannot do this if we wish to remain true to our pedagogical methods. We can only support what is helpful for man's progress. If we wish to open centres for further education we must do it in such a way that the children will benefit in their human education." (23.3.21)

Steiner obviously did not want to have anything to do with the established forms of evening classes or compulsory commercial schools, nor with countless colleges training students for many different specialised trades. He expressed his own picture of such a school in the following way:

"We must decide what kind of school we want to create. No one can doubt that S. (a teacher) was called to a comprehensive school of further education. It was supposed to be a college combining both the practical and the humanistic aspect of education. To build up anything different could not be our motive." (ibid.)

He wanted to unite the "practical vocational training" with that of a secondary school (Gymnasium (*3)) in the sense of the Waldorf School. But at that time he saw no possibility of realising such an aim within the Waldorf School, because the authorities of schools and centres for apprenticeships would not yield an inch from their established forms of training.

"What is missing is the possibility to educate the children from fifteen years onwards according to our curriculum. This has been stated previously. The question is therefore settled for the time being." (ibid.)

"This problem of using the time gap between school and adult training is most acute. If we could get the authorities to recognise us we should be absolutely overrun." (ibid.)

Stating that nothing could be done within the established forms of vocational training because "everything was sealed within watertight compartments", he nevertheless believed that new attempts should be made:

*'We should study the question of how to create centres for further education which could become places of education in the sense of the "Volkspädagogischen Aufsätze" (*9,9). The school ought to try to push this idea through to the authorities. We ought to gain more official recognition for the school." (ibid.)*

It is clear what Steiner meant in this last statement: to give young apprentices a broad general education, as was being done for the children who aspired to more academic professions. He wanted to stop the exploitation of apprentices by industry in order to gain time for their more general education, apart from an economically run training for their trade. The aim which he wanted to achieve for them became clear from the remark quoted above: "The most acute question is how to make use of the time between primary school ("Volksschule") and college ("Hochschule")". He wanted to use the four or five years which lie between the two schools in such a way that the apprentices who had been trained for their jobs would still have the possibility of attending a college or university, apart from receiving a broad general education in a Steiner school ("Hochschule"). The idea was to have Steiner schools in which – possibly side by side with classes of the more academic education – there should be courses for apprentice-pupils in which they would be trained for their jobs apart from receiving a broad general education. In the first lecture of the Volkspädagogische Vorträge (*9) Steiner had already mentioned the necessity of organising such schools.

This new type of school was never opened in Steiner's lifetime. Only during the years of rebuilding, after the collapse of Nazi Germany, several centres of education were opened in industrial enterprises, in which these ideas were seriously considered. In the Steiner schools of to-day the introduction of courses preparing for life, and technological courses, could be considered a beginning in this direction, but a full training in crafts and trades cannot yet be given. For such an extension of the Waldorf School would only be possible if sufficiently large numbers of such "practically-minded" pupils gave it a sound financial basis (since this was written full training in crafts and trades has been established in two or three schools, particularly in The Hibernia School in Wanna-Eikel in the Ruhr). For the time being the Waldorf School must remain unbalanced because in actual fact it cannot become a truly social unit. On the other hand, as long as we are unable to offer something really worth while to the non-academic type of pupil, we are bound to lose very substantial numbers of pupils after Class 8 year after year, because they have to go in for a practical training. They probably do not realise what a loss this means for their lives, but even if they knew they would still have to leave prematurely in order to earn a living at an early age.

Steiner, recognising this situation, arranged the curriculum in such a way that early leavers (at 14 plus) would at least take something into their lives which they could not get from their vocational training. In his last educational course he said:

> "We must also consider those children who have to leave school at puberty, at the end of the Elementary School period, and who cannot therefore participate in the upper classes. We must make it our aim that by this time, through the whole tenor of our teaching, they will have come to a perception of the world which is in accordance with life itself. This can be done in a twofold way. On the one hand we can develop all our lessons on science and history in such a manner that at the end of their schooling the children have some knowledge of the being of man and some idea of the place of man in the world. Everything must lead up to a knowledge of man, reaching a measure of whole-ness when the children come to the 7th and 8th classes, that is when they have reached their thirteenth and fourteenth year. Then all that they have already learnt will enable them to understand what laws, forces and substances are at work in man himself, and how man is connected with the physical matter of the world, how he is related to everything which is of a soul na-ture and how he is linked with the spirit-world, so that the child, naturally in his own way, will know how man is related to the whole cosmos. This is what we strive to achieve on the one hand.

> On the other hand we try to give the children an under-standing of life. It is actually the case today that most people, especially those who grow up in the town, have no idea how a substance, paper for instance, is made. There are a great many people who do not know how the paper on which they write or the material they are wearing is manufactured, nor, if they wear leather shoes, how the leather is prepared.

> Think how many people there are who drink beer and have no idea how beer is made. This is really a mon-strous state of affairs. Now we cannot of course achieve everything in this direction, but we can try to make it our aim as far as possible to give the children some knowledge of the work done in the most varied trades, and to see that they themselves also learn how to do certain kinds of work which are done in real life." (40)

Shoemaking

Steiner continues:

> "I should have dearly liked to have a shoemaker as a teacher in the Waldorf School if this had been possible. It could not be done because such a thing does not fit into a curriculum based on present-day requirements, but in order that the children might really learn to make shoes, and to know, not theoretically but through their own work, what this entails, I should have dearly liked from the very beginning to have a shoemaker on the staff of the school. But it simply could not be done be-cause one would have run into trouble with the authori-ties, although in real life such a skill would enable peo-ple to avoid trouble." (ibid.)

A small beginning in this direction was made in the Stutt-gart Waldorf School: a Class teacher had a very difficult boy in his last class and Steiner gave the advice that this boy should be instructed how to make shoes and that he should make a pair himself. Another teacher therefore spe-cially learned the art of shoemaking and taught the boy. This however was the only case and must be considered more as a therapeutic measure.

Anthroposophy for the Young

This title may surprise the reader who has been told repeat-edly that Steiner schools are not ideological schools, i.e., that Anthroposophy is not to be taught in them. Therefore this section can only deal with matters strictly outside the scope of the school. It is written for the benefit of maturing adolescents who approach their teachers with questions because they have heard or know that the teacher is an anthroposophist.

Towards the end of the last teachers' meeting of the year 1923/24 Steiner said spontaneously:

> "There is one more point to be mentioned. It is some-thing which is linked with all kinds of possibilities for the further development of our Anthroposophical Society. It is that in the near future something will evolve in Dornach which must be used to further our

pedagogy, namely that courses should be given to the students Of our "Fortbildungsschule" (College of Further Education) so that a new Anthroposophical Youth Group may evolve. I have often mentioned that Anthroposophy, as it is now, is really there for adults and that we should work towards an Anthroposophy for younger people. Anthroposophy is of course available for the young adults, as one calls young men and women. I am speaking about the kind of Anthroposophy which is suitable for the youths in their rough years of later puberty. This would have to he taught in real lessons." (9.4.24)

Introductory Lessons to Philosophy

This introduction to philosophy does not form part of the curriculum of the original Waldorf School. It was nevertheless given in the class which was preparing pupils for the examinations. Steiner spoke about it on several occasions. In his course on Comprehensive Steiner education (*9) he said:

*"You see, at the time when the Gymnasium (*3) – which nowadays is a terrifying spectre with regard to what is needed today – was the only place in which one could be prepared for higher education, when it still followed the pattern of the old monastery schools, which at their proper time were not bad, it still retained a quality which could be characterised in the following way: Man absorbed something which led him towards a point of view within a general world philosophy. An introduction to Philosophy (Philosophische Propädeutik) was one of the subjects in the curriculum of these schools. Admittedly it was only taught during the last two years; and in most schools it happened that the content of the second year was taught in the first year and vice versa... but at least something was there. It was a remnant of something for which the older High Schools catered so that during the first years the student was given the possibility of absorbing something of a general world philosophy, and only this would earn him the right to specialise for a profession. For nobody can be of any real use, when studying for a profession, who has not gained the possibility of forming reasonable judgments about human affairs.*

Today it is deemed unnecessary to teach man some logical and some psychological concepts which correspond to truth. Nobody can study higher spiritual life with advantage if he has not undergone the discipline of such logical and psychological ideas, if he has not earned for himself the right to follow such a path. All this has been completely wiped out by the later cultural and spiritual life which no longer wishes to look at man at all. This later cultural and spiritual life wants to force quite alien impulses upon man." (9 lecture 3)

This introductory course to philosophy was only mentioned during curriculum meetings when discussions were held about the preparation of Class 12 for examinations.

Steiner said:

"One could introduce philosophy (Propädeutik) in the last half year... It is better for the pupils of Class 12 to be prepared for this examination during the first half of the year rather than during the second half." (3.5.23)

So this philosophy course was to be given during the latter half of the year which was less crowded.

Steiner emphatically refused exercises in logic as a means of schooling the forming of judgments. In the Supplementary Course he said:

"It was by no means a mere whim when the request was made that all boys should learn how to knit etc. In this activity of the hands something is built up, is formed which actually considerably increases the power to form judgments. This ability to form judgments is helped least if one makes pupils do exercises in logic, for these exercises are not at all suitable for enhancing the power of forming judgments. If one makes the pupil join subject and predicate, if one teaches him logic in this way, one not only contributes nothing towards his ability to form judgments, but one even makes this ability quite sclerotic. The pupil will become the kind of person who in later life can only judge schematically. If one gives too many of such thinking exercises one educates man's mind to run on tramlines. Apart from this, such exercises cause too much salt to be deposited so that man becomes "pickled". He then tends towards sweating which we can observe only too well if we strain children too much by making them come to logical conclusions." (26)

Here exercises in logic are rejected, but not the introduction to philosophy.

School Leaving Examinations and University Training

Steiner had already spoken about school leaving examinations and university training in his early years, as far back as 1898, and his remarks have already been quoted in this book in the section on the different phases in the development of the Steiner School curriculum.

His observations on the same theme are a somewhat drastic evaluation of the situation which finally led to a plan to prepare pupils for the school leaving examination in a Class 13 which was added to the 12 classes of the Waldorf School.

In his lectures on "Comprehensive Steiner Education" (*9) Steiner spoke about the demands made by a university training:

"Naturally anyone caring for the cultural life cannot hope, nor even wish, that specialisation should be changed into universal dilettantism. However, it ought to be the aim to organise the entire education in such a way that the student always has the possibility, in what I should like to call the lower levels of his consciousness, to spin threads from his particular realm of specialisation which will link him to the universal culture of mankind. This can only be achieved if in every place of further education a general course is given before specialisation begins. Pedants will object: well, how can we cope with specialisation if this is done? One should really examine how economically one could

teach specialised subjects on the basis of such a general education, i.e., when teaching students who have been encouraged to develop their human potential." (9 lecture 3)

When, after its first year of existence a new Class 9 was to be opened as the first class of the upper school Steiner warned of the dangers of State interference in examination matters, which any negotiations concerning State aid might bring. He said:

> "There is no point in opening a Class 9 unless we contemplate the opening of a completely free university at the same time... Then we can be indifferent about their decision regarding the examination procedure. What matters then is the problem of recognition of our university. This is a problem which we cannot discuss at present. By then, conditions will have changed so that one can (not?) refuse the recognition of such a university." (29.7.20)

In the spring of 1923 in the Dornach Easter course on pedagogy Steiner said about the school leaving examinations (Abitur (*1)):

> "For a natural way of teaching and for a natural education the only question can be: does man learn to make the social contact in life which is an essential requirement of human nature? For after all, the people who make demands in their examination papers are also human beings, even though the style of these papers today is wrong. But if one wishes to adapt the Waldorf School pedagogy to the social demands of today, one is forced to do things with which one cannot inwardly agree. Therefore an official, when inspecting our top class, may well think: I do not find here what the ideal Waldorf School pedagogy sets out to do. But I can give you the guarantee: if we really were to carry out our education, which is read out of the nature of the child, especially if we tried to establish the proper links with the different branches of practical life, then all our pupils would fail their examinations. This is how matters are today." (34)

A few days later the whole complex of problems brought about by the first examination (Abitur (*1)) to be taken by Waldorf School pupils was discussed in every detail. Steiner remarked:

> "If we should succeed in getting our school reports recognised (by the authorities) our pupils could well follow a specialised study on the basis of what they have learned according to our curriculum. But the problem is that none of the stuff which they have to swot up for this examination (Abitur (*1)) is of use for the study of a specialised subject. You could build on Kolisko's chemistry. The specialists would at first feel shocked about the lack of knowledge as regards chemical formulae but our pupils can catch up on them. What is far more important is that one has the understanding of the inner relationship between the different substances and their chemical reactions. These are the points I wished to mention." (25.4.23)

After dealing with another question he continued:

> "To be able to make our own examination syllabus, which is our final aim, will not be possible for a long time. This would have been possible with the help of the Kulturrat (*5) which died a natural death after a few weeks' sitting. It would be desirable to create the conditions in which many private 'Realschulen' (*3a) and private 'Gymnasien' (*3) existed in Austria. There were many 'Gymnasien' attached to religious Orders which were allowed to mark their own examination papers. There were 'Realschulen' which were allowed to issue recognised examination results. There are no such schools in Germany as far as I know.
>
> What should be granted to us is that an official inspector is present during the examinations which, however, our own teachers would organise. After all, the inspector could hardly expect to give the marks if the examinations were held in the Waldorf School under the guidance of its teachers." (ibid.)

About a year later when the first Class 12 was about to take examinations Steiner summed up the whole problem:

> "It was the wish of the majority of our parents that we should give our pupils the possibility of continuing their education at colleges or universities. This wish comes from parents and pupils alike. In the beginning the pupils did not expect this to become a painful business and they were anxious to take their examinations. It is quite possible that they will do it but we do not solve the problem by sending our pupils to other schools. The question is whether it is right to solve it in the way which we have found extremely problematic and which we have already turned down. Now the question is whether we should consider a compromise instead of insisting on following our curriculum rigidly – instead of refusing to allow a preparation class for intensive coaching to be part of the school. We have turned down this idea because we thought it to be very unpedagogical. To introduce a preparation class for intensive coaching or to neglect our curriculum, that is the question. I think it would be best not to send our pupils to other schools, where they would have to pass some kind of entrance examination, and to carry out our curriculum up to Class 12 inclusive. Then we could take a thirteenth year for examination preparation. Let us assume – speaking only from a pedagogical point of view – that a child comes into the first class between its sixth and seventh year, then it will pass through Class 12 between its eighteenth and nineteenth year. This would be the right time for changing over to college or university, not later. To add a further year to the school would show the same intelligence as that of the State authorities which added another year to the medical study because they believed that there was more matter to be covered. Those things (adding an extra year for examination preparation) could drive you crazy. Those pupils who do not wish to go to a college or university must find their way into life without it. They will become useful people even without examinations for they will gain what they need for life. Those who wish to go on to further education could well stay on for another year in order to become a little more stupid. I think one could look at this thirteenth year as a year of 'drumming it in'. But it is for us to see that the pupils take their examinations for we must not send them away to another place. We ought to separate

this Class 13 from the rest of the Waldorf School. We could employ a coach, which means that the number of teachers would have to be increased because of this Class 13. If we were to employ coaches to work under the supervision of the teachers it could be done. I think it could be done." (5.2.24)

When, in spring 1924, the results of the first examinations were known, in which five out of nine pupils had passed Steiner said:

"On the whole I find that the results of the examination have shown in a striking way that all the things which we have discussed here are valid for the future. Of course it would be better if we could add this special class without bringing an alien influence into the Waldorf School. Needless to say, what we have agreed upon will stand. We do not wish to undermine that. However, the poor results seem to indicate that the pupils were unable to cope adequately when they were left to themselves, they were too much used to working in groups... There was not enough time, but nevertheless it seems that our pupils were not taught to solve their problems on their own... This shows a lack of understanding of the pupil's individuality. This seems to be the essence of what went wrong." (27.3.24)

On 29th April Steiner spoke to the pupils of the newly opened second Class 12 about the problems of taking examinations, and on the following day he reported this conversation at the teacher's meeting:

"All the pupils of Class 12, with the exception of one only, have declared that they do not think it important to take their examinations at the end of this year, but possibly a year later after the full course of the Waldorf School and after an examination preparation class. However, they do think it important that this preparation class should be given at the Waldorf School." (30.4.24)

This preparation for the examination was finally characterised by Steiner at the last teachers' meeting which he attended at the Stuttgart Waldorf School:

"This year (1924/25) we do not reckon with an examination and we shall carry out the Waldorf School curriculum. We don't reckon with an examination. But we shall endeavour to offer the coaching ourselves for the examination in the following year. You have heard the discussions today. They show how much these young people depend on the Waldorf School. The pupils of Class 12 would not find it at all to their liking if they were asked to take the examination this year. We can't avoid the intensive "crash-course" becoming distasteful to them, but the children love the teachers and the school. We shall not call the new class 'Class 13' but 'Preparation Class for the Abitur' (* 1)." (3.9.24)

This way of changing over from the Waldorf School to a college or university is still generally accepted today. At the time of its introduction it had a very beneficial effect as it gave the possibility of carrying out the work for twelve years without interference. Later it was adapted to meet the demands of the official curricula and examination papers, but this has to be considered as incompatible with the spirit of

the Steiner Schools. Adaptations to the State school system will still be necessary today but these should be limited to the acceptance of the thirteenth year of preparation, which would bring the number of school years to a level with those of the State schools (in Germany). This thirteenth year could be used for preparing our pupils for quite a different kind of examination which would not be at loggerheads with the Steiner School pedagogy. Steiner has made suggestions for such an examination and these were given at the beginning of this chapter in the quotations from the "Magazine for Literature" of 1898.

Advice on Careers

Steiner has said very little about this important point. On 5th February 1924, shortly before the first examination was to be taken and during the time of discussions about the next one, he said:

"One can do this only in special cases. Generally speaking one can hardly make decisions. Altogether the school has little influence on the choice of careers. The different aspects of such a choice are not so simple. Really the whole affair should happen in such a way that when a boy of eighteen or nineteen is of the opinion that he should train for this or that profession, one accepts his wish and gives him advice accordingly. This is a very responsible matter." (5.2.24)

3   About the Timetable

A distinguishing feature of the Steiner School timetable is the introduction of main lesson periods for a number of subjects, for which such an arrangement is both possible and advantageous. This means that each of these subjects – which belong to the more intellectual subjects but do not include the languages – is taught during the first two and sometimes even three periods of the day for about four weeks, after which it is replaced by another main lesson subject. The history of this new arrangement of the timetable can be read in the section "Aims and Problems" under the sub-title "Replanning the Foreign Language Lessons – Two Streams in the Upper School". At this point we shall only mention that to begin with English and French were also main lesson subjects. In the meeting which Steiner held on 8th September 1919, i.e., immediately after the curriculum lectures were given to the new College of teachers (*12), languages no longer belonged to the main lesson subjects, but formed part of the remaining timetable. It was recommended that they should be given during the morning sessions but that they could be put into the afternoon if necessary. The main lesson subjects were: German (including reading and writing), mathematics, geography, nature study, history, physics and chemistry. Later on art courses were added. Soon afterwards subjects taught in periods of some four weeks at a time became known as "main lesson subjects".

Speaking about the main lessons, which at that time were not yet known by that name, Steiner said:

"But the lessons will be given in such a way that the attention of the child is concentrated for several weeks upon the same subject. At the end of the school year there will be periods of recapitulation in which subject matter taught earlier on will be brought back to mind again." (13 session 1)

This plan was to be used for the main lesson subjects which were to be given in periods during the first three quarters of the year and in turns during the last quarter (8.9.19). This means that the main lesson subject matter was to be covered within three quarters of the year and that during the last quarter the teacher was to repeat systematically all the main lesson subjects taken previously.

This has not become the practice in our schools although Steiner never altered his views. On the contrary he spoke clearly about this plan in the Christmas Course for Teachers:

"It goes without saying that when the end of the school year approaches, everything taught earlier during the year will be brought back again to the soul of the child – and one can do this quite attractively." (27)

And again in Oxford:

"People may criticise the fact that our children are liable to forget what was taught in main lesson periods. But this must be balanced by economy of lesson time and by the efficiency of the teachers. The main lesson subjects will only be repeated during the last weeks of the school year, so that a kind of recapitulation of the whole year is given. In this way the child really grows into his subjects." (29)

The lessons after the daily main lesson were arranged in the following manner (taken from notes):

"In the first class, one lesson of English and French could possibly be put into the afternoon, also in Classes 2 and 3; the same in Class 4 (apparently every day except Wednesdays and Saturdays). Latin in the afternoon also ~ two lessons every day except Wednesdays and Saturdays i.e., eight lessons per week – but if possible these lessons should be put into the morning session, Greek in Class 6 and 7, But from Class 6 only three lessons of English and French a week, and one and a half hours' lesson each of Latin and Greek. (Lesson and hour are the same words in German (Stunde) but school lessons do not usually last one hour). All language lessons are to be placed between breaks... Handwork lessons could be put anywhere in the afternoons – music, religion and eurythmy should be given from 2.00 pm onwards. Latin (beginning with Class 4) Greek (beginning with Class 6) should be given after the main lesson like the modern languages, or they could be placed in the afternoon." (8.9.19)

In the succeeding years the timetable became somewhat obscure and unpedagogical because of the need to split large classes in certain subjects, such as languages, eurythmy and handwork.

In Autumn 1922 several teachers' meetings were given up to making a new timetable and Steiner introduced this task with the following words:

"The timetable has become quite impossible. Though trying to apply methods based on the knowledge of Man

and his development, we are actually managing to become as unpedagogical as possible." (28.10.22)

In this meeting the following principles were formulated for the timetable. They naturally have to be considered as desirable guiding lines which time and again will have to be adapted to the manifold needs of the circumstances:

"Remaining for the morning sessions, there would be main lessons, Latin and Greek (for pupils wanting to take the Abitur (*1)), eurythmy and singing. Then we would start the afternoons with choir practice and orchestral rehearsals. And those who take French and English should have these language lessons while the others are having Latin and Greek, so that we keep the languages together. For the upper classes (Class 7 upwards) one should see if handwork lessons could be put into the afternoons. Handwork and gymnastics should be postponed until the afternoons, especially in the upper classes. In this way it should be possible to arrive at a reasonable timetable. Gymnastics lessons should be in the afternoons if possible. Gymnastics lessons are not to be considered as a kind of recreation. It is not good to sandwich these lessons between other lessons. Two classes can be taken together. I must talk to the gymnastics teacher about the method – I have only given a few hints so far. But in gymnastics lessons one can always have two large groups (squads)." (28.10.22)

After this remark about the proper place of gymnastics in the timetable, which will be discussed in detail in the chapter on eurythmy and gymnastics, Steiner continued:

"But there remain the religion lessons which one may have to think about, and also the handicraft lessons. Those lessons ought to be put into the afternoons... artistic handicrafts can be given in the afternoons." (ibid.)

The place of handicrafts in the timetable has already been discussed. When the handicraft teacher asked for more time for his work with Class 9 Steiner answered:

'"It is not possible to give more time to this subject. Contrary to the method of splitting into groups, which is pedagogical nonsense, it would be better if one were to contract the work into eight days, (one full week is often referred to as 'eight days' in German) so that one would work with one group of pupils every day for 'eight days'. It is of great importance for life that the children feel sorry to have to drop a certain subject for a longer time. This feeling of being torn away from the work is of definite importance. Perhaps this is another case of having to work with our principle of contraction... perhaps it could be done so that only 1/3, 1/3, 1/3 of the class has handicraft lessons (apparently it is meant that only one third at a time of a class should have those lessons for one week). The only subjects which do not suffer so much from being taught in a less concentrated form are the languages. The main lessons and the artistic lessons suffer not only from a psychological point of view, but something becomes spoilt, something becomes really spoilt in human nature." (16.11.21)

At that time the problem remained unsolved but the handicraft teacher renewed his request. Steiner answered:

"To begin with it is like this: one could consider teaching handicrafts in periods, but it is quite impossible to have such periods during the main lesson time. One ought to weigh up whether it would not be possible to drop the languages for a time in order to make time for such a period. This would also bring about a certain amount of relief for teachers... One can do it for a fortnight at a time with regard to the language lessons, beginning with Class 9. One could make this arrangement every six weeks and distribute it over the year." (22.6.22)

However, a decision was not reached until 28th October 1922 when in answer to a further request for more time from the handicraft teacher Steiner said:

"You will be able to manage by teaching in periods. If one first gives the main lesson, then Latin and Greek, to be followed by eurythmy and singing, and in the afternoons the subjects just mentioned (religion, handwork and shorthand) then one can come to a satisfactory arrangement." (28.10.22)

Steiner looked upon these fundamentals of the timetable with great earnestness. He gave his reasons repeatedly. Thus in the first lecture of his "Supplementary Course" he says:

"We can't give someone food and then say: now you are satisfied. He must become hungry again, must eat again. This must become a living process, it must form a rhythm. Man must become musical again, must live in rhythms again. He must live in rhythms in such a way that in being thrown entirely upon himself he must undergo great tension, to be followed by release. If you teach him concepts of the stomach, the lungs, the liver you create a certain disposition within him – this becomes relaxed through singing just as hunger is balanced by eating, and in this way a rhythm is set up." (26)

After a description of the effect of eurythmy and singing lessons upon the supersensible being of man, one can read in lecture 3 of the same Course:

"One can make excellent use of these facts in education. If one could arrange for instance – I am speaking of an ideal situation, but teachers could at least endeavour to move towards such an ideal – if one could arrange that a eurythmy lesson were given one afternoon and then allowed to have its full spiritual effect during the night, and the next day a gymnastics lesson given in the way I described yesterday (2nd lecture), then these lessons would permeate the body in such a way that the gymnastics lesson would have a health-giving effect. In this way one can achieve a great deal through alternating eurythmy and gymnastics. And again one could achieve a great deal if for example one let the children sing one day – and after they have carried into the spiritual world during sleep whatever they have experienced in the singing lesson, the next day, conditions permitting, one will let them play together on musical instruments – which involves listening as well as being active. Then what has been done on the previous day will again make itself felt in an extremely healthy manner through the kind of condensing process which takes place within man when he is listening to instrumental music. You see, if one could achieve ideal conditions, one could work with

immeasurable advantage towards the health of the child by making a timetable which is in sympathy with the child's conditions. In these matters we wish to go much further." (26 lecture 3)

In the Dornach Course of Christmas 1921/22, the importance of giving gymnastics lessons the right place in the timetable is again stressed:

"It is absolutely right that all teaching which appeals more directly to the head should be given during the morning sessions. Only when these lessons are over are the children led to what is directed more towards the bodily-physical, if they have not already let off steam during the short breaks between the morning lessons. And after this more physical gymnastic training has taken place the child should not be brought back to doing any more head-work – I have already indicated that this would have a destructive effect upon the life forces, for while the children are practising whatever is related to the bodily-physical supersensible forces are working in the child unconsciously, and the head is no longer able to return to headwork after having given itself over to bodily-physical activities. It is quite wrong to believe that something positive has been achieved by inserting a gymnastics lesson, or even less than a full lesson, between other lessons, merely to give the children a change of activity. The homogeneous character of the morning and afternoon activities proves to be of great benefit for the development of man." (27)

About the proper place of religion lessons in the timetable Steiner had already said:

"If, after the children have written a business letter in the morning, you meet them again in the afternoon to teach them religion, and if whatever has been set in motion in their subconscious through writing that business letter is now having its effect, you are fortunate because you yourself have created the mood which needs to be balanced by its opposite pole." (12 lecture 12)

In actual fact it proved impossible to put the religion lessons into the afternoons because they were taken by teachers sent by various communities and sects, who had to fit their lessons at the Waldorf School into their already existing timetables.

In the autumn of 1922 the following guidelines for the timetable were agreed upon: the main lesson was to take place from 8.00 am to 10.00 am and, in the upper classes from 8.00 am to 11.00 am on two days a week, and was to be followed by the language lessons. From Class 9 upwards English and Greek were to be taught at the same time. Immediately after the language lessons and still during the morning sessions, singing and eurythmy were to be taught. On the other hand religion, gymnastics, handwork and the handicrafts (the latter taught in periods in the upper classes) choir practice and orchestra were to be in the afternoons. (28.10.22 – 5.12.22)

Details such as the number of weekly lessons per subject or the usual length of the main lesson periods are given in the section dealing with the different subjects.

SECTION 2 – THE CURRICULUM ARRANGED ACCORDING TO SUBJECTS

1 German (the Mother Tongue)

German was the mother tongue; English would take its place in an English school.

Main lessons throughout all classes; in Classes 1 – 8 painting and drawing form part of the main lessons.

Class 1 to 3	14 weeks each
Class 4 to 5	12 weeks each
Class 6 to 8	10 weeks each
Class 9 to 12	6 weeks each

Before going into details of the curriculum, some of Steiner's remarks will be quoted whose significance extends beyond the scope of each individual class. However, any matters which, though being part of the German main lessons belong to a separate subject, such as painting, modelling and drawing, have been omitted here and will be found in the section on "Painting, Modelling and Drawing".

Instructions concerning telling and retelling of stories, the introduction of writing and grammar, appreciation of style and descriptive writing, as well as indications about essay writing will be quoted before the content of each individual class.

Stories and reading matter for the lower classes

In the first lecture of "Discussions with Teachers" after having outlined an introduction to main lessons which were to be taught in periods Steiner said:

"All that has to be taught through the medium of telling stories belongs to this main lesson. In the first school year we shall mainly tell fairy tales. In the second year we shall try to bring the life of animals to the child in story form. We shall go from the fable to how animals live together in real life... I believe it would be good if you thought about what kind of content you would choose for these story lessons... You will have to choose material for story telling and retelling which is to be introduced to the children from their 7th to their 14th year in a free and narrative style. It will be necessary to have a certain stock of fairy tale material at your disposal. Later on you will have to occupy yourselves with the introduction of animal stories in connection with the fable. Then Biblical stories form part of these story telling lessons, quite separately from the religion lessons. Scenes from ancient history should follow and then scenes from medieval history and from later history. Then you should be able to tell stories about the different tribes, showing the differences which are more or less brought about by natural living conditions; then the reciprocal relationship of the different tribes (probably meaning races) – the Indians, Chinese, Americans – showing their individual characteristics – in other words, knowledge of nations. This is of particular

importance for our present epoch." (13 first session)

In a text duplicated for teachers we find the following summary:

"1 A certain repertoire of fairy tales
2 Stories from the animal world introduced through fables
3 Biblical stories as part of general history
4 Scenes from ancient history
5 Scenes from medieval history
6 Scenes from later history
7 Stories illustrating tribal life
8 Knowledge of nations (races)." (ibid.)

As far as I can remember this summary was also written on the blackboard. As it was not published in Heydebrand's "Curriculum" it is likely to have remained unknown to many teachers. One might easily consider this list of story telling material to be merely an index which bore no relation to the different ages. However, I feel sure that the eight themes, given in such precise form, are related to the first eight classes. The introductory sentence shows the unmistakable style of Rudolf Steiner.

How seriously he took this choice of story material and how seriously he wanted it to be taken by the teachers can be seen by the fact that he ended the first session of the "Discussions" with this theme and also began the curriculum lectures by pointing out the necessity of finding suitable material for telling and retelling:

"You see, when we receive the children in Class 1 we must first of all try to find the right material for telling and retelling stories. Through this telling of fairy tales, of legends, and also of outwardly realistic happenings, and through the children retelling these stories, we train their actual mode of speaking. We form the transition from dialect to educated speech. If we see to it that the child speaks correctly we lay the foundations for a correct style of writing." (16 lecture 1)

In the Basle Course Steiner stressed the importance of the form in which the stories are retold, and why these stories should be told and not read from textbooks:

"If only you could realise, ladies and gentlemen, what an immense difference there is between merely reading a fairy tale to a child and making one up yourself! However many fairy tales you may first read and then retell your children, they will not have the same impact as stories invented by yourselves, even if your own efforts are far inferior to the existing stories. It is this imaginative process of creating – and that is what I mean by a living element – which will communicate itself and work upon the child. These are the imponderables in one's relationship with the child." (23 lecture 5)

It has never been clarified how Steiner wanted the above story material fitted into the main lesson. It appears to me that he wanted the teachers to set apart a special time during

17

the lessons, when educational and artistic treasures should be offered to the children without any compulsion to learn, purely because of the inherent educational value, so that the children should learn to know the world in a way which they could enjoy.

This does not exclude the possibility of explaining what was freely given if a child expressed the wish to understand more fully, so that what was received in a more dreamy manner would then become more conscious.

Speech and Grammar

Before quoting from Steiner's numerous indications about language and speech, we will begin with a paragraph taken from the Basle Course for Teachers which though dealing with the child's painting and drawing nevertheless belongs to our subject:

> "When I look at a child's drawings, however primitive and schematic they may be, I find in every one of them a combination of the child's outward perception with an experience of his own organic life. One can recognise in almost every line of these drawings where the child has tried to copy something seen with the eye and where he has added something arising from inner feeling." (23 lecture 6)

He then goes on to the teaching of the mother tongue and shows how this subject together with arithmetic forms the counterbalance to the forces awakened through artistic and musical activities:

> "If an inner experience of the organs is not nurtured between the 6th, 7th and 9th years an unhealthy growth of the intellect results. And this intellect is fundamentally speaking the enemy of the real intellectual human life as well as of the social life. I am not trying to advocate stupidity for mankind, my dear friends – it is a question of recognising the intellect in its parasitical nature and of learning to regard it as complete only when it comes forth from the whole human being and does not appear in a one-sided way. But nothing will be achieved in this direction unless the artistic drawing and musical education is at the same time supported by other branches of education – above all through speech and by the teaching of arithmetic. With regard to the teaching of language, one must first learn to understand the whole meaning of language teaching. I must say that the meaning really became clear to me when I had the opportunity to observe what happened when children who spoke dialect sat together in the school with children who did not. It was just the observation and training of these dialect-speaking children which proved so important and interesting. Dialect – every dialect – has peculiarities of its own. It proceeds from what I might call the inner feeling of the human being exactly as if it were the inner experiencing of the organs – although this has largely been stunted by our present intellectualism. It is an inner experience which really draws the whole human being into the speech. But in our so-called cultured speech, which has become so abstract, there is no longer any real connection between the inner experience and what is expressed*

*outwardly in the succession of sounds." (ibid.)

After a remark about the logic inherent in languages he continues:

> "There is in certain primitive languages a remarkable inner logic in the speech which then becomes much more abstract and simple as it becomes more civilised. And it is the same with dialect. As a matter of fact there is much more inner logic in it than in our cultured speech, and a very great deal can be achieved when, for instance, in the village school, one starts directly from the dialect, for then one must talk dialect with the children and endeavour to bring to consciousness what is already unconsciously within the speech – that is the grammar. Grammar should be taught in an essentially living way, so livingly indeed that one starts with the presupposition that it is already there when the child speaks... One lets the child utter sentences which accord with its nature and whose inner connection and plasticity the child feels. And then one is able to draw the child's attention to how what it performs unconsciously can become conscious...

> One can indeed presuppose that the whole of grammar is already inherent in the human organism, and if this presupposition is acted upon in earnest then, my dear friends, a man will learn to say to himself: In drawing forth the conscious knowledge of grammar from the unconscious life of grammar at the right time and in a living way you are simply working at the bringing forth of the Ego consciousness of the child. And with this knowledge in your bones, if I may use this expression, then towards the 9th year, when the Ego consciousness normally awakes properly, you lift the unconscious up into consciousness. Then the child will reach this Rubicon in its development in the right way. Then one works with those forces within the child that want to develop, not with forces which are imposed on him from without. And this way of teaching language so that one begins with the child's way of speaking (viz. his dialect) and supports this through a living intercourse between the children who speak the ordinary cultured language and those who speak dialect, measuring one with the other, not in an abstract but in a feeling way, taking a word or a sentence of the dialect and translating it into the other – in working in this way in language lessons one is introducing the artistic element which was laid down in the lessons in drawing and music. An hour and a half of such language teaching makes you really perspire!" (23 lecture 6)

Though an attempt has been made to illustrate the essentials of language teaching to classes in which dialect is spoken, I strongly recommend the reader not to be satisfied with this excerpt but to study the Basle Course in full.

In the 9th lecture of the same course Steiner gives more details about language teaching, this time showing how this subject can help the child to become more awake to his earthly surroundings.

> "The aim of learning and teaching grammar is essentially to stimulate the awakening of the child, to increase his consciousness. In this way we call upon inner forces which can develop at about nine years old in the sense

which I have characterised. We must make use of language teaching in order to make the child more wide awake. We shall be able to do this better if we make use of the dialect spoken by the pupils. For if the child has only been taught the ordinary cultured language, if it has learnt this before the age of seven, then it becomes extremely difficult to get at the unconscious forces in the child, for in a sense they have already been killed – the unconscious has a quite definite natural relationship with the logical formation of speech. So that when we have children who speak dialect together with those who do not it is a good thing to relate our grammar teaching to what the dialect-speaking children bring to the lessons." (23 lecture 9)

Later on in the same lecture he says:

"And as dialect is linked more directly with the unconscious element we can really build up grammar and syntax using dialect as a basis and then appealing more to the powers of reasoning. However, if we only teach children who have been brought up on educated forms of speech, we must not expect this intellect to develop a kind of grammar which will act like a plumb line so that the child blindly follows this rule of the plumb line by using the dative or accusative case, or by making a full stop here or a comma there. Something different must now come to the fore – if we have to reach children who have never lived with dialect we must introduce an artistic element into our teaching of grammar, we must appeal to a feeling for the different kinds of style in language. The child brings to school a sound instinct for language, but we must try to develop this appreciation of style in language in the child up to his ninth year. However, we can only achieve this if we work towards this feeling for style in an artistic (i.e., not in an intellectual) way. This can be done by using the child's natural instinct to follow authority, even though such a method may be looked down upon by educators who wish to do away with the teacher's authority. We can develop grammar and syntax if we make the child aware of the difference between sentences expressing general statements, questions or exclamations – if we make him conscious of the different inflection of the voice when it is uttering such different kinds of sentences. We can show how a statement is made in a neutral, objective kind of voice, whereas an exclamation expresses a certain nuance of feeling. Out of this artistic element in the language we can lead over to grammar and syntax.

Thus, if we use what the dialect-speaking children bring to us and also what the children whose speech is free of dialect bring, if we use the first to develop man's natural instinct for language, and the second to awaken the inner feeling for style, then we shall attain what language teaching can contribute to the child's development." (23 lecture 9)

In the 11th lecture of the same course Steiner's request for an artistic approach to grammar is considerably supplemented:

"You see, everybody knows what a melody is and also what a sentence is. However, very few people realise today that a sentence consisting of subject, predicate and object is in reality a melody in man's subconscious realm.

In the same way in which we can make clear to ourselves that what is experienced in sleep as an increase and fading away of feelings like a curve, rises into consciousness when clothed in dream pictures, so we also experience in the depths of our being the sentence as something musical. In adapting ourselves to the world around us we clothe what we feel musically within with a plastic picture –

| the child | writes | the exercise |
| subject | predicate | object |

In the innermost being of man a triad is experienced. It is really a triad he experiences inwardly. In this sentence the triad works in this way: the first tone is, so to speak, directed to 'the child', the second to 'writes' (the act of writing), and the third to 'the exercise'." (23 lecture 11)

In lecture 12 of the same course another indication is given illustrating the importance of language hygiene.

"It is just in childhood that the right handling of the soul has such immense importance for the body. It is also of immense importance that one continually sees to it that the child learns to speak in clear, full tones and, as I have already emphasised, that he rounds off his speech, that he learns to pronounce his sentences completely, giving each syllable its full due. For in the human being right breathing depends on right speaking. Indirectly the right formation of the organs of the human breast is dependent on right speech. It would be well for once to look at the statistics of chest diseases, which are so devastating today, from this point of view. One should ask oneself how much of the blame for chest tuberculosis today is due to the fact that too little care was taken at school over measured rhythmical speech and, above all, that there was insufficient awareness on the part of the teacher as to whether the child was breathing fully and deeply. Speech must not proceed from breathing – on the contrary breathing must proceed from speech. It is the speaking that must be right – the feeling for right speech, for the length and shortness of syllables and words must be developed – then breathing accommodates itself to it. It is nonsense to believe that one must train the breathing in order to come to the right way of speaking. Breathing, right breathing, must be a result of rightly felt speech." (23 lecture 12)

Soon afterwards, in answer to a question in a teacher's meeting Steiner indicated how he would explain the perfect tense. (In German the imperfect tense conveys a quality of still living in the past, of still experiencing the past, whereas the perfect tense indicated that some activity is completed, finished, over and done with.):

"I would discuss with the children in varied ways the parallels between what belongs to the past and what is perfect. What is a perfect human being, a perfect table? Get the children to feel the connection between what is perfect or finished and then speak about the

perfect tense. Then I would tackle the imperfect tense, a tense which shows that one is still in the process of perfecting.

Had I enough time today I should have read the story to the children in the perfect tense – such a thing would bring life into the lessons. Naturally one cannot change the tense in every sentence." (12.6.20)

Then he continues – and here one meets Steiner as a real educator:

"And eurythmy too brings life to the formative forces of the head. I should do lots of things between the lines as it were. As I have already mentioned today, I can understand the objection to digressing. (Yet) bringing in such things should be looked upon as ideal. For example, today I have felt so tempted to treat your children to the 'hurtig toch', for this is one way in which one can broaden their thoughts – it means (in Dutch) the fast train. This is the kind of thing I should do between the lines with the children." (12.6.20)

Before the observations on the perfect tense were made the different talents of the children were discussed:

"Those who are clever-heads, the gifted head-children, will write good compositions; the gifted body-children will be good at eurythmy. One must try to balance this through conversations. If you converse with the children this activity will lead away from the head – that is if you talk about something which has been taken from outer life and then deepen it." (ibid.)

After this Steiner continued with his observations on the perfect tense...

In lecture 12 of the Dornach Course of 1921/22 a relevant passage about the teaching of grammar can be found:

"In our times there is a tendency towards fanaticism – one finds quite sound educational ideas becoming one-sided because they are taken too far in a fanatical way. We find an example of such an attitude in language teaching. The young child learns his mother tongue quite naturally and without learning any grammar, and this is of course the right way to learn it. When the child reaches school age and has to learn foreign languages he should also do so without learning any grammar – in a similar though more mature way to that in which he learned to speak his mother tongue.

However, when the child reaches the turning point between the 9th and 10th year his own development demands that he acquires some knowledge of grammar which must not be given in a pedantic way, for at this stage the child must find the transition towards his ego-development. He must now learn to do everything more consciously than he has done hitherto. One therefore needs to introduce an element of thinking into the teaching of the language with which the child is already familiar, though in a feeling way. He now needs to discover and recognise the rules in exercises which are stimulating but never pedantic. At this important point between his 9th and 10th year the child needs to occupy himself with grammar in order to be able to express himself with certainty, supported by the logic of

grammar. For one must realise that two elements are always working together in language – an element of thinking and an element of feeling." (27)

After a further observation about the working together of the two elements in the language Steiner continues:

"But these two streams of the more thinking and the more feeling elements in language always flow together... In modern languages much of this has become less pliable but in the earlier stages of development there was always an active, formative element in the languages which allowed the thinking and feeling streams to mingle freely.

Before the ninth year the child's relationship to his language is an entirely feeling one. However, his self-consciousness could not develop if we did not introduce him to the more thinking quality of the language. It is therefore so important to bring this thinking element to the child via grammatical rules, taught in an appropriate way – especially with regard to his mother tongue, but also with foreign languages, where the rules must follow in the wake of learning the language and not vice versa.

The following points now become relevant: between the 9th and 10th year the child should have the feeling that he has made a living connection with the language, as I have already mentioned. In this way the right sense of grammar could be implanted in the child. Towards the 12th year – and this should now become the aim – the child should have developed a feeling for the beauty of the language, an aesthetic sense of the language. Towards the 12th year he should endeavour to learn to speak with what one could call a taste for the beauty of the language. Only when this stage has been reached, and continuing until puberty, should the pupil learn to express himself in such a way that he could convince someone else of his own opinion – in other words he should practise the dialectical element of language. The pupil should only experience this latter element when he is approaching school leaving age."

We can summarise what has been said in the following way:

"First we must learn to appreciate the correctness, the rightness, inherent in a language, then we must gain a feeling for its beauty, and finally we must experience the power a language can bestow on whoever can speak it. Language teaching should be planned in this way.

It is more important for the teacher to occupy himself with such matters than to be given a detailed curriculum. In this way he will find the right material and the right time to introduce it. Up to the pupil's 9th and 10th year he will deal in a sensitive and artistic manner with the formative part of language which lets one take an active part, and thereafter, without however neglecting this formative part, he will add the descriptive part of language." (27)

In the second of the two lectures held in Stuttgart in 1922 Steiner gives an example of how to look at sentence construction in a pictorial way and how children can practise such sentence constructions:

"It should not be too difficult to present these matters pictorially in a language, if one thinks it is worth while to bring out the pictorial element in the lessons. Really one ought not to miss a single opportunity to show even 10, 11 and 12 year olds how sentences are built up by, let us say, a main clause, a relative clause and a conditional clause. The actual grammar involved is not what matters most – it should only be a means of arriving at a picture. We should not miss the opportunity of giving the child what one could call a spatial picture of a main and a relative clause. Naturally this can be done in the most varied ways. Without wanting to theorise one could represent the main clause as a large circle and the relative clause as a small one, perhaps an eccentric circle. The conditional clause, the "if-sentence", could now be shown by lines drawn towards the circle like rays indicating the conditioning factors... It is really necessary, after appropriate preparation of one's material, to come back to these matters again and again, and even with 10, 11 and 12 year olds to go into the moral-characterological aspect of style made visible by pictures. This does not imply teaching syntax, for the pupil should grasp these matters in a more intuitive way. One can really go a long way here. For instance one can introduce a short story from the point of view of the temperaments, having thoroughly prepared it beforehand.

One can talk – not about the content, but about the style – about a melancholy or a choleric style quite apart from the content, even from the poetical content. I am referring to sentence construction. There is no need to dissect sentences – this should be avoided – but one should cultivate this transformation into the pictorial element showing the moral and characteristic quality. One will find that it is possible to teach children aged 10, 11, 12 and 13 in a stimulating way if one struggles hard enough with the necessary preparation." (28 lecture 2)

On 9th December 1922 a teacher said that one could experience different degrees of reality by building upon the verb, and that one entered the language very directly in this way. Steiner answered:

"It is quite right to begin with the verb. The preposition is also very alive. One should not begin with the noun. We will say more about this." (9.12.22)

He apparently wanted to give further details but this did not happen.

The teaching of grammar also came into the conversation when the question of school hygiene was discussed:

"One can easily sin against these matters (of school hygiene). For instance you may be sinning against the healthy condition of the child if you occupy him for an hour with what is usually called grammar. If the children have to occupy themselves distinguishing between what one calls subject, object, attribute, indicative, subjunctive etc. – all things in which they have only a half-hearted interest – then they are put into a state where their breakfasts are boiling in their organisms quite uninfluenced by their soul lives. Then one is cultivating real stomach trouble, for example enteric illnesses, in the child – though

this may only reveal itself some fifteen to twenty years later. Enteric illnesses very often are caused by grammar lessons. This aspect is of the utmost importance and really the whole mood which a teacher brings into his lessons, by a web of innumerable threads, has a far reaching effect upon the children." (6.2.23)

In the published report of the same teacher's meeting we find the following passage about teaching grammar:

"The actual language lessons of most of the language teachers here are better than their grammar lessons. Above all, I find that the main shortcoming is that the teachers do not know their own grammar. Don't feel offended: perhaps you could use the teachers' meetings to learn a bit of grammar yourselves... I find the way grammatical terms are used terrible. (If I were a pupil) I myself would raise a riot if I did not know why such things were being thrown at my head. The point is that the teachers have not taken enough time to find out how a reasonable grammatical knowledge can he acquired. (Only) then does it stimulate the pupils. If I may speak plainly, the grammar lessons are just horrible. All the stuff which you find printed in books ought to be burnt. Something living must enter... The pupils do not learn to experience what a perfect tense or a present tense is, whereas it is essential for them to experience it. The genius of the language must live in the teacher. This applies equally to the German lessons. There too the torture of undigested terminology is being inflicted upon the children." (ibid.)

A short and very beautiful summary of the character of the language and of the different aspects of language teaching can be found in the Torquay Course. There, in the second half of lecture 6, every language teacher can find a little treasure which he is well advised to use. It seems impossible to take out just a few excerpts. (40)

To conclude this section covering Steiner's indications about how to teach the mother tongue (in as far as these do not refer to a particular class (I will give a survey of grammatical steps for Classes 1 to 7 as formulated in the curriculum lectures:

Class 1   "Hardly touch it at all."

Class 2   "Build up concepts of what is a noun and a verb with its tenses... conversations about the structure of sentences."

Class 3   "Conscious feeling... for short, long, expanded sounds, etc... A feeling approach towards articulation of language and general language-configuration.... Different parts of speech, and parts of sentences... Structure of a sentence, punctuation."

Class 4   "A clear idea of the tenses, of what is expressed by the changing forms of the verb... Prepositions governing cases (applies to German grammar)... Modulate the language plastically."

Class 5   "Difference between active and passive voice... Indirect speech... Difference between writing one's own opinion and reporting another person's opinion... Complete punctuation."

Class 6   "A feeling for the subjunctive... A strong

feeling for the plasticity of the language."

Class 7 "A sensitive appreciation of forms expressing wish, wonder and surprise."

After speaking about how the teacher should approach his language lessons I should like to mention a passage in the "Conferences" (*4) where Steiner criticises the faults made in such lessons. The passage is too long to be quoted in full but ought to be looked up by each teacher. (6.2.23)

Writing and Reading

In his 10th lecture of the Practical Course for Teachers Steiner said about learning how to write:

"When man adjusts himself to writing he is obviously assimilating something very foreign to the universe. But if we link the written forms with the universal forms – f with the fish etc. – at least we lead man back to the world again." (12 lecture 10)

Steiner dealt with the teaching of writing in practically every lecture course he gave. He paid so much attention to this responsible task that he approached it from a new angle whenever and wherever he spoke about it.

In lecture 1 of the "Practical Course of Teachers" he sketched out the new way of teaching writing for the first time. (12)

In "Discussions with Teachers" he speaks about drawing free shapes which should precede the introduction of writing. (13 "Discussions" 3 and 4)

In the Practical Course the beginning of the very first school lesson shows a very simple drawing exercise. In lecture 5 of the same course the introduction of writing is the main theme, with detailed instructions:

"Let us now suppose that you have pursued such exercises with pencil and with colour for some time. It is an essential condition of well-founded teaching that a certain intimacy with drawing should be developed before writing is taught, so that writing is in a sense derived from drawing, And another condition is that the reading of printed characters should only be developed from the reading of handwriting. We shall then try to find the transition from drawing to handwriting, from writing to the reading of handwriting, and from the reading of handwriting to the reading of print. I assume for this purpose that you have succeeded, through the medium of drawing, in giving the child a certain mastery of the round and straight-lined forms which he will need for writing, Then from this point we would seek the transition to what we have already mentioned as the foundation of teaching in reading and writing... We assume then that the child is already able to master round and straight-lined forms with his little hands. Then you must try to indicate to the child (that there are written characters)." (12 lecture 5)

Here it is clearly pointed out that writing lessons should only begin when elementary drawing exercises have reached the stage of the controlled drawing of shapes with straight and curved lines. In the same lecture, after the example of the letter F, there follows a detailed description of writing lessons, of which every Waldorf teacher should avail himself.

Writing is spoken about again in lecture 10 of this course, as part of the plan for a curriculum, and in the 13th lecture there is an outline of what a teacher of Class 1 should cover in writing and reading.

In the Basle Course Steiner approaches writing lessons again from quite a different point of view. In the 5th and 10th lectures he develops what he calls the analysing method (compare with the "Look and Say Method" in England) in contrast to the usual synthesising methods (i.e., adding letters together to form words) and it is astonishing to see with what freedom he modifies his own methods as expressed in the Stuttgart courses, thus giving the lie to anyone who wishes to hold to these. These observations he concludes with the following sentences:

"How does it come about that in our time we have developed what I might call an inclination to atomism? It has come about through the fact that in our day the analytical faculty is too little developed in children. If only the analytical activity of children, that proceeds by analysis from the finished word picture to the letters, were developed then the child would be using this analytical faculty at a time when he has a natural inclination to do so, and it would not linger until the later activity of thinking uses it in devising atomistic structures, etc. It is simply the unsatisfied impulse for analysis that fosters materialism... Therefore in the Waldorf School we do not start from the letters and synthesise into words, but we start first with the complete sentence; within the sentence we analyse the words and then we take the words and analyse the letters, and finally we take the letters and analyse the sounds. Thus we actually come to a true inwardness (Verinnerlichung). For the child already knows the sentences and the words, so, in order to awaken his consciousness, we analyse these sentences and words." (23 lecture 10)

As already mentioned, indications about the teaching of writing can be found in practically every pedagogical course:

In the Dornach Christmas Course it is shown how the consonant "U' can be brought near to the child entirely out of movement. (27 lecture 9)

In the Supplementary Course the learning of writing is described as a process which in itself is alien to the natural development of the child's spiritual, soul and physical being from its pre-earthly state to its earthly incarnation, a process which is bound to have a disturbing influence unless it is directed in the right way. (26 lecture 8)

Lecture 3 of the Oxford Course also contains passages dealing with writing. (29)

In the Dornach Easter Conference we find the following thought: "One must introduce reading and writing in such a way that the formative forces which have been active within the child up to the seventh year and which are now becoming free for the outer activity of the soul, really do become active outwardly." (34 lecture 4)

In the Ilkley Course the consonant "S" is developed out of movement. A special approach to vowels is also given in this course. (35 lecture 7)

The Stuttgart Course of 1924 also deals with the introduction of writing:

> "Now the point is that we should spare the child of six or seven from learning to write as it has to today. What we have to do is to bring to the child something that is akin to what can flow out of its very self, out of the actions of its arms and fingers. The letters are then brought into existence out of our activity!" (37 lecture 2)

The Berne Course stresses the fact that the historically-developed letter forms are alien to the soul of the child, and then describes the new methods of teaching writing.

The Arnheim Course of 1924 looks at the learning of writing from the point of view of the development of the language which, with its "Wau-wau" and "Bim-bam" theories, offers starting points for the introduction of vowels as well as consonants. (39 lecture 3)

The Torquay Course of 1924 deals in great detail with the introduction of writing, thus becoming a summary of previous indications. (40 lecture 2)

May these manifold possibilities of introducing writing guide the teacher towards the true fundamentals. Then his own imagination will show him how to use these indications for his own good and for the benefit of his pupils.

Punctuation

In a teachers' meeting on 3rd July 1923 Steiner pointed out that the pupils of Class 9 were not using any punctuation marks. He then proceeded to give some very revealing guidance for the teaching of punctuation. Apparently however this guidance was not meant specifically for Class 9. Steiner pointed out during the meeting that it was high time for that Class to begin using punctuation marks:

> "Beginning with the older forms of the German language, it is for instance possible to show in quite a fascinating way how the relative clause came into existence as writing gradually changed over from the Gothic to the Latin script. This relative clause can become the foundation for the study of the use of commas. The pupils will apply commas quite differently if they are shown how every relative clause needs to be enclosed by commas. This relative clause can become very interesting because it did not exist in the older German language. Neither is it used in dialects. You can trace it back to the Song of the Nibelungs where the relative clause first made its appearance, bringing about the necessity to introduce this form of logic into the language. If you have shown how the relative clause must be put into commas, you can explain the idea of a sentence to the children. Then they must learn that every sentence needs to be separated from the next one by a punctuation mark. The other matters are not so terribly important. Then you show how thought is developed in the language and so you come to the semi-colon, which indicates a great incision. They are already using full stops (in Class 9).
>
> Now it is high time for Class 9 to begin. One should be able to work it out of positive language forms, going into the deeper meaning of punctuation marks. This must be made especially stimulating and never become boring. Children find pure grammar most boring.
>
> When speaking or dictating one must make it clear through the inflection of the voice how sentences begin and end. This should be achieved not by dictating the punctuation, but by the children learning to distinguish the use of punctuation through listening to the spoken words. To dictate punctuation is a doubtful business. I would not dictate punctuation, but let the pupils hear it." (3.7.23)

This is followed by indications about the artistic structure of the sentences, which can be looked up in the appropriate place and which end with the words:

> "This can be done in such a way that by the time they reach Class 9 a certain feeling for a complete sentence has been developed." (ibid.)

These words indicate that the understanding of the structure of sentences, which is expressed by punctuation marks, ought to have been dealt with before Class 9. The teaching of punctuation is supposed to begin in Class 3 and the syllabus for the later classes offers so many opportunities to acquaint the children with the forms of the language that by Class 9 they really ought to "have a certain feeling for the complete sentence."

Style and Figuration – Metrics and Poetics

Steiner spoke about these themes for the first time when the syllabus for Class 10 was discussed:

> "You should now begin, or continue, with a coherent presentation of what is generally called metrics and poetics. On the basis of what they have learnt already in connection with Jean Paul... our pupils will be well able to enter these themes. The pedantic methods in which these subjects are usually taught should be avoided. This so-called metrics and poetics must appear reasonable and must be dealt with in a living way, in connection with living poetry." (17.6.21)

When asked on the same day which text book he would recommend for the study of metrics Steiner answered:

> "Every one of them is equally good or equally bad. Take Göschen (a text book), which represents one of the worst methods because it strictly adheres to a terminological sequence. There is no good book on metrics and poetics in German. Bartsch, Lachmann, the Song of the Nibelungs put into German by Simrock; he tried to stick to the rules. I have given the fundamentals based on physiology in a lecture called "Between pulse beat and breathing", given in Dornach. If one adds the caesura one can study the hexameter by observing the pulse beat and the breathing. It is not possible today to go into details about the theory of metrics." (ibid.)

It is clear how seriously Steiner took the task of bringing young people to an appreciation of an artistic style in language by his attitude towards a disciplinary case which was discussed on 21st June 1923:

"The years of transition are a difficult time for these children. One realises that something must happen.

There is too little vitality and impetus in the German lessons of Classes 8 and 9. The psyche of these children feels this lack... The children's interest ought to be awakened in a stimulating way for the structure of sentences, for the style of sentences. A feeling for the style of the language ought to be developed through compositions. This should happen in their twelfth year. I have indicated appropriate points in the course about children reaching puberty (26). We ought to discuss descriptive writing, tropes, metaphors; there is a total lack of these as far as I could observe. Neither shall we ever get them to use proper punctuation if they have not grasped the value of each word in the style (sentence ?). As a matter of fact, the kind of lessons in style and composition which they are receiving in German is such that they cannot mature properly. In Class 9b they still don't know what a sentence is ... they have not developed a feeling for writing in different styles. This must become part of the German lessons. These German lessons are not what they ought to be and this is of immense importance for the development of the children. They experience the mutation of voice as much in the written language as in the spoken language. The children will develop inner defects if one does not take note of this." (21.6.23)

In the next teachers' meeting, which took place hardly a fortnight later, Steiner spoke again about the artistic treatment of the language because he was feeling concerned about the state of the one Class 9. Concluding a discussion about punctuation he turned to a more artistic approach to the problem:

"It would be much nicer if something different could be done. It would be much nicer if one could construct sentences in such a way that each sentence occupies one line in the exercise book. This is possible in old German but not in modern German which has been moulded according to the Latin sentence construction.

It is definitely possible to discuss the artistic structure of a sentence with the children in a stimulating way and without becoming pedantic. It is quite possible to evoke a feeling in them of what a sentence is, to make them conscious of what a sentence is. One ought to achieve that the children show a positive attitude towards learning how to construct sentences. The style of Hermann Grimm could illustrate how language can be used pictorially – for he still writes proper sentences, whereas nowadays you usually read not sentences but tapeworms of sentences. Sentences are being quite mishandled (by Class 9b)... This can be cured in Class 9 if one develops in them a definite feeling for a complete sentence. There is something else in our curriculum which could help a great deal, namely a kind of poetics. This is lacking here altogether – it has not been taught at all. I have noticed that the children do not know what a metaphor is. They must know metaphors, metonymy and synecdoche. Something wonderful can come about if one uses these themes. It was put into the curriculum but it has never been

taught. This tropology is a great help in getting the children to write good sentences. If they use pictorial language they learn how to form good sentences. One can take examples, such as: 'O water-lily, thou blossoming swan, O swan, thou floating water-lily'; then one can ask them to explain what is meant by such a sentence. In this way, through metaphorical expressions, they can gain a clear feeling for the artistic wholeness of a sentence." (3.7.23)

Steiner's reminder of what was put into the curriculum referred to oral indications given on 17th June 1921 for Class 10. The strange fact is that on 17th June 1921 he asked that metrics and poetics be given to Class 10, but on 3rd July 1923 he suggested that it be taught in Class 9. Then a year later on 2nd June 1924, when Steiner gave the curriculum for modern languages, he asked that the rudiments of poetics and metrics of foreign languages be taught in Class 8 and "Some aesthetics of language" in Class 11. In my opinion the reason for putting forward metrics and poetics twice can only be explained in the following way: the pupils of the first Class 8 and those of the following Class 8, most of whom had entered the Waldorf School after having attended the German State schools during World War I, did not bring with them the fundamentals necessary for studying the above subjects. Because of this particular situation it was evidently only possible to introduce metrics and poetics in Class 10. This however means that one should teach metrics and poetics in Class 8 with ordinary pupils who entered the Waldorf School in their early years, first in German lessons (i.e., mother tongue) and then in the foreign languages, of which the "rudiments" were supposed to be taught in Class 8. In Class 9 one should certainly continue and in Class 10 one should begin and continue "a somewhat coherent presentation of what is generally called metrics and poetics".

During the next teachers' meeting a teacher referred to these indications, asking how they should be understood:

"Metrics deals with the structure of verse and stanza, poetics with the different kinds of poetry, with lyrical, epic and dramatic poetry. This is what is called metrics and poetics. Then you go on to tropology and to figuration. Illustrate these by examples, let the children use many metaphors, etc. In the aesthetics of the language you draw attention to whether a language is rich in the vowels u (pronounced oo) and o, or in i (pronounced ee) and e ('a' as in table). The pupils have quite a good vocabulary by the time you introduce this: you can take examples from German, French or English and you can compare the different languages. In this way you bring about a feeling for how much more musical a language is in which there are plenty of o and u (oo) sounds than another language which uses more e (a) and i (ee) sounds. One tries to convey an appreciation of how the aesthetic beauty of a language decreases if it loses the possibility of changes due to the inflections of the different cases. So the syntax of the language is part of the aesthetics of the language – whether it is plastic (mobile) or lyrical, whether it offers the possibility to use complicated interjections, etc. This is quite different from metrics and poetics. Aesthetics reveals the inherent beauty of a language." (19.6.24)

Immediately afterwards Steiner gave the answer to a riddle he had asked in one of his lectures held at Ilkley in the summer of 1923 (35). He then made a remark about metrics in French which should perhaps be quoted in the chapter about foreign languages but which nevertheless is also relevant in this context:

"However little one may realise it, French metrics is based on a sense of systematic classification, on the mathematics of the language. Normally one is not conscious of this. In French metrics everything is accounted for rationally. This is only thinly veiled and toned down by rhetoric. It is audible reasoning. This is rhetoric (may mean: This has become rhetoric)." (19.6.24)

On the same day, in answer to a question, there followed this remark about tropes and figuration:

"Tropes and figures of speech contain the element of imagination. First you find that the greatest part of poetry, 99% of poetry, is absolutely unpoetical. There remains the 1%. If the poets whose works represent this 1% want to reach beyond the physical plane, they need to express what hovers above pictorial and figurative language through a medium existing above ordinary prose. How can one express the meaning of: 'O water-lily, thou blossoming swan, O swan, thou floating water-lily'? What these lines express hovers between the two pictures, and this 'something' cannot be expressed in prose. It is the same with the figure of speech. But it is also possible to express adequately what is metaphysical with falling back on pictures of speech as Goethe managed to do. He does not always need to express his ideas in pictures for you to experience what he wishes to express. Goethe achieved it, sometimes also Martin Greif, who achieved what one could call objective lyricism. At times Shakespeare also succeeded entirely in the lyrical passages of his dramatic works." (19.6.24)

The following short summary shows how metrics and poetics and the aesthetics of language are supposed to be distributed over the main lessons, beginning with Class 8:

Class 8   German (and foreign languages) – "Rudiments" (2.6.24)

Class 9   German – (history of art lessons deal with paintings and sculptures)

Class 10   German – coherent representation of metrics and poetics (17.6.21)

Class 11   Art lessons – Aesthetics of language (21.6.22 and 19.6.24)

Essay Writing – Fundamentals

After speaking about essay writing in his 10th lecture of the "Practical Course" Steiner gave some clear indications about the teaching of foreign languages which are also relevant to the teaching of the pupil's mother tongue.

"To make children write compositions in a foreign language, compositions which are not related to life, is real nonsense. The teacher should not go beyond setting tasks concerned with letter writing or with business correspondence and similar matters. At most the children could practise writing down in simple sentences stories which they had heard." (12 lecture 10)

The above lines refer to foreign language lessons, but are also applicable to German lessons. However, the following sentences certainly concern the German teachers as much as the foreign language teachers.

"In primary education, we should practise the recounting of incidents which have occurred or of adventures children have had rather than give them compositions to write. Free compositions do not yet belong to the lower classes. However, oral descriptions of events which the children have witnessed do belong to primary education, for it is essential for the child to learn how to report happenings. Otherwise he will not be able to play his proper part within the social structure of mankind." (ibid.)

This is followed by remarks about the lack of ability in modern people to observe and report accurately what they have witnessed. Steiner describes a criminological-psychological attempt to get witnesses in court to report more accurately and continues:

"We ought to see that our civilization develops in such a way that more reliance can be placed on witnesses and that people speak the truth more and more. But to achieve this aim we must begin with childhood. And for this reason it is important to let the children practise how to report what they have seen and heard rather than to give them compositions to write. In this way the habit of describing accurately, be it in ordinary life or in a court of law, will become inculcated in the children, so that they will learn to respect the truth. Here, too, the will-element ought to be considered more than the intellect... Therefore we need to observe such details in education so that we ask the children, once they have learnt how to write and particularly after the age of twelve, to write down accurately what they have witnessed rather than give them free compositions which in any case do not really belong to this stage of childhood." (ibid.)

Here Steiner points out the consequences which result in a general social failing of our times, namely most people's inability to speak the truth in serious life situations. The education of the past and present is to blame for the lack of truthfulness. Education must change so that this social damage may be repaired. Whoever cannot report truthfully what he has experienced, is not fit to play his proper part within the civilisation of his time.

Towards the end of the Waldorf School's first year, in a conversation about eurythmy lessons, Steiner also spoke about essay-writing:

"It should be our task to talk to the children far more freely about the subjects which they are studying, and to aim more towards a general development of their life of thinking and feeling. In mathematics lessons one can make sure that the pupils grasp the idea behind the terms: -5, -a; one enables the pupil to see that he has five less than he needs to give to his neighbours. Go into precise details in a conversation. Sometimes it is good to stray from the main theme. You may

notice that the children will not become perfect in their essay writing quite so quickly, but you will also realise that this is not a matter of great importance. Those who are cleverheads, the gifted head children, will write good compositions – the gifted body children will be good at eurythmy. One must try to balance this through conversations. If you converse with the children, this activity will lead away from the head – if you talk about something which has been taken from outer life, and then deepen it." (12.6.20)

The business composition which Steiner included in the curriculum as part of German was always a headache for the teachers. While discussing the syllabus for Class 10 and in answer to a question, Steiner referred to a previous complaint about improper and negligent work which however was not directly connected with the school:

"One must try to grasp the case in question, and see the whole course of a business transaction, and then one must try to write a report about it. This is best done with a critical attitude. Try to do it. Then try to fathom what the gibberish is all about and then try to put it into decent German." (17.6.21)

The teachers were asked to occupy themselves with any concrete business situations and transactions which were available to them in order to acquire an understanding of a given situation, which they were to put down in clear German. Steiner then continued:

"Business composition: If in any business you need a specialist's judgement about something and you ask for an expert opinion such a written opinion is an example of a business composition. Written information, an agent's report, these are business compositions. It isn't so terribly serious if one makes a slip (in one's attempts). Those who have expertise manage better than someone without previous experience. Nevertheless, the experts also make blunders." (ibid.)

Many faults were found in an example of such a business composition:

"This is the result of superficiality, because one does not realise that these matters must be dealt with in an exact way - one should only write down the essentials. Even a naive way of doing so is better than business jargon... This sort of thing need not terrify you. One only needs to grasp the essentials and put them down in writing. Anybody will then be able to understand your efforts." (ibid.)

When a teacher remarked that the pupils of Class 7 ought to have a sense of duty towards their homework Steiner said:

"One ought to ensure that the children's curiosity is roused when they have to do homework. If you set them the kind of task which would make them curious about the results or answers which they have to find then they feel stimulated. This is how I should do it. A sense of duty cannot be developed in the child before he can understand the full meaning and consequences of duty. Give him composition themes such as these: 'The steam engine, a witness of human strength – The steam engine, a witness of human weakness'. Let one such theme follow the other. I believe that in this way you will create interest. One can arrange one's lesson in a way which will excite interest." (28.4.22)

As Steiner recommended this kind of theme several times it can safely be assumed that he did not wish to restrict it merely to Class 7. On the same day he once more recommended this type of theme to a German teacher who had reported that he was going to give his class a composition about the character of Faust. Steiner answered:

"But surely this is beyond them: consider that not even Kuno Fischer has written well on that theme. I should choose themes which are based more on observation of life like the one mentioned previously (about the steam engine), or let us say: 'What is beautiful about Nature?' – and then: 'What is beautiful about the Human Soul?'. Choose the kind of theme which compels children to concentrate while they are writing." (ibid.)

A third question about essay-writing was put on the same day, viz, should one discuss a composition theme when it is set? Steiner answered:

"The theme should be built up within the general context of the lesson and not be treated as a separate entity. One should have said quite a lot (about the theme). While talking about Jean Paul you had many possibilities for fruitful themes. Your themes were aimed too high." (ibid.)

Thereupon a teacher asked: how would you use the subject of Schiller's and Goethe's friendship for a composition? (in Class 9). Steiner replied:

"I would describe the scene of Goethe walking through Weimar to Tiefurt. Then I would ask the class to describe a walk with Goethe as concretely as possible. In this way you can bring everything together." (ibid.)

During a discussion about any special tasks for the coming new school year 1923/24, in which the first Class 12 was to be opened, Steiner said that not enough attention had been given to composition lessons:

"It is essential that children get into the habit of writing German compositions. One could make use of the content of the lessons for such compositions." (25.5.23)

When a teacher thought it necessary to tell the children something about the technique of essay writing Steiner answered:

"Let them learn from their mistakes. I should avoid any theoretical splitting up of their work which would only make them lose heart, especially if their compositions were poor." (ibid.)

In the Berne Course Steiner spoke about the teacher who is able "to read" Man:

"If he can read then the educator will find in each child a book of the soul. Children can become 'reading matter of the soul' for their teachers, even in quite large classes. If this is so then the teacher will find, simply out of his own inner tact, that before the ninth or tenth year the child does not differentiate between the world and his own I, and that before this time he will not be able to write anything in the way of a composition out of himself. The most he can do will be to retell what he has heard of fairy tales or legends. It is only at nine or ten that you can gradually begin to approach the child with images and thoughts which you can get him to write about out of his own free thoughts and feelings. The inner thought structure which a child needs before he

can pass over to essay-writing is not present until towards the twelfth year. He should not write essays before this time. If he does it too early (I am speaking of this because a question was asked about it) then there will set in, not in this case sclerosis of the soul, but rickets of the soul. At a later age of life the child will be inwardly weak and ineffective." (38 lecture 5)

In the 7th lecture of the Torquay Course Steiner emphasised the necessity of appealing only to the rhythmic system in the child of primary school age. He said that in order to do so one did not need the intellectual but the pictorial approach, viz, what comes from the imagination. After a few explanatory words he continued:

"Now this fantasy should above all be the guiding principle in what are called compositions, when the children have to write about something and work it out for themselves. Here what must be strictly avoided is to let the children write a composition about anything that you have not first talked over with them in great detail so that the subject is familiar to them. You yourself, with the authority of the teacher and educator, should have first spoken about the subject with the children; then the child should produce his composition under the influence of what you yourself have said. Even when the children are approaching puberty you must still not depart from this principle, Even then the child should not just write whatever occurs to him; he should always feel that a certain mood has been aroused in him through having discussed the subject with his teacher, and all that he then writes in his essay must preserve this mood. Here again it is 'aliveness' that must be the guiding principle. 'Aliveness' in the teacher must pass over to 'aliveness' in the children." (40 lecture 7)

Curriculum indications for each class

Class 1

"The first thing we have to do when we get the children in the first class is to find suitable material for telling stories and having them retold. Through telling and retelling of fairy tales and legends, as well as through recounting actual happenings, we develop real speech; we form a transition from dialect to cultured colloquial language. In our efforts to teach the young children to speak properly, we are also laying the foundations for correct writing. Running parallel with the practice of listening and retelling of stories, we also introduce the children to an inner experience of different forms and shapes. We let them draw simple curved and angular forms, not with the intention of teaching them how to copy external objects, but in order for them to become familiar with the 'language of forms'. Apart from this form drawing we practise painting by placing one colour next to another in such a way that the child can experience the quality of colour intervals, such as red next to green, red next to yellow, etc. From this we lead on to writing in the way outlined in previous talks on teaching methods. It would be a natural step to lead over from form-drawing to the Roman alphabet and

later from the Roman to the Gothic letters (In Steiner's days children in all schools were taught two alphabets for handwriting – the Gothic (the German script) and the Roman (the 'modern' German) alphabet. Finally we introduce printed letters, but only after the child has learnt the shapes of the drawn letters and when he can read and write simple words. When introducing printed letters, begin again with the Roman alphabet before introducing the German printed type.

If we approach our task with common sense we shall enable the children during this first year to put down in writing a few simple words or short sentences spoken to them, and they will learn to read simple words and sentences. One need not fix a definite standard to be reached during the first year – indeed this would be quite wrong. The aim during the first year should be that the child becomes familiar with printed letters and that he can write a few simple words and sentences out of himself." (16 lecture 1)

Story material – Fairy tales

Teachers are recommended to look up lecture 13 of the Practical Course, in order to find out more about the standards to be reached by the end of Class 1. (12)

For teaching poems see the section on Class 4.

Class 2

"In the second school year continue with the telling of stories and having them retold, and try to develop this further. The child will gradually be led to write down what has been recounted to him. When he is able to do this you can let him reproduce, in quite small compositions, descriptions of what he has heard about animals, plants, meadows and woods in his neighbourhood. It is important not to touch upon grammar in the first school year, but in the second school year one should let the child know what a noun is, an adjective and a verb. This should lead to a talk about the fundamental construction of sentences." (16 lecture 1)

On 15th March 1922 Steiner further elucidated the above passage, after a teacher had complained that the grammatical points which he was bringing to the children had remained obscure:

"It depends on how one does it. Under certain circumstances it is not necessary to teach the children the grammatical terms noun and verb, but merely to begin with their contrasting nature. A child of 7 years old will be able to distinguish between a verb and a noun. This difference he will be able to appreciate. The terminology is not essential, but begin with stories and then make clear the difference between noun and verb. This the child can grasp at that age. It must be able to grasp the difference between running or jumping and man or some other noun. It must be able to grasp that. Definitions should be especially avoided with children in the lower classes." (15.3.22)

Story material – Stories from the animal world introduced through the fable.

For treatment of poems see under the section on Class 4.

Class 3

"The third year will essentially be a continuation of what was done in the second as regards speaking, reading, writing and much else. The capacity to write down what has been seen, heard and read will be increased. One will also however attempt to bring out in the children a conscious feeling for short, long and lengthened sounds and so on. This feeling for articulation in speech, and speech formation altogether, is something that can be profitably dealt with between the ages of 8 and 9, when one has the child in the third class. The child is then given an idea of the parts of speech, the parts of a sentence and the structure of sentences and also of the linking up of a sentence by punctuation - comma, full stop etc." (16 lecture 1)

Story material – Biblical stories as part of ancient history.

Class 4

"In the fourth year the telling of stories by the teacher and the retelling by the children is continued. Whereas in the first two years the teacher has led the children to experience the rhythm, rhyme and beat of short poems in an instinctive way, in Classes 3 and 4 it is a good thing to lead them to an appreciation of the form and inner beauty of the poems. When the children have learnt to write simple stories and descriptions, letter writing of all kinds is introduced.

It is at this time that one endeavours to call up in the children a clear idea of the tenses of the verb. In this way a child is given just the ideas suitable for his stage of development (we are speaking about children of 9 and 10 years). A child must feel clearly that he cannot say 'the man ran' when he means 'the man has run'; that he does not confuse the imperfect tense with the perfect tense and that he acquires a feeling for when he should say 'the man stood' and 'the man has stood', and so with all the things that come to expression by changing the form of the verb. We also try to stimulate an instinctive feeling for the connection, let us say, of a preposition with the noun before which it stands. We see to it that the child feels the difference between saying 'in' in one case and 'at' in another. Forming language plastically is what he should practise in his mother tongue when he is about ten years old – a feeling for the plastic forming of speech." (ibid.)

Story material – Scenes from ancient history.

Class 5

"In the fifth school year the teacher recapitulates and continues what he has fostered in the fourth year. At this point he introduces the active and passive moods of the verb. Just at this time, too, we ask the child not merely to reproduce freely what he has seen and heard but, if possible, to render it in direct speech – as though put in inverted commas. We try to give the child plenty of practice in distinguishing between giving his own opinions and those of somebody else. Later on we show him how to express in writing the marked difference in style between reproducing one's own ideas and report-

ing other peoples' views. In connection with this, one again tries to improve punctuation. Letter-writing is also developed further." (ibid.)

Story material – Scenes from medieval history.

Class 6

"In the sixth school year we naturally repeat and continue what we have been doing in the fifth and we try to let the children experience the style of the subjunctive mood. We speak of these things, giving plenty of examples, so that the child learns to distinguish between what can be expressed as a direct affirmation and what needs to be expressed in the subjunctive mood. We give the child exercises in speaking where we pay strict attention to this difference and we allow nothing to pass that is faulty as regards the application of the subjunctive. For instance when the child should say 'I take care that my little sister may learn to walk' we never let him say 'I take care that my sister learns to walk', so that a strong sense of the plasticity of language may flow into the feeling for speech.

At this time letter-writing takes the form of simple straightforward business essays, in which themes are dealt with that are already familiar to the child. One can refer back to what was already taught about meadows and woods in Class 3, and use information given at that time as a basis for simple business correspondence." (ibid.)

Story material – Scenes from later history.

Class 7

"In the seventh school year one will have to follow up what was done in the sixth. One must try to develop in the child an appreciation of the plasticity of the language which can be illustrated by the difference in style between a wish, wonder and surprise. The child should form sentences which really do bear an inner relationship to the form of the feeling itself. This, however, ought not to be done by using, or rather misusing, an existing poem in order to show how its author has formed a sentence expressing a wish. No, you should tackle the matter directly by making the child express a wish quite spontaneously and then by helping him to clothe this wish into a proper sentence. The same can be done with other feelings, such as wonder or surprise. When comparing the different sentences, you bring to light the formative power in the language whose conscious appreciation you must try to develop further...

What has been brought out in natural history will enable the child to characterise in essays, let us say the wolf, the lion, the bee, and so on.

Parallel with these themes of a more general human character, practical business affairs should be studied especially at this time. The teacher must take the trouble to familiarise himself with matters of this kind and to get such ideas (worked out in a suitable form) into the heads of the pupils." (ibid.)

Story material – Stories about different tribes.

Class 8

"In the eighth class, one will have to give the children a comprehensive understanding for lengthier poems and prose: one reads with them something dramatic or epic. Consideration must be given to what I have said about all explanations and interpretations preceding the reading, so that the actual reading is always the final climax of all that has been built up previously.

Especially in Class 8 practical business correspondence should not be neglected." (ibid.)

Story material – Knowledge of different peoples.

It should be noted that for the foreign languages in Class 8 "the rudiments of poetics and metrics of the foreign languages" were meant to be given (2.6.24). Therefore metrics and poetics were also to be taken this far in German. For details see the heading "Style and figurative writing – metrics and poetics" in this section.

Indications given for the upper classes, each of which can be found in the "Conferences" (teachers' meetings), are listed below.

Class 9

Indications were given after the German teacher had reported that he had taken Goethe, Schiller and Herder and that he had added individual reviews such as on Dante's "Divine Comedy":

"With regard to literature you could now try taking Jean Paul, particularly certain passages from 'Aesthetics or an Introduction to Beauty'... more especially those passages which deal with humour... Then go on to Herman Grimm's Goethe lectures. This may take six months. Without going into detail, read and discuss separate chapters... With regard to language I recommend you not to concentrate on pedantic grammar during the first half of the year, but on Grimm's law of sound-shifting. Discuss it from its different aspects... Concerning essays: I should leave everything belonging to grammar and syntax until you discuss corrections in class. I should recommend that you try to set compositions with historical themes, in which the pupils use the material which you yourself have taught them during the last year's history courses. Before setting the composition you will have to ask the old pupils to cover the theme orally for the sake of the newcomers." (22.9.20)

Later on in the same year the English teacher of Class 9 reported that he had read "Julius Caesar" with his class and that the play had been much appreciated, and Steiner commented:
"Could you not repeat the same theme in writing, as a kind of composition? It is necessary for such a task to be given in German lessons too... so that pupils produce something in writing and really formulate their thoughts." (15.11.20)

He then turned to the German teacher of the class:
"Don't you set them any kind of themes (for compositions)? It would not matter if the content were first repeated orally. As long as they bring their own written formulation." (ibid.)

From Class 9 onwards art lessons are taught side by side with German lessons and it is worth noting what Steiner said about this arrangement: "It would be a good thing to balance the art lessons with history and history of literature lessons." (24.4.23). This instruction to the art teacher is equally applicable to the German teacher.

As mentioned before Steiner did not determine in which class the question of the artistic treatment of the language should be explored – therefore all relevant indications given to the Waldorf School have been added to the chapter on German (the mother tongue) under the separate heading: "Style and figuration – metrics and poetics."

Class 10

The syllabus for Class 10 was finished on 17th June 1921. The following instructions were given for German:
"You should now begin, or continue, with a somewhat coherent presentation of what is generally called metrics and poetics. On the basis of what they have learnt already in connection with Jean Paul... our pupils will be well able to enter into these themes. The usually pedantic methods of teaching these subjects should be avoided. This so-called metrics and poetics must appear reasonable and must be dealt with in a living way, in connection with living poetry. Then the Song of the Nibelungs and Gudrun should be given. If possible, endeavour to take it in the Middle High German language. Time permitting, one should teach some Middle High German and describe the entire milieu out of which the work has grown. One would discuss the artistic and national importance of the work and – apart from reading some passages as samples – one should tell the pupils the entire content of the great narrative poems. Finally, in connection with the Song of the Nibelungs, one should teach them some Middle High German grammar and compare it with the Modern High German grammar... Begin with metrics." (17.6.21)

A year later the German teacher remarked that the children would like to know something about contemporary literature:
"They are still too young for the later German poetry. One cannot introduce Geibel and Marlitt yet. One could take C. F. Meyer, but even this would be too early. One needs to be more mature to understand Jordan. This they could only understand in the 12th and 13th Class. It would be no good to introduce it in 'governess-style'. If you wish to go in for 'Demiourgos' you need children of 16, 17 years. Otherwise, in a certain sense, it could be very confusing to introduce pupils to the latest trends in poetry." (20.6.22)

On 14th February 1923 Steiner answered a question about how one should treat the Song of the Nibelungs:
"What matters is that you first introduce the children to the whole atmosphere of the Song of the Nibelungs, so that they can understand its historical context. Do this as vividly and pictorially as possible, in the way in which I tried to characterise Parsifal and Christianity. That would be the era of mass-migration. Make it really alive and then read some sample passages. First

prepare the ground by giving a picture of the whole scene, not in a monotonous prose but in an entertaining and pictorial way, and then read the passage. Above all see to it that it is not only you who are reading but that the children also read, and after having been given your preliminary picture they will not read in a flat and monotonous manner. It is not possible for them to read in a boring way if you have given them a good picture beforehand. Sometimes you can interrupt the reading to observe an interesting passage and discuss words of interest. One can strike sparks from many a word or sentence construction which can shed light upon the entire era. If you do it in this way, you will give the children sufficient introduction." (14.2.23). [The above mentioned characterisation of Parsifal and Christianity can be found in the reported teachers' meetings. (Conferences 9.12.22)]*

Class 11

The syllabus for Class 11 was completed on 21st June 1922, after a new arrangement for the distribution of teachers of different subjects had been made on the previous day. Steiner spoke about the German lessons:

"For Class 11 the history of literature comes into question first of all. In our discussions we will link what has to be taught now with what has already been covered in Class 10. What have we taught? – The Song of the Nibelungs, Gudrun, metrics and poetics.

Now we have to refer to what should be done in metrics and poetics in this class, to what I called yesterday the aesthetic element when speaking about art lessons for this class. First you must place the literature into the foreground in such a way that you build a bridge from the Song of the Nibelungs and Gudrun to the great literature of the Middle Ages, to Parsifal, Poor Henry (Armer Heinrich) and such like. Above all, try by a preliminary cursory treatment to create a picture of the whole work, so that the children know the Parsifal legend, so that they look upon the passages which you read from the original version as samples seen within the totality of the work." (21.6.22)

After this the treatment of Parsifal in the religion lessons was discussed, as well as the history course which ran parallel with the art course. It was stated that poetics, metrics and appreciation of style should be given within the art course, etc. This shows clearly that the interpretation of the sentence about poetics in the above syllabus text for Class 11 is correct. This sentence has a proper meaning only if it is read in the following way: "Now we have to refer to what should be done in metrics and poetics in this class, what I called yesterday the aesthetic element (to the lessons on aesthetics)". (ibid.)

Steiner spoke about the Parsifal legend in greater detail on 9th December 1922 in the reported teachers' meetings (Conferences). On 6th February 1923 he also made an important comment on this theme.

Class 12

On 25th April 1923 Steiner gave the curriculum for the first Class 12. This class was to be prepared for the forthcoming examination right from the beginning. Steiner showed what should be taught in this class if one were not forced to work exclusively for the examination. Because of the difficult situation he had already said on the previous day:

"But in order not to compromise to the exclusion of our own rights, I would think it right if we were to indicate here what could be considered the curriculum of Class 12."

"A great number of Goethe's literary works can be traced back to pictorial impressions. On the other hand, a great number of romantic works of art can be traced back to musical impressions. This contact between the two different arts (should be the basis of study for Class 12)." (24.4.23)

The following words of 25th April 1923 are also guide lines for a Class 12 syllabus, free from compromise:

"It would be desirable, if just at this age – the pupils are about eighteen years old – they could gain a rounding-off of the historical-artistic element and already receive a spiritual background in literature, history of art and history, without, however, being taught 'anthroposophical dogma'. We ought to make the attempt to bring the spiritual element into literature, history of art and history, not only a part of the content, but in the way these subjects are treated." (25.4.23)

A year later the decision was taken to teach the new Class 12 according to the Steiner School curriculum and then to add a special preparation class during the thirteenth school year for those who wished to take the examination (see the section on school leaving examinations and university training). For this new Class 12 the following outlines were given:

"Yesterday I indicated that, since the syllabus of the history of literature has not been covered in general, it would be sufficient to give a cursory survey of the missing parts. On the other hand, a complete survey ought to be given, in the appropriate place, of German history of literature in connection with foreign works. One would have to start with the greatest works of ancient literature as part of this survey – the old monumental literature. Start properly with the Gothic period, then go on to the old German period, taking the whole development up to the Song of the Nibelungs; take Gudrun cursorily so that an impression of completeness can be gained – then the middle ages, then the pre-classical period, the classical period and the romantic period right up to the present day. Give a general survey, but a survey which allows the pupils to appreciate the contents – a survey of substance, so that it becomes evident what a person would need for his life, if he wished to know something of Walter von der Vogelweide, of Klopstock, or Logau, for instance. I think this could be done in five to six hours. It could be done in five to six hours.

This ought to be followed mainly by a study of present day literature. This period should be dealt with more extensively in this oldest class. By present day literature I mean that a shortish introduction should be given to the most outstanding literary works of the years 1850, 1860 and 1870 so that the latest literary works can be studied at greater depth, so that the young people can gain an insight into the works of Nietzsche, Ibsen and also foreign authors like Tolstoi, Dostoevsky, etc., so that they will leave school as educated people." (30.4.24)

2   Art, Aesthetics and History of Art

From Class 9 to Class 12 five to six weeks' main lessons each.

The specific intentions underlying the art lessons which begin in Class 9, are perhaps most clearly explained by the words from the Ilkley Course which are quoted below:

"At a certain age, as I told you yesterday, the child must be led on from the plant- and animal-lore which he grasps more with his faculties of soul, to mineralogy, physics and chemistry, where greater claims are made on his conceptual faculties and intellect – though it is all important that these subjects are not taught too soon. During this period of life when we are conveying the idea of causality to the child and he learns of cause and effect in nature it is essential to balance the inorganic, lifeless elements in nature-study by leading him into the domain of art.

If we are to introduce art to the child in the right way not only must all our teaching be artistic from the beginning but art itself must play its proper part in education. You can see that the plastic arts are cultivated, if only from the fact that the writing lessons begin with a kind of painting. Thus, according to the Waldorf School principle, we begin to give painting and drawing lessons to children of a very tender age. Modelling too is cultivated as much as possible, albeit only from the ninth or tenth year and in a primitive way. It has a wonderfully vitalizing effect on the child's physical sight and on the inner quality of soul in his sight if, at the right age, he begins to model plastic forms and figures. So many people go through life without even noticing what is most significant in the objects and events in their environment. As a matter of fact, we have to learn how to do this before we can see and observe in the way that gives us our true position in the world. And if the child is to learn to observe aright it is a very good thing for him to begin to occupy himself with modelling as early as possible, to guide what he has seen from his head and eyes into the movements of fingers and hand. In this way we shall not only awaken the child's taste for the artistic around him – in the arrangement of a room perhaps – and distaste for the inartistic, but he will begin to observe those things in the world which ought to flow into the heart and soul of man." (35 lecture 11)

And after some remarks about musical instruction he concludes:

"At the age when the child must realise that nature is ruled by abstract law to be grasped by reason, when he must learn in physics the link between cause and effect in given cases, we must promote an understanding of art as a necessary counter balance. The child must realise how the several arts have developed in the different epochs of human history, how this or that motif in art plays its part in a particular epoch. Only in this way will those elements which a human being needs for all-round unfoldment of his being be truly stimulated. Its this way too we can unfold the qualities which, as I shall show in tomorrow's lecture, are essential in moral instruction." (ibid.)

In these art lessons, taught as a separate subject in main lessons, the generally artistic atmosphere of the education reaches its climax and its conclusion. In the first years the child is allowed to live within a generally artistic atmosphere. Then, strengthened by this, the child has to find its way towards the more intellectual work and understanding. At the same time its artistic abilities should mature until, during the last school years, it is led to full appreciation of the arts and their historical development. (12 lecture 3)

The art lessons were given their first concrete aims only at the beginning of the third year of the Waldorf School on 17th June 1921, when the syllabus for the new Class 10 was planned. On this occasion Steiner said, turning towards Max Wolfhügel the handicrafts teacher:

"The handicraft lessons now need to be led into a genuinely artistic realm. You have already done this in modelling. Modelling can be alternated with painting for those who have sufficient skill. With regard to those now entering Class 10, we must take into account their previous training in the Gymnasium (*3). Nevertheless we must move more towards an artistic conception of life. We need something more than art, applied arts or handicraft lessons, we need some kind of aesthetics, and here Dr. Schwebsch could help to link through aesthetics what belongs to the realm of sculpture and painting to what belongs to the musical sphere. He has occupied himself a great deal with music in its widest context. In order to introduce pupils to aesthetics of music – which would have to be given in an elementary way – various colleagues would have to work together, forming a kind of sub-group, so that the handicraft lessons could lead over into applied arts and then into the musical sphere – but in such a way that the aesthetic side of music rather than its theoretical side would be cultivated. I think that one should enable the children at the earliest possible age to distinguish whether a chair or a table is beautiful or ugly. Do not let them think that a chair is beautiful only when its shape is pleasant to the eye. The chair's beauty should be felt when sitting in it. In this fitness for purpose lies its beauty. Yesterday I spoke to you about kindred things when telling you that the children should arrange the patterns of their embroidery in handwork lessons in such a way that anyone looking at it could feel which side is the one to be opened up. Altogether I believe that the development of a refined artistic sense will bring together the different branches of handwork and handicrafts. This needs to be brought about in quite a natural way, but in a proper way so that pupils will outgrow their present weaknesses." (17.6.21)

Here we come to a decisive point in the development of the Waldorf School idea. Steiner realised that in Erich Schwebsch he had found the person whom he knew to be capable of building up the art lessons in the way he had wanted them to be. His above remarks about the beauty of an object show that he wanted the concept of beauty freed from mere eye or ear appeal in order to spread it also to the so-called lower senses (see Aeppli: The Twelve Senses) so that plastic forms were not just a matter for the eyes but for a full experience in space. This theme resounds again and again throughout Steiner's art of education.

In the Autumn of the same year, on 11th September 1921, Erich Schwebsch asked for further directions for his art lessons and Steiner's answer can be looked upon not so much as an aim for a particular class, but as a more general guide. It should be remembered that at that time Classes 11 and 12 did not yet exist and that apart from Classes 9 and 10, Class 8 was also receiving art lessons during this and the following year.

> *"I should try – we are dealing with children between 14 and 16 years of age – to get them to develop by real and practical examples a sense of beauty, a sense of what is truly artistic. Let them experience the metamorphoses of beauty in the different periods: the Greek ideal of beauty, the Renaissance ideal of beauty. It is of special importance at this young age that the pupils work out concretely what is usually taught in abstract form. Works on aesthetics such as von Vischer's and Carriere's are mere husks. On the other hand, it ennobles the character if at this age the children are given the possibility to understand: What is beautiful? What is sublime? What is comical? How is the comical expressed in music and how in poetry? The soul of the child cannot yet absorb more general concepts. Therefore, at this age, one should ask them: What is the meaning of declaiming, of reciting?" (11.9.21)*

This is followed by a further remark about reciting and declaiming which can be looked up in the Conferences.

At the beginning of the next school year Steiner said, when asked a question about the art lessons in Class 8:

> *"(Take) the motives of Albrecht Dürer – also what is related to them musically, e.g., Bach. Make the black and white drawing lessons very alive." (28.4.22)*

At this time the fourth year of the Waldorf School was just beginning. Class 8 once more received art lessons but a definite syllabus for art lessons did not yet exist. On 10th May 1922 Steiner gave directions for Class 11, and when Erich Schwebsch asked for fundamentals for Classes 8, 9, 10 and 11, he replied:

> *"In Class 8 take the motives of Albrecht Dürer. I should like to think about what to take for Class 9." (10.5.22)*

Class 9

On 9th December 1922 Erich Schwebsch asked how the periods of the different art courses should be handled. He reported that he was going to take Class 9 and that in Class 8 he had taken Albrecht Dürer's motives for his black and white period. Steiner replied:

> *"One can do this very well. Do you really think that all the many objects in Dürer's 'Melancholia' are mere attributes (added to the picture)? I believe that the difference between Dürer and Rembrandt consists in*

> *Rembrandt's looking at the problem of light and darkness simply as that of light and darkness 'kat' exochen' (par excellence), whereas Dürer wants to solve the problem by showing the light and darkness in as many objects as possible. The many objects in the 'Melancholia' are not to be looked upon as attributes, but more as objects reflecting light and casting shadows. With Dürer I see the problem more in this way: how does the light appear if it is reflected by different objects? With Rembrandt the interaction of light and darkness in itself is the problem. This I think is the difference. Rembrandt would not have solved the problem of the 'Melancholia' in this way. He would have solved it more abstractly. So I think one can draw the lines very distinctly." (9.12.22)*

Erich Schwebsch mentioned that he wanted to bring the problem of Northern and Southern art into his course and later also the problem of Western and Eastern art. Steiner answered:

> *"In the lessons one can contrast the effect of light and darkness in Rembrandt's works, which he paints qualitatively, with the paintings of Southern art. In this way one can introduce the two streams. One can do this quite naturally if one shows how Rembrandt, whose paintings are three dimensional, solves the light-dark problem qualitatively so that space becomes only an opportunity of solving the problem as a painter. If you contrast this with sculpture whose problem is entirely one of space, you can lead over to the study of sculpture. And perhaps it is best also to link this to the later French sculptors of classicism (whose art is based on the Graeco-Roman model). In the Rococo period – naturally you must choose good examples of this period – you find the extreme sculptural counterpart to Rembrandt. One can show in the works of the Rococo period how light and darkness have a totally different effect from that in Rembrandt's works. One must always point out that Rococo art, even if it may not be appreciated as much as Baroque art by many people, represents a higher stage in the development of art." (ibid.)*

When asked whether certain stages in the history of art were to be worked out, Steiner answered:

> *"I should point out how these stages find their expression differently in different parts of the earth. It is interesting to show how at the time of Dürer the style in Holland was quite different from Rembrandt's style: different times for different places.*

> *I should begin first in Class 9, only bearing this class in mind.*

> *On the other hand, I should work out the stages more and more clearly as the pupils become older, so that when giving a summary in Class 11 I could awaken in the pupils a clear concept of the different stages." (ibid.)*

On 24th April 1923 Erich Schwebsch once more asked for plans showing successive stages for art lessons. He explained that he intended to link up with history and the history of literature when teaching Class 9 on the following morning. He wanted to show how the arts had their origin in mythology. Steiner answered:

"It would be good to link the art lessons with history and history of literature. It would be good to try to begin with Germanic mythology but then to pause and perhaps to show how later the Germanic myths reappear as something aesthetic, though in a different form of artistic development. It is absolutely possible to bring together Dürer as artist with the way in which the forms of Germanic mythology are expressed. We are dealing with children of fifteen years old. One could prove that the old Teutons used to paint their gods in the same way as Dürer painted his figures." (24.4.23)

Class 10

After the above remarks on Class 9 Steiner then continued on the subject of Class 10, apparently referring to the teacher's report of his lessons:

"Then in Class 10 you would go on to Goethe's lyrical poetry and style. The syllabus is prepared through the preliminary work in Class 9. This can remain. Bring together the musical and the poetical element in Class 11." (24.4.23)

In these sentences the aims for Class 10 are mentioned for the first time. Soon afterwards Erich Schwebsch once more asked for advice about art lessons for Class 10, mentioning Goethe's lyrical poetry and tropology, which he wanted to teach. Steiner answered:

"It is a subject which could almost cover the whole of Class 10. Of course one can teach tropology and figuration. One can give the children a feeling for poetical forms. One must not tell them that Goethe was able to master poetical form only at a definite age, that he was able to write a stanza only at the age of 40. Such things which call forth reactions, which may create a mood of resistance, one needs to watch very carefully. It is quite possible to teach it, In art lessons the subject matter is the motive. One can adapt it according to the pupils' capacities." (31.7.23)

Class 11

Steiner gave the following information when asked about art in Class 11, which was being opened for the first time:

"It would certainly be possible to teach and to achieve good understanding in this class with a theme such as: The position of art in the entire development of culture. Draw their attention to questions like: Why did music as we know it today develop comparatively late? What did the Greeks call music? etc. – such points. Then one naturally has to discuss in detail what was indicated today in German from a literary point of view: Why does landscape painting begin at a certain point of time? Especially such questions. Then art and religion." (10. 5.22)

A few weeks later Steiner gave some more information about the art syllabus for Class 11:

"What has been taught? – Song of the Nibelungs, Gudrun, metrics, poetics. Metrics and poetics and what I yesterday called the aesthetics in art lessons, should be taught in the art lessons." (21.6.22)

This shows that aesthetics in this class should be part of art and not of German, as previously metrics and poetics had been.

The remark "What I yesterday called the aesthetics in art lessons" refers to the first of the two lectures given to the Waldorf teachers in 1922 (28), the study of which would make a deeper understanding possible.

On the same day the following indications were given for Class 11:

"Poetics, metrics and study of style will have to be part of aesthetics and art for this class, whereby one need not limit style to literary style. It could also be extended to cover other arts, music and sculpture. For the last third I should use Gottfried Semper's definition of style and would show through this work how one can bring other characteristics of style to the children." (21.6.22)

On 6th February 1923 Erich Schwebsch reported that in Class 10 he had developed the theme of how in "The Bride of Messina" Schiller had wanted to gain a musical effect through the spoken word and how in his 9th Symphony Beethoven had moved towards the spoken word through the text of the chorus and that Richard Wagner had experienced this deeply. Steiner replied – and his words must be looked upon as an educational aim for Class 11:

"It will be specially important to place this relationship of Schiller to Beethoven right into the centre. Children of this age will be able to experience this most deeply. If you make this observation a kind of dramatic centre – viz. the chorus in Schiller's 'Bride of Messina' – then you will succeed best in bringing to them what you wish to say about Parsifal." (6.2.23)

A further indication for the syllabus of Class 11 is contained in the short summary of 24th April 1923, which has already been quoted in connection with Class 10:

"Bringing together the musical and the poetical element." (24.4.23)

Classes 9-11 (Summary)

Finally, in the teachers meeting of 29th April 1924, a short synopsis was given of the art lesson syllabus for each class:

"In Class 9 selections from the art of painting. Class 10 classical poetry. Class 11 the reciprocal relationship between music and poetry. The theme for Class 11 had been the observation of how, since Goethe, poetry and music were continuing to develop below the surface." (29.4.24)

Class 12

Steiner first spoke about art in Class 12 on 25th April 1923, during anxious discussions about the first examinations, which at that time had to be taken in Class 12. The teaching of art in Classes 9 and 10 had been discussed and Erich Schwebsch had proposed – somewhat under the shadow of the forthcoming examination work – to treat artistically the German curriculum, namely literature beginning with the year 1740. Steiner agreed and said the following words (already quoted in the section about teaching German):

"But in order not to compromise to the exclusion of our own rights I would think it right to act in the following way: A great number of Goethe's literary works can be traced back to pictorial impressions. On the other hand, a great number of romantic works can be traced back to musical impressions. Take this point of

contact between the different arts." (24.4.23)

On the following day the syllabus for the examination Class 12 was discussed in detail and Steiner introduced it with the words already quoted:

> *'It would be desirable if just at this age – about eighteen years old – the pupils gained a rounding-off of the historical-artistic element and if they received a spiritual background in literature, history of art and history, without however, being taught 'anthroposophical dogma'. We ought to make the attempt to bring the spiritual element into literature, history of art and history, not only as part of the content, but rather in the way these subjects are treated." (25.4.23)*

This is an outline of what could be considered an ideal curriculum of a future Steiner School, a curriculum based only on pedagogical considerations, something that does not seem a practical possibility today.

Towards the end of the same teachers' meeting, when a teacher asked for a further lesson in English and French for Class 12, Steiner said with a deep sigh:

> *"I would like to do all kinds of things. It is scandalous that the pupils in Class 12 cannot be given an introductory course in architecture." (ibid.)*

Then, turning to the teacher who had asked for more lesson time, he continued in a consoling voice:

> *"If we all help, it will be possible." (ibid.)*

Almost exactly one year later when a "pure" Class 12 was planned, and after the experience of the first examination, Steiner said: referring to Class 12:

> *"Elements of architecture. Architecture ought to be included. When architecture and building are taught in Class 12 discussions about the different styles of building should also be included." (29.4.24)*

On the same day Steiner added further remarks about the teaching of art in Class 12, which could be a guide for the lessons on style in building.

> *"Here Hegel's aesthetic order is extremely important: symbolic art, classical art and romantic art. Symbolic art is the oldest, it is the art of revelation. Classical art expresses itself in outer forms which romantic art deepens again. In Greek art all three kinds are represented, even though the first one is somewhat neglected. During later times we find the classical and romantic art predominating and symbolic art lacking. Hegel's work on aesthetics is interesting even in its details; it really is a classic work on aesthetics. This for Class 12. Symbolic art reveals its fundamental character in Egyptian art. There the other two kinds are quite rudimentary. In Greek art the classical lines are fully developed, but the 'before' and 'after' are neglected. The later art is classical and romantic, as shown by Hegel. The latest art is actually always romantic." (29.4.24)*

After a short recapitulation of the syllabus already given in connection with Class 11 Steiner said:

> *"In Class 12 work towards what I have outlined. Otherwise, what has already been done so far is quite good. (ibid.)*

The first sentence refers to the indications about architecture and about Hegel's order. The second confirms the aims of the other classes.

On the following day, after the pupils of the new Class 12 had agreed to take their examination after a year of special preparation, the curriculum for a "pure" Class 12 was fixed. Here is the excerpt on art:

> *"For aesthetics and art lessons the divisions of symbolic, classical and romantic art have already been given. Now the possibility exists of not only treating aesthetics in this way: Egypt: symbolic art; Greece: classical art; what follows: romantic art; but the arts themselves can be arranged in the same way: Architecture, the symbolic art; sculpture, the classical art; and painting, music, and poetry, the romantic arts. One can look at the arts themselves in this way. This indicates an inner structure (for the lessons)." (30.4.24)*

A little later during a summary of the same meeting Steiner concluded, still on the subject of Class 12:

> *"Aesthetics of architecture. The beginnings of architecture from an aesthetics point of view; one should get far enough for the young people to gain a concrete idea of how a house is constructed. Building materials, roof constructions, seen as part of aesthetics." (ibid.)*

Erich Schwebsch's summary of Steiner's indications for the teaching of art:

> *"The aim of teaching art should be to convey the concept of beauty to the pupils. When doing so one should try to relate the development of the arts to the entire development of the different civilisations and to follow up how the concept of beauty has changed throughout the different periods of style. At the age when the child must realise that nature is ruled by abstract law to be grasped by reason, when he must learn in physics the link between cause and effect in given cases, we must promote an understanding of art as a necessary counterbalance. The child must realise how the several arts have developed in the different epochs of human history, how this or that motif in art plays its part in a particular epoch." (35)*

This passage from the Ilkley Course heads Erich Schwebsch's summary. He then outlines the aims for each class, basing them on his experience of long standing. After the closure of the Waldorf School in 1938 he placed his notes at my disposal:

Class 9

The development of painting and sculpture from ancient times until approximately Rembrandt is shown in the simplest possible way by selecting great works of southern and northern artists. The pupils should gain a concrete idea of beauty through seeing important examples of works; an appreciation of art itself is to be developed and of the metamorphoses of beauty, such as the Greek ideal of beauty, the Renaissance ideal of beauty, etc. In this way, by following the development of style from Giotto's paintings to those of Rembrandt, the pupils can observe quite objectively the solution of soul problems which they themselves are experiencing at their particular stage of development.

Class 10

The teaching of art now deals with artistic-aesthetic facts from the realm of poetry. The pupil is to get hold of poetical language through speaking. Practical speech exercises are given as a preparation towards this aim. In this way a feeling for the elements of poetry can be developed. Linking up with the experience of rhythms gained in previous eurythmy lessons the fundamentals of metrics are now brought to consciousness, including figuration and tropology. In this context Goethe's lyrical poetry and style offer specially suitable examples.

Class 11

The teaching of art again picks up the theme of the two previous years, but in an entirely new way. It now endeavours to show how in the later German spiritual life the sculptural-painterly elements flowed together with the musical-poetical elements. In this context the development of music is characterised as the determining influence in the later spiritual life.

Class 12

Beginning with building and its development, art lessons are to awaken the understanding for the elements of architecture in its great forms and styles throughout the history of civilisation. This is followed by a synopsis of the entire artistic field, which reveals, for instance, the natural division of the arts and their development into the three stages of symbolic, classical and romantic art.

3 Language Lessons

In his second lecture of the Practical Course for Teachers, Steiner describes the fundamentals of language teaching in the Waldorf School which was then about to be opened. In this lecture he speaks about language as the working together of antipathy and sympathy within the life of feeling, and as accompanying this process into the imagery of thinking.

He follows up this thought into the elements of language, into the working together of vowels and consonants . In this way he outlines in a few sentences the significance of a new linguistics which looks upon language as a means by which man both reveals and forms his relationship to the cosmos. This interpretation of linguistics was already mentioned by Steiner on 25th April 1919 in a conversation within a restricted circle (referred to at the beginning of this book) where he called it "Study of the origin of words." In the Philological Course (22) this new philology based on spiritual science is further developed. It represents the basis of speech education in the Steiner Schools.

Guidance for the teaching practice of foreign languages was given by Steiner in lecture 9 of the Practical Course for Teachers (12), where he bore in mind the fact that in the school about to be opened one would have to deal with pupils who had – or had not – already been taught languages by various methods and who had reached different standards. Just this lecture contains important information about the teaching and its aims with regard to old and modern languages which

Steiner never altered later. Despite the anxieties of teachers who felt unable to cover the ground adequately, he stuck to his first claims whose carrying out he considered essential for successful language teaching. The presence of newly admitted children, who had not learned languages through listening and speaking and who were consequently holding up proper progress, was a source of serious concern to Steiner. In the reported teachers' meetings questions arising from just this complication are dealt with time and again. In those early days language problems appear to have taken up more discussion time than almost any other subject.

In the curriculum lectures (16) no detailed information is given for teaching modern languages in the different classes. Much can be found in the "Conferences" (*4) and also in the pedagogical courses held abroad.

In this section, general information for all age groups will be quoted first, to be followed by indications for each separate class. Finally a summary of the curriculum for modern languages agreed upon during the meeting on 2nd June 1924 will be given for each class in turn.

Information regarding Greek and Latin will be added in a separate section.

The entire 9th lecture of the Practical Course for Teachers ought to head this section for it contains all the essential principles. However, as this course is bound to be readily available to any Steiner School teacher, only one short passage will be quoted from this lecture, because in it we find perhaps the most difficult demand which Steiner makes upon the language teacher in a Steiner School:

> *"You will achieve a great deal by simply remembering that for all so-called foreign language teaching the greatest waste of time lies in translation from the foreign language and translation into it from the native language... Much more should be read (in the foreign language), and the pupils ought to express their own thoughts far more readily in the foreign language." (12 lecture 9)*

In one of the first teachers' meetings with Steiner the following question was put: Was it right to withhold reading and writing in the foreign language so that pupils would learn the language orally only, even if a class had already learnt how to write? Steiner's short reply was:

> *"Yes, in foreign languages introduce reading and writing as late as possible. This is very important." (25.9.19)*

Much of importance can be found in the Basle Course of 1920 about the development of speech in the formative years:

> *"The secret of the development of human speech is really hidden from the natural-scientific thought of today, from the whole of contemporary science – so that it is not known that in exactly the same way as the first teeth are received through a kind of inheritance from parents, so speech is received through a kind of external influence of environment, by means of the principle of imitation, which now, however, becomes an organic principle.*
>
> *During the first years of life, one learns speech from one's environment, but this speech which is learnt and spoken by the child until its fifth or sixth year is related*

to the whole human being in the same way as are the milk teeth. What man really possesses in his speech after he has reached puberty, after he is 14 or 15 years old – what he speaks, what is at work in him when he speaks – is acquired a second time, newly acquired and gained by man, in exactly the same way as the second teeth. In the development of the boy this becomes outwardly apparent in the change of voice. In the girl's development it recedes more into the inner life, but it is still there. Because these forces work differently in the larynx of the boy this also shows itself outwardly. That is a manifestation of what is happening during these important school years in the entire human being – not only in the human physical body and in the human soul, but in the human soul-body, body-soul, continually, from year to year, and from month to month, in connection with things relating to the inner acquirement of what man has already gained externally as speech in early childhood from his environment." (23 lecture 1)*

These sentences are only the beginning of a longer explanation which can be read in the appropriate place, for excerpts can never do justice to the whole lecture.

Steiner answered a question put to him in a teachers' meeting in the following way:

"The earlier you start teaching a language the easier it is learnt and the better and purer the pronunciation will be. The gift of learning languages decreases as age increases after the seventh year. It is very good to speak in chorus, for language is a social medium. It is also easier to speak in chorus than alone." (12.6.20)

But six weeks later he also said:

"In language lessons there exists this great difference between speaking in chorus and speaking alone. All children will speak in chorus without hesitation but they can't do it individually. One should make use of this. We shall deal with it when discussing teaching practice. One should try to let the children repeat singly what has been spoken in chorus by the class. There is no doubt that this is the basis for learning languages." (24.7.20)

After a remark about the pupils' attitude towards language lessons Steiner said:

"They learn best from readers. To find a way into a coherent reader is a great help. Memorising is only an aid. Take the reading matter sentence by sentence. With young ones always speak first. (26.5.21)

In the Dornach Christmas Course of 1921/22 the following passage about learning foreign languages can be found:

"The rest of the morning is given over to freer subjects... and there, above all, the foreign languages play the most important part. Because they are to enter the children's lives in a really practical way they are taught right from the entry into school at the age of six or seven. Foreign languages are introduced in such a way that the children can really grow into them. The medium of the mother tongue is therefore avoided when learning a foreign tongue.

Naturally one must consider when forming one's lessons that the children in the class are older than they were when they were learning their mother tongue. This is essential if one takes one's lead from the age of the children. Nevertheless the children must grow into the foreign language in such a way that they do not inwardly translate whenever they try to express something in the new language. This method of translating should be completely avoided. The new language should be taught by leading the children into it directly, so that they first learn to speak and later to translate, provided the latter should ever prove desirable in particular cases. One really finds that by avoiding the usual teaching of grammar, etc., something can be achieved which the children absorb in a living way." (27)

After the syllabus for Class 11 was planned in the spring of 1922 Steiner again spoke quite spontaneously about language teaching:

"What matters is that you give your language lessons in the form of dialogues. Dr. Schwebsch has assured the little ones in Class 1 repeatedly that he can't understand a word of German (their mother tongue and his own). You can use your readers as a basis but weave them into the conversation. Do not be the only one who does the talking but let the children talk as much as possible. This is something which the children cannot yet do. You must think about how you can get them to speak. They must find the opportunity to speak about what they have read. This is particularly important for it is in the upper classes that lessons are still behind schedule. The lower classes are much better in foreign languages; in the lower classes this is achieved more easily. It is in the upper classes that the teachers have failed." (21.6.22)

After a few remarks about foreign readers, during which Taine's "Les Origines de la France Contemporaine" was praised as a good reader, Steiner continued:

"Something which does not belong here is slovenliness. Yet slovenliness has crept in because one has allowed oneself to take the easiest way. What matters is to realise that if the children speak in chorus – though this in itself is very good – it is no proof that they know their subject, because they are carried by a group spirit... Always tackle the matter directly so that the word links immediately to the point in question... In order to establish certain figures of speech it is good to link up with learning poems. In order to make a link with such a poem it is good if it is memorised. When one has taken two, three, four such poems one can come back to them again later in order to practise pronunciation. All this has been discussed here previously. This way of letting children learn poems has led to slovenliness. It has come about because, on the one hand, in this school languages are given a second place, because they have to be given as a side-line –the teachers are already tired when teaching languages – and on the other hand, many a teacher shirks proper preparation because he realises this situation. They use their time for preparing other lessons. In this case it is quite good to make use of an artificial and stereotyped 'prop'. The situation forces me to make reprimands. Preparation of language lessons cannot be as it ought to be. We must make efforts to bring out of

unless it happened in a Latin lesson?... I am not imply-
ing that one should get rid of grammatical terms, but
one should handle them in such a way that they make
sense for the children. Above all I find that the main
trouble is that the teachers do not know their own gram-
mar... The way in which grammatical terms are used is
quite abominable. (Were I a pupil) I would raise a riot
if I did not know why such things were being thrown at
my head. The point is that not enough time has been
taken by the teachers to acquire a reasonable amount
of grammatical knowledge. (Only) then does it stimu-
late the pupils. The grammar lessons are horrible, if I
may speak plainly. All the stuff which you find printed
in books ought to be burnt. Something living must en-
ter... the pupils are unable to experience what a perfect
tense or a present tense is, whereas it is essential for
them to experience it. The genius of the language must
live in the teacher. This applies just as much to the Ger-
man lessons..." (ibid)

Steiner's answer to Professor D. Karutz's request to drop
French from the curriculum is a valuable key to the understanding of his attitude towards language teaching. Unfortunately it cannot be reprinted in this context. (14.2.23)

In the curriculum lectures of 1919 Steiner graded the teaching of grammar (see the chapter "German: syllabus for the
different classes"). When a teacher asked him whether grammar teaching in foreign languages could be graded in a similar way he answered:

"What I have indicated there tallies exactly with the
needs of the appropriate ages. It simply belongs to a
particular age to experience a particular mood of soul.
It is by far the easiest for the child to appreciate and
understand such a mood in his own language. After this
first introduction one can link up what has been learnt
in the mother tongue with a foreign language; perhaps
to show how the same mood of soul is expressed differ-
ently in another language. It is absolutely possible to
draw comparisons. As you know, one does not really
begin to teach grammar before the ninth and tenth year.
During the early classes one develops the language les-
sons entirely out of speaking and out of the feeling for
the word, so that the children learn to speak out of feel-
ing. At this stage, which has no clear cut line of demar-
cation, between the ninth and tenth year – this stage is
not a single point and has a wide margin – at this stage
one begins to introduce grammar. And teaching gram-
mar is related to the development of the ego. Not that
one should ask: How does one develop the ego forces
through teaching grammar, for grammar in itself has
this effect. It is not necessary to arrange special prac-
tice periods of grammar with this aim in view. One does
not introduce grammar any earlier, but tries to develop
the grammar out of the substance of the language."
(19.6.24)

In the Torquay Course Steiner approaches language teaching again in a different way. Some passages will be quoted
but a study of the complete course is strongly recommended:

"But for the teaching of languages it is specially im-
portant to consider this epoch between the ninth and
tenth year.

Before this point of time is reached language teaching
must under no circumstances be of an intellectual na-
ture – that is to say it must not include any grammar or
syntax. Up to the ninth or tenth year the child must learn
to speak the foreign language just as he acquires any
other habit. It is only when he learns to differentiate
himself from his environment that he may begin to ex-
amine what he himself is bringing forth in his speech. It
is only now that one can begin to speak of noun, adjec-
tive, verb and so on, not before. Before this time the
child should simply speak and be kept to this speaking.

We have a good opportunity for carrying this out in the
Waldorf School, because as soon as the child comes to
us at the beginning of his school life he learns two for-
eign languages besides his mother tongue.

The child comes to school and begins with Main Lessons
in periods, as I have already described: he has the Main
Lesson for the early part of the morning, and then di-
rectly after that the little ones have a lesson which for
German children is either English or French. In these
language lessons we try not to consider the relationship
of one language to the other. Up until the point of time I
have described to you between the ninth and tenth year
we disregard the fact that a table for instance is called
'Tisch' in German and 'table' in English, that to eat is
'essen' in German and 'eat' in English; we connect each
language not with the words of another language, but
directly with the objects. The child learns to call the ceil-
ing, the lamp, the chair, by their names, whether it is in
French or in English. Thus from the seventh to the ninth
year we should not attach importance to translation, that
is to say rendering a word in one language by a word in
another, but the children simply learn to speak in the lan-
guage, connecting their words with the external objects
– so that the child does not need to know or rather does
not need to think of the fact that when he says 'table' in
English it is called 'Tisch' in German, and so on; he does
not concern himself with this at all. This does not occur
to the children, for they have not been taught to compare
the language in any way.

In this manner the child learns every language out of
the element from which it stems, namely, the element of
feeling." (40 lecture 6)

After this passage observations are made about the origin
of language stemming from human feelings: about the archetypal human language – observations regarding the comparison of languages and their limited yet important task in
education, and also hints about the teaching of grammar.

During the same course Steiner answered a question about
foreign languages at the Waldorf School in the following
way:

"We have introduced French and English in the Waldorf
School because in French much can be gained inwardly
which cannot be learned from any other language, a
certain feeling for rhetoric, which has its value. And
English is taught because it is a world language and
will become so more and more." (ibid)

The reader has been repeatedly advised to deepen his

understanding of the quoted passages by studying the lectures and courses in full. I should like to emphasise once more this need to study the complete works. It is really fundamental to the teaching of foreign languages to have an adequate picture of the whole being of language which will permeate and enliven all language teaching.

Indications for each class are given below and also the final curriculum for modern languages given on June 2nd 1924 (see Conference *4).

French and English

Class 1 to 5:	3 lessons each	for each
Class 6 to 8:	2 lessons each	language
Class 9 to 12:	3 lessons each	per week

Class 1

Asked whether the children of Class 1 would not have too many lessons through the introduction of languages Steiner answered:

"It is better to drop the language lessons in the first two classes if the children become tired... If they tire it will be better to give the little ones only two lessons a day altogether." (2.6.24)

This apparently does not mean that language teaching should be dropped in the first two classes but that it should only be omitted if the children show signs of marked tiredness.

Class 3

When asked whether one should let children of Class 3 write in the foreign languages Steiner replied:

"They can begin to write short easy sentences which express a simple thought." (26.5.21)

Class 1 to 3 (from the curriculum of June 2nd 1924)

"Generally speaking, the children should already be learning languages in Class 1. The lessons are to be given in such a way that the children learn the new language through speaking it. They should avoid the use of the mother tongue when learning new words or phrases. One should make sure that the children link words or phrases immediately to objects (shown). This means that one does not teach the foreign word via its German counterpart but that one remains entirely within the new language. This should be carried out especially during the first three years. During this stage grammar should be left out altogether.

When attempting something bigger, one must not mind if the children learn a verse or a poem entirely through the sounds, and if they only have a rough idea of its exact meaning. In extreme cases it may happen that a child learns four, six or eight lines which it remembers only as sounds. Under certain circumstances this way of learning, which is followed by subsequent understanding via the memory, can contribute a great deal towards the eventual mastery of the language.

In the first three years poetry is definitely preferable to prose.

This should make it clear that during the first three years all lessons have a similar character." (2.6.24)

Class 4

"Now it would be good not to postpone the introduction of grammar any longer. However, it should not be introduced through memorising rules but by making use of the already existing vocabulary. In this way one should finally formulate grammatical rules by deduction. Once such rules have been deduced one should insist that the children really remember them. One must not fall into the extreme of thinking that children should not learn any rules at all: once the rules have been discovered and recognised they should be memorised thoroughly. Remembering rules belongs to the development of the ego between the ninth and tenth year. The ego development can be strengthened by the children grasping grammatical rules.

Then one can move on to prose which should be used as little as possible in the first three years. Beginning with Class 4 one can choose a theme which is first introduced and where the grammatical learning goes parallel with the absorption of the content. For this stage prose only should be used. Abstracting grammatical rules from poetry would be treating poetry very pedantically. But it is absolutely possible to treat prose in this way. One can also gradually move towards a kind of translating (compare with the indications for Classes 5 and 6).

Of course, efforts have been made to follow these lines. But it has happened time and time again that a teacher took the 'dictionary approach', that he did not try to make the direct link between an object and its foreign name, but that he fell back on the German word before giving the equivalent foreign word. This may be more convenient for the teacher but it follows the general trend in language teaching today where the reciprocal relationship of the languages is treated in such a way that a true feeling for the foreign language cannot grow. Now this (translating) would have to start in Class 4. In Class 4 we would have to limit ourselves on the whole to word-inflections." (ibid)

Class 6

In answer to a question as to whether it would be good to have a printed reader in Class 6 Steiner said:

"One would have to choose a fairly long story. One would have to find a story, a novel, something of substance, nothing superficial. It would be possible to read something like a historical account from Mignet. There the pupils could learn a great deal." (26.5.21)

Classes 5 and 6 (from the curriculum of June 2nd 1924)

"In Class 5 syntax; in Class 6 continue with syntax, taking its more complicated forms.

Running parallel with grammar teaching one would always have a reader.

Translations from German into the foreign language should not really be practised (compare with Class 4).

Then short and simple compositions should be written.

The children should only be asked to do free translations, retelling in the foreign language what the teacher has said in the original German language. Translating should be treated in this way right up to Class 6. In any case, longer translations from German into foreign languages should be avoided.

Reading matter should be freely discussed. Take only humorous stories. With joyous inner participation the teacher should talk about all kinds of things which are connected with the customs, habits and soul-conditions of the people who speak the foreign language. In other words, the study of national customs should be brought in a humorous way into the lessons of Classes 5 and 6. From Class 5 upwards attention should also be paid to peculiarities of expression.

Then, beginning with Class 5, one should weave into the lessons the wealth of proverbs and idiomatic phrases of the foreign language.

Describe a situation which can be characterised by a proverb in the mother tongue and show how this same situation is expressed quite differently by the foreign proverb." (2.6.24)

Class 7

To the question as to whether it was possible to read parts of an English book in Class 7 Steiner answered:

"Perhaps this is possible after all... How could one arrange to read 'A Christmas Carol'? It is most instructive if each child has the book so that one can call different pupils to the front to read to the others in a free and easy manner, so that they read thoughtfully together." (23.3.21)

When asked what Class 7 should read in French Steiner answered:

"Read La Fontaine's fables". (17.6.21)

The teacher for whose Class 7 "A Christmas Carol" had been recommended found the book too difficult for his class and asked whether he should not use a textbook. Steiner answered:

"I have nothing against the use of textbooks. All textbooks are very poor. The class then has no common link. Try to find a suitable textbook and show it to me when I return. About Dickens: I cannot admit that it is too difficult. In Class 7 one can read him. You can choose prose passages yourself. It (Dickens) has only been mentioned as an example..." (11.9.21)

When a teacher said "I have finished the fables of La Fontaine with Class 7 some of them contain doubtful moralisations", Steiner answered:

"One cracks a joke about it. One must take it as a fable. Surely one can summon up the necessary humour. One can cause misunderstandings using a different source too. What matters is that one enters into the spirit of the story. If you have finished La Fontaine you could choose passages from great works of prose. One could possibly take Mignet with these children." (14.1.22)

A teacher asked: "Should one read 'The Tempest' after 'A Christmas Carol'?" Another teacher said: "I have read 'The Tempest' in class with the roles divided up." Steiner replied:

"This is just the right kind of problem. The children

know the plot, they don't learn anything new about it but perhaps this is the best way of introducing them to the spirit of the language." (ibid.)

In answer to another question from a teacher, "Would you recommend the use of short stories?" Steiner replied:

"They would be suitable for pupils of thirteen to fourteen. This is what I meant when I suggested Mignet. One must choose characteristic stories." (ibid.)

Class 8

An English teacher found Dickens' "Christmas Carol" too difficult for Class 8. Steiner said:

"You may be certain that it is possible to read this book of Dickens with children who hardly know any English at all. You can use this book best as a basis for what they could learn. Tell (them) how it goes on. Would it not be best to tell the children the story first and then choose passages which are specially suitable for discussion, passages which are less difficult? It ought to be possible to overcome the difficulties. Just for the ones who know nothing, this story is most suitable." (24.4.23)

Asked whether to use Jules Verne as reading matter for Class 8 Steiner said:

"I don't object to your taking Jules Verne as long as you treat him in such a way that the children's imagination does not run riot." (16.1.22)

Classes 7 and 8 (from the curriculum of June 2nd 1924)

"When planning the syllabus for Class 7, we have to bear in mind that a large proportion of the pupils will leave school after Class 8. In Classes 7 and 8 one should lay the main emphasis on reading matter and on observing the character of the language through studying sentences. The children should meet what is typical of the life and activities of the people whose language they are learning. The printed text should be the basis for practice, and through retelling the children should practice expressing themselves in the foreign language. Translations should only be done occasionally. On the other hand, one should ask the children to retell what has been read, even dramatic parts. Do not choose lyrical or epic passages but dramatic passages for retelling (in the foreign language) in their own words,

In Class 8 the rudiments of poetics and metrics of the foreign language should be given.

And in these two latter classes a very short summary of the history of literature of the foreign language should follow." (2.6.24)

Class 9

Answering a question Steiner said:

"I should try to stress the element of recitation at that age, so that they will learn even better to master the language. Clarify the meaning of idioms contained in the recitation and use them in another context." (22.9.20)

"Concerning history of literature: to make a few remarks about Shakespeare while reading his text or... while dealing with one thing or another, and to make *the children acquainted with some appropriate facts, is really all the history of literature which you need for the children." (15.11.20)*

Class 9 (from the curriculum of June 2nd 1924)

"Here a kind of revision of grammar would be essential but done in a humorous way. Choose humorous examples all the time. By giving such examples one can cover the entire grammar. At the same time, obviously, read stimulating material with this class." (2.6.24)

Class 10

When the French syllabus for the first Class 10 was fixed Steiner said:

"Literature, culture. I should begin with later times and work backwards towards older periods. I should reverse the order." (17.6.21)

Then (after answering a question about the old languages) he returned to French:

"One could read 'Le Cid'. One should enable them to begin to understand French classical poetry. Take Molière later. I should prefer it if you did not hurry from one to the next. If you like it, take the whole of 'Le Cid'. During the course of the year we can find the next reader." (17.6.21)

With regard to English Steiner said on the same day, after a teacher had reported that he had taken the entire previous history ("Vorgeschichte") during the past year:

"This should be continued. Then find out whether the children are able to write a few sentences about this theme on their own as their independent work... One burdens the pupils if one does not work economically. Therefore one must avoid wasting time. One must not deal with some matters as if time was unlimited. It has become evident that some teachers don't consider this aspect of time." (ibid)

To the remark of the French teacher that some pupils in Class 10 had asked for a partition (of the class) and that he wanted to know whether to choose a continuous story Steiner answered:

"One could choose a different reader. One ought to go through the whole reader even if they only read little. Have you any suggestions yourself? I think it would be good to take something short which could be finished in these two and a half months. I don't know whether it would not be best to read something biographical in such a class. There is a nice little book: 'La vie de Molière'." (17.1.23)

After a remark about Latin readers, an English teacher reported that he had finished "The Tempest" and that he had taken excerpts from "Childe Harold's Pilgrimage". Steiner replied:

"I should prefer to take something in its entirety. The choice in English is not easy. As soon as one has gone beyond Shakespeare matters become difficult. It is possible to read Macaulay in Class 10, but it depends entirely on how this is done.

This is the age when the children should get used to characterising in a rather broad and easy style. On the other hand I think it would also be acceptable to read Carlyle and Emerson in Classes 11 and 12. One should recommend Walter Scott only for private reading. Emerson and Carlyle are suitable for reading in class. The biographical characterisations, for instance the Luther biography, are very useful in the fifteenth year. Emerson's style has very short sentences." (ibid.)

When asked whether Poincaré was suitable French reading matter for Class 10 Steiner said:

"It is still a dangerous, strange matter. In principle you can do something of this kind, but not with Poincaré, because there is so much misrepresentation in it. On the other hand, for those who are leaving, ought it not to be something which apparently turns from what is usually done in life and then comes back to it – that you would have in 'The Coming Race' by Bulwer Lytton. There is a collection of French essays brought out by Hachette and in that there are essays by the other Poincaré, the mathematician; in the second part of it there is also one about technical thinking. That is something which can well be used." (18.12.23)

Class 11

At the opening of Class 11 on June 20th 1922, the teacher, looking back over the past year, reported that he had read "The Tempest." Steiner said:

"I recommend you not to drop the play, but to hold conversation about it with your class tomorrow. It does not matter whether the pupils know a great deal about it or only a little. Talk about what they do know and in such a way that they feel compelled to answer, and so guide them along. In French one could use the same technique. They ought to read prose. Don't think that H. Taine is impossible – 'Origines' (Les Origines de la France contemporaine). Also writings expressing a philosophy of life are suitable, e.g., 'Voyage en Italie'." (20.6.22)

A remark quoted above made on 17th January 1923 about English lessons in Class 10 also refers to Class 11.

In answer to a question about English in Class 11 in which Warren Hastings by Macaulay had been read Steiner said:

"Besides prose, English lyrics should be read i.e. the lyrical ballads of the poets of the Lake School. Then chapters from Emerson with his disjointed, aphoristic style; let us say the chapter about Shakespeare and Goethe. You should try to point out what is aphoristic and not aphoristic. This should be discussed. His method of writing consisted of spreading a whole library about in his room and then walking about, now reading, now writing a sentence. He used his library as a stimulant and this is the reason why you will notice mental jumps in his writings. Nietzsche had the habit of drawing rings around key words in his copies which he proceeded to number. So much for lyrics and Emerson." (18.12.23)

Classes 11 and 12

On the question of English prose for Class 12 after Carlyle's "Heroes and Hero Worship" and after studying the "Athenaeum", Steiner said:

"The Athenaeum is a magazine which has been revised in a truly practical manner. You should not pass it into the hands of the pupils, but select individual articles. It should be considered also for Class 11. In Germany we have no longer such a well-edited magazine." (25.4.23)

Class 12

After a remark about French reading matter for Class 10, Steiner said about Class 12:

"In English one could take Mackenzie's 'Humanism' for Class 12." (18.12.23)

When planning the Waldorf School curriculum for Class 12 on 30th April 1924 he said:

"Concerning languages, it would be better to state the aims, namely that the pupils should gain an appreciation of present day English and French literature." (30.4.24)

Classes 10, 11 and 12 (from the curriculum of 2nd June 1924 (*4))

"In Class 10 take the metrics of the language. In Class 11 we must introduce dramatic literature side by side with some prose and aesthetics of the language. Poetics should be developed from the dramatic readings, and this should be expanded in Class 12 where lyrical and epic poetry should also be included. And here we must introduce subject matter which is related to present day conditions. In addition some knowledge of modern foreign literature is to be aimed at." (2.6.24)

Concluding remarks about the curriculum of 2nd June 1924

"This could be the draft of the curriculum which we wish to follow in the future. Do not let the pupils begin to read their text without first having made them acquainted with its entire content. In Class 5 or 4 you can begin with the elements of grammar. As far as possible pass on to letting the children practise conversation. There is still the following to be said with regard to the grammar in Classes 7 and 8. Seek out some longer passage which you want to read. Make the children acquainted with it in a humorous way, as dramatically as possible, and then read the extract.

We have in the course of the years made small additions to what was said earlier; in principle it must remain as it is. Written work only from the stages outlined in the different courses." (2.6.24)

With regard to the last sentence see lecture 10 of the Practical Course (12).

An instructive passage about reading matter for English lessons in the three top classes can be found in the "Conferences" of 19th June 1924 (*4).

Regarding the place of language lessons within the curriculum, the reader is recommended to read the section "Aims and Problems" under the heading "Replanning the foreign language lessons – streaming in the upper school." Steiner's views on how these subjects can be taught in cross sections will be found there.

Latin and Greek

From Classes 5 to 9, four joint lessons for both languages in each class. All pupils capable of learning these two ancient languages as well as the two modern languages are to attend these classes. The decision about possible exemptions is to be taken by the school in co-operation with the parents. Beginning with Class 9 the pupils are to choose whether to take the two modern languages apart from Latin or the two ancient languages plus French. From then on there are to be three lessons per week for each of the ancient languages.

Steiner did not give any detailed instructions about Latin and Greek lessons for each separate class, but in the curriculum lectures of 1919 (16) he recommended that the syllabus of the classical Gymnasium (*3) should be followed.

Regarding the practical side of teaching, however, there are so many essential indications that the teacher does gain a concrete picture of how to approach the ancient languages.

The following is an extract from the "Social Basis" (*9):

"The ancient Greeks and Romans were able to acquire a contemporary education which united them with their own personal lives. In our present times there is nothing which links us to our totally different ways of life during our most formative years of education. Indeed, many people who enter leading positions today have acquired the same education as the ancient Greeks and Romans, and this causes them to be torn away from the life of their own times. As well as this, during their education they absorb the most uneconomical spiritual substance. We have reached a point in the development of mankind – and only few people are aware of this – when it is absolutely unnecessary for our relationship to classical times to receive a classical education. For what mankind needs to learn from it has already been absorbed by our education for a long time and in such a way that we can reap its benefits without having to live for many years in an atmosphere which has become alien to us. Our knowledge of the ancient Greeks and Romans is by no means perfect, although great improvements have indeed been made lately, but this is more a matter for specialists and has nothing whatever to do with a general, social education. What we need to absorb from classical times in our education has already reached a conclusion through the spiritual activity of the past. It exists and is available without our having to learn Greek and Latin. It is no longer essential to speak these classical languages and in many ways knowledge of them is of little value." (9)

In lecture 13 of the Practical Course for Teachers, which deals mainly with the problem of how a Steiner School can adapt its ideal timetable to the practical conditions which it has to face, the following passage can be found about Latin and Greek:

'Now let us suppose the child has already learnt Latin and Greek. I try to make the children not only speak

Latin and Greek but listen to one another as well, listen to each other systematically when one speaks Latin, another Greek. And I try to make the difference which exists between the nature of the Greek and Latin languages live vividly for them. I should not need to do this in the ordinary course of teaching, for this realisation would result of itself in the ideal timetable. But we need it with the children from outside, because the child must feel that when he speaks Greek he really only speaks with the larynx and chest but that when he speaks Latin there is something of the whole being accompanying the sound of the language." (12)

Similar observations follow about French and English.

In the curriculum lectures of 1919 we find guiding lines to the ordinary teaching of ancient languages in the Waldorf School:

"When the children are in the fourth class we include Latin for them in the syllabus. While we begin English and French with children as soon as they enter school, though in quite a simple way, we begin Latin with them in the fourth class. The children listen to begin with and reproduce as far as they are able. As soon as this has been developed a little they repeat short pieces.

The start is made from listening and speaking, trying, through the spoken word, to reach the stage that is usually set for the first year.

These Latin lessons will be conducted as indicated in the Practical Course and carried on, so that by the eighth class the standard of the 'Tertia' is reached." (16 lecture 1)

Here it should be pointed out that in 1919 the regulations for elementary schools issued by the Weimar Constitution were not yet in operation. Through these regulations our Class 4 was made to correspond with the fourth year; the fifth year corresponded with the "sexta" (first year in the Gymnasium (*3) (the sixth year to the "quinta", etc., and the eighth year of the Waldorf School corresponded to the "Untertertia", i.e., the fourth year in the Gymnasium).

After a few words about modern languages we come to the following passage about Greek lessons:

"In Class 6 we leave it free for those who wish to begin with the elements of Greek. Here also we follow the lines given in the Study Courses, i.e., we endeavour to employ once again the drawing of forms for the upbuilding of the Greek letters. And it will be extraordinarily beneficial for those who will now learn Greek to repeat with another alphabet what they did right at the beginning when they arrived at writing through the drawing of forms." (16 lecture 1)

In the third lecture of the curriculum lectures Steiner once more gave details about the teaching of ancient languages:

"In Class 4 we introduce Latin and in Class 6 Greek as optional subjects. To avoid putting too much strain on the pupils learning these two languages we need to balance their timetable, and this is quite feasible because a great deal of grammar taught in Latin and Greek can replace German grammar. Other adjustments can also be made. We will apply the same methods of teach-

ing (as in the case of modern languages) but we must realise that now we can use the curriculum (of the State schools) with the exception of what I pointed out this morning (ibid), because their curriculum still stems from the pedagogically most fertile period of the Middle Ages. In it there is still much of value for teaching Greek and Latin. The State schools still carry on the ancient traditions which is quite a reasonable thing to do. The old textbooks on the other hand are no longer suitable. One ought to drop the somewhat clumsy rules for memorising which appear a little childish to the modern generation, especially in their German translations. Otherwise the methods of the State schools are not too bad." (16 lecture 3)

What is here called an exception ("with the exception of what I pointed out this morning") apparently refers to the remark made during the morning of 6th September 1919:

"One should certainly begin by first speaking the language to the pupils and then trying to achieve through their listening what needs to be learned."

This then is the exception to the otherwise accepted rule that in the ancient languages one could generally follow the curriculum of the State schools. For this curriculum is based on learning through writing and grammar and not through speaking and listening.

Indications from the "Conferences" and lectures (in chronological order)

In the teachers' meeting of November 15th 1920 Steiner spoke about the methods and the curriculum for the ancient languages in the State schools, comparing them with the situation in the Waldorf School:

"Our pupils must reach a level which would enable them to switch over to other schools. When we have worked out our methods properly, our pupils should be able to take their place in other schools. However our methods have not yet been established sufficiently. I believe that once this problem is solved you will no longer be hamstrung by problems of discipline and that you will reach this goal. The trouble is that the children get beyond you every four or five minutes in the lessons.

The Austrian Classical schools were model institutions, Their curriculum was indeed the very best imaginable if only people would admit it." (15.11.20)

Steiner thought it very important that the pupils of the Waldorf School should be given the opportunity to learn ancient languages and that at least some classical scholars should emerge from among them. This becomes specially evident when reading the answer which he gave to the teacher who had remarked upon the poor attendance at classics lessons:

"Even if you have only one pupil, if there is only one, he must be taught. It can't be helped, it must be done." (16.6.21)

On 17th June 1921, when the curriculum for the first Class 10 was made, Steiner said:

"We should give as much Latin and Greek as we can. We do not need to be like the Gymnasium with its strictly defined methods. That is nonsense. You must attach

somewhat more importance to Latin and Greek, somewhat less to modern languages. Get so far in the lower classes that you do not need to spend too much time later. We have indeed the task with many of the pupils of making them believe that it is a good subject to take. I cannot understand why there are not more boys who wish to learn it. In the upper classes rather more hours for Latin and Greek " (17.6.21)

In September 1921 Steiner outlined orally to the specialist teacher Dr. Maria Röschl the fundamental curriculum for ancient languages. These guide lines, as written down from memory by Dr. Röschl, are quoted at the end of this chapter.

On 15th March 1922 Steiner answered the question whether Greek and Latin were to be taught simultaneously right from the beginning:

"It would be right, ideally, to take Greek earlier and only begin Latin two years later. But it would be difficult to carry this out practically. We should really have to leave out something else in order to have Greek and this we are reluctant to do. Our curriculum is arranged in accordance with the development of the pupil, but this problem is due to external conditions. What I have explained in the lecture (apparently the foreword to the Eurythmy performance in Stuttgart on 13.3.22 is meant) could be of help towards an understanding step by step of the Greek language.

I have founded the entire evolution of language on an imagination. K. on the contrary talked of Inspiration and Intuition. People do not seem to be conscientious about listening accurately any more. Such things need very careful consideration. You must gradually develop a feeling for what I have put before you. It can well be made use of when teaching Greek. Latin is of less importance, for it does not call up the corresponding feelings in the same way." (15.3.22)

After these somewhat puzzling remarks a teacher asked how one should select suitable pupils for these lessons. Steiner answered:

"As long as we only have isolated schools we are naturally not able to do anything about this. Only if our schools spread should we be able to make the selection ourselves according to the characteristic qualities of the child if we are to have any influence on the later course of his life. Only 33% take part now; still too few to influence our curriculum. Every subject that we have (in our curriculum) is necessary, so nothing can be omitted (even by those who are taking ancient languages)." (ibid)

On 28th April 1922 Steiner said in answer to a question about translating ancient languages:

"Since these are not living languages the pupils can do translations." (28.4.22)

When the curriculum was being planned for Class 11 Steiner said about the ancient languages:

"Latin and Greek in the eleventh class – while discussing the reading matter with the pupils, we must also teach them an appreciation of the different styles as well as some grammar, and then compare Greek syntax with Latin syntax. Weave into it an

understanding of etymology. In ancient languages you ought to pay more attention to the etymology of words. Livy will do. Choose any suitable reading matter in Greek." (21.6.22)

On 24th November 1922 it was finally decided that in future there should be partial streaming beginning with Class 9; pupils entering for the "Abitur" (*1) should have Latin, Greek and French, and the modern languages stream should have French, English and Latin (24.11.22) – see section "Replanning of language lessons – streaming in the upper school" and the section about the "Development of the Curriculum".

On 2nd June 1924, after the curriculum for modern languages was fixed, Steiner also gave the prospect of a more detailed curriculum for Latin and Greek:

"Now since the teaching of classical languages takes a special place with us, it must also have a special curriculum. I should work out an exact curriculum and will bring it to you. It has come into being by degrees." (2.6.24)

This remark clearly shows that on account of the experience gained in teaching ancient languages Steiner deemed it necessary after all to drop the original curriculum of the "Gymnasium" (*3). Unfortunately he was not able to fulfil his intention to give a new syllabus for ancient languages.

The last information about teaching ancient languages is taken from the Torquay Course of August 1924 in which Rudolf Steiner answered the question of whether Greek and Latin should also be taught by "direct method", i.e., without translation from one language into the other:

"In this respect a special exception must be made with regard to Latin and Greek. It is not necessary to connect these directly with practical life, for they are no longer alive, and we have them with us only as dead languages. Now Greek and Latin (for Greek should actually precede Latin in teaching) can only be taught when the children are somewhat older, and therefore the translation method for these languages is, in a certain way, fully justified.

There is no question for our having to converse in Latin and Greek, but our aim is to understand the ancient authors. We use these languages first and foremost for the purposes of translation." (40 Questions and Answers)

Guide lines for the teaching of Latin and Greek (September 1921)

Summary of a conversation written down from memory by Dr. Maria Röschl:

The aim is the mastery of Greek and Latin to the extent that after Class 12 the pupils of the Waldorf School are able to pass examinations in these languages.

The pupils who have decided to take these two languages, have to consider them as main subjects and – since they are likely to be under too much pressure in the upper school – they must occasionally be prepared to forego some other lessons, such as handwork or other similar subjects, if this should prove inevitable.

Greek is not to be taught as a separate subject but is to

be worked in with the Latin lessons.

Concerning the actual teaching: the pupils are to be instructed in three stages of four lessons per week (see below):

1st Stage. A practical contact is to be made with the foreign language; the pupil is to become familiar with forms of grammar and with its peculiarities through reading easy readers.

2nd Stage. Raising these characteristic features of the language into the sphere of consciousness; conversations about the grammar.

3rd Stage. Deeper penetration into the spirit of the language, development of the feeling for the language (virtue).

During the lessons special attention is to be paid to the psychology of the language (testa – tête – Kopf; pes – Fuss; virtus – Tugend (virtue 1).

Further, during grammar practice such forms as 'I swim, I have swum' should be avoided because they contain an element of untruth – the child saying them may not even be able to swim. When such inevitable exercises have to be made their fictitious nature should first be made clear by appealing to the imagination, e.g., 'Let us imagine that all of us present here were able to swim; how would we say (in Greek or Latin): I have swum?' or 'Let us imagine a garden with lots of flowers; how would we say: The rose is blooming?'.

Only texts of actual Latin or Greek authors should be used as reading material, not practical courses whose foreign language text has been composed by the publisher. However, not only classical authors are to be used but also, especially in the highest stages, medieval and later writers of prose and lyric style, such as Erasmus of Rotterdam, Jakob Balde and others.

When I asked Dr. Steiner whether instruction in Latin and Greek was still altogether desirable, he answered: With regard to Latin, the Roman influence is now so firmly woven into our spiritual life that one could not protect oneself from its harmful effects merely by remaining ignorant of the Latin language but only by assimilating it in the right way and being able to understand it. It was therefore desirable that some pupils should learn Latin. Learning Greek, on the other hand was important because one was able to gain concepts through this language which one's own language could no longer give, e.g., the word "idea" which was now being used in quite a different and wrong way. Only through an intimate knowledge of the Greek language could one gain a true feeling for the exact meaning of "idea" (ιδεα – stem: ϝιδ (early Greek) – video ... viz ιδεα the concept which can still be inwardly seen). It was therefore particularly desirable that the pupils should be able to learn this language.

Note by Dr. M. Röschl:

For the period of "transition" Steiner found it right to increase the number of lessons and to introduce beginners' courses and extra coaching.

The concluding remarks are notes by a teacher of classical languages, Verene Gildemeister, after her introductory talk with Steiner. The date of this conversation is unfortunately not known.

"In the long conversation with Rudolf Steiner granted me before engaging me as teacher of ancient languages, he said among other things, that he would leave me free to choose whether I would teach syntax systematically, or whether I would clarify grammatical points as they came along when studying a reader, so that the pupils could understand their text. On principle he wanted me to begin directly with the foreign language, never with German and he completely condemned specially prepared German exercises or texts for use in translating into the foreign language. On the other hand he was entirely in agreement with the idea of letting advanced pupils, who had already lived themselves into the language, occasionally translate original German texts into Latin, or simple Greek prose into Latin. This of course is very difficult but interesting work for the pupils and demands great ability and mastery of Latin from the teacher. For the rest Dr. Steiner said that I could follow the methods of the 'Gymnasium' (*3)."

4 Shorthand

In Classes 9 and 10 two periods a week each.

First of all I should like to recommend to the reader the relevant passage about shorthand which is to be found in the 10th lecture of the Practical Course for Teachers. There Steiner speaks of the "unimaginable" picture of a stenographer sitting at the feet of a venerable bard in ancient Greece in order to take down in shorthand the bard's chanting of Homer. (12 lecture 10)

When making the timetable for Class 10 in the early summer of 1921, and after pleading for greater economy in teaching time, Steiner said:

"Other questions arise. If we add shorthand to our curriculum, we must begin it now...

We must ask ourselves if we are to use a further two hours in the week in the tenth class in order to study shorthand, and which system. It seems to me that Gabelsberger would be the least death-dealing to the spirit. It would indeed have been good if shorthand had never been discovered. Since it is here, we can no more dispense with it than we can with the telephone. Gabelsberger. Two hours' shorthand." (17.6.21)

A few months later, after the first experience of shorthand teaching had become available Steiner said:

"People should learn shorthand as though they were asleep, without any special concentration. That shorthand is learnt at all is really vandalism, the height of Ahrimanism. It would be ideal, therefore, to learn it as though asleep. But since that cannot be, it is most important for it to be learnt without any concentration at all because it is nonsense. Shorthand is a cultural folly." (16.11.21)

When the question arose whether shorthand should become a compulsory subject Steiner said:

> *"There are many reasons for making it compulsory. It is something which should really only begin in the tenth class. We will make an alteration and have a weekly lesson in shorthand in the afternoon. It is indeed quite good for the children to learn shorthand." (28.10.22)*

On 9th December 1922 during a discussion about the newly introduced timetable, when the teacher asked that shorthand should become an optional subject Steiner said:

> *"It is a pity. When do we begin the lesson? In Class 10. I cannot understand why they should not want it."*

> *"Many things are judged too critically so that we forget the difference between our methods and curricula and those of other schools."*

> *"Unfortunately I was not able to observe your method. How do you explain shorthand to the pupils?" (9.12.22)*

When the teacher answered that he had given his pupils a talk about the history of shorthand before introducing the vowels Steiner said:

> *"You will stimulate the pupils considerably if you teach grammalogues at the same time as the sounds. This is a way of overcoming the difficulties. What do you mean by 'The pupils do not like it?' " (9.12.22)*

When a teacher reported a pupil's remark that there was no need for her to learn shorthand because she was only interested in artistic subjects Steiner replied:

> *"The two sides are complementary. The question 'What use is this subject to me?' should not enter at all. Our attitude should lead the teacher to say to the pupil: 'Look, if you want to be an artist, then you need all kinds of other abilities which will help you in your work. You must realise that one cannot just be an artist, for one needs to be able to do all kinds of other things as well, even if they are not directly connected with art.' There once was a poet called Hamerling, who maintained that he could not possibly have done his work without his shorthand.*

> *We must arrange our education in such a way that a teacher's remark immediately produces an effect. This is something which we must achieve. We begin shorthand in Class 10. By that time the pupils ought to be mature enough to understand the situation so that they would not ask the question: 'What use is this subject going to be for me?' " (9.12.22)*

When the teacher mentioned that some pupils had already learned the Stolze-Schrey (system) Steiner said:

> *"That is really different. That might lead to giving special lessons if there are enough children who want to learn Stolze-Schrey." (9.12.22)*

When the language timetable was discussed on 2nd June 1924 Steiner answered a question about the difficulties caused by newly admitted pupils who had not been taught shorthand previously:

> *"Then there would be no alternative but to allow shorthand lessons to become optional. Nevertheless we look upon them as something our pupils ought to learn.*

> *Let us suppose a pupil enters Class 11 who in all his previous classes has been taught natural history by a Catholic, and who refuses to be taught natural history by anyone who does not do so out of a Catholic background. We must not exempt such a pupil from natural history lessons.*

> *In shorthand we teach the best system and we make it a compulsory subject because at the present time it is a necessary part of education. I do not think that we are prejudiced. It is the only system which has an inner reality. All other systems are thought out. We should however consider whether we should introduce this subject in an earlier class." (2.6.24)*

As far as we know this is Steiner's last remark about shorthand teaching. According to his wishes shorthand was later introduced in Class 9, as mentioned at the beginning of the chapter.

5 Mathematics

1st – 5th school years	12 weeks each	Main
6th – 8th school years	10 weeks each	lessons
9th –12th school years	8 weeks each	

In addition, from the 6th school year onwards within the framework of the main lesson one hour each week is given for repetition and practice, but only when a subject other than mathematics is being taken in main lessons.

In the first lecture of the Practical Course Steiner shows where the arithmetic and mathematics lesson stands in the whole context of the education and he then develops the introduction to the 4 rules. These indications are somewhat more developed in lecture 4 of Discussions with Teachers. In both places he points very significantly to his "Theory of Knowledge" (end of chapter 12 on Intellect and Reason). It was important to him that the teacher of the lowest school class should bring before the children such a thing as addition out of the sum and corresponding things for the other rules on the basis of a trained philosophical consciousness in the teacher. He wanted it to be known that these beginnings of arithmetical thinking should be valued right from the start through understanding their significance for the proper development of the child into the world. That does not mean bringing the theory of knowledge before the child, but it does mean that instead of making arithmetic more elegant in the sense of these indications, the duty which the teacher bears towards the Spirit should be remembered in the very first steps in education. On account of its extraordinary importance I will quote the whole of the corresponding passages in Steiner's philosophical work:

> *"Kant decides that the propositions of maths and pure natural science are a priori such valid synthetic judgements. (That was the subject of the preceding deliber-ations in the book.) He takes for example the proposition 7 + 5 = 12. In 7 + 5 the sum 12, Kant concludes, is by no means contained. I must go beyond 7 and 5 and call upon my sense-observation, whereupon I find the concept 12. My sense-observation makes it*

necessary that the proposition 7 + 5 = 12 shall be accepted. But the objects of experience must approach me through the medium of my sense-observations, thus blending themselves with its principles. If experience is to be possible at all, such propositions must be true. Before an objective examination, this whole artificial thought-structure of Kant fails to maintain itself. It is impossible that I have no clue in the subject-concept which directs me to the predicate-concept. For both concepts are attained by my intellect, and that in reference to a thing which in itself constitutes a unit. Let no one be deceived at this point. The mathematical unit which lies at the basis of number is not primary. The primary thing is the magnitude (the whole thing we are dealing with), which is a certain number of repetitions of the unit. I must assume a magnitude when I speak of a unit. The unit is an image created by our intellect which separates it from a totality just as it separates effect from cause, substances from their attributes, etc. When I think of 7 + 5, I really hold 12 mathematical units in my mind, only not all at once, but in two parts. If I think the group of mathematical units all at once, this is absolutely the same thing. This identity I express in the judgement 7 + 5 = 12." (2)

This is what the teacher has to carry within himself when, together with the children, he wishes to approach arithmetic, in that he develops addition from the concept of the sum, etc. He knows then that he lets the concept of the sum become an experience for the children by dividing the concrete number into various groups. The reader can read up the details in the places indicated, where they are sometimes contained within a larger context. Yet we must beware, especially in the Seminar Course (13) that the presentation is spoilt through various stenographical mistakes. An attempt to interpret it will therefore be appended to the end of the paragraph on the first school year.

The following quotations from Steiner throw light on the whole of mathematics teaching.

In the lectures of 1919 on "Volkspaedagogik" we reach a point where we are led right into the middle of the problem of mathematics' teaching:

"I have often said: provided we choose the right age we can lead young people in 3 or 4 hours from the beginning of geometry, the straight line and the angle, to the theorem of Pythagoras (once known as the Bridge of Asses). And you should have seen when I tried to do this what a tremendous joy the people had when the Pythagorean theorem suddenly became clear for them as a result of from 3 to 4 hours teaching! But think for a moment what rubbish often goes on in present-day teaching before people reach this theorem! The point is that we have wasted a tremendous amount of spiritual effort, and that shows itself in life. It streams forth over the whole of life." (9)

One can feel that to be risky. One can also feel oneself called upon to test with due care what really is necessary from the structure of elementary geometry in order to arrive at the theorem of Pythagoras. For there lies in the words of the above lectures the beginning of a complete reconstruction of geometry.

Light is shed on the geometry lesson from a quite different direction in the 6th lecture of the Basle Course for Teachers (1920). The observations made there are intended to bring about in the child a concrete experience of space with the whole body. Steiner says there:

"In the Waldorf School the teacher should not be satisfied when the children can draw a circle – our children must learn to feel the circle, the triangle, the square. They must draw the circle in such a way as to have the roundness in their feeling. They must so learn to draw the triangle that they have the 3 corners in their feeling, that already in drawing the first corner they have the feeling that 3 corners are emerging. In the same way they draw the square so that they feel the emergence of angularity, that the feeling permeates the whole line-development right from the start. A child has to learn from us what a curve is, what a horizontal line is, what a vertical line is, but not merely for his observation, but for following it inwardly with his arm, with his hand. That should also be done as a foundation for the writing lesson. No child should learn from us how to write a "P" without first having an experience of a vertical and of a curve. It should not merely be that the child gets an abstract outwardly directed perception of the vertical and the curve, but he should have a way of observing tempered by feeling, a feeling tempered experience of things." (23 lecture 6)

As a first introduction to arithmetic Steiner gives a very significant viewpoint in the same 1920 Basle Course, which should be placed before the other observations about the introduction to arithmetic.

"There is always present in the soul an urge to proceed from a unity to a multiplicity (its parts). It is just because people take so little notice of this that they also have such little understanding of what human freedom in the soul actually is. If human soul activity were to be an exclusively synthetic one – if man were to stand in such a relationship with the outer world that he could only synthesise, form concepts of type and species and also could so arrange his life that he became able to strive as much as possible to arrange it according to concepts – which is certainly one of man's main activities – then man could in fact scarcely speak of freedom. For the way in which we proceed there is indeed usually prescribed for us by outer nature. Over against all our outer activity stands an analytical activity in the soul, and this analytical activity brings about our ability to develop freedom straightaway in the pure life of ideation." (23 lecture 10)

In the same course of lectures Steiner expounds upon the problem of how one can lead geometry from a static state to a living one:

"That which is geometrical can really be felt by one who has had some experience of geometry as something which should be gradually raised from a state of rest into one of livingness. We really express something of a very general nature when we say that the sum of the angles of a triangle is 180°. That is the case with every triangle, is it not? But can we picture for ourselves every triangle?... It would, however be good to bring before our children a movement-endowed concept of a

triangle, not a dead concept, not let them merely draw a triangle which is indeed always a special, individual one, but say to them: here I have a line – then I develop the matter so far that in some way I divide the angle of 180° into 3 parts for the child. I can do this in innumerable ways. Each time that I have divided this angle into 3 parts I can pass over to the triangle by showing the child how the angle which is here

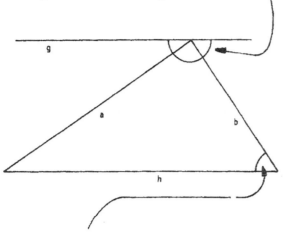

now appears here. (Apparently a remark is missing to the effect that to the original line g one has to draw a parallel h which cuts the lines a and b dividing up the angle of 180°.) Thus I shall obtain such a triangle in following such a method. By starting from the 3 fan-like angles lying side by side, I can picture innumerable triangles which move, and these innumerable triangles have, needless to say, the characteristic of having an angle sum of 180° for they arise through dividing up the 180° of the angle sum.

Thus it is good to call forth in the child the thought-picture of the triangle, which really is in inner movement, so that one never gets the thought-picture of a triangle at rest, but of one in movement, which might just as well be an acute-angled one as an obtuse-angled or a right-angled one, because at no time do I grasp the mental picture of a triangle at rest but the mental picture of a triangle in movement. Just think how transparent the whole theory of the triangle would become by starting out from such an inwardly moving concept, and then developing the metric of the angle.

We could very well use this as a support, if we would build up for the child a proper feeling for space, a concrete, a true feeling for space. When we have used the concept of movement for the plane figure in this way, the whole spiritual configuration of the child then receives mobility of such a kind that I can easily pass over to that perspective element – when a body passes in front of another one or behind it. This passing in front and behind can be the first stage in calling forth a corresponding feeling for space." (23 lecture 13)

A few pages later Steiner explains the connection of the feeling for space with this "play of movement":

"Let us look at these drawings of the child. Children younger than 7, 8 or even 9 actually have not yet got what we could call a true feeling for space. That comes later, when the other force gradually finds its way into the development of the child. Up to the 7th year there

works on the child's organisation that which later becomes the power of thought; up to puberty the will works on the child's organisation, which then (as I told you) is dammed up and actually shows itself in the change of voice in the boy, being shot into the body. It is this will which is adapted to develop in itself the feeling for space. Thus through all the things I have mentioned, through this development of a feeling for space in "plays of movement", through observing what happens when shadow-pictures arise, namely through what arises in the movement and is retained (by the soul), – through all this the will is developed and man achieves a much better understanding of the things than through the intellectual approach, even if it is the playlike childish intellect, which expresses itself on the surface and wants to be communicative." (23 lecture 13)

An extract from the small Course of 1922 in Stuttgart may be repeated at this point:

"After the 14th and 15th year one must take every opportunity to seek out connections with the more pictorial things brought forward in earlier years. Let us suppose that in mathematics we are striving towards the knowledge of Carnot's theorem in trigonometry (the Cosine Law), which we described yesterday. Now it is of extraordinarily great benefit when one does not let the opportunity go by of going through in every detail with the children every relationship which can present itself between Carnot's theorem and the ordinary Pythagorean theorem, so that the judgement is directly stimulated as to how a metamorphosis of Pythagoras' theorem lies before one in Carnot's theorem. Thus this recalling of what was pictorially nurtured in earlier years can be born in mind just as well in mathematics as in religion lessons, indeed in all subjects. What has been pictorially nurtured in earlier years must always come to one's aid. It is this recalling which stimulates the power of judgement." (28)

The Oxford Course of 1922 provides an important passage on the introduction to arithmetic lessons:

"A child is able to take in the elements of arithmetic at quite an early age. But particularly in arithmetic we observe how very easily an intellectual element can be given the child too soon. It arises in human nature; the operations of mathematics are not foreign in a succeeding civilisation. But it is exceedingly important that the child should be introduced to arithmetic and mathematics in the right way. And what this is can really only be judged by one who is enabled to observe the whole human life from a certain spiritual standpoint. There are two things which in logic seem very far removed from one another: arithmetic and moral principles. It is not usual to connect arithmetic and moral principles because there appears to be no obvious logical connection between them. But it is apparent to one who looks at the matter not logically but livingly, that the child who has a right introduction to arithmetic will have quite a different feeling of moral responsibility in later life from the child who has not. The following may seem extremely paradoxical to you, but since I am speaking in realities and not of the illusions current in our age, I will not be afraid of seeming paradoxical, for in this

age truth often seems paradoxical. If men had known how to permeate the soul with mathematics in the right way in the arithmetic lessons during these past years we should not now have Bolshevism in Eastern Europe." (29 lecture 5)

And after a short description of the foundation of number on the parts of a whole and the introduction of the concept of sum through dividing up into parts as one pleases Steiner continues:

"In this way we get the child to enter into life with the ability to grasp a whole, not always to proceed from the lesser to the greater. And this has an extraordinarily strong influence upon the child's whole life of soul. When a child has acquired the habit of adding things together we get a disposition which tends to be desirous and craving. In proceeding from the whole to the parts and in treating multiplication similarly, the child has less tendency to acquisitiveness, rather it tends to develop what, in the Platonic sense, the noblest sense of the word, can be called considerateness, moderation; and one's moral likes and dislikes are intimately bound up with the manner in which one has learned to deal with number. At first sight there seems to be no logical connection between the treatment of numbers and moral ideas, moral impulses, so little indeed that one who will only regard things from the intellectual point of view may well laugh when one speaks of it. It may seem to him absurd." (ibid)

A year later, in the 1923 course in Dornach, Steiner spoke once again about our consciousness of space:

"To-day in our abstract intellectual age people have the idea that the 3 dimensions of space hover about somewhere in the air. These are indeed 3 mutually perpendicular lines which are thought of as going into the infinite. You can of course gradually win through to that by means of abstraction, but it is not something we experience. But the 3 dimensions become an experience – more in the unconscious – when the child learns to raise itself from the awkward crawling condition, in which it loses its balance everywhere, and come into balance with the world. There you have the 3 dimensions present in a real way. We cannot draw 3 lines in space, but there is one line which coincides with the upright axis of the body. This is something which we put to the test when we lie down and sleep and are not within our body. This line also reveals itself as a most important characteristic distinguishing us from the animal, which has its spine parallel to the Earth, whereas we have ours upright. The second dimension is that which we unconsciously attain when we stretch out our arms. The third dimension is the one going from front to back and vice versa... Man experiences what he describes in geometrical figures in himself, but only at that age where there is still much of an unconscious, half-dreamlike condition. Later it becomes raised up and appears abstract.

Now with the change of teeth precisely that thing is consolidated which gives man an inner hold on himself. Between the ages when the child raises itself upright and when it experiences inner hardening (the change of teeth), the child tries out geometry and drawing

unconsciously in its own body. Thereafter it becomes ensouled. It becomes ensouled just at the time of the change of teeth and we have on the one hand something physiological, something hard we have built up within ourselves, our own strengthened skeleton like a sediment – just as when we cool a solution a sediment can appear making the remaining part so much the clearer – and on the other hand, we have the soul element which has remained behind and has become geometry, drawing, etc. We see characteristics of the soul streaming out of man. And just think what an interest in man that stimulates." (34)

There is a reference to the time for beginning arithmetic lessons in the 10th lecture of the Practical Course. It follows straight after a remark *explaining how* the art lesson, and the writing and reading lessons built upon it should form the beginning of the work in the school.

"For you see, arithmetic should be begun somewhat later. This can be adjusted according to outer necessities as there is no point marked for it in man's life-development. Thus man should begin somewhat later with arithmetic." (12 lecture 10)

Class 1

In the lectures on the Curriculum of 1919 the work of the 1st school year is not expressly divided from that of the 2nd school year. There is however one place in the 4th discussion which is being included here at the beginning on account of its general importance. It can help to separate these two years' work:

"It is especially important not to go on working in a monotonous way, doing nothing but add for six mouths, etc., but where possible one should take all four arithmetic rules fairly quickly one after another and then practice them. So we shall not teach arithmetic in accordance with the ordinary curriculum, but we shall take all four rules at once and be careful that through practice these four rules are mastered almost at the same time. You will find this way of doing things very economical." (13, Discussion 4)

There now follow references from the 2nd part of the Lectures on the Curriculum.

Class 1

"The ordinary method describes dealing with numbers up to 100 in the first year. One can keep to that for it is of very slight importance how far up one counts in the first class, so long as one keeps to simple counting. The main thing is that in so far as you use figures you pursue the kind of reckoning I have indicated: addition developed first out of the sum, subtraction out of the remainder, multiplication out of the product and division out of the quotient, that is to say the exact opposite of the usual procedure. Only after having shown that 5 is 3 + 2 one shows the opposite, through addition, that 3 + 2 makes 5. For one must arouse in the child the strong idea that 5 = 3 + 2, but that 5 is also 4 + 1, and so on. Therefore addition (of the ordinary sort) comes after the splitting up of the sum into parts, subtraction (of the ordinary sort) after one has asked, 'From what minuend must I take away something in order to leave

a particular remainder?' As already said, it is taken for granted that one does this with the simpler numbers in the first school year. Whether one goes up to 95 or 100 or 105 is immaterial. Then however, as soon as the child has gone through the change of teeth one begins straightaway to teach the tables, and for that matter, one plus one up to six or seven. You get the child to memorise the multiplication and addition tables as early as possible, as soon as the child has had the principle explained, just with the very simplest multiplication as has been shown. That is to say then, that as soon as it is possible to bring the idea of multiplication to the child you give him the task of learning the tables by heart." (16 lecture 2)

Thus far this passage apparently refers to the 1st school year, where the learning of the four rules and the tables is required: the four rules "all at once" and the tables off by heart "as soon as it is possible to bring the concept of multiplication to the child!" What follows afterwards in our passage in the Lectures on the Curriculum refers apparently to the 2nd school year:

Class 2

"Then you carry on with these ways of reckoning for a greater range of numbers. You try to get the pupil to solve simple problems without any writing, just in his head", and so on. That can be read up in the place indicated. (16 lecture 2)

But counting obviously belongs to the first school year too, though it is not mentioned here. We read about that in the 1921/22 Christmas Course for Teachers in Dornach.

"The child is indeed suited for arithmetic without more ado the moment it reaches school age. Only it is a matter of having to go into the inner needs of the child's organisation. In this direction the child has an inclination towards rhythm, beat, a grasping in feeling of a harmonising element... Of course, the child must learn to count... In the course of civilisation we have gradually come to the point of dealing with this working with numbers in a certain synthetic way: we have a unity, a second unity, a third unity and in counting up, in the additive element, we strive to bring the one to the other so that then, so far as our counting is concerned, the one lies near the other. The child does not meet us with an inner understanding for that approach, as we can see for ourselves. In this way the fundamentally human has once again not developed as far as the counting process. At all events counting started out from the unity; but the 2 was not an outer repetition of the unity, but was inherent in it. The 1 gives the 2 and the 2 are contained in the 1. The 1 divided gives the 3 and the 3 are contained in the 1. When people began to write "one" (in modern times, no longer "the one") they did not step out of the unity in arriving at the 2 or the 3. But the unity embraces everything and the numbers are organic members of the unity." (27)

It was then shown there how you obtain the numbers from a simple separation. That may be read up in the place indicated. For all that it is extraordinarily instructive when you come across variations of the procedure indicated at Stuttgart, which show how much scope the methods given by Steiner offer the teacher. Drawing as a preliminary step towards geometry can be looked up later under the 4th school year.

A summarised interpretation of the arithmetic for Class 1

Through dividing up a given observable whole into 2, 3, 4 and more equal parts you lead the children to the first coming to grips with the being of number, and from then on you let them count – on the fingers. Straight after that all the four rules are introduced – simultaneously if possible – and to start with are practised with a small compass of numbers. You set out from a real quantity of given things (SUM) and divide them up in front of the children into just as real smaller quantities (ADDENDA). By comprehending the quantitative identity of both conditions the child grasps hold of ADDITION.

You set out from a real objective quantity as MINUEND, and from the quite similar quantity of the REMAINDER which still remains lying before the children after removing a part. The question as to what was taken away in order to leave just this remainder causes the children to grasp what is more transitory, the SUBTRAHEND, and with it SUBTRACTION.

You set out from something real and simple (MULTIPLICAND) and from something manifold and equally real (PRODUCT) and leave the child to find the more transitory MULTIPLIER which is given by a real number. Thus it learns to know MULTIPLICATION.

You set out from a real quantity to be divided (DIVIDEND) and from the equally real part (QUOTIENT) and let the child find the dividing number, the DIVISOR.

You set out from the real quantity to be divided (DIVIDEND) and from the equally real measurement or number of parts conceived (QUOTIENT) and let the child find the measure or share. In these two tasks you let the child experience DIVISION in both its forms – dividing or cutting up and measuring up or sharing out.

After first building up such introductory exercises, in which you proceed as far as possible from things ready to hand and graspable, leaving the more transitory and abstract to be sought and found, you go over to the usual kinds of arithmetic with the so-called concrete numbers.

The following compilation has been made to give the teacher a survey:

1 Addition: Sum total = that which is seen + what addendum? How much (addendum) has to be added to what is seen so that just this sum total is attained?

2 Subtraction: Difference = minuend – what subtrahend? How much (subtrahend) has to be taken from the minuend so that just this remainder is left?

3 Multiplication: Product = multiplicand X what multiplier? How many times (multiplier) must you multiply this multiplicand so that just this product arises?

4 Division:

   a) Dividing or cutting-up: Part = dividend ÷ what

number of parts? Into how many (divisor) parts must you divide this dividend so that just this size of part is obtained?

b) Measuring-up or sharing out: Measurement or number of parts = dividend ÷ what size of part? With what measure or share must you measure up (pace off, compare) this dividend so as to obtain just this measurement or number of parts?

On the introduction to arithmetic one can also refer to the 1921/22 Dornach Course, the 1923 Ilkley Course and particularly the 1924 Torquay course.

Class 2

The Lectures on the Curriculum deal with this immediately after the passages above on Class 1:

"Then you carry on with these ways of reckoning for a greater range of numbers. You try to get the pupil to solve simple problems without any writing, just in his head. You try at first to develop abstract numbers in connection with objects. I have already shown how you can develop abstract numbers in connection with beans, etc. But do not lose sight of reckoning with concrete numbers as well. " (16 lecture 2)

Drawing and geometry can be looked up later under the 4th school year. There it is shown in detail how to take care of the development of the inner perception of the spatial in Classes 2 and 3, for example the feeling for symmetry and similar things.

Class 3

The Lectures on the Curriculum say:

"In Class 3 everything to do with more complicated numbers will be continued and at this stage applied to certain simple things in practical life, and the 4 rules continued as for Class 2." (ibid)

You can also compare this with the 1924 Torquay Course lecture 7.

It has become usual in Class 3 to begin with written arithmetic but you might compare this with what is said with respect to Class 2. Drawing and geometry can be looked up later. You can also refer to the 1924 Torquay Course lecture 7.

Class 4

"In Class 4 what has been fostered in the first school years will be continued. But we must now go over to fractions and in particular decimal fractions." (ibid)

On the matter of dealing with decimal fractions you should especially refer to the 1920 Basle Course lecture 14.

Geometry

As far as geometry is concerned a difficulty arises. In the tenth lecture of the Practical Course, Steiner says the following, in particular connection with the stage of life between the years of 9 and 12:

"You see, at this stage of life of the human being we can go on to geometry through our having hitherto wholly restricted the element of geometry to drawing. In drawing, of course, we can evolve for him the triangle, the square, the circle and the line. That is, we evolve the actual forms in drawing by drawing them and then saying, 'This is a triangle, this is a square'. But what geometry adds to these, with its search for the relations between the forms, is only introduced at about nine years of age." (12 lecture 10).

At the end of the lecture just quoted he says:

"Geometry offers you an extraordinarily good example of how to combine the object lesson with the subject matter of geometry itself." (ibid)

A proof of Pythagoras' theorem is then set forth – a proof wholly built up on the basis of observation, at first for the special case of the isosceles right-angled triangle, but which can be so developed that it can also be applied to any given right-angled triangle. Thereupon Steiner says:

"That is an object lesson. You can turn geometry into an object lesson. But there is a certain value – and I have often tested it myself – if you wish to give the child over nine a visual idea of the theorem of Pythagoras – in constructing the whole theorem for him directly from the separate parts of the square on the hypotenuse. And if as a teacher you realise what is taking place in a geometry lesson you can teach the child in at the most 7 or 8 hours all the geometry necessary to introduce a lesson on the theorem of Pythagoras, the famous Pons Asinorum. You will proceed with tremendous economy if you demonstrate the first rudiments of geometry graphically in this way. You will save a great deal of time, and besides that, you will save something very important for the child – which prevents a disturbing effect on teaching – and that is: you keep him from forming abstract thoughts in order to grasp the theorem of Pythagoras. Instead of this let him form concrete thoughts and go from the simple to the composite." (ibid)

Another reference to Pythagoras' theorem occurs in Study of Man, 14th lecture.

On the other hand it says in the Lectures on the Curriculum for Class 6:

"Now I should like to draw your attention to the fact that up to the 6th school year we have taken geometrical forms – circle, triangle – out of drawing, when we were doing drawing in the first school years-for the writing lessons." (Up to and not including the 6th school year is meant – this follows from a comparison with the indications in the same Lectures on the Curriculum, dealing with drawing and painting. For a different aim is quite definitely given for the 6th class itself.) "Then we gradually made the transition from employing drawing in the writing to the development of more complicated forms for their own sake, drawing them for drawing's sake; also doing painting for painting's sake. We guide the drawing and painting lessons into this sphere in the 4th class. In drawing we learn what a circle is, what an ellipse is, and so on, This is taught in the drawing lesson. This you take further always leading to plastic forms, using plasticine if you have it – if not, mud will do – in order to bring about sensitivity and a fine feeling for form. What has been taught in this way in drawing is now taken over into the mathematics lesson. What the children have acquired so far is now

incorporated in geometry. Only now does one begin to explain what a triangle is, a circle, a square etc., geometrically. Therefore the spatial conception of these forms is brought out of drawing, and in Class 6 the child learns the geometrical conceptions of the forms which he previously made in drawing. By this it will be seen that we absorb something different in the drawing element.” (16 lecture 2)

There appears to be a contradiction between the previous quotation from the Practical Course, in which the geometrical approach to drawing, "about the 9th year", was spoken of, and the above quotation from the lectures on the Curriculum, in which the entering with geometrical concepts into what has been learnt from drawing "in the 6th class" was spoken of.

The explanation is found by referring to other places: first of all out of the 13th lecture of the Basle Course for Teachers in 1920. After a discussion as to the necessity for living concepts we find:

"That which is geometrical can really be felt by one who has had some experience of geometry as something which should be gradually raised from a state of rest into one of livingness.” (23 lecture 13)

It is then shown how one can use the theorem of the sum of the angles of a triangle to call forth "a mental picture of the triangle which is actually in inner movement"... and then it says:

"We could very well use this as a support if we then want to build up for the child a proper feeling for space, a concrete, a true feeling for space. .... The same thing is necessary when we want to judge the relations of one being to another in space, when we want to penetrate their inner beings. And if we have fully realised this then we are led to develop in the children the sense for space by making use of the play of movement itself, by letting the children run certain figures. ... Furthermore it is of special importance that we now really proceed from this type of observation to the retention of what we have observed. Especially for developing the sense of space... it is of great significance if I allow shadows of various curved bodies to fall on various curved surfaces and then try to call forth an understanding for the special configuration of the shadows. One can definitely assert: if a child is in a position to grasp why a sphere throws an elliptical shadow under certain conditions – that is something which the child can already understand from the 9th year – then this interpenetration, this arising of surfaces in space works powerfully upon the whole inner mobility of the child's ability to feel and make mental pictures. Because of this one should look upon the development of the feeling for space during the school years as being something important.” (23 lecture 13)

There is indicated here a comparatively difficult task in understanding space for a quite early age, in which there can naturally be no question of deductive proof from axioms in the Euclidean manner, but rather an understanding developed from the feeling for space.

You find something different in the so-called Dornach

Christmas Course of 1921/22 in the 12th lecture. After speaking about the inner division of the period of life between the change of teeth and puberty and the necessity of adapting the lesson in accordance with this division, Steiner said:

"It is much more important that the teacher, the educator, finds his own way into such things, rather than receive a ready made curriculum with goals to achieve. Indeed in this way he will do the right thing for each life period. By means of art and artistic presentation up to the 9th and 10th year he will let the descriptive element approach the form-making element, in which the human being himself still takes part – without therewith neglecting the form-making element in itself.” (27 lecture 12)

There then follow sentences on other subjects which should be dealt with at this age and then the thread returns to the division of the lesson according to the form-making and describing elements.

"With the approach of the 12th year there now can be added to the form-making and describing elements the explaining elements, the taking into account of cause and effect, that through which the intellect is exerted. The child first grows into that between the 11th and 12th years. Now something must diffuse itself over this whole period, namely the presentation of the mathematical in its most widely different realms, suited to the age of the child naturally. The presentation to the child of the mathematical, of what is arithmetical and geometrical, is something which engenders quite special difficulties for instruction and education. For it is really true that things of a mathematical nature taught prior to the 9th year in a simple form must first be approached entirely out of the artistic element. Here, too, in all kinds of ways we must present the mathematical and geometrical to the child artistically, i.e., here again we shall pass over to the description of forms between the 9th and 10th years. For when we go about things properly the child can grasp a very great deal before the 9th year – and afterwards throughout his entire school life over an increasingly comprehensive, more complicated field. The child should only learn to observe angles, triangles, quadrilaterals, etc., in this descriptive way; and above all only towards the age of 12 should we begin to actually prove things.” (27)

We read in the 9th lecture of the Ilkley Course 1923:

"Arithmetic and geometry, indeed all mathematics, occupy a unique position in education.” (35 lecture 9)

– and after describing the supersensible members of the human being and the special ways in which the lessons work upon the different members of the child's being, we read further:

"Thus on the one hand, the study of the plant kingdom and the rudiments of writing and reading of which I spoke yesterday affect the physical and etheric bodies – I shall speak about the teaching of history later on. On the other hand all that is learnt of man's relation to the animal kingdom affects the astral body and Ego-organisation, those higher members which pass out of the physical and etheric bodies during sleep. But the remarkable thing is that arithmetic and geometry work

upon both the physical-etheric and the astral and Ego. As regards their role in education arithmetic and geometry are really like a chameleon – by their very nature they are related to every part of man's being. Whereas lessons on the plant and animal kingdoms should be given at a definite age arithmetic and geometry must be taught throughout the whole period of childhood, though naturally in a form suited to the changing characteristics of the different life-periods." (ibid)

– and after describing what happens during sleep to what has been worked at in the lesson, we read:

"During sleep, however, our body of formative forces continues to calculate, continues all that it has received as arithmetic and the like. We ourselves are then no longer within the physical and etheric bodies - but supersensibly they continue to calculate or to draw geometrical figures and to perfect them. If we are aware of this fact and plan our teaching accordingly great liveliness can be brought about in the being of the child. To achieve this in geometry, for example, we must not take as our starting-point the abstractions and intellectual formulae that are usually considered the right groundwork. We must begin with inner, not outer perception, by awakening in the child a strong sense of symmetry for instance. Even in the case of the youngest children we can begin to do this." (ibid)

Then there follow indications for suitable drawing exercises similar to those of the Discussions with Teachers and Steiner later speaks about how they work on further during sleep. Finally we read:

"It is possible to assist the continued activity of the etheric body during sleep if instead of beginning geometry with triangles and the like, when the intellectual element is already in evidence, we begin by conveying a concrete conception of space." (ibid)

In the last educational course which Steiner gave (in Torquay 1924) we read about the building up of the geometry lesson upon symmetry exercises and this is followed by these remarks on Pythagoras' theorem:

"Pythagoras' theorem shows us what we can set up as a goal where geometry is concerned. We can really build up our geometry in such a way that we can say that we want to form everything so that it culminates in the theorem of Pythagoras, that the square on the hypotenuse of a right-angled triangle is equal to the sum of the squares on the other 2 sides. It is really wonderful if this is really born in mind."

After demonstrating a particularly suitable proof, the same as can be found in Discussions with Teachers, and after further discourses on how one is ever and again astonished by new aspects of it (which the reader is especially recommended to read), the subject is concluded with the following sentences:

"With 11 or 12-year-olds you can really bring geometry to the point when you explain the theorem of Pythagoras by comparing areas; and the children will be filled with joy and enthusiasm when they have understood it. Now they want to do it again and again especially if they are allowed to cut it out. There will only be a few intellectual good-for-nothings, who remembering it fairly well will

always succeed in doing it. Most of the more normal children will always cut it out wrongly and then keep making corrections until they find how it has to be done. But that is quite in keeping with the wonder of the theorem of Pythagoras and one ought not to evade this wonder but remain in it." (40 lecture 5)

Summary

1   It is to be noted that arithmetic and geometry are to be taken right through the whole of the child's school life – reshaped from time to time according to the stages of development of the latter. (35)

2   Because of the crucial points of development occurring at the ages of 9 and 11 there arises a division of the mathematical and geometrical instruction, which can be characterised as "artistic form-making", "describing" and "explaining and proving". (27)

3   The actual building up of geometry according to the proof-procedure is in its right place after the ages 11 and 12. (16 & 27)

4   Previously, however, the children should have already been intensively occupied with geometrical forms and figures and so have become familiar with them. This occupation with plane and spatial forms which can be presented in drawing goes through 2 stages, that of the "artistic form-making" (up to the 9th year) and that of the "descriptive observation" (up to the age 11 or 12). (27)

In the first stage – apart from the preparatory exercises leading to handwriting – the exercises on symmetry are taken by giving artistic tasks to the children; in the 2nd stage we go over to the usual geometrical forms and figures and at the same time to ruler and compasses.

We should take into account here that Steiner required mineralogy – using geometrical forms – to be taken in Class 6.

5   In the Practical Course the transition from the artistic form-making stage to the descriptive observation stage is already made about the age of 9, whilst in the Curriculum lectures and the Dornach 1921/22 Course, the describing geometry only begins during the 9th year.

From all these indications we can deduce the following aims for the teaching of elementary geometry.

Aims for the Teaching of Geometry

Class 1

Drawing for the sake of handwriting.

Classes 2 and 3

Drawing of simpler and more complicated forms for their own sake and without any dependence on perceptible objects, for the nurture of the consciousness of space in its form-creating quality (symmetry and the like).

Classes 4 and 5

Getting to know geometrical figures by means of drawing, grasping their interrelationships by describing, i.e., triangle, square, circle, ellipse, etc., up to the theorem of Pythagoras, at least as far as the isosceles right-angled triangle.

Classes 6 to 8

That which up to now has been treated by means of drawing and describing is now to be grasped by means of proving things geometrically. At the same time simple projection and shadow drawing are taught in the drawing lesson which has once more become independent.

Really there result – apart from the drawing for handwriting – three teaching stages each of which is a whole in itself.

Stage 1

Before the age of 9 the free artistic form-making (symmetry, deviation from symmetry, intensification and elaboration, etc.) independent of perceptible objects, is nurtured by drawing, painting and modelling.

Stage 2

At the age of 9 at the latest the first actual teaching of geometry is begun, which embraces the usual geometrical figures and reveals their interrelationships but at the same time is to remain purely within the realm of inner perception. Its goal is the theorem of Pythagoras.

Stage 3

Only now, beginning in the 11th or 12th year of life, will one lead over to the precise method of building up mathematical knowledge and therefore the knowledge hitherto acquired by observation will have to be worked through anew from first principles.

Steiner also considered the stage when the child learns by means of observation to be true geometry. This is shown by his advocacy of the pictorial proof of Pythagoras' theorem already in the time between the ages of 9 and 11 or 12. This way of developing geometry is obviously meant in the Practical Course – according to which geometry proper is already begun after the 9th year of age.

But the Curriculum lectures mean the strict proof-demanding geometry when they describe how the knowledge which the children have acquired out of the drawing element should be begun to be understood geometrically in Class 6. By this the apparent contradiction between these 2 courses (the Practical Course and the Curriculum lectures) is resolved and the way is open again for the further treatment of class aims.

Class 4

Geometry – Attempt at a formulation:

After having first carried out, in the first three school years, the drawing exercises, which give service to learning to write, and the drawing and modelling purely for the sake of forms in themselves and without reference to perceptible objects, one begins in the 4th class at the latest with the drawing of elementary geometrical forms and teaches their relationships, finding them purely by observation.

Class 5

The Curriculum lectures say:

"We shall proceed further in Class 5 with the teaching of fractions and decimals and bring before the child everything that induces in him the ability to move about freely in reckoning with numbers, whether whole or fractional or expressed in decimals." (16)

In Geometry the description of geometrical forms and figures through observation will be taken further and be made more advanced.

Class 6

In the Curriculum Lectures:

"Then in Class 6 we go over to the calculation of interest and percentage, discount and simple exchange and thence establish formula calculation, as I have indicated."

One can compare this most especially with the Seminar Course (13) where it is explained how the transition is made from calculating interest to working with letters in formulae.

"In geometry a beginning must be made – in the sense of what has been followed through under the heading of the 4th Class – with building up proofs – about as far as understanding congruent triangles and their applications. In this manner those concepts which the children made their own in the previous years through geometrical drawing are to be employed, illuminated and extended and in particular the concept of locus is to he introduced."

On the commercial arithmetic that has to be begun in Class 6 we read the following in the 14th lecture of the Practical Course:

"And the actual power of discernment, the rational, intellectual comprehension of the human being which can be relied upon, belongs to the last school period. For this reason we employ precisely the 12th year in the child's life, when he is gravitating in the direction of the power of discernment for merging this power of judgment in the activities still partly prompted by instinct, but already very thickly overlaid with discerning power. These are, as it were, the twilight instincts of the soul, which we must overcome by the power of judgment. At this stage it must be remembered that man has an instinct for gain, for profiteering, for the principle of discount, etc., which appeals to the instincts. But we must be sure to impose the power of discernment very forcibly upon this and consequently we must use this stage of development for studying the relations existing between calculation and the circulation of commodities and finance, that is for doing calculations in percentages, interest, discount, etc." (12 lecture 14)

Class 7

The Curriculum lectures say:

"Then in Class 7 we try to teach raising numbers to powers and obtaining roots, also what is called reckoning with positive and negative numbers. And above all we try to bring them to what is called the theory of equations in connection with general application to practical life." (16)

For this the supplement to the 14th lecture of Discussions with Teachers might be drawn upon.

In geometry the following is proposed – the building up by

means of proof should be carried further, say through the treatment of the circle, the quadrilateral and the polygon. In this way the concept of the geometrical locus is fostered further, because it concerns the freeing of geometrical figures from their rigidity and endowing them with movement.

Class 8

The Curriculum Lectures say:

"Then in Class 8 we develop further what is connected with the theory of equations and take the children as far in it as we can relating it to calculations of length and areas of figures and surfaces, and the theory of loci, as we at least endeavoured to do yesterday." (16)

On the treatment of loci we can also consult the afterword to the Discussions with Teachers (13) and also the Conferences (22.9.20).

The geometrical aspect has already been given consideration in the Curriculum lectures, but it should be pointed out in that connection that besides calculations on surfaces, simple calculations on solids should also be done. Furthermore the concept of locus might now be applied to the following curves: ellipses, hyperbolae, Cassini ovals and Apollonian circles. Here we might also consult the Discussions with Teachers (13). Furthermore raising any kind of number to a power and finding its root should be practised; also equations with more than one unknown.

It is clear that from the results of the mathematics teaching up to now it is still true to say that many class teachers do not possess a sufficiently strong relationship to mathematics to be able to really fulfil the demands required by Steiner. This is especially true in the case of geometry – the lie of the land is strange to many in the first place – their own school days have not endeared them to it. And now something quite different is to be put in its place – indeed there are two replacements: to begin with, drawings of figures which have to be transformed and which have to be obtained purely from one's inner being without support from external objects or perceptible events; and afterwards one has to move to those geometrical figures which are indeed "abstract" and one has to master their characteristics, the nature of the laws of their transformations, purely from observation, and therewith work with such mechanical aids as ruler and compasses; and then finally one has yet to pursue a "proper" geometry with proofs!

There lies here an exceedingly important task, that of developing really concretely this completely new way of approach to geometry; incidentally Steiner expressed himself on the question of one's own geometry book on February 14th 1923 in the Conferences.

Class 9

From Class 9 onward the position of the Geometry Lesson is quite different. For this lesson rests in the hands of the mathematician and he finds again and again that the elementary geometry on which he has to build is completely strange to the children, whom he takes over from the class teacher.

At the original opening of a 9th class on September 22 1920 Steiner asked the mathematics teacher how he had dealt with raising numbers to powers and finding their roots, particularly the squaring and cubing of particular numbers and the extraction of square and cube roots in what had previously been Class 8. He then remarked:

"It is not important for things to be done in the way they are required later, but rather that certain forms of thinking are practised. This peculiarity in the form of thinking practised in cubing, squaring and finding roots – where one abstracts so to speak from the concreteness of numbers and unites the numbers in a new way, groups them together in a different way – leads so deeply into the being of number, is so formative for one's thinking, that we really should do it. Then practical arithmetic will be necessary, for example I would certainly consider it good if you were to work out with the children such things as the practical calculation of volumes. Here is an example: suppose a can is conically cylindrical and it contains a certain quantity of water: how great is the quantity of water if the base has a diameter which is half that of the top?"

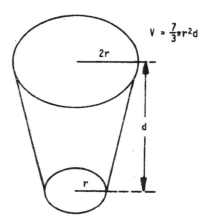

"Then I would add to that the study of approximations so that the children get hold of such concepts. I would set out from the way the "Nivellier Dioptre" is used – this kind of thing can take place here all the time, and the working out of mean values arising from all kinds of similar practical problems, e.g., weighing with apothecary's scales. In addition take what in more advanced calculations still has to do with systems of exchange. As far as geometry is concerned –you must have preceded this with calculations of the cubical contents of bodies – I would then advise you to take the first elements of Descriptive Geometry." (22.9.20)

(Note: The Nivellier Dioptre is a simple surveying instrument employing a spirit level. With all such instruments it is necessary to take several readings and then calculate their arithmetic mean value. In the case of apothecary's scales there is the well-known formula: true weight = geometric mean value of the two weighings obtained by alternating the functions of the two scale pans.)

On the occasion of the formulation of the Curriculum for Class 10 a year later a few things were also said about what is important for Class 9. The teacher had described how he had dealt with what had just been indicated for Class 9 and Steiner commented:

"You can introduce the concept of π. When you introduce the concept π then it cannot be a matter of obtaining theories about decimals. They can get to

know the numerical value of π to so many decimal places." (17.6.21)

As a result of the teacher's replying to the question as to what curves the children were familiar with – the ellipse, hyperbola and parabola as geometrical loci which he had taken in Class 8 – Steiner said:

"It might come about that the children get to know the first elements of Plane Trigonometry. I believe we could at first regard that as a task. Then comes Descriptive Geometry..."

And after the teacher had described how the children had understood the idea of interpenetrating planes and surfaces, how they were already able to make drawings of two interpenetrating triangular surfaces and also of the intersection point of a line and a plane, Steiner said:

"Perhaps that is not necessary. You must actually so form your method that you set out from projection, orthogonal projection, point, line, that you take the idea of the plane as plane, not the plane as a triangle." (17.6.21)

Up to this point what has been followed through is clearly related to Class 9, where the task in the realm of Descriptive Geometry is indicated to be somewhat more advanced than in the previous year (1920) but also easier than that for which the teacher had formed his lessons in Class 9.

Class 10

Immediately after the last quoted words Steiner said the following, which is obviously more related to Class 10:

"The theory of planes and the intersection of two planes must be added to the treatment of the plane as plane. And thereto the first elements of Projective Geometry fit in, do they not? Above all, you bring to the children the concept of duality. You need only teach the most elementary things." (17.6.21)

Since the teacher had then referred to the fact that one also needs logarithms for trigonometry Steiner said (this was just before the opening of the 1st Class 10) – obviously in reference back to Class 9:

"Haven't you yet taken the concept of logarithms? Naturally that must be done in the mathematics lessons. That belongs to it all. You need only get to know the basic concepts: sine, cosine, tangent. A pair of theorems that can be understood on their own merits – so that you begin to understand:

$$cos\,^2A + sin\,^2A = 1$$

and understand it as pictorially as possible." (17.6.21)

The teacher gathered from this that Steiner wanted to have logarithms already in Class 9 and asked about it. Steiner replied:

"It is enough if you get so far with logarithms that they can carry out simple logarithmic calculations." (17.6.21)

The last remark clearly applies to the 9th school year.

In the course of the school year at the beginning of which these indications for the mathematics lessons were given, Steiner said more about Class 10:

"If they get the first fundamentals of Projective Geometry from you as far as the Principle of Duality in perspective, in such a way that the children are "perplexed and astounded", and if you awaken interest for some of the figures in the new dissertation of Dr. Baravalle, then you have accomplished everything which you should have done." (11.9.21)

Class 11

On the occasion of the formation of the first Class 11 in 1922 the following aim was given for the mathematics lesson:

"In mathematics we should go in for as advanced a treatment as possible of Trigonometry and Analytical Geometry. In Descriptive Geometry we should get so far that the children understand and can draw the curve of intersection of a cone with a cylinder." (21.6.22)

This advice received a special colouring a year later when Steiner answered a question from the mathematics teacher concerning the Algebra curriculum:

"I made my suggestions in such a way that I said that the mathematical material should be taken so far that an understanding of Carnot's theorem (The Cosine Law) and its applications is obtained. In saying this the whole curriculum is indicated. A great deal of algebra is contained in it – necessarily so – the theory of series, etc. We can indeed keep to this curriculum, and in such a way that we can give the children problems, by solving which they have to master Carnot's theorem in all directions." (1923)

A third formulation of the curriculum for Class 11 was given on April 30 1924:

"Class 11: Sections and interpenetrations, shadow constructions, Diophantine equations, analytical geometry as far as conic sections. In Class 11 one should take the functions more inwardly, so that one has within one the ratio-principle in the sine and cosine. Of course one has to set out from the geometrical aspect in this case." (30.4.24)

The last sentence may seem rather pointless. It was said because Steiner had spoken on the goals of Class 12 immediately beforehand and in so doing had advised against beginning differential calculus from geometrical considerations. Therefore he expressly emphasised here in the treatment of trigonometry that one should set out from geometrical considerations.

Class 12

For Class 12 Steiner also gave the mathematics curriculum twice – in 1923 for the single class which took their exams immediately after the 12th Class and in 1924 for the later 12th Classes which had a preparation year for the exams after Class 12. The difference between these two curricula is nowhere so strongly marked as in mathematics. In considering them it should not now be our purpose to enquire as to what goals were sought for in 1923 with the State curriculum in mind, but rather how Steiner let the ideal goal of a pure 12th Class in a Waldorf School illuminate and run alongside the one laid down:

"It would certainly be desirable that just at this age –

they are about 18 years old – the scholars should gain a mature understanding for the historical-artistic and should already take up what is spiritual – without teaching them anthroposophical dogma – in literature, the history of art and history." (24.4.23)

Goals of intrinsic worth were indicated then for various subjects by means of examples; the concrete manner, and indeed spiritually concrete manner, in which this was done was not repeated on the occasion of the second treatment of the curriculum for the 12th Class given in 1924. The following was given for mathematics in particular:

"For example it is quite impossible to develop the theory of space as I indicated it in the recent course for Teachers in Dornach (1923) with the 3 dimensions above-below, right-left, in front and behind. Because of this a deplorable state of affairs undoubtedly arises where the propagation of anthroposophical truths above all is concerned. For you see today there exists absolutely no public interest for such things, things for which in the widest sense there ought to be public interest.

Consider discussing the following: everything of the nature of will works three-dimensionally within the earth-sphere; everything of a feeling nature works not three-dimensionally but two-dimensionally so that we are always obliged, when passing in the soul-realm from the domain of will to that of feeling, to project the 3rd dimension not on to a plane but in a planar direction, which thus corresponds to the in front-behind. In this connection we should notice that although we can reduce it on to the plane of symmetry in the human being we should not merely do that, we cannot allow it to be confined to that. The phenomenon is two-dimensional everywhere. Thinking leads us into the one-dimensionality, the ego into the null dimension. In this manner the matter becomes very clear. Now may I ask you – how can one present such things in a lecture today – even if they are elementary things? Today there is no possibility of making them plausible to an audience. There is simply no public interest in such things." (25.4.23)

The curriculum for Class 12 given on April 30 1924 shows the second formulation. The class had taken its lessons in the Waldorf School curriculum since it was Class 7 and had furthermore learnt about complex numbers up to De Moivre's theorem, and also about identities and the theory of combinations. Steiner said on this subject:

"The very lessons as given last year in Class 12 have shown that we simply cannot do things in that way. To do things in that way (as the approaching Abitur required things to be done for the Class 12) is quite dreadful for the human soul. It is necessary to take spherical trigonometry and the elements of the analytical geometry of space in as clear a way as possible. Then take Cavalier perspective in Descriptive Geometry. The scholars ought to reach the point of being able to represent a complicated house in Cavalier perspective and also the inside of the house. In algebra it is necessary to take only the first beginnings of Differential and Integral Calculus. It is not necessary to get as far as Maxima and Minima. That already belongs to the University. Just work properly through the concept of differential and integral." (30.4.24)

Amplifying these indications he went on to say:

"You should lay emphasis on the value of developing spherical trigonometry and its applications to Astronomy and Geodesy in a manner quite befitting the age, so that they become understood comprehensively. The analytical geometry of space should be developed so as to make clear how geometrical forms are expressible in equations. I would not hold back here from letting the lessons culminate for example in comprehending what sort of curve, or rather surface is expressed by

$$x^{2/3} \quad y^{2/3} \quad z^{2/3} = a$$

that gives an Astroid – so that as much as possible of a general character is included. Above all, make equations transparent so that one acquires a feeling for how the essence of things is actually contained in them. Conversely, we should especially foster the following: I draw a curve on the board or describe a curve or surface in space and without having to pause for a moment we should know the equation which applies, so that we have a sense for the equation.

I do not consider it good for one's general mathematical education when differential and integral calculus are derived from geometrical considerations – they should rather be derived from quotients. I would set out from the difference calculation, i.e., from

$$\frac{\Delta y}{\Delta x}$$

I would grasp hold of that as quotient and would only develop the differential quotient through making the numerator and denominator grow ever smaller, reach it purely out of number. I would not set out from this business of continuity – by that means you acquire no concept of differential quotients.

If you set out from series and then only at the end go over the tangent problem in geometry, i.e., from secant to tangent, if the whole differential quotient is understood purely from the standpoint of number, numerical calculation, and only then proceed to what is geometrical, the scholar will gain the insight that what is geometrical is only an illustration of what is arithmetical. Then you obtain the integral as the converse. Then you obtain the possibility of not setting out from the idea that arithmetic (or calculus) is an embodiment of geometry but that geometry is an illustration for arithmetic. One should observe this principle more generally; for example, do not look upon positive and negative numbers as being things in themselves; one ought to consider the number series as follows: 5 – 1, 5 – 2, 5 – 3, 5 – 4, 5 – 5, 5 – 6... now I haven't got enough, because one is lacking for me and I write it as – 1. You then remain in the realm of number. The negative number is the quantity which is not present, the deficiency of the minuend. Much more inner activity! In this way one has the possibility of arousing capacities in the scholars which are much more real than when one only derives everything from geometry." (30.4.24)

To a question of a teacher as to the point where he ought to begin, Steiner expounded further:

"When the class has reached the point of starting spherical trigonometry you must pass over from trigonometry to developing the concept of the sphere, qualitatively, without immediately launching into calculation. Instead of drawing on the plane you must draw on the globe, so that they get the concept of spherical triangle, the concept of the triangle lying on the sphere. You must make that graphic for the children – that in this case the angle sum is not equal to 180 degrees but is greater. You must really teach this concept, the triangle on the sphere with curved boundaries. Only in conclusion to this do you go on to calculate. In trigonometry calculation is the interpretation of the sphere. I would prefer you not to observe the sphere from its centre but from its curved surface, so that you can also immediately pass on to a general discussion on curvature, for example, and how the corresponding figure to a spherical triangle on the globe would appear on an ellipsoid, how it would look on a paraboloid of rotation where it is not closed on both sides but is open. Do not set out from the centre, but from the curvature of the surface, otherwise you will not be able to deal with other bodies. You must think yourself into the surface. You must, so to speak, build for yourself the thought: what do I experience when I set out from a triangle, which corresponds to a spherical triangle, on an ellipsoid? Then make the scholars aware in this connection how matters stand when you apply the ordinary Pythagoras' theorem to the spherical triangle. You can't consider squares, naturally. These things contribute to general education, whilst otherwise you only develop the intellect.

Permutations and combinations have already been taken (the teacher had already taken the theory of combinations in Class 11). If there is time, take the first elements of Probability, for example the probable length of life of a human being." (30.4.24)

On Cavalier perspective there is a further remark on 2nd June 1924:

"The realistic thing is Cavalier perspective. All possibilities should be taken for Cavalier perspective. Architectural work is that for which Cavalier perspective is fitted. I would only prefer that you practice freehand sketching of the constructions along with the actual drawing done with rule and compasses."

6 Home Surroundings

Classes 1 to 3, ten weeks main lesson each.

In lecture 10 of the Dornach Christmas Course for teachers 1921/22 the following passages were found dealing with Home Surroundings (*7), out of which nature study, history and geography are developed after Class 4.

"When one is called upon to educate children of this age, one needs artistic sensitivity to imbue with life everything that is brought before the children. The teacher

must reanimate, he must be able to let the plants speak, to let the animals act morally. The teacher must be able to transform everything into a fairy tale, a fable, into living substance. But here we need to consider one important point." (27 lecture 10)

And, after pointing out how not to teach, Steiner continues:

"Ideally, after very careful preparation, for this kind of teaching demands special preparation, the teacher should be in a position to create out of his own resources conversations between different plants so that the story of the rose and the lily or the conversation between the sun and the moon reach the children directly out of the teacher's individual imagination. Why should this be so? I should like to answer by a living example: if one tells children what one has read in books, the effect of one's words is bound to be that of a dried-up person, even if one is full of life outside the classroom. Through the workings of the imponderables, one's words would become those of a person who is withered, who is not covered by living skin but by parchment... On the other hand, what has been invented by oneself is still imbued with life-giving forces which work upon the children. It has a wholesome effect upon the children if the teacher who has created his story – and such a task is by no means an easy one – goes to his lessons in the morning with steps which reveal his eagerness to bring the story to his class. In fact, his story remains incomplete until the radiantly happy faces of his children give it its proper conclusion.

Up to the end of the ninth year everything the child learns about plants, animals and minerals, about the sun and the moon, mountains and rivers, would be rendered in this way, for the child is still united with his surroundings. World and child, child and world, are a unity during these years." (ibid)

Indications for the individual classes

These have been taken from the curriculum lectures, in which the lessons on home surroundings come immediately after the passages about reading and writing:

Class 1

"To what has just been described must be added what can stimulate the child to reflection; you explain to him what lies near at hand and this will later be brought to him again arranged in an orderly way as Geography and Natural History. These subjects are brought close to his understanding by linking them to things familiar to him – plants, animals, configuration of the land, mountains and rivers. This is called in school 'Study of Home Surroundings', knowledge of the homeland. But the point is that we bring about a certain soul-awakening in the child just in this very first year of his school life, an awakening as regards his environment, so that he learns to connect himself with it." (16 lecture 1)

Class 2

"With regard to a description of the surroundings one should continue with what has begun in Class 1." (ibid)

Class 3

"Now you see that the material you have gathered

through describing the environment you employ in a free way for forming your lesson on practical occupations. The child of about nine in the third class can very well gain an idea, through such a lesson – I can only give instances – of preparing mortar as it is employed in house-building. The child can also have an idea of how to manure and how to plough; what rye and wheat look like. In short, in a free way, you let the child enter into his surroundings as far as he can with understanding." (ibid)

With the entry into Class 4 this study of home surroundings leads over to history, geography, nature study and, later on, physics and chemistry.

7 History

Beginning with Class 4, 6 weeks of main lessons a year.

In his Practical Course of 1919 Steiner spoke about the meaning of history lessons in the future:
"I shall only touch on history, as far as it is more than stories, after the child has reached his twelfth year. At this point he begins to take an inner interest in the great historical connections. This will be quite especially important in the future, for it will become more and more obviously necessary to educate people to a comprehension of historical connections, where hitherto they have never arrived at a real conception of history. They have been more like members of an economic State system whose demands and interests they have followed as if they were machines. It has been considered sufficient to know a few paltry anecdotes about rulers and wars, and the dates of battles and famous people.

A special subject of teaching in the future will have to be the development of the impulse in humanity towards culture. But teaching will then have to include the study of historical impulses, and these will have to be timed in the curriculum to answer to the appropriate moment in the child's development." (12 lecture 8)

During the previous day the Crusades were chosen as an example to show how history should be dealt with in this sense. (13)

In the 14th session of "Discussions with Teachers" Steiner recommends two English works as a basis for teaching the history of civilisation, viz. Buckle's "History of Civilisation" and Lecky's "History of the Age of Enlightenment".

In the Basle Course of 1920 Steiner also showed how history should be taught, and above all, how one should link up with what is still living and working at the present time as a consequence of the period of historical development which has been studied:
"If we introduce the children to Greek history in an abstract way, even if they have already entered the Gymnasium (*3), we are merely putting them back quite abstractly into an earlier age; they do not understand why the present needs this Greek age. On the other hand they will see the point at once if they are shown that in

the midst of our present-day life there are still immediate living forces at work which have their roots in the Greek ages. We must first of all get this over to the children. We may already have found an opportunity to prepare for this understanding through teaching other subjects. At any rate, when teaching history we must start from those factors which are still influencing our present times." (23 lecture 12)

Then Steiner continued to speak about Greek history:
"We have inherited all our universal concepts from the Greek civilisation. Certain artistic experiences which are still active in our soul life today, we have received purely as heredity from the Greek civilisation." (ibid)

He then made this clear through the basic concepts of our cognition and through our artistic experiences and activities, showing how in all that the Greeks have contributed as "treasures of life" nothing Christian can as yet be found.

How to portray historical figures during the first stage of history teaching before the great change in the eleventh to twelfth year, is described particularly graphically in the Supplementary Course:
"Suppose you are telling a child about Julius Caesar. You will not be content merely to relate what Caesar did, but you will try to give the child at the same time an imaginative picture of him. You will paint the historical situation in such a way that the child cannot help having in imagination a kind of picture of Julius Caesar – he sees him walk, he follows him about. If he really imagines Julius Caesar in this way – not only painting, but also modelling him in imagination – then, if he goes to a class in handwork immediately afterwards, you may be sure he will knit better than he would have done without Julius Caesar!" (26)

In his 2nd lecture of the same course the following passage can be found, also showing how historical characters or events can be described in an imaginative way:
"This will mean that when you are teaching history you will need to collect and bring into play all your own temperamental tendencies and imbue the lessons with strong personal interest. The child will have time enough in later life for objectivity. To make our teaching entirely objective when we are telling the children, for instance, about Brutus and Julius Caesar, to refrain from showing any emotion in the picture we give of these two contrasting characters, is to teach history badly. We must be there with our heart. No need to get wildly excited and rave about the situation; but we should show quite openly where we are moved to sympathy and antipathy, and show it in such a way that the children are stirred to feel for themselves what we have felt. It is, above all, subjects of this kind – history, geography, geology – that should be put before the children with real feeling. Geology, for instance, becomes quite fascinating when the teacher has a deep and sympathetic understanding of various rocks and stones that he describes. In this connection I would recommend every teacher to read Goethe's treatise on granite, to read it right through, entering into it with heart and soul. He will find there a proof of how, by entering into the world of Nature not merely in thought but with the whole of

his being, man is brought into a human relationship with that primeval father, the sacred granite of remote antiquity. Other things can be approached in the same way." (26)

In the 14th session of the "Discussions" it was shown how to give children a concrete idea of the historical conditions of the times in their history lessons. This point is once more taken up in the Supplementary Course of 1921 in lecture 3:

"The history lesson works in quite a different way. History has to do with time; and if we want to teach it rightly, we must give due consideration to the time element in it. We shall be failing to do this if we only give pictures in our lessons. Suppose I were to tell a child about Charlemagne almost as though he might be the child's grandfather, who is still living! I should be leading that child astray. If I speak to him of Charlemagne I must see that he realises how far removed Charlemagne is from us in time. I could bring it home to him, for example, by saying: 'Imagine you are standing here, and holding your father's hand.' The child can picture that. Then I must make sure he understands that his father is much older than himself. And now I tell him: 'Imagine that your father is holding the hand of his father, and that he is holding the hand of your father's grandfather.' I shall then have led the child back about 60 years. And now I can go still further back and get the child to think of a series of, let us say, 30 ancestors one behind the other, and explain that the thirtieth might have been Charlemagne. In this way the child gets a feeling of distance in time. He should never have isolated facts presented to him; the history lesson should always create a sense of distance in time. This is important.

And then in treating the different epochs we must point to the characteristic features of each, giving the children in this way an idea of how the various epochs differ from one another. Our aim throughout must be to let history live chiefly in time concepts, so that the children see it all from the aspect of time. This will work powerfully upon them; they will be stirred and stimulated in their inner being." (26)

After this passage follow some remarks about the effects of a wrong approach to history teaching upon the later life of the pupils.

A little earlier in the same course Steiner speaks about the actual history teaching in the lesson:

"When I am teaching history, I shall take care not to place the facts before the children in a purely external way, but to put forth my skill and ingenuity to adapt the lesson once again to the life-processes in the child; and this time in the following way: first, I tell the facts – the bare facts, that take place in space and time. In doing this I am once more claiming – laying hands on – the child's whole being. As with the physics experiments, the child is again under necessity to picture it all in space. And this is right. He must have a picture of what I tell him, he must see it in the spirit, see it spread out before him as a continuous whole; and he must also picture it in time.

When I have done this, I shall try to add some details concerning the characters or the events in my narration. In this way I shall keep the children's attention on the facts, but I am no longer simply narrating, I am describing. I have, you see, again gone through the same two stages – the first stage making demands upon the child's whole being, and the second appealing to his rhythmic system. Now the lesson is finished, and the child is dismissed.

Next morning the child comes to me again, bringing with him once more in his head the spiritual photographs of the lesson of the previous day. I shall be meeting him in the right way if I now go on to suggest discussions that can arise on the subject of yesterday's lesson. We might, for example, consider together whether Mithridates, or let us say Alcibiades, could be regarded as a respectable character or not. You see I must give narration and description on the first day and then on the following day I must lead the children to reflect and to form their own opinions. By this method I shall bring it about that the three members of the threefold human being interwork and interweave with one another in the right way.

An example of this kind can give you some idea of what you could achieve if you were in a position to adapt the whole of your teaching to the life-conditions of the children." (ibid)

In lecture XI of the Christmas Course 1921/22, which is especially helpful for the understanding of the development of the child's thinking, Steiner says this about the lessons after the twelfth year:

"We are only now at the point when the human being himself is placed into the world as a physical being with the attributes of dynamics and mechanics and, as such, with the equivalent experience. And only now is the possibility offered of approaching the human being with what is also the simplest element in physics and chemistry, with the laws of chemistry, of dynamics, to which the earth as earth is subject, with mineralogy, the knowledge of the minerals. If actual mineralogy, dynamics, physics, chemistry, are brought to the human being before this, one is – unconsciously – working detrimentally into human nature. On the other hand, the comprehension of so-called historical connections, of a historical survey, the comprehension of the dominant impulses in history, in social development, is only the polar opposite of the comprehension of what is connected with the physical, with mineralogy. For this, too, the child will only be mature enough when he is approaching the twelfth year. The nature of historical ideas, the impulses which run their course through the life of history, which work into social forms, these – although of course they are something quite different – are nevertheless the skeleton in the historical sphere, whereas the flesh, the muscles, are the living people with their biographies, and the immediate, concrete, historical events. Hence, in the treatment of history, which is also introduced between the tenth and twelfth years, we so go about matters that we conjure up isolated pictures which can kindle warmth in the feelings, to which the

feelings can aspire: biographies, individual character-
istic events – not the course of abstract impulses. These
come to the child when he has arrived at the twelfth
year, where there now enters what is conditioned by the
fact that man stands in the external world; and one can
also learn to understand what seizes upon an individual
person as a historical impulse from outside." (27)

Right at the beginning of the first of the two Stuttgart lectures of 1922, the transition which takes place in the young person between Class 9 and Class 10 is described, the transition from "knowledge to cognition" ("von der Kenntnis zur Erkenntnis") and history teaching is used to illustrate it:

"Let us assume, in order to clarify this point, that we
happen to talk about Julius Caesar with the children.
Earlier on we shall endeavour to describe his deeds,
perhaps also the tribes through which he passed; we
shall try to describe how he himself was a writer, how
alive and characteristic his style was, etc. If we talk
about Julius Caesar after Class 10 we shall speak about
the underlying intentions of his deeds; we can point out
how one or the other event in Caesar's life might have
happened differently and why it did not take a different
course. When we describe other scenes we shall try to
consider favourable or unfavourable circumstances.
Speaking about Goethe, for instance – after having given
to the children below Class 10 mainly pictures of his
life and works, we shall now try to speak about him in
such a way that we shall consider how his creative work
changed its character after the year 1790. At this new
stage in the life of the children we shall endeavour to
describe his longing for Italy, whereas previously we
have simply described the experiences of his youth and,
in the same way, what he experienced later on. In short,
we shall try to bring out more and more the causal and
similar relationships. As mentioned in previous courses,
one hints at such causal links already before the twelfth
year, but from this stage on the inner need for causality
must above all be fulfilled (Steiner refers to the age of
transition to Class 10). If one does not recognise this,
the most various short-comings may result within the
children. One must realise that the human soul has quite
definite needs at every stage of development, and if one
gives the child something unsuitable he will react in an
unfavourable manner. He will react specially unfavour-
ably if one does not make a clear difference between
the before and after. If one continues the same teaching
methods from Class 9 to Class 10 without changing their
character, then the child's soul will react in an unfa-
vourable way." (28 lecture 1)

The theme of the transition from Class 9 to Class 10 is developed further but only one sentence will be quoted here to indicate the general direction of Steiner's indications:

"Altogether it needs to be realised that when the child
reaches puberty it is essential to awaken in him an unu-
sually keen interest in the outer world." (ibid)

What follows after this statement is so relevant to all other subjects that it seems right to quote it in the section dealing with more general aspects of teaching. It will be found under "The curriculum arranged according to different ages" (this section has not been translated).

The real essence of history teaching is brought to light with particular clarity in the Dornach Easter Course of 1923. After some remarks about the first appearance of this need for causality in the twelfth year the following lines about teaching history are found:

"On the other hand until children are approaching their
twelfth year they cannot really begin to grasp historical
connections. Before that age you must give them pictures
of isolated human situations which either arouse pleas-
ure through their goodness, truth and so on, or displeas-
ure through the opposite qualities. History too must be
related to the life of feeling, to sympathy and antipathy.
Give the children complete pictures of events and per-
sonalities, but pictures which are kept mobile and alive
in the way I have indicated. (Compare what is said a few
pages later in the same lecture (34) about pictorial teach-
ing.) On the other hand causal connections between what
happened at an earlier and at a later period in history
can only be brought to the children at the first glimmer-
ing of the astral body's "moving backwards" (which was
also spoken of in the lecture), which increases in strength
at the approach of the fourteenth year. And so, at about
twelve years old, the child begins to enter this period of
retrospection, and this is the time when one can intro-
duce the concept of cause and effect in history. If atten-
tion is drawn earlier to this link between cause and ef-
fect, and to its inherent intellectual judgment, something
is introduced which is harmful to the later development
of the child." (34)

A comprehensive exposition of history teaching can be found in the Ilkley Course in the lecture held on 14th August, the study of which would be helpful for any history teacher, particularly for teachers of the middle school.

Curriculum indications for individual classes

Those for the middle school are based on the Curriculum Lectures and those for the upper school on the "Conferences" (*4).

Class 4

"In Class 4 a transition will be made from these les-
sons (Steiner refers to the lessons on Home Surround-
ings) towards a first presentation of local history, in-
troduced in a free and simple manner.

The children can for instance be told how it happened
that wine was cultivated in their home surroundings, if
this should be the case, or how fruit-growing became
established, how this or that industry was built up, and
similar matters." (16 lecture 1)

Class 5

"In the fifth class every effort will be made to make a
beginning with actual historical ideas, and just at this
time in the fifth class there must be no faltering in get-
ting the children to grasp ideas of the cultures of the
Oriental and Greek peoples. The reluctance to look
back into ancient times has only grown up in
present-day man, and he has no capacity for applying
the right ideas to what he sees when he looks back. A
child between 10 and 11 can do this very well, that is
if one continually rouses his feelings in making him

aware of all that can give him understanding for the Orientals and Greeks." (16)

(Suitable stories for reading and telling: "Scenes from medieval history").

Class 6

"Historical accounts of the Greeks and Romans, and the effects of Greek and Roman history up to the beginning of the fifteenth century, form the content of this sixth school year." (ibid)

(Suitable stories for reading and telling: "Scenes from later history".)

In a teachers' meeting which took place a few weeks after the beginning of the term Steiner was asked to speak about teaching Greek and Roman history. Since his answer is important, both as far as the syllabus of Class 6 is concerned and also for the style of teaching, it is reproduced in full. When asked whether one should not omit the Persian Wars in order to gain more time for the history of Greek culture he said:

"The Persian wars can be treated in such a way that they become part of the history of culture. It is possible to treat wars in ancient times from a cultural-historical aspect. Since then wars have become more and more negative. One can look upon the Persian wars as a symptom of cultural history." (25.9.19)

The teacher then asked whether the domestic politics of the Greeks were of less importance and Steiner answered:

"They are important, e.g., the way money came to be used." (ibid)

When asked whether one could deal briefly with the different constitutions he said:

"Yes, but you must describe the spirit of the constitution of Lycurgus and, for example, the difference between the Athenian and the Spartan way of life." (ibid)

When it was mentioned that the constitution of the Roman government was described extensively in textbooks he replied:

"In textbooks it is treated in detail and often quite wrongly. The Roman knew no constitution, but he knew from memory not only the Twelve-Table Laws but also a large number of law books. You will get a false picture of the Roman constitution if you do not show to the children that the Roman was a man of law, and that that was known. This is set forth in the textbooks in a very boring way, but with regard to the Roman constitution you must awaken the picture that every Roman was a law-fanatic and could count up the laws on his fingers. The Twelve-Table Laws were taught there as the multiplication tables are taught in our times." (25.9.19)

Class 7

"In the seventh class the main thing will be to make really comprehensible to the children the kind of life mankind evolved in the fifteenth century, and to describe European and extra-European conditions up to the beginning of the seventeenth century. This is the all-important period on which much care must be lavished. It is of even greater importance than the period which follows." (16)

(Suitable stories for reading and telling: "Stories about different tribes").

Class 8

"In the eighth class one tries to bring history up to present times, giving great consideration to cultural history.

Most of what forms the content of history today will be merely mentioned in passing. It is much more important for the child to learn how the steam engine or the mechanical loom, etc., transformed the world than that he should learn about incidents such as the altering of the Emser telegram.

Much of what is still found in our history books is of little value for the education of the child and even Charlemagne and similar historical figures should be treated without too much detail.

What I told you yesterday about helping children to experience historical time quite concretely (see "Discussions" session 14) should be applied consistently and with real zest." (ibid)

Further recommendations for the syllabus of Class 8 were made by Steiner on 23rd March 1921:

"It is of great educational value to read with Class 8 the first chapters of Schiller's 'Thirty Years' War'. Much is contained in them which penetrates right into our present times." (23.3.21)

(Suitable reading and telling material: "Knowledge of different peoples".)

I should like to conclude the indications for the curriculum of the middle school (Volksschulklassen) with some advice given by Steiner referring to the situation in Autumn 1919 when the school was being opened, because it may be of help in similar situations today:

"In almost every class you will have to begin from the beginning. You must simply limit your teaching as you find it necessary. If, for instance, you are obliged to begin at the beginning in the eighth year, then you must only take a little, but try nevertheless to give a complete picture of the whole evolution of humanity, only in an abbreviated form. In the eighth school year you would have to go through the whole world history as we understand it." (25.9.19)

Class 9

The transition of history teaching from the middle school to the upper school is marked by a surprising statement Steiner made on 22nd September 1920 after the opening of the first Class 9, when the history teacher gave an account of how he had tried to carry out the curriculum in his Class 8 – which had rather a mixed background. He reported how he had based his teaching on Buckle's "History of Civilisation" and how he had tried to throw light upon our present times. Steiner replied:

"Now I should like to recommend that you do not continue, but work through the whole period once more, basing the preparation on a more spiritual approach, and then take Lecky's 'History of Modern Civilisation'!" (22.9.20)

Steiner's indications of 15th November 1910, which were given specially for Class 9, make the above quotation clear:

"The point would be to deal with the history of the sixteenth, seventeenth, eighteenth and nineteenth centuries at least in the ninth class. Perhaps you could do it in this way: As Class 9 has not had it, it would be necessary now to deal with these centuries. In this connection the important thing would be to aim at giving your pupils an understanding of the present – they are already fifteen years old. You could take your themes as they are given in Herman Grimm's chapter for each century, the nineteenth century as a convergence of national histories – I mean the themes for the last four centuries as your guiding motif – they should really be covered in both classes. You would be able to take it in different ways: in the eighth class more in the form of a narrative, in the ninth entering more into the ideas of the last centuries.

You would have to make it your aim to bring the leading ideas before the children. A great deal of material can be found in my lecture cycles which can be expanded in a simple way by your getting literature from other sources." (15.11.20)

On 24th April 1923 Steiner was asked on what the teacher should concentrate after the pupils had been taught history in Class 8 mainly through descriptive accounts and biographies:

"According to our curriculum the children in the two Classes 8 and 9 should get a picture of the inner historical motifs, the main features. They should see how the fifteenth and sixteenth centuries bring about a widening of man's horizon, geographically and astronomically – how these effects are shown in history. Then in the sixteenth and seventeenth centuries the transition from the old social to the new political associations takes place; in the seventeenth and eighteenth centuries the effect of the more enlightened view of historical life; and in the nineteenth century the intermingling of the peoples and all that this implies. These centuries give the opportunity for presenting the facts which belong to these points of view. As a preparation for the teacher it would be extremely good if you could imagine to yourselves what kind of history would have arisen if Schiller's 'History of the Thirty Years' War' had been continued up to our day. For Middle Europe the short essays written by Treitschke are very good. There you will find all the necessary threads." (24.4.23)

The following syllabus of Class 10 was given twice, on 17th June 1921, and on 24th April 1923:

Class 10

"As to history teaching in Class 10, it is essential to be well prepared. In the tenth class you would go back to the earliest historical times and from there right through the downfall of the freedom of Greece, arranged in the following way: oldest Indian time, Persian time, Egypto-Chaldean time, Greek time up till the downfall of Greek freedom, until the battle of Cheronea 338." (17.6.21)

This was confirmed at the beginning of the school year 1921/22. Two years later after hearing an account of the history teacher referring to oriental history and to middle high German literature Steiner said:

"They would have to accord with one another. Even if you hate historical documents (in a lecture the teacher had railed against historical documents) we must start from them as a basis. We should have to take an older historical statement as a basis and then bring forward our view as history. Could you not take, for example, Heeren, as a foundation? It would be equally good to look for help in Rotteck – he is somewhat antiquated and has a certain bias. Then it would be a good thing to relate this to your lessons on artistic style. Young people could receive a great deal of permanent value if you read with them certain chapters of Johannes Müller's '24 Books of Universal History'. That has historical style, almost like Tacitus. These attempts to start from the whole have always been made and they must be renewed from our point of view." (24.4.23)

Steiner then told the history teacher not to spend too much time on the geological background of his historical scenes:

"If you go back too much to geology you are in danger of taking the cellar, leaving out the ground floor and taking the second storey, whereas you ought to begin with a historical motif which can be established by geology – the migrations of the nations and their dependence on the territories of the Earth. For this subject you can use one of the public lectures given in Stuttgart: 'Die Völker der Erde' (The Peoples of the Earth). You cannot use it directly in the class – it was given for enlightened older Stuttgartians – you must adapt it for the young.

If you begin your preparation at once then you must take something like Heeren, Rotteck or Johannes Müller. It is of course not right to transform history merely into a history of religion – that would be the task of the religion teacher." (24.4.23)

After a teacher had again asked where he should begin Steiner said, elaborating the last passage:

"You yourself have specified that you wish to start from dependence upon the earth – climate, zones, formations of the earth – and to build your history on this foundation. Dependence on mountains and plains, but historically not geographically, and thus dealing with a definite people at a definite time. But the facts must be correct." (24.4.23)

Class 11

Steiner laid great stress on bringing together German and history in Class 11, as can be seen in all following indications. The main task of these literary-historical lessons is Parsifal and Poor Henry. The aesthetic side of this theme is passed on to the art and history lessons so as to give the historical background which needless to say has to be taken before the literary approach. When the first Class 11 was opened and the German syllabus was made for this class on 21st June 1922 Steiner spoke the following words which should be considered as part of the curriculum:

"Then it is a good thing if the historical element of this

period is dealt with at the same time, but at this age you must draw deductions for the present, linking on to the present time and showing the children which figures of modern history are like those of the past – and especially those which are different but ought to be similar. In this way bring into the whole subject something in the nature of forming judgments. The children should above all realise that the whole structure of the nineteenth century has grown out of the previous centuries." (21.6.22)

This uniting of literature with history was not really understood by the teachers at first, and a year later Steiner answered a question about German and history in the new Class 11 with the following words:

"You have recently had a kind of review of the literature. You cannot leave everything for Class 12. Why do you not go on with it? You could cover all that belongs to the literature in a few paragraphs. In the teaching of history, however, it is assumed that you take up the thread again. For the time when there is no history of mankind to be given you must try to follow some historical thread. Class 10 finishes with the battle of Cheronea: in Class 11 you must work at the history of the Middle Ages. You will not succeed in enabling the young people to acquire an understanding of Parsifal if you do not give them a picture of the historical background.

Properly speaking the historical tableau should have come first. Today you spoke of Friedrich Barbarossa. You are taking the history of the Middle Ages. In the curriculum it is even said that these literary historical questions should form part of a historical tableau. There are also the literary themes which form a counterpart to history. There is much historical matter treated in this period." (3.7.23)

These indications of 1922 and 1923 together form the syllabus for Class 11. The indications found under German also belong to it.

Class 12

When dealing with history in Class 12 we must go back to Steiner's words of 25th April 1923 which have already been mentioned prior to the indications for German and art lessons. They can be found under geography. On the same day Steiner gave the first Class 12 its history syllabus:

"I have told you this so that you may know how to think in accordance with the Waldorf School principles if you have to deal with young people of eighteen years. Young people of eighteen should be brought to understand the historical epochs in a living way, including the 'becoming younger' of humanity; that would have a considerable influence on humanity. In the most ancient epoch people experienced their own soul development up to their sixtieth year. At the time of the Mystery of Golgotha this age had fallen to the thirty-third year, and today this awareness only reaches the twenty-seventh year. This is a universal feature which should be understood before professional study is taken up at a University. It should belong to general education and would have an immeasurably beneficial influence on the soul life." (25.4.23)

This was said in view of the task of preparing a Class 12 for the examination within one year; hence the use of the conditional "This should belong to general education". Steiner spoke a month later about the actual tasks of this unique Class 12 of 1923/24, when he was asked to recommend a history textbook. What he said there is of far-reaching importance and might have been put into the chapter on general observations. Up to the present day it belongs to those aims of the Waldorf School which have not yet been realised:

"History lessons in the last class are usually a kind of repetition. That is also the case with us. Would it not be possible to enable the children to remember all they have learnt through the introduction of written notes so that a textbook would be unnecessary?

You see it is most important to select with the greatest economy what needs to be known by the pupils. I remember with great joy how through all the classes we had no geometry textbook because the essentials were summarised in dictation. If a pupil writes his own textbook it will greatly help him to know its content. It is obvious that if the children had to learn to select the essentials they could not do it. If these essentials were recapitulated in a living way it would be possible to summarise what the children must know.

Examination requirements only need some 50-60 written pages. It is obvious that not even a history specialist is familiar with everything to be found in Ploetz – it is only an illusion to give a book of this kind into the children's hands. There they will only find titles and headings whereas all they need to know could be contained in 50-60 pages. You might wish to introduce such books of notes for every subject." (25.5.23)

This remark about a suitable textbook for history lessons in Class 12 – whether it be dictated or printed does not concern us here – shows the aims for this class, namely the revision of the entire history syllabus condensed into 50-60 pages. Because of the somewhat unusual circumstances it was not decided from which point of view those 50-60 pages should be arranged. There were two possibilities – either what "ought" to be taught or what "needed" to be taught to satisfy the demands of the examiners. However this was done a year later when a "real" Class 12 was opened for the first time and the class received its syllabus:

"You have covered it all, haven't you? (All periods of history had been covered, first biographically and pictorially, and then again according to historical motifs). Now in Class 12 you should give a survey of the whole of history. You know what I have shown how the concept of causality can only be grasped at the age of 12. Now this sense of causality needs to be developed further. It must be experienced quite concretely by each individual pupil. (This was an indication that the handling of the material for Class 12 was to be raised to a third level. How this was to be done was to be explained later). In Class 12 you have to penetrate more deeply into the inner aspects of history. When summarising the whole picture of history you can show how, let us say during ancient Greece itself, one can discover a time of antiquity, of middle-ages and 'modern' times. The most ancient past – namely the time of Homer – represents

antiquity, the time of the great tragic poets would correspond to the middle-ages whereas the time of Platonism and Aristotelianism could be compared with modern times. The same natural division can be found in Roman history. Present history in such a way that lines of development can be traced in the history of the different peoples or civilisations. The characteristic features of an antiquity can be traced in the different periods of history – you can find such symptoms even in our so-called Middle Ages, resembling certain aspects of Greek Mythology. The study of incoherent or incomplete civilisations could then be introduced, such as the history of the American civilisation which has no definite beginning, or that of the Chinese people which never reached a final conclusion but became fixed in a kind of rigidity. Instead of giving sketchy outlines of history we should endeavour to teach history so that it hangs together like intersecting circles." (29.4.24)*

A day after this discussion about the three periods of each cultural development the plan for the history lessons of Class 12 was considered once more. With the exception of one girl all pupils had decided not to take their examination at the end of Class 12, so that a genuine Class 12 became reality. Steiner therefore gave the following guide lines for history:

"In history too, give a survey covering the entire historical background, beginning with oriental history, to be followed by Greek history and reaching the later Christian development. You are then quite free to introduce content of real inner spirituality – without teaching anthroposophical dogma. For instance, I once showed at the workmen's school how the seven Roman kings represent the seven principles of man, for this is really the case. Of course, you cannot say in an external way that Romulus is the physical body, etc, but the inner plan of Livy's history of the kings is such that in its composition you can see that Tarquinius Priscus, the fifth, who is a pronounced individualist (intellectual man?) corresponds with man's ego-principle; as far as the spirit-self is concerned, a new impetus comes into being through the Etruscan element. And the last king, Tarquinius Superbus, shows how what should have reached the greatest heights sank to the greatest depths, for it was natural for the Romans to sink down into earthly materialism.

Similarly the development of oriental history is built up in a very beautiful way: in the Indian history we witness a fashioning of the physical body, in the Persian of the etheric body, and in the Egypto-Chaldaic of the astral body, but of course you cannot give it in this form. Show how people living in the astral element have developed astronomy, how the Jews expressed the ego-principle in the Jehovah-principle and how the Greeks were the first people to develop a real conception of nature. Earlier conceptions of nature were merely part of a whole world outlook. You can give a survey which will stand the test of time and which will show how historical events really unfold in the manner described." (30.4.24)

Further information about the pre-Grecian civilisations can be found in the last Conference Steiner gave to the Waldorf School teachers. (3.9.24)

A short summary of the history syllabus for the different classes

Course 1: biographical and episodical

Class 4   Transition from study of home surroundings lessons (*7) to history lessons via local history.

Class 5   First historical concepts; civilisations of the Oriental people and of Greeks.

Class 6   Greeks and Romans and the consequences of their history up to the beginning of the fifteenth century.

Class 7   Fifteenth century until the beginning of the seventeenth century – the most important period of time.

Class 8   Seventeenth century until present times (biographically and episodically).

Course 2: following historical motifs

Class 9   Modern times once more according to the inner historical motifs beginning with the fifteenth century.

Class 10   Ancient history up to the loss of Greek freedom in 338 BC.

Class 11   Middle Ages (with special reference to Parsifal and Poor Henry).

Course 3: survey (inner spirituality)

Class 12   Survey of the whole history which needs to be remembered. Periodical development of civilisations – inner structure of the total development of history.

8 Geography

Classes 4 to 6 four weeks' main lesson each
Classes 7 to 12 three weeks' main lesson each

In the three lectures about Comprehensive Steiner Education (*9) Steiner said after speaking about the education of the will:

"In this sphere particularly, however, we shall have to go to work with common sense. In the way instruction is given combinations will have to be made little dreamt of today – for instance, drawing will go hand in hand with geography. It would be of the greatest importance for the growing pupil to have really intelligent lessons in drawing; during the lessons he would be led to draw the globe from various sides, to draw the mountains and rivers of the earth in their relation to one another, then to turn to astronomy and to draw the planetary system. It goes without saying that this would have to be introduced at the right age, not for the 7-year-olds, but certainly before they have reached 15, perhaps from the 12th year onwards, when if done in the right way it would work on growing youth very beneficially." (9 lecture 1)

In the Stuttgart pedagogical lectures geography is mentioned for the first time. There he said:

"If you make your geography lessons really graphic, if you describe the countries well and show the distribution of vegetation, the distribution of the products of the earth in the different countries and in this way make your lessons thoroughly alive you will notice that this is the very lesson in which you do not find any general dullness in your scholars. If you further enliven your geography lesson first by describing the country, drawing it, letting the children draw it on the board, sketching in the rivers, mountains, distribution of the vegetation, of forest and meadow land, and then reading books of travel with your pupils, if you do all this you will find that you usually have very few dull scholars – and indeed you can use your geography lessons in order to arouse the vivacity of your pupils and to draw forth other powers. If you can make geography itself interesting you will actually notice that other capacities are awakened in your pupils." (13)

Geography is also mentioned in lecture 10 of the Practical Course; in the short survey of the curriculum which forms part of this lecture and which characterises it we read that at about the twelfth year one should speak about the mineral kingdom with reference to physics (das Physikalische) and that history could also be gone into. He continues:

"All this time we study geography, which we can always reinforce with natural history by introducing physical concepts and with geometry by drawing of maps, and finally we connect geography with history – that is, we show how the different peoples developed their characteristics. We study this subject throughout these entire stages of childhood, from nine to twelve, and from twelve to fifteen." (12 lecture 10)

Thus geography is given a special place in the curriculum. Like mathematics it accompanies the other subjects in constant transformation and intensification; it is supported and illuminated by the other subjects and it again also supports their progress.

A detailed description of the methods of teaching geography is given in the 11th lecture of the 'Practical Course", which every teacher is advised to study. It contains in concentrated form the syllabus of this subject to the end of the middle school; and it shows how one finds the transition from the so-called home surrounding lessons of the first years to the geography lessons in Class 4 through the "transformation of the known surroundings into a first geographical map". This is shown in a concrete and direct way right to the introduction of geographical symbols for maps which connect the natural configuration with the resulting "human living conditions". The study of the different means of transport in the direct vicinity concludes this elementary picture of life. In Class 5 this introduction to geography is extended to further parts of the earth and in Class 6 to the whole of the earth. In Classes 7 and 8, however, geography links up with the historical background and includes the "spiritual relationships", the character-forming conditions of man, up to the end of the middle school. What is meant by the "spiritual relationships of the people" is shown concretely by the example of the geography of Japan,

during which the teacher was asked to encourage the pupils to try to paint as the Japanese paint, etc. The following quotation illustrates clearly how geography lessons should be taught and planned to the end of the middle school.

"We describe to the child from nine to twelve years old first the economic and external aspects of the geography lessons. We then lead him on to understand the cultural conditions, the spiritual conditions of the different peoples. At this point, saving up everything else for a later time, we touch upon the prevailing laws of the people, upon their legal conditions... For the child cannot yet understand legal systems." (ibid)

Here Steiner wants geography lessons to throw light upon the human conditions on earth, beginning with known home surroundings and ending with a picture of the whole earth. He wants economics, man's spiritual life, and finally – but only in a cursory way – human rights brought to the children as described in his book 'Towards Social Renewal' (7). Here we have reached an important point which enables us to understand what is meant by the three main aims of the geography lessons:

"The whole of this living complex of processes, that begin with man's relation to nature and continue through all that man has to do to transform nature's products, down to the point where they are ready for consumption – these processes, and these alone form a healthy social organism, comprise its economic system."

"Next comes the life of public rights – political life in the proper sense. This must be recognised as forming a second branch of the body social. To this branch belongs what one might term the true life of the State – taking 'State' in the sense in which it was formerly applied to a community possessing common rights." (ibid)

"The third realm within the body social, which must be looked upon as coequal and independent from the other two, contains everything which belong to the spiritual life. To put it more concisely, as the expression 'spiritual culture' or everything pertaining to the spiritual life is too vague, one could say: Everything which is the outcome of the natural gifts of each individual person and which needs must flow into the life of the body social as contribution of each individual's aptitude – both spiritual and physical – helps to weave the fabric of this third spiritual-cultural realm." (ibid)

It should not be necessary to point out that this does not imply that we should teach the children about the threefold social organism. The real task of the teacher is to open the eyes of the pupils to the fact that there are three spheres in the human community, spread all over the earth, and that they have their own laws and development. A study of "Towards Social Renewal" would assist the teacher in this task. Then the earth can become a colourful picture for him and his pupils, showing how human beings live together.

It is worth noting that on the two separate occasions when he spoke about map drawing Steiner suggested the same sequence in drawing geographical maps. In the 8th session of the "Discussions" he arranged the drawing of maps in the following order: rivers, mountains, distribution of vegetation, forests and fields. In the 11th lecture of "Practical Course" he said:

> *"We enter in our maps the rivers and brooks of the surroundings, thus transforming the picture of our neighbourhood into a geographical map. We also draw into these maps the lay-out of the mountains." (12)*

One might wonder why he mentioned this sequence twice. It might be accidental in the first instance but it is definitely intentional in the second. There actually exists another passage where Steiner mentioned an inverted sequence, but the passage taken from the 11th lecture of the "Practical Course" implies a definite order.

Mountains and rivers cannot be separated in reality; on a large scale one can look upon the mountains as causing the rivers, and on a small scale they can be the result of rivers. When drawing maps one could think of first drawing the mountains as causing the rivers and then, after that, the rivers. This aspect would be related to reality. However, this would mean beginning with something entirely unknown, something intangible, with hypothetical primeval mountains. One then would have to begin with the movement of the earth's crust which is supposed to have caused the mountains, in other words, with a mere theory. One would then introduce map drawing with a problem which has not yet been solved by geography as a science. If on the other hand one begins with rivers and brooks one allows the child to experience the immediate present conditions and presents an organic arrangement of the earth, of its separate landscapes with their natural shapes, their elevations, valleys, ridges, watersheds and passes. All forms become clearly visible if the river net is drawn first. Step by step one can deduce geographical details and change them into geographical concepts. The mountains are practically there if one begins with the river courses. Other specific features also become perceptible, such as bifurcations and seepages. Furthermore the sequence: rivers – mountains, is in accordance with Steiner's indications about the layers of the earth, which suggests that one should begin with the uppermost layers (25.9.19). These indications are considerably supplemented by the following sentences taken from the third lecture of the Supplementary Course held by Steiner in the summer of 1921 at the opening of the first Class 10.

> *"Now remember what I explained to you about the drawing of conclusions. When we consider the part of man that is active in coming to conclusions, and note how it stands right in the world – not dissolving away out of it through the head – we can see at once that this member of man's being is unthinkable without space. In so far as I am a man of legs and feet, I am a part of the world of space; and when I am considering things in their spatial aspect, this has the effect of setting my astral body firmly, so to speak, on its legs.*
>
> *When therefore we teach a child geography, his astral body does actually grow – down below – denser and more powerful. In dealing with space we densify the spirit and soul of the child, we drive it down onto the ground. By teaching geography in such a way that the child sees what we are telling him we bring this consolidation in him. But there must be the true seeing in space. The child must, for example, be conscious that*

the Niagara Falls are not on the river Elbe! We must help him to realise what a vast space stretches between the two." (26 lecture 3)

This is the proper place to quote a conversation from the Conferences (4*) of 1921 which followed a complaint by a teacher about the poor memory of children:

> *"They remember the pyramids and obelisks. In this connection you must ask yourself whether you have described everything in detail so as to give all the children a picture of the real position of Egypt, so that the child has no gaps when he is expected to know about Egypt. If you just say Egypt, and he has no clear picture, then it is very easy to forget. Perhaps you must take great care to give every detail so that the children may have a completely plastic picture. The child will know something about the pyramids and obelisks but he may not know that they are to be found in Egypt. You must consider very carefully whether you have done everything possible to give a full picture. Do you let the children draw Africa alone? Perhaps it would always be better if besides drawing special maps they drew a European map or some other, in order to obtain a bird's eye view and the connection between one part and another. Perhaps you should seek out the towns which you would pass in going from here to Egypt. This kind of lack of memory is due to the fact that in some way they have not had sufficient opportunity of making mental pictures. If the children get complete pictures then there is no doubt that their memory improves." (26.5.21)*

Further information about how to develop concrete mental pictures, not only in geography, but also in history, can be found immediately after the last quotation.

This connection between the study of geography by the child and his incarnating fully into earthly life and space should be ever present in the mind of the geography teacher, not merely as an idea but as a real experience, so that the teacher feels connected with the space surrounding him just as much as he does with his own body. Then he will also realise the importance of the sentences which Steiner spoke immediately after the words quoted above:

> *"Teaching the child in this way we place him into space: and he will begin to be interested in the world, in the whole wide world. And we shall see the results of this in many directions. A child with whom we study geography in an intelligent way will have a more loving relationship to his fellow men than one who has no feeling of what proximity in space means; for he will learn to feel that he lives alongside other human beings and he will come to have regard and respect for them. Such things play no little part in the moral training of the children, and the lack of attention to geography is partly responsible for the terrible decline in recent years of the brotherly love that should prevail among men. A connection of this kind may escape observation altogether but it is there and it plays its part for there is a sort of subconscious intelligence – or unintelligence – operating in the events that we see happening around us." (26 lecture 3)*

In the Basle Course of 1920 Steiner spoke about the link between geography lessons and history lessons, which has already been mentioned in the quotation from the 10th lecture of the Practical Course. Steiner's words follow a discourse about history teaching and its proper preparation through nature study:

"I have shown how the children can be led to an understanding of the life of the earth by the teaching of botany in the way I have described. Then they will be ready at this age to pass over to geography. And this geography, which is geography proper, can be further built up upon all kinds of descriptions which have been given earlier in preparation. One can even describe distant countries, but one must have described these previously, have told the children something about them. If one has properly prepared them through such descriptions, let us say of some region in America or in Africa, then at about the twelfth year the moment has arrived to lead them on to instruction in geography. What is of importance for geography is – and as I have said, this has already been prepared for by showing how the growth of plants is connected with the earth – what is of importance is that now we can show how the development of history itself depends upon what comes from the earth, from its climate and from all that it brings forth in its various regions, in its formations and structures.

For instance, after having given an idea of the connections between sea and land and the climate of ancient Greece we can then lead back to what we have already developed concerning the character of the Greeks purely as a symptom of the inner evolution of humanity. Then an inner connection can be found between the geographical picture we have given of the earth, and historical developments. And really these two things should always play into one another, the description of regions of the earth and the description of historical development. America should not really he dealt with before the discovery of America has been taken in history. It is necessary to bear in mind that the horizon of mankind was widened in the course of evolution, and that human feeling should not be led too strongly to what I should like to call something absolute." (23 lecture 12)

This connection between geography and history also includes an elementary idea of world space, which must not be omitted if one wishes to build up concrete space consciousness in the pupils:

"It is not advisable in so-called mathematical geography to proceed dogmatically from a drawing of the Copernican system or Kepler's system of the universe – rather the attempt should be made to indicate to the children how such concepts were arrived at. By this means the children are not given ideas reaching beyond their present stage of development, which is a recapitulation of mankind's development. It is necessary that the children should at least have an idea of how the positions of stars have become a familiar pattern which in itself can lead towards a system of the universe. They should not gain the impression that such a world system was the result of someone sitting on a chair outside in space and merely observing the universe from out there. How can a child possibly appreciate what has led mankind to the Copernican world system if you confront him straightaway with a diagram on the blackboard? He must

gain a living conception of how such things have arisen – otherwise he will pass through the whole of life with confused ideas, which seem to him however absolutely certain. It is through matters of this kind that a false belief in authority is created, but not the way in which a right feeling for authority is achieved in children between 7 and 14 years old." (23 lecture 12)

A remark made in a teachers' meeting about astronomy in Class 8 also belongs to this chapter:

"When it is a matter of evoking the right feeling you can certainly obtain it in the very best way by looking at the real picture of the sky but trying, as you have done in earlier classes, to retain this picture by means of memory. The children will acquire a certain reverence if from time to time you take them out into the presence of the starry heavens itself and talk to them there. It is harder to produce reverence by looking at our maps than by standing in the presence of the starry heavens. Maps kill reverence." (22.6.22)

Passages from the Ilkley course also illuminate geography lessons but from a different angle. They are found after a passage about botany:

"From a study of the living, weaving forces of the earth itself we can lead on to a characterization of all different plants. And when a child has been given living ideas of the growth of the plants we can pass on from this study of the living plant to a conception of the whole surface of the earth.

In some regions yellow flowers abound, in others the plants are stunted in their growth, and in each case the face of the earth is different. Thus we reach geography, which can play a great part in the child's development, if we lead up to it from the plants.

We should try to give an idea of the face of the earth by connecting the forces at work on its surface with the varied plant life we find in the different regions. Thus we unfold a living instead of a dead intellectual faculty in the child." (35 lecture 8)

Syllabus for the middle school

From the curriculum lectures of September 1919. This is in full agreement with the quotations already given.

Class 4

"Begin with the geography of the home surroundings, as I have shown." (12 lecture 11, and 16)

Class 5

"Begin geography as I have illustrated with the configuration of the land, and show how this is connected with the economics sphere – take a region of the earth which is near to the child." (16 lecture 1)

Class 6

"Continue the work of Class 5 by taking other regions of the earth and try to find the link between climatic conditions and astronomical conditions – of which I gave examples here yesterday." (not available)

Supplement: The syllabus for nature study contains the following remark for Class 6:

"... one should proceed to study minerals. But this study of the minerals should be absolutely part of geography." (ibid lecture 2)

The climatic conditions are characteristic of the earth's immediate neighbourhood; the astronomical conditions depend on one's position on earth. They define the space consciousness and make it possible to see the earth as a totality.

Class 7

"In geography try to extend the pupils' knowledge of the heavens, and begin to introduce the spiritual cultural relations of the inhabitants of the earth. But this should always be related to knowledge of the material cultural conditions, gained in the first two years (or three) of geography, especially to economic conditions." (16 lecture 1)

This is all that can be found in the Curriculum lectures about geography as a separate subject. There is however another remark in the second lecture which also belongs to Class 7:

"Together with concepts gained so far in physics and chemistry lessons, endeavour to give a picture of a totality which comprises conditions of earning through this or that industry, conditions of transportation – all this in connection with physics, chemistry and geography lessons which have grown out of nature study." (ibid lecture 2)

These sentences obviously refer to geography lessons in Class 7, changing them into something which touches physics, chemistry, nature study, technology and history. This remains a characteristic feature for the next year, for the curriculum lectures contain only the one short paragraph quoted for Class 8:

Class 8

After a remark about nature study (physiology?) which is supposed to deal with the mechanics of bones, muscles and the inner structure of the sense organs, Steiner continued:

"Then give a summary of industry and transportation in connection with physics and chemistry." (ibid)

Classes 7 and 8

If one tries to understand the task which has thus been set for Classes 7 and 8 one could formulate it in this way:

In Class 7, through studying the individual countries of the earth, together with their astronomical and material conditions, the spiritual conditions of the different nations should be discussed. When dealing with sources of income the relevant factors of physics and chemistry should be included. In Class 8 this theme will be broadened into a physical-chemical, biological, astronomical and ethnographical picture of the earth as a totality. The political and constitutional conditions should be touched upon only lightly.

Class 8

When during the first month of the Waldorf School the history teacher of Class 8 asked Steiner how one could bring about a link between geology teaching and the Akashic Records, he said the following:

"It would of course be a good thing to begin by mak-

ing the children aware of the formation of the stratification, to give them a concept of how the Alps have been formed, and to deal with the whole complex proceeding from the Alps, the Pyrenees, Alps, Carpathians, Altai, which form one chain or wave. Make the whole wave clear to the children. Then the other chain or wave, which goes from North America through South America. From this you get this one wave running as far as the Altai, the Asiatic mountains. That is one wave, going from west to east. Above we have the North and South American mountains. We start from this distribution. We then add the vegetation and the animals; then try to study the fauna and flora on the west coast of Europe and east coast of America and the strata of the mountains. Then we call up the concept of the connection between the East of America and the West of Europe, and of the Atlantic Ocean as simply sunken land. Then proceeding from these concepts, try to explain in a natural way that there is an up and down movement. Let us start from the concept of rhythm. We can show that the British Isles have ascended and descended four times. Then we come back to the concept of old Atlantis by way of geology.

Then we can pass on to trying to call up in the children a picture of how different it was when this region was above and that one below. We start with the fact that the British Isles have ascended and descended four times – that can be established simply by the strata. We try in this way to show the connection between these things, but we must not shrink from speaking to the children about the land of Atlantis. We must not pass this by. We can establish a link also in connection with history. Only you will have then to discard the usual geology. For the Atlantic catastrophe must be placed in the 7th to 8th millennium." (25.9.19)

This is followed by further remarks about geology. Only a short practical hint will be quoted:

"Yes, give as much as possible about the strata. You can teach it from a chart of the strata, but never without the children knowing something about the kinds of rocks – they must get an idea of what kinds of minerals are there. In explaining you begin at the top and work downwards because then you can more easily show them what breaks through." (25.9.19)

The last two quotations cannot be considered as applying only to Class 8 because in the original curriculum (curriculum lectures) geology is not mentioned and in lecture 11 of the Practical Course which gives the basis for geography teaching, geology is limited to the distinction between limestone and igneous rock in the Alps. The question to which the last two quotations refer appears to have been asked out of general interest, perhaps with the intention of passing on the answer to the pupils. At any rate, Steiner did answer it and the teacher reported at the end of the school year on September 22nd 1920, what he had taught to his Class 8: Chiefly the ice-ages, changes in the distribution of water and land, altogether a great deal belonging to the geology period of that time. Steiner then proceeded to give the syllabus for Class 9:

Class 9

"In addition to all that can be brought into such a subject I should recommend you to go through the whole structure of the Alps: Northern limestone Alps, southern limestone Alps, with all the river valleys which form the boundaries, the mountain chains, the structure, then the landscapes of the country, something about its geological constitution from the maritime Alps right over to the Austrian Alps, through the whole of Switzerland. As you talk about the Alps you can introduce the fact that in the structure of the earth there is really a kind of cross to which the external mountain formations point. Continue the Alps through the Pyrenees, then through the Carpathians, go over to the wooded mountains as far as the Altai, and in this way you have an extended east-west chain of mountains which, continuing subterraneously, encloses the earth like a ring, which is crossed perpendicularly by the Andes-Cordillera course which forms another ring. You can very beautifully make clear to the children how two cruciform rings, one on another, give the structure of the earth. You get a picture of the earth as a body with an inner organisation. Do not attempt to rush through this content, for you need not cover the entire geographical theme in one geography period." (22.9.20)

Here Steiner gave Class 9 the same theme (mountain cross of the earth) which he had given to Class 8 on September 23rd 1919, at that time linking it to Atlantis and the ice ages as well as to the rising and submerging of continents – and he told the teacher that there was no need to complete this theme all at once! More needs to be said about this later on. The Curriculum lectures mention astronomical conditions in Classes 6 and 7 but not in Class 8. However, since in Class 8 the syllabus of Class 7 has to be broadened and brought to a conclusion, astronomy cannot be omitted:

"Doppler's principle would naturally follow on after that, the movement of the stars in the line of sight. You have omitted the movement of the stars in the line of sight. Take everything which leads up to this. You must work up to it." (22.9.20)

When the teacher remarked that the necessary knowledge of optics was lacking in Class 9 for the understanding and the use of the Doppler's principle and that for physics only heat, mechanics and electricity had been planned, Steiner replied:

"You can include enough optics for them to understand Doppler's principle. Discuss too the related phenomenon in acoustics." (22.9.20)

During a conversation about the Doppler's principle which followed Steiner recommended using this only for double stars, not for the sun. More about it can be found in the appropriate place. My personal opinion about this conversation is that Steiner did not really want teachers to give details of the wave theory of light in Class 9 so that pupils should be able to deduce the Doppler's principle in order to use it for star-spectra, but that he was not against it being explained to the children in a satisfactory way. I believe that he wanted the name Doppler's principle used at first only as a formula for everything which would serve to find out the movement of stars in the line of sight:

"Use everything which helps to find out the movements in the direction of sight."

Class 10

A year later Steiner gave the teachers the syllabus for Class 10, saying this about geography:

"Description of the earth as a morphological and physical whole. In geology you must describe the earth as being a kind of cross in its whole formation, the two rings intersecting one above the other, the one in the direction of east-west, the other in the direction of north-south. The forms of the continents. The origin of the mountains. What passes over into the physical. Then the rivers. The geological, the physical aspects: isotherms, the earth as a magnet, northern and southern magnetic poles. Proceed morphologically in this manner. Continue with ocean currents, air currents, trade winds, the earth's interior – in short, with everything which affects the earth as a totality." (17.6.21)

At the same time lessons on surveying enable pupils to get at least an elementary introduction into geographical surveying.

Class 11

We do not find a strictly geographical theme for Class 11 in the Conferences (*4) but among the indicators for technology, and linked to the course of surveying in Class 10, Steiner said when the first Class 11 was opened (these words should be considered as part of the curriculum):

"Now I would like you to link surveying with geography, so that the children will get a concrete picture of what a Mercater world map is. To do this you need to explain how the metric measure has come into existence." (21.6.22)

Class 12

Like the other subjects, so also geography for Class 12 was discussed twice: on April 25th 1923 Steiner told the teachers what they should cover if they were not forced to adapt their lessons to examination demands:

"It would be desirable that just at this age – about 18 years old – the pupils should gain a comprehensive understanding for the historical-artistic element, and that they should indeed take in what pertains to the spiritual in literature, the history of art and history without giving them anthroposophical dogma. In literature, the history of art and history we must make the attempt to bring in the spiritual, not only as a matter of content but also in our way of treating the subjects; we must, that is, at least achieve for these pupils what I have myself striven for in the case of the workmen in Dornach, to whom I have been able to make it clear that really, let us say, such islands as the British Isles, float in the sea and are held firm from outside by stellar forces. We are dealing with an island. It does not rest on the ground, it floats; it is fixed from outside. On the whole, in principle, the continental and the island formations are brought about from outside by the cosmos. Generally speaking that is the case of the configuration of the continents. These continents are formed by the cosmos – they are the results of the activities of the starry worlds.

The earth altogether mirrors the universe and is not at all formed from within. We cannot teach such things because our pupils would pass them on to their examiners when sitting for their exams and this would give us a very bad reputation. But this really ought to be taught to our pupils in geography lessons." (25.4.23)

After a further question the remark about the floating continents was enlarged upon by Steiner. This can be looked up in the Conference of 25.9.19.

On April 30th 1924 the final syllabus for Class 12 was given:

Class 12 (1924)

"The aim of our geography lessons (as well as the history lessons) should be to give a broad survey. The main task in these two subjects is that the pupils should gain a comprehensive view. Once they have gained such a bird's eye view they can easily look up any details needed." (30.4.24)

This survey of geography in Class 12 was more clearly defined in the meetings on July 12th 1923 and April 25th 1924. On July 12th 1923 we read about the planned first examination:

"When speaking about geology I should recommend you to go backwards, from the present, from alluvium to diluvium, then to discuss the Ice Age, evoke the concept of the connection of such phenomena as the Ice Age with what is outside the earth (extratelluric), even with the alteration in the earth's axis; then, from there, go back to the tertiary period. Make clear to the children when the second and when the first world of mammals appeared. If you go back to carbon you can simply take the turning point. It would be better to take the transition in the following way: in the later strata you have separately the mineralised element, the fossilised vegetable and the fossilised animal. Now we come back to carbon. Then the fossilised animal element ceases. We have only fossilised vegetable. The whole of the carbon is plant. There the differentiation ceases; there is nothing else besides plant; we come back to what is completely undifferentiated." (12.7.23)

Steiner then drew the attention to two lectures about geology which he had given to the workmen at the Goetheanum (38a) and continued:

"Earlier the forms were only ether forms. At that time we have to picture the carbon without the definite individualising into separate plants, which is usually imagined. Today people picture ferns. It was much more an undifferentiated pap which became petrified. And in this pap the etheric forces were constantly active. Secretions precipitated which really were organic substances in the state of becoming (status nascendi) and which subsequently became petrified." (12.7.23)

On April 30th 1924 Steiner recommended that in nature study for Class 12 one should go on from zoology and botany to palaeontology. Geography in Class 12 is thus given a first concrete task, viz. palaeontology; and the request of April 30th 1924 to give a total survey of geography is herewith fulfilled. However, part of this request includes ethnography, which, as mentioned before, was to be taken later (see natural study, Class 10). The aim of the geography survey is to unite the animal kingdom and the plant kingdom palaeontologically with the earth and to bring to a conclusion the study of man, not only from the point of view of individual man but also from the aspect of the different nations and races. There is no other possibility of including ethnography, mentioned in connection with the nature study of Class 10.

The few indications for geography in Class 12 could be summed up in the following way:

On the one hand, the survey of geography should include palaeontology of plants and animals after botany and zoology; on the other, it should include ethnography to be linked to the previous study-of-man periods.

A short synopsis for geography

Class 4   (6.9.19) "home surroundings" – nature and human activities.

Class 5   (6.9.19) "extend the territory" – the same.

Class 6   (6.9.19) "other parts of the earth" – the same, but in addition climatology and astronomy.

Class 7   (6.9.19) View of the whole earth – spiritual relationships of civilisation in connection with economic relationships; in addition study of trade and industry and study of transportation.

Class 8   (6.9.19) The whole earth – industries and transport facilities together with spiritual relationships of the different countries.

Class 8   (23.9.19) Geological strata; origin of the Alps, the mountain cross; rising and submerging of the continents, the Atlantean catastrophe.

Class 9   (22.9.21) Formation of the Alps; the mountain cross ("Not the entire geographical theme all at once"); Doppler's principle in astronomy.

Class 10   (17.6.21) Earth as a morphological and physical totality, the mountain cross, shapes of the continents, origin of mountains, matters pertaining to physics in the widest sense (at the same time surveying).

Class 11   (21.6.22) Geographical survey; map projection.

Class 12   (25.4.23) (Floating islands and continents as a result of the activity of stellar forces – (30.4.24) page 21 and page 23 as well as nature study Class 10). Survey: palaeontology and ethnography.

The mountain cross of the earth is mentioned three times: first for Class 8, but here in such a way that, together with what is called the floating of the continents, one needs to consider it as a theme for the years from Classes 8 or 9 to Class 12. In Classes 9 and 10 it is again mentioned as a kind of reminder that one should continue the theme. The floating continents are also mentioned several times: in Class 8 as a rising and falling through the activity of stellar forces; in Class 10 it remains hidden as a theme when the origin of the mountains is taken and in Class 12 it again comes to the fore with the example of the floating British Isles. This is "the entire geographical theme" mentioned in connection with Class 9 (22.9.20) which was "not to be dealt with all at once". It was obviously meant to be a keynote for the entire upper school to which every year was to bring its contribution.

In Class 9 geology and the Doppler principle are to be studied. Penetration into the depths of the earth and into the depths of cosmic space, i.e., the extension of space consciousness both in a downward and upward direction forms part of the syllabus; and time consciousness is to be awakened through geology and astronomy.

In Class 10 the earth's form is to be studied and also the earth as field of physical happenings in the widest possible context.

In Class 11, through surveying, an exact knowledge of the earth's shape should be gained, leading to accurate map–drawing.

In Class 12 a broad survey should be given, containing a systematic classification of "the entire geographical theme" as a basis for palaeontology and ethnography.

9 Surveying

Surveying is taught during a practical course lasting one week, during which the pupils of Class 10 stay in a youth hostel or in other accommodation situated in suitable surroundings. Work continues throughout the days of this week.

Originally Steiner gave the following instructions when the first Class 10 was opened in the early summer of 1921:

"For technical mechanics we only need 1 hour a week; for surveying and topographical drawing, only 1 hour a week. Six months for mechanics, six months for surveying and topographical drawing." (17.6.21)

Class 10

"For surveying it is enough if you first manage to teach the treatment and finding of the horizontal and show how to draw small features: vineyards, pastures, orchards... so that they have an idea of how one reproduces this on a map." (ibid)

This course was first carried out on the school grounds of the first Waldorf School but soon afterwards Class 10 was taken to a youth hostel. Ever since, the pupils have become familiar with the fundamental instruments and with methods of surveying through their own practical experience. These regular courses end with the pupils making a survey map with the measurements taken by all participants. The full cooperation and support among the pupils is considered an important feature of this course.

After a report by the teacher about a course of surveying given to Class 10 Steiner said:

Class 11

"I now wish you to make a link between surveying and geography, so that the children get an idea of what a Mercator world map is like. To do this you need to show how the metric measure has come into existence." (21.6.22)

10 Nature Study

Class 4 to 6 four weeks each
Class 7 to 12 three weeks each   Main lessons

In Waldorf Schools nature study is a subject which occupies rather a special position in the curriculum. Apart from a change in teaching methods, a new point of view and new ways of observation and interpretation are called for in this subject even more than in other subjects. Again and again one is prompted to seek recourse to "The Study of Man" and to the other lectures given at that time viz. the "Practical Course for Teachers" and "Discussions with Teachers" (11, 12, 13). When trying to collect relevant information from Rudolf Steiner's various lecture courses, it appears extraordinarily difficult to come to a clear picture of how Steiner wanted us to present this subject; far more difficult than in the case of other subjects in the curriculum.

By way of introduction a number of lectures, especially those from the great Stuttgart courses, will be characterised so as to throw light upon the chief problems of this subject. It can surely be taken for granted that these lectures are available to the reader. Here we shall keep to their chronological order. Apart from a close study of the entire Stuttgart Courses, which cannot be recommended strongly enough, the teacher of nature study is advised to work out the selected passages and lectures one after the other in order to become familiar with the fundamental outlines of Steiner's teaching.

1   Study of Man, lecture 4: How the animal forms reveal the animals' instinctive behaviour; the relationship of animal forms to the different stages in man's will life.

2   Practical Course for Teachers, lecture 7: The beginning of animal study after the ninth year; the animal world and its relationship to the human body; cuttle-fish, mouse (lamb), man. (12)

3   Discussions with teachers, sessions 9 to 11: A discussion with the teachers about plant-study and its relationship to the whole earth and to man's soul. A specially important sentence from the ninth session runs as follows:
"Whereas you need to compare the animal kingdom more with the corporeality of man, you must compare the plant kingdom with the soul life of man, with what permeates man (literally fills him up) when he awakens in the morning." (13 session 9)

This "filling up" of man refers to his soul which unites itself with the body on awakening, as in the plant world the formative forces of the plants unite themselves with the earth.

4   Study of Man, lecture 10: The threefold nature of man's body and the development of the animals and of man. (11)

5   Study of Man, lecture 12: The relationship between the functions of man's head and, the animal forms; between the functions of his trunk and the world of plants; and the relationship of the functions of his limbs to the mineral world:

"The human body is only to be explained when we know the processes that take place in it – when we know that the human being must dissolve within him the mineral, must reverse within him the plant kingdom, must raise above him, that is, must spiritualise, the animal kingdom." (11)

6   The Practical Course, lecture 14, shows how knowledge of nutrition and hygiene has to be woven into the lessons during the last years of the middle school. (12)

In this connection I should like to recommend the two books of Gerbert Grohmann as a valuable help in teaching nature study: "Plant – Earth – Man's Soul", Stuttgart 1953 and "Animal form – Human Spirit", Stuttgart 1954. ("Pflanze – Erdenwesen – Menschenseele" and "Tierform – Menschengeist").

For teaching the study of man the whole of Steiner's "Study of Man" (11) should be read as a basis for the preparation.

After this somewhat general synopsis, more detailed information with regard to the different ages will be given.

After speaking about the changes taking place after the ninth year Steiner continued in lecture 7 of the Practical Course:

"When we approach this period in their lives we shall have to feel the need to introduce natural history into the time-table in addition to the other subjects, Before this the children will have grown familiar with natural history in narrative form, as I showed yesterday in our training class (13 Session 6) when speaking about the relationship of the animal and plant worlds to man. The method used so far to familiarise the child with natural history has been chiefly narrative, descriptive. But with natural history, before the Rubicon of the ninth year has been crossed, you will hardly have started.

Now here it is of great importance to know that the development to be aimed at in the child by means of natural history is radically defeated unless the teaching starts with the exposition of man. You may say with justice that the child at nine years old can be told little natural history about man. But be it ever so little, the little that a child can be taught about man should be taught as a preparation for all other teaching in natural history." (12 lecture 7)

More information can be gained in the actual lecture. There Steiner introduces a strange way of looking at man, only hinting at the human figure but nevertheless making the child familiar with its typical features and functions.

Now to lecture 5 of the Dornach Pedagogical Course of Easter 1923. After the passages about the plant world and after the remarks that a child younger than nine would show an aversion to the teacher's describing the human being to him, Steiner continued:

"Now this horror – for so it may be called – aroused by a description of the human being, actually remains until towards the 12th year of life. We can quite well put forward what I spoke about yesterday (the study of the animals in their relationship to man) between the 9th and 12th years. We can, as I explained yesterday, present the plant world to the children as the hair which grows upon the Earth – but we must keep to a

pictorial characterisation. We can also bring the animal world to the children in a manner adapted to them, by conceiving each animal form as a part of the human being which has developed one-sidedly. At this age however, we must not pass over to any kind of description of man himself. With this in view, it is even quite a good thing if in our teaching we influence the child by speaking about the members of the human being and relating these members in their one-sided development to this or that animal form. But the child has as yet no understanding at all of how to connect these with the human being. Only towards the 12th year does he get the longing to see in man a synthesis of the whole animal world. And this can be pursued in those classes which follow the period of life between the 11th and 12th years. In first describing the whole animal kingdom as a distributed human being there lies an apparent contradiction. It is however right to do it in this way before describing the human being himself in his completeness as a space-form. The child must first gain some kind of feeling for the fact that the whole earth is inhabited by what is comprised in mail, though in a dismembered state - that the animal world is the entirety of what is human but dismembered into its separate constituents. And then the child must experience the great moment when everything spread out in the animal world is brought together for him, concentrated into man. The important thing in teaching is to let the child really experience the decisive moments in life, at the opportune time to allow the idea to pass through the child's soul that, on a higher level, the human being as physical man is the synthetic combination of the whole animal world." (34)

The last two quotations seem to contradict each other – the Practical Course gives a very definite description of the human figure and indicates that it should be introduced before animal and plant study; the Dornach Easter Course, on the other hand, suggests that the description of man should not be given before the important point of change in the eleventh and twelfth years.

In the Ilkley Course, we find the following passage, after a remark about the great changes taking place in the ninth year, after which the child can be guided towards an understanding of the world:

"When we have given sufficient time to speaking of the plants as articulate beings, allowing the child as he looks at the plant world to experience it in living pictures, we can then introduce something he can learn in the best possible way from the plants if we begin to speak of it between the ninth and tenth year, gradually carrying it further during the tenth and eleventh. The human organism is now at this stage ready to relate itself inwardly to the plant-world by way of ideas." (35 lecture 8)

This is followed by a detailed description of elementary botany lessons, which begin immediately after the changes in, the ninth year. Steiner then says of the child who can now experience the plant world:

"Just as the world of the plants should be related to the earth and the child should learn to think of them as the offspring, the last, outward-growing product of a living earth organism, so should the animal world as a whole

be related to man. The child is thus enabled – in a living way – to find his own place in nature and in the world. He begins to understand that the plant-world belongs to the earth. On the other hand, however, we teach him to realize that the various animal-species spread over the world represent, in a certain sense, the path towards human development. The plants have kinship to the earth, the animals to man – this should be the basis from which we start. I can only justify it here as a principle; the actual details of what is taught to a child of ten, eleven or twelve years concerning the animal world, must be worked out with true artistic feeling.

In a very simple, even primitive way, we begin by calling the child's attention to the nature of man. This is quite possible if the preliminary artistic foundations have already been laid." (35 lecture 8)

Then follows a thorough description of man in his threefoldness of head-organisation, rhythmic system and metabolic and limb system. He continues:

"Thus we find these three members in man and if the teacher has sufficient artistic sense and teaches in a pictorial way, he can certainly give the child a feeling for the threefoldness of man." (ibid)

The introduction of the animal world at this age follows:

"The animal kingdom is experienced as a spread-out human being, as a man spread out fan-wise over the whole earth." (ibid)

In the Ilkley Course Steiner puts the study of plants right at the beginning of nature study but, in contradiction to the Dornach course of 1923, he suggests that the study of man as a threefold being should be taken as the second theme to be followed by animal study from the aspect of a spread-out human being. He says:

"When the child is approaching the twelfth year, one can again return to the subject of man, for now he can understand as a matter of course that because man bears his spirit within him, he is a synthetic unity (in the text we find 'symptomatic unity' which makes no sense, whereas the expression 'synthesis' or 'synthetic unity' is used several times). The child can now experience man as a work of art, as an artistic organism uniting the separate parts which are mirrored in the various animal species throughout the world." (35)

There is yet another difference between the Stuttgart Courses of 1919 and the later ones which were given abroad.

In the Practical Course we find the following passage regarding the order in which animal study and plant study should be taken:

"Only in the second stage (of the middle school), from nine to about twelve, do we begin to develop the self-consciousness more"... then after a few lines about grammar... *"We embark on the natural history of the animal kingdom, as I showed you with the cuttle-fish, mouse and, human being. And only later do we add the plant kingdom." (See 13 Session 10)*

At the end of this course we read once more about cuttle-fish, mouse and man:

"These ideas of things must be rooted in feeling during

the middle period of the elementary school course, when the instincts are still alive to this feeling of intimacy with the animals, with the plants, and when, after all, even if the experience never emerges into the ordinary light of reasoning consciousness, the child feels himself now a cat, now a wolf, now a lion or eagle. This identification of one-self now with one animal, now with another, only occurs up to about the age of nine. Before this age it is even more profound but it cannot be used, because the power to grasp it consciously is non-existent. If children are very precocious and talk a great deal about themselves when they are still only four or five, their comparisons of themselves with the eagle, with the mouse, etc., are very common indeed. But if we start at the ninth year to teach natural history on the lines I have suggested we come upon a good deal of the child's instinctive feeling of relationship with animals. Later this instinctive feeling ripens into a feeling of relationship with the plant world. Therefore, first of all the natural history of the animal kingdom, then the natural history of the plant kingdom. We leave the minerals till the last because they require almost exclusively the power of judgement and do not appeal to anything that relates man to the outer world. Indeed man is not related to the mineral kingdom. (12)*

A few lines further on he continues:

"The intermediate school period, from nine to eleven, presents a fine balance between the instincts and the powers of discernment. We can always assume that the child will respond intelligently if we rely on a certain instinctive understanding, if we are not – especially in natural history and botany – too obvious. We must avoid drawing external analogies particularly with the plant world, for that is really contrary to natural feeling. Natural feeling is itself predisposed to seek psychic qualities in plants; not the external physical form of man in this tree or that, but soul-relations such as we tried to discover in the plant system." (ibid)

Here the animal study is taken first, in order to make use as much as possible of the child's kindred instinctive feeling for animals. Plant study is taken later because the "instinctive feeling for the plant world matures later." And in the ninth session of Discussions with Teachers it is suggested that animal study should be taken before the study of plants.

The Dornach Course of 1921/22 begins with the study of plants, but it goes on to a description of man and his connection with the animal world which, however, was not meant for children but for his listening audience. Steiner said at the end:

"By all means translate (what I have told you) into the world of children so that they can understand it too." (27 lecture 10)

Then follows the animal study.

In the Dornach Easter Course of 1923 the time between the ninth and tenth years is suggested for the introduction of plant study. About animal study Steiner said:

"You can expect a little more from the child there because animal study begins only in the tenth, eleventh year." (34 lecture 4)

Here plant study is clearly put before animal study.

It has already been pointed out that the Ilkley course puts plant study first, then the threefold man and lastly animal study.

In the later course held abroad plant study is also taken before animal study and it is interesting to see how Steiner again and again introduces new aspects.

The following table shows the difference of the order suggested in the various courses:

Survey of the order for the introduction of the different branches of natural history in Steiner's pedagogical courses:

1 Stuttgart 1919	Study of Man (preliminary) – Animals – Plants (Earth) – Man
2 Basle 1920	Animals (Man) – Plants (Earth)
3 Dornach 1921/22	Plants (Earth) – Man and Animals
4 Oxford 1922	Plants (Earth) – Animals (Man)
5 Dornach 1923	Plants (Earth) – Animals (Man) – Man (Synthesis)
6 Ilkley 1923	Plants (Earth) – Man (Threefoldness) – Animals
7 Berne 1924	Plants (Earth) – Animals (Man)
8 Arnheim 1924	Plants (Earth) – Animals (Man)
9 Torquay 1924	Plants (Earth) – Animals (Man)

This summary shows a gradual change of sequence from the Stuttgart Courses in 1919 – via the Basle Course which, though keeping the same sequence, suggests an abbreviation; via the first Dornach Course (1921/22) in which the study of plants is put at the beginning for the first time; viz the second Dornach course (1923) in which the study of man is put right at the end; and finally to the Ilkley Course in which the new position of the study of plants is retained but in which the study of Man is placed before animal study with the emphatic instructions about how to illustrate the threefold nature of Man to children. In the later courses, and also during the first Dornach course, the study of Man is no longer given a separate heading, which might have been due to lack of time during the actual lecture courses. And so we are faced with the apparent contradiction between the courses given at Stuttgart, Dornach (1923) and Ilkley. The order of the above mentioned subjects found in the Stuttgart Courses was given because it seemed important to begin with the study of Man, introduced artistically, as otherwise "the teacher might thoroughly ruin all his efforts"; the study of animals had to follow quite naturally.

In the Dornach Course of 1923 Steiner mentioned that before the 12th year the child had an aversion to the kind of picture of Man presented in the usual textbooks. During the Ilkley Course he stated that it would be feasible to introduce the study of Man before the animal study, provided this was done in a suitable and artistic manner.

During the Stuttgart Courses such an artistic presentation was taken for granted and therefore the study of Man could form the great opening theme.

In the Dornach course 1923 a description of Man was discouraged because at that time the audience consisted of teachers to whom these ideas were still quite new and who consequently could not be expected to have developed the necessary skill and ability to teach such a subject in a suitable way.

According to the Ilkley Course the study of Man, artistically prepared and based on the threefoldness of the human organisation, was to be introduced as late as possible in order to avoid the "aversion" mentioned above, but nevertheless before the animal study. Hence the sequence: plant study from the aspect of the whole earth – study of Man – animal study in connection with Man – and finally, after the threshold of the 11th and 12th years the more detailed study of Man.

The later courses of Berne, Arnheim and Torquay show the same sequence though in abbreviated form as the Ilkley course, so that the placing of the study of Man does not present any new problems.

The three problematic courses remain those given at Stuttgart in 1919, in Dornach in 1923 and at Ilkley. However, Steiner appears to have had good reasons for the changes which should not be considered as mere inconsistencies on his part. Rather one should try to solve the apparent contradictions by recognising inherent and deeper reasons.

First of all it seems obvious that the Stuttgart Course holds a unique position because of its great aim to prepare the original teachers for their tasks in the Waldorf School. In this course details are given at greater depth and if Steiner places the study of Man as the opening theme, we can only see in it his real intentions. This is also confirmed by the first and biggest course held in England, the Ilkley Course, according to which the threefolded Man should be introduced at an early stage if the teacher has the necessary artistic ability. In the Ilkley Course the study of plants is actually put first with the result that the study of Man period is given at a later time when the pupils are more ready for such a theme. The Dornach Course of 1923 on the other hand, discourages a "description" of Man and this must be clearly recognised.

If the teacher has the necessary artistry, he will begin with the study of Man, introducing the animals and plants later on, in order to return to the theme of Man in Class 7. From Class 7 to Class 10 this will remain the central theme in natural history. However, if the teacher does not feel capable of following this ideal order, because he may lack confidence in introducing these subjects with the necessary imagination he could begin with plant study and take the study of Man later when his children are more receptive. Then animal study, and finally again study of Man.

The sequence according to the Ilkley Course naturally assumes that the teacher will spare no effort to arrange his lessons artistically (which should not be confused with "anthroposophical mannerisms").

The remark that the teacher who is to give the child "a description of Man" should wait until after the 12th year is of no interest here because it does not apply to a Waldorf School. Neither does it come into question to delay the first artistic introduction to the study of Man until the plants have been studied.

What is meant by "the necessary artistry" can be found in Steiner's Course "Study of Man" a work imbued with artistic spirit, a work to be studied and practised time and again.

One easily gains the impression that the artistic way of handling this subject in accordance with Steiner's aims lacks certainty on the part of our teachers and all too often one has to witness that his fundamental course "The Study of Man" is not taken seriously enough so that the teachers cannot develop the artistic sense which is prerequisite to fulfilling the demands of Steiner's curriculum.

After these observations the reader will understand why the original Stuttgart sequence will henceforth be followed.

The last branch of natural history, mineralogy, has not been mentioned because its placing does not seem problematic.

Various quotations will follow – first, one from the Basle Course about teaching natural history in general:

> "I really have taken a good deal of trouble to observe the effects of a premature introduction to natural history. I found that it leads to the child later becoming atrophied so that a careful observer notices that the skin has a tendency to become yellow. The ninth year is the time when we may begin to bring such concepts to the child, but they should at first be living concepts. Avoid as far as possible at this period speaking about what is mineral and dead. What is living in the outer world – and we see it in two realms, i.e., in the animals and plants – is what may be brought to the child. But if we give the children popular short books with descriptions of animals and plants according to science, if we try to talk about animals and plants in an external and popular way we do not really reach the children. It can be observed that ordinary natural history text books are only filtered down natural scientific learning. This is terrible. On the other side, admittedly, an attempt is made to build up object lessons based on natural science. For these too there are books of a kind, but they fail in the opposite direction. They are full of trivialities and have a content with which the child is already familiar. The attempt is made as far as possible, only to introduce a subject matter with which the child is already familiar and to draw forth in a concrete and pictorial way from the very nature of the child itself It is easy to fall into trivialities in this way. Many a textbook exists whose instructional methods drive one to despair because they are so dreadfully trivial and because one feels that if these methods were to be put into effect in the schools all the harm that triviality can cause would be implanted into man. This feeding on trivialities in childhood expresses itself later, as indeed does much else in what I have already mentioned, as a void, an emptiness in human life, or at least in the fashioning of life in such a way that the human being is unable to look back on his childhood with pleasure. But man really needs this, for it is necessary that throughout our life we should be able to look back upon our childhood school days as on something like Paradise – and not only because we have experienced joy there – that is not the point." (23 lecture 8)

In lecture 1 of the Stuttgart Course 1920, now called "Meditatively Acquired Knowledge of Man" Steiner characterised the spirit of nature study from the point of view of the demands made by modern spiritual life, with special reference to Herbert Spencer:

> "Spencer was of the opinion that the way of giving object lessons should be such that they would lead over into the investigations of the naturalist, into the research work of the man of Science. What then would have to be done in school? According to that we should have to teach the children in school in such a way that when they are grown up and have the opportunity they can continue what they have learnt in school about plants, minerals, animals, etc., so that they can become regular scientists or natural philosophers. It is true that this kind of idea is frequently attacked, but at the same time people really put this principle into practice and for this reason: our textbooks are composed with this aim in view, and no one thinks of altering or doing away with our textbooks... Now the remarkable thing is that we ought to strive for the exact opposite of what Spencer has laid down as a true educational principle. In our lessons when we are teaching the children of the lower and middle school about plants and animals, we could hardly imagine a greater mistake in our method of education than to treat the subject as an introduction to the studies which would be required to enable the child later to become a botanist or zoologist. If on the contrary, you could have arranged your lessons so that your way of teaching about plants and animals would hinder the children from becoming botanists or zoologists, then you would have acted more wisely than by following Spencer's principle. For no one should become a botanist or zoologist through what he learns in these years. That he can only become through his special gifts which are revealed by his choice of vocation and which would be sure to appear during his life, if there is a true art of education." (25)

In lecture 7 of the Supplementary Course nature study is described from the aspect of Greek thinking and the Greek way of looking at life. As this cannot possibly be characterised through appropriate quotations the reader is recommended to study the entire lecture. (26)

The Dornach Christmas Course of 1921/22 in lecture 10, following some remarks about the great change after the ninth year there is a detailed description of natural history. This lecture ought to be studied in full. (27)

In lecture 5 of the Oxford Course there is the short description of nature study which has already been mentioned. (29)

In the lecture given at Ilkley on August 15th 1923 there is a passage about teaching mineralogy, after a short observation about the change occurring during the eleventh and twelfth years:

> "Then comes the age when, for the first time, we may draw the child's attention to process going on in the outer world independently of man. Between the eleventh and twelfth year, and not until then, we may begin to teach about the minerals and stones. The plants as they grow out of the earth are in this sense related to stone and mineral. Earlier teaching about the mineral kingdom in any other form than this utterly spoils the child's inner mobility of soul. That which has no relationship with man is mineral in its nature. We should only begin to deal with the mineral kingdom when the child has properly found his own place in the world – when in thought and especially in feeling he has grasped the life of the plants and his will has been strengthened

by a true conception of the animals – the two kingdoms of nature which are nearest to him." (35)

In the same course, in the lecture of August 16th Steiner relates knowledge of nature to artistic activity and understanding:

"If he acquires an understanding of art, the relation of the human being to his fellow men will be quite different from what it could be without such understanding. For what is the essence of understanding the world, my dear friends? It is to be able, at the right moment, to reject abstract concepts in order to attain insight into and true understanding of the world.

The mineral kingdom can be understood in the light of cause and effect. The physical can be grasped in this way. When we come to the plant world, however, it is impossible to grasp everything through logic, reason and intellect. The plastic faculties of man's being must here come into play, for concepts and ideas have to pass into pictures. Any plastic skill that we develop in the child helps him to understand the formations contained in the plants. The animal kingdom can only be comprehended if the ideas for its understanding are first implanted and developed in us by moral education. This alone will activate such inner powers as enable us to understand the forces building up the animal structure from the invisible world. How few people, how few physiologists today know whence the form of an animal is derived! As a matter of fact the origin of the animal form comes out of the structure of those organs of speech and song. That is the centre of the origin of the forms and structure of the animal. The animal does not come to the point of articulate speech – it only comes to the point of song as we know it in the birds. In speech and song, form-giving forces stream outwards, giving shape to the air waves and sound arises. That which in the organism of speech and song develops from out of a vital principle, passes back into the form of the animal. It is only possible to understand the form of an animal if we realise that it develops, musically as it were, from organs which, at a later stage, are metamorphosed in the human being, into the organic structures connected with the element of music.

To understand man we need an all-round conception of art for the faculty of reason can only comprehend the inorganic constituents in man's being. If at the right moment we know how to lead over the faculty of mental representation to artistic understanding, then, and only then, is a true understanding of man possible. This understanding of man's being must be awakened by the teaching we give on the subject of art... if nature and history alike are imbued with an inner quality of soul through teaching that conveys an understanding of art then we are bringing the human element into all education." (35)

These passages from the Ilkley Course are further elucidated by lectures 3 and 4 of "Essentials of Education" (37) which are warmly recommended to every teacher of natural history.

An excerpt from the Torquay Course relates nature study to the soul life of the child:

"All this must be brought to him through the feelings in an artistic way, for it is through learning to feel how plants belong to the earth and to the soil that the child really becomes clever and intelligent. His thinking will then be in accordance with nature. Through our efforts to show the child how he is related to the animal world he will see how the force of will which is in all animals lives again in man, but differentiated, in individualised forms suited to man's nature. All animal qualities, all feeling of form which is stamped into the animal nature lives in the human being. Human will receives its impulses in this way and man himself thereby takes his place rightly in the world according to his own nature." (40 lecture 3)

To conclude this more general aspect of the teaching of natural history a passage from the third lecture of the Practical Course will be given, in which Steiner speaks about the children's experience of nature outside the classroom. Previously he had shown how the sculptural-pictorial arts make men reproduce the order found in the world and cosmos, whereas the musical-poetical arts prepare him for a reincarnation of the earth in the Jupiter-Venus-Vulcan development. He then continues:

"Only in linking up in this way with the great facts of the world do we acquire a right understanding of teaching. Only this can confer on it the right consecration, and in receiving this consecration it is really transformed into a kind of divine service. I have set up more or less an ideal. But surely our concrete practice can be ranged in the realm of the ideal. There is one thing we ought not to neglect, for instance, when we go with the children we are teaching – as we shall, of course – into the mountains and the fields, when, that is, we take them out to nature. In introducing these children like this to nature we should always remember that natural science teaching itself only belongs to the school building... We ought to lay stress on the difference between studying dead nature in the classroom and contemplating nature in its beauty out of doors. We should compare these two experiences side by side." (12 lecture 3).

Curriculum indications

Now follows the syllabus for each year; first the suggestions from the curriculum lectures for the classes of the lower school:

Class 3

"Let us be very clear that towards the ninth year, i.e., in Class 3, we begin to introduce animal study, selecting animals in such a way that we can relate them to man in the way I have already indicated." (16 lecture 2)

Examples can be found in the 7th lecture of the Practical Course.

Class 4

"This we continue in Class 4, so that we relate the animal world to man in a scientific manner during the third and fourth years." (ibid)

The nature of this relationship of animal to man can be seen by an answer which Steiner gave during a teachers' meeting on June 17th 1921:

"That must be done according to the children's age. In the fourth class you would keep to what is more external; this is possible in almost every class. The skeleton is of course the most abstract part of the human body. Do not take the skeleton as a separate entity but only as part of the whole organism. Not even in Class 10 would I take the skeleton separately but I should always begin with the whole human being. Try to group together certain ideas in order to make them intelligible to the pupils." (17.6.21)

Class 5

"In Class 5 we bring lesser known animal forms and introduce the study of plants in the way which has been shown in the practical sessions of our discussions." (See 13 sessions 9, 10 and 11) (16 lecture 2)

Class 6

"Continue botany in Class 6 and introduce elementary mineralogy. However, this study of the minerals must be part of geography." (ibid)

Some important information about teaching mineralogy is contained in the Practical Course. In lecture 10, after a remark about the threshold of the twelfth year we read:

"Here too the time has come when, using geometrical forms, we can go on to the mineral kingdom. We take the mineral kingdom in constant conjunction with physical phenomena which we then apply to man, as I have already explained: light refraction – the lens in the eye." (literally – the story of the lenses for the eye). (12 lecture 10)

The expression "story of the lenses" may remind us that the function of the eye's lens should be taught after the significant changes of the twelfth year mentioned above, as will be explained in detail in the chapter on physics.

Another relevant passage comes form the eleventh lecture of the same course:

"And if I have told you that mineralogy is to be introduced only as a third step (in the middle school), round about the twelfth year, a study of the minerals can already be woven into geography during an earlier stage, but only in a descriptive, pictorial manner." (ibid)

This remark can be clarified by the example of the Alps which Steiner gave in the same lecture when speaking about geography:

"And now you show him – here the teaching of mineralogy springs from geography – a piece of Jura limestone, for instance, and say, 'You see, the mountain masses above the top red line are made of limestone like this, and the mountains beneath the red line are made of different limestone.' And for the mountains lying between show him a piece of granite, or gneiss and say, 'The mountain range between the two is made of rock like this, which is primary rock.' And he will be tremendously interested in this Alpine structure..." (ibid lecture 11)

Towards the end this lecture returns once more to the study of minerals:

"Geography can really be a vast channel into which everything flows, from which in return much can be drawn. For instance, you have shown the child in geography the difference between limestone mountains and primary mountains. You show him the constituents of the primary mountain-rock, granite or gneiss. You show him how they contain different minerals, how one of these is a sparkling substance whose presence is shown by a glitter – the mica. And then you show him all the others that are contained in granite or gneiss. Then you show him quartz and try to evolve the mineral element from rock-substance. Particularly here you can do a great deal towards developing a sense for the association of facts and a united whole. It is much more helpful to show the child granite and gneiss first and then the minerals of which they consist, than to teach him first of all: granite consists of quartz, mica, felspar, etc., and only afterwards show him that these are combined in granite or gneiss. Particularly in mineralogy you can go from the whole to the part, from the structure of mountains to mineralogy. And it helps the child." (ibid)

Thus mineralogy, which should follow simple zoology and botany, is meant to be taught as a part of geography and in this way a much wider relationship to the world in general and to man is achieved.

Class 7

"In the seventh class we return to man and try to bring what should be taught in connection with food and health, as I mentioned yesterday. The teacher should try, with the ideas he has been able to evoke in physics and chemistry, to build up a comprehensive survey of industrial and economic conditions, transport and business management. All this should arise out of the study of nature in connection with the teaching of chemistry, physics and geography." (16 lecture 2)

In this year the curriculum should return to the study of man. One is reminded of "the big moment" mentioned in the Dornach Course 1923, in which the child should experience how "everything which is spread out over the animal kingdom is found within man in concentrated form."

The concrete aim for these lessons is a study of nutrition and hygiene. Through this theme the teacher will have to reveal "the big moment" in which the synthesis of the animal world in man is experienced.

The background for teaching nutrition and hygiene can be found in lecture 14 of the Practical course.

On February 6th 1923 Steiner spoke at length about hygiene, referring, however, mainly to the teachers' and school doctors' measures of hygiene and to the advice regarding health to be given to parents, rather than to actual lesson content. (6.2.23)

When thinking about the above indications for Class 7 and for the ones to follow for Class 8, one may wonder whether to include the theme "industrial and economic conditions and transport" in nature study or in geography. Since Steiner looked upon geography as being a "vast channel" for much which can illuminate the earthly sphere in a practical, imaginative and lucid way, it appears best to apportion this theme to geography, which in Class 7 should introduce the chosen countries from the aspect of economics, industries and transport. The picture of such a country would then be a concrete one, reaching far beyond the picture from a mere map, when everything is thus brought together from the astronomical, climatic, geological and biological points of view, apart from the study of man's living conditions, his spiritual conditions of culture, his economic conditions and his means of transport. For all these different branches meet in the one wide subject called geography. One must, however, be careful not to lose sight of the earth as a totality when approaching a single country from so many aspects.

Each class from Class 7 to Class 10 has been allocated a definite aspect within the general study of man. It therefore appears evident that What has been said in the various lectures about man being the synthesis of the animal world implies that in each class a contribution should be made towards this climax of experiencing the synthesis. And since Steiner looked upon the understanding of man's threefold nature as being the aim of the study of man lessons, the syllabus of each class ought to move towards this aim. This is actually the case, as can be seen from the survey of tasks in natural history lessons which is added to the end of this chapter.

Class 8

"In the eighth class you will have to prepare your study of man lesson in such a way that you describe what has been built into him from outside: the mechanics of the bones and muscles, the inner structure of the eye, and so on. Once again you make a comprehensive survey of conditions in industry, commerce and transport in connection with physics and chemistry. When you prepare the natural history lessons in this way you will make them extraordinarily alive, and through natural history you will awaken in the child an interest in everything belonging to the world and man." (16 lecture 2)

In this class it is also advisable to deal with the study of man in the actual natural history lessons and to relegate what has been mentioned otherwise to geography lessons. These should give a picture of the entire earth of which single parts were studied in Class 7, as mentioned in the syllabus of Class 7.

The outlines of the natural history courses in the upper classes are taken from the conferences (*4).

Class 9

"Continue the study of man so that the pupils receive a proper grounding in anthropology. This should be fitted into the natural scientific subjects in cycles, widening from class to class." (22.9.20)

Class 10

"Above all a certain amount of mineralogy is now essential. We should now reach the study of man in Class 10. And mineralogy must be taught. We must now tackle mineralogy." (17.6.21)

On the same day he said:
"It ought to be possible to enable pupils to gain an understanding of what a human being is, at least to a certain extent. You must, of course, make use of your opportunity to help the children to understand man as an individual being, so that you may pass on later to ethnography. Make man intelligible as an individual being. You can find a great deal for this in Anthroposophy. There is no other theme where you can gather so much information out of Anthroposophy without running the risk of being blamed for teaching Anthroposophy. This is the objective truth; physical man with his organs and their processes seen as part of his soul and spirit." (17.6.21)

The last sentence about physical man with his soul and spirit clearly refers to what Steiner called the threefoldness of man as a physical being, described for the first time in his book "Riddles of the Soul" (6a) and developed further and further in the different lecture cycles. The most detailed exposition of this theme can be found in the "Study of Man".

Ethnography is not mentioned again in the curriculum and therefore the question of when to teach it has to remain open for the time being. It has already been mentioned in connection with story and reading material for Class 8 and it can reappear in geography lessons, when the cultural background of nations is discussed in Classes 7 and 8. Steiner's suggestion in lecture 11 of the Practical Course to encourage the children during a study of Japan to paint in Japanese style, also shows how he wanted ethnography to be part of the lessons. If it is not possible to bring ethnography in Class 10 after the study of individual man (which probably was not intended) then in Class 12 ethnography will receive an appropriate place in the synopsis and culmination of the geography survey.

Class 11

"At this stage it would be important to study the Theory of Cells. And then, though not in detail, to characterise the plants from the lowest up to the monocotyledons, working from below upwards. But refer to the dicotyledons by drawing parallels between blossoms and mushrooms, Always notice the mycelium, the formation of spores. You must also go back to the mycelium if you describe the formation of shrubs. In teleology, bring the connection of the separate parts of the organisation (one might say organism) into a reasonable relationship; the relationship of reciprocal causes, not purely causal relationships. Treat the theory of cells cosmologically." (21.6.22)

In the first of the Stuttgart pedagogical lectures of 1922 the following remark about the study of cells appears:
"For the pedantic type of professor it is a matter of course to introduce the study of cells via the microscope. This is done in the universities, and schools imitate it at a lower level. One does something dreadfully wrong by this approach. One should never introduce the cells to pupils of the age with which we are now dealing without also bringing the cosmological aspect, without really considering what is happening within the cell as a little cosmos. Naturally one must not bring anything which is not based upon one's own conviction, and unless it is the result of one's own

observation of the nucleus and the various particles of the cell." (28 lecture 1)

Further information about the relationship between the study of the cell and cosmology can be found in the lecture cycle on astronomy held in Stuttgart in January 1921 (25a). A close study of this course is urgently recommended to the teacher of natural history in the upper school.

Class 12 (1923)

As in the subjects already dealt with we must again distinguish in this class between the syllabus planned in 1923 and the other syllabus of 1924. On April 25th 1923 Steiner said in answer to a question:

"In Class 5 there is zoology – later (Class 7), man. Then zoology comes again. If there were no examination I should consider it eminently possible (from Class 12) to give the children 3 wonderful weeks of zoology; 18 mornings, 12 classes of animals. The whole bony system is familiar (osteology), The essential thing is for the pupils to gain an understanding of how the various animal species fall into a definite order. You begin with the amoebae, go through the medusae – you find 12 if you consider the vertebrates (they can just as well be called mammals) as one class." (25.4.23)

On the same day Steiner gave the following indications with regard to zoology:

"On this occasion I should like to give you a classification of the animal groups, albeit with certain reservations, which could serve as a guide-line. One should divide the entire zoology into three major groups, of which each group is again sub-divided into four parts, thus obtaining twelve different categories or types of animals.

No 1 Principle Group would be:

1 Prostista, quite undifferentiated infusoria, protozoa.
2 Sponges, corals, anemones.
3 Echinoderms, from the starfish to the sea-urchins.
4 unicates, where there is no longer such a proper external shell-formation, where this is already receding.

No 2 Principle Group would be:

5 Molluscs
6 Worms
7 Arthropoda
8 Fishes

No 3 Principle Group would be:

9 Amphibians
10 Reptiles
11 Birds
12 Mammals"

(12.7.23)

This is followed by an arrangement of the different animal types in accordance with the zodiac, further by a second one related to threefold man; other interrelations to geology and animal-geography are also given. (See "Conferences" [*4] same date)

Still Class 12 (1924)

"Zoology has already been discussed. For geology and palaeontology start from zoology, then it has only an inner value (should probably read: only then does it have an inner value). From zoology you pass over to palaeontology and by this means you also come to the layers of the earth. Botany: phanerogams. Here too you pass over into geology." (30.4.24)

The sentence "Zoology has already been discussed" can only refer to what was given on July 12th 1923 with regard to zoology. This then is to be the syllabus for Class 12. But one goes on to palaeontology from there. One is also supposed to go on to palaeontology from botany, which has as its aim the phanerogams (flowering plants) and which passes over once more to the monocotyledons.

Since geology has been taught from Class 5 onward as part of geography, this could also be done in Class 12, i.e., one should try first to take natural history, zoology and botany (phanerogams) before geography; then begin geography with geology-palaeontology and end up with a survey of the earth as an organism.

One could therefore formulate the aims of natural history in Class 12 thus:

The twelve animal groups are taken first and related to man. Their development through previous earth periods will lead to the study of the earth's layers and its fossils.

The plant kingdom will be treated similarly and thus become a preparation for the big synthesis in geography.

Survey of the natural history syllabus:

Classes 3 – 4 Picture of man animal study (cuttle-fish, mouse, man).

Class 5 Animal study – plant study and earth.

Class 6 Plant study and earth – (minerals in geography).

Class 7 Study of man: nutrition and hygiene (economics, industries and transport in geography).

Class 8 "Mechanics of bones and muscles", "structure of the eye" and similar matters.

Class 9 "Proper anthropology".

Class 10 "Physical man, his organs and their functions in connection with soul and spirit".

Class 11 "Study of cells from a cosmological aspect". Lower plants including monocotyledons. Causes of changes.

Class 12 Zoology (to palaeontology in geography), Botany: phanerogams (also to palaeontology in geography, ethnography in geography).

In Conclusion

In the pedagogical course of Basle 1920, the following sentences about natural history teaching and its relationship to history can be found:

"If one can bring to life in a simple and elementary way

what is otherwise only experienced as dead – a living characterization of earth, plant life, animal life and man – then something grows up with the child which also brings him into a right relationship with the historical life of humanity on earth. Then only does the feeling develop which can take up history in the right way. To what has formerly been dealt with only in the form of stories and biographies can be added in the tenth and eleventh years, natural history teaching; but always so that, wherever feeling has been kindled through natural history, its teaching should be closely linked to what one can make alive in the concepts, ideas and feeling of historical teaching. It is only in the twelfth year that the possibility to develop actual judgment is really there." (23 lecture 8)

11 Physics and Chemistry (General)

Before going into the teaching of physics and chemistry, which is introduced during the time of great changes in the eleventh and twelfth years, words which Steiner spoke in the Supplementary Course of 1921 will be quoted. These stress the importance of bringing anything appealing directly to thinking and reasoning in a way that awakens strong soul powers in the child.

"And fundamentally what we impart with feeling, fosters the growth of the child's own inner life, whilst what we give him merely in ideas, is dead, and remains so for him. For in ideas we are giving the child reflected pictures, and to do this we work with his head – the head that is, as we have seen, of value only in its relation to the past, to the time when it was in the spiritual world. In order to reach what is found in the blood, and has its significance here and now, on earth, we need to imbue our lessons with feeling.

You must for example, experience within you something of the hostile, destructive force of space under the receiver of an air pump. The more vividly you are able to describe how terrible a thing space is when all the air has been pumped out of it, the further you will find you can go with the children. In earlier ages these feelings were expressed in the very words that were used to describe the processes. Horror vacui: what streams out from a space that has been emptied of air, inspires horror. It was all in the language itself; but we have to find it again. We must learn, for example, to feel the relationship that exists between a vacuum and a very thin and shrivelled human being." (26 lecture 2)

Here are some more characteristic words of Steiner's about a subject which, generally speaking, deals with lifeless matter:

"In physics and chemistry one ought to be able to put into practice the principle that the whole system of chemistry and physics is one organism, a unity and not an aggregate, as it is seen today." (25.4.23)

This quotation comes form the "Conferences" (*4) in which the syllabus of Class 12 was discussed for the first time.

Though it contains something which has not yet been realised, it nevertheless should be borne in mind by the teacher who prepares himself for these subjects. The two natural-scientific courses, viz. The First Science Course (20) and The Heat Course (21) can give further guidance in this respect and a study of these courses is an important preparation for teaching the two subjects in a Steiner school.

Technology, based on physics and chemistry, has created a new world which can be looked upon as part of nature only as far as natural laws operate in it, i.e., no other powers than those active in lifeless matter. But it has also been newly created and added to the old kingdoms of nature, viz the mineral, plant, animal and human kingdom. This new kingdom – technology – affects and continually changes the life of man in the strongest possible way.

What this means for man has been shown by Steiner in the Practical Course in an urgent argument about the latest phase of development of the social life and its corresponding demands upon education:

"Just think how many people today see a steam engine or a railway engine steam past them, without any idea of the physical and mechanical processes involved in the motion of the steam engine. But think further, in what relation, in view of such ignorance, we stand as human beings to the surroundings of which we even make a convenience. We live in a world produced by human beings, moulded by human thought, of which we make use, and which we do not understand in the least. This lack of comprehension for human creation, or for the results of human thought, is of great significance for the entire complexion of the human soul and spirit. In fact, people must benumb themselves to escape the realization of influences from this source – and there is at least some pleasure in seeing people who are completely ignorant of the workings of an electric railway, get in and out of it with a slight feeling of discomfort. For this feeling of discomfort is at least the first glimmering of an improvement in attitude. The worst thing is participation in a world made by human heads and hands without bothering in the least about that world. We can only fight against this attitude if we begin our fight as early as the last stage of the elementary school course, if we simply do not let the child of fifteen or sixteen leave school without at least a few elementary notions of the most important functions of the outside world. The child must leave with a craving to know, an insatiable curiosity about everything that goes on around him, and then convert this curiosity and craving for knowledge into further knowledge." (12 lecture 12)

A further quotation from Steiner, taken from the Conference (*4), classifies the general attitude towards physical and chemical facts. It was given during the very first days of the Waldorf School.

"Why does it present difficulties? You must strive to lead these things gradually over to what Goethe called the Original Phenomenon, thus only dealing with phenomena. The Law of Conservation of Energy ought not to be treated as it has been up till now. It is a postulate, no law. And secondly there is something quite different

here. You can deal with the spectrum, that is the phenomenon: but the Law of Conservation of Energy is treated as a philosophical law (that is to say, it should be so handled). The mechanical equivalent to heat has to be treated as something different. That is the phenomenon. Why not then remain strictly within phenomenology? i.e., I should say, work out such laws as really are phenomena. It is nonsense (then) to call them 'laws', as, i.e., Law of the Rate of Falling Bodies. Those are phenomena, they are not laws. And you will find that you can keep the whole of physics free from so-called laws and transform them into phenomena, and group them into secondary (and) original phenomena; the whole theory of the Rate of Falling Bodies, for instance. If you begin to describe the so-called laws of Atwood's Machine, these are phenomena and not laws." (25.9.19)

When asked how to achieve that Steiner said:
"You can simply draw it if you have no Atwood's Machine. In the first second it falls so, in the second so, in the third so. You simply get the series of numbers, and out of them you make what is called the law, which however is only a phenomenon." (25.9.19)

When asked about gravity, he said:
"It would be wonderful if you could really get used to applying this term no longer. This is possible if one only takes the actual phenomena. This would be the best way, for gravity is only a phrase." (ibid)

When asked whether the same applied to the forces of electricity, he said:
"Today you can talk about electricity without speaking of forces. You can keep strictly to phenomena. You can reduce it to the theory of ions and electrons without speaking of anything but phenomena. To do this would be enormously important educationally." (25.9.19)

The teacher still doubted whether he could manage without using the concept of force because of the measuring system in physics:
"What then have forces to do with it? Of course when you have calculations, in which you can exchange one thing with another, you can use it." (Force as a means of measuring?) (25.9.19)

When a teacher suggested a new word to replace the word 'force' Steiner said:
"As long as the pupil is clear that 'force' is nothing more than the 'product of mass and velocity', as long as he connects no metaphysical concept with it, treats it always phenomenologically, you can speak of force." (ibid)

It is only possible to understand this discussion if one can see it within the context of Steiner's theory of knowledge. We shall therefore mention those of his works which can be of help:

The Theory of Knowledge implicit in Goethe's World Conception (2 bibliography)
Goethe the Scientist (1 bibliography)
Truth and Science (3 bibliography)
The Philosophy of Freedom (4 bibliography)

A careful study, above all of the first two works mentioned,

must be considered as an important preparation for a teacher of physics and chemistry, especially since there exists a vast amount of literature on these two subjects which points in a completely different direction from Steiner's approach. It is therefore necessary to reassess existing textbooks before teaching the subjects in a Steiner school. The four books mentioned above will make this possible.

In the third lecture of the Supplementary Course there is a definite and practical indication of how to teach physics. As this passage is relevant to any subject in which many experiments have to be carried out, e.g., chemistry, it will be quoted in full despite its length:

"Take for instance, a lesson in physics. We do some experiment together with the children. Now remember what I said yesterday – that man thinks with his head, but it is the rhythmic man who appraises and judges, whilst it is the metabolism-and-limbs man (more particularly legs and feet) that draws conclusions. Once you realise this and realise also the nature of the act of perception as such, you will be ready to admit that when we perceive an action that we ourselves perform of our own accord, the act of perception is in that case very closely connected with the drawing of conclusions, – more so indeed than it is with thought. When I see my own body, my body is itself a conclusion. Thought is present only in the moment of turning my eyes to my body. For then I immediately carry out a semi-conscious or subconscious process, which consists in gathering together all the details I have perceived into a 'whole' and pronouncing judgement on them in the words: that is a body. This is then the perception of a conclusion. The fact is, whenever I perceive with understanding, I am at the same time drawing conclusions; consequently my whole human being is involved in the process. And this is how it is when I do scientific experiments. I am all the time receiving – absorbing – something, and doing so through the medium of my whole being; and 'conclusions' are continually entering into the process. The 'judgements' are of course there too, but are as a rule not perceived; they are too deeply hidden within. So long as I am making experiments, my whole being is thus called into action.

But now, looking at the matter from the educational standpoint, we are not really doing the children very much good with these experiments of ours! They will perhaps be quite interested in them; but man is too weak, normally, to stand being compelled in this way to make constant effort with his whole being... Whenever you make experiments in front of him or direct his attention to something in the world outside, he comes too strongly out of himself. Right regard and care for the three members of the threefold human being is the mark of true education. We have to see that each member plays its part, and we have also to see that all three interact rightly in and with one another.

Suppose however I take the lesson in the following way. First I conduct an experiment. This means, I am making demands upon the child's whole being. That is asking a great deal! Then I turn his attention away from the apparatus that is standing there in front of him, and go through the whole thing again, appealing now to his recollection of the experiment. When we recapitulate in this way, letting the child review the experiment in thought without seeing it take place, then his rhythmic system is stirred and animated. After first making demand upon the whole human being, I make demand now upon rhythmic system and head system – for naturally recapitulation brings the head system also into activity. And then I can close the lesson, and let the child go home. Later on, he goes to sleep. While he is asleep and his astral body and ego are away, what I have set going, first in the child's whole being and then in this rhythmic system, lives on in him, lives on also in his limbs.

Let us now concentrate our attention upon the sleeping child, as he lies in bed. What I managed to achieve with him in the Physics lesson, echoes on in his physical and ether bodies. All the development that the lesson evoked first in the child as a whole, and then more especially in the rhythmic system, streams up now into the head-man. Pictures of it all begin to form in the head. And when the child wakes up in the morning and goes to school, these pictures are in his head; we find them there. It is actually so, When the children come to school next day, they have in their head, without knowing it, pictures – photographs – of the experiment I showed them the day before and of which I afterwards gave them a graphic description. It is all there in picture form.

On the next day I can begin to lead the children to reflect upon the experiment. When I went over it again with them the day before, I appealed rather to their faculty of imagination. Now I want them to consider what they have seen and heard. We have reached a further stage: the pictures have to become conscious. I must lead the children to recognise the laws that underlie the experiment. Thus the pictures they still carry – unconsciously – in their heads will not be compelled to lead a meaningless existence. But now consider what would happen if, instead of giving the children nourishment in this way by leading them to reflect on yesterday's experiment, I were to go straight ahead next morning with further experiments. Once again I would be taxing their whole being; and the exertion I aroused in them would push its way into every part of their system and bring confusion and chaos into the pictures that are there from the day before. No, before I pass on to new experiments, I must always – without exception – consolidate first what is trying to establish its existence. I must give it food. And so here I have found the right way to order and arrange my Physics lessons, adapting them throughout to the life-processes in the child." (26 lecture 3)

The Oxford Course gives a helpful account of how between the eleventh and thirteenth years the child experiences the mechanics and dynamics of his own body:

"Between the 11th and 12th years a very great change takes place in the human being. The rhythmic system – breathing system and system of blood circulation – is dominant between the change of teeth and puberty. When the child is nearly ten years old the beat and rhythm of the blood circulation and breathing system begin to develop and pass into the muscular system. The muscles become saturated with blood and the blood pushes through the muscles in intimate response to man's inner nature – to his heart. So that between his ninth and eleventh years the human being builds up his own rhythmic system in the way which corresponds to its inner disposition. When the eleventh or twelfth year is reached, then what is in the rhythmic system and muscular system passes over into the bony system, into the whole skeleton. Up to the eleventh year the bony system is entirely embedded in the muscular system. It conforms to the muscular system. Between the eleventh and twelfth years the skeleton adapts itself to the outer world. A mechanics and dynamics which is independent of the human being passes into the skeleton. We must accustom ourselves to treating the skeleton as though it was an entirely objective thing, not concerned with man.

If you will observe children under eleven years old you will see that all their movements still come out of their inner being. If you observe children of over twelve years old you will see from the way they step how they are trying to find their balance, how they are inwardly adapting themselves to the leverage and balance, to the mechanical nature of the skeletal system. This means that between the eleventh and twelfth year the soul and spirit nature is much more inward. And only now that he has taken hold of that remotest part of his humanity, the bony system, does man's adaptation to the outer world become complete. Only now is man a true child of the world, only now must he live with the mechanics and dynamics of the world, only now does he experience what is called causality of life." (29 lecture 6)

A little further on these sentences follow:

"Before his eleventh year a human being has in reality no understanding of cause and effect. He hears the words used. We think he understands them. But he does not, because he is controlling his bony system from out of his muscular system. Later, after the twelfth year, the bony system, which is adjusting itself to the outer world, dominates the muscular system, and through it, influences spirit and soul. And in consequence man now gets an understanding of cause and effect based on inner experience – an understanding of force, and of his own experience of the perpendicular, the horizontal, etc.

For this reason, you see, when we teach the child mineralogy, physics, chemistry, mechanics before his eleventh year in too intellectual a way we harm his development, for he cannot as yet have a corresponding experience of the mechanics and dynamics within his whole being. Neither, before his eleventh year can he inwardly participate in the causal connection in history." (ibid lecture 6)

After a few more sentences about history:

"If before his eleventh year we teach the child the principle of the lever or of the steam engine he can experience nothing of it inwardly because as yet he has no dynamics or mechanics in his own body, in his physical nature. When we begin physics, mechanics and dynamics at the right time with the child, namely about

his eleventh or twelfth year, what we present to him in thought goes into his head and it is met by what comes from his inner being – the experience the child has of his own bony system. And what we say to the child unites with the impulse and experience which comes from the child's body.

Thus there arises, not an abstract intellectual understanding but a psychic understanding, an understanding in the soul. And it is this we must aim at." (ibid lecture 6)

These remarks of Steiner about teaching physics and chemistry as an organic unity will be concluded by a passage from the Torquay Course. There he said after speaking about teaching mineralogy:

"For physical phenomena also it is just as important to start from life itself. You should not begin your teaching of Physics as set forth in the text books of today, but simply by lighting a match for instance and letting the children observe how it begins to burn; you must draw their attention to all the details, what the flame looks like, what it is like outside, what it is like further in, and how a black spot, a little black cap is left when you blow out the flame, and only when you have done this, begin to explain how the fire in the match came about. The fire came about through the generation of warmth, and so on. Thus you must connect everything with life itself.

Or take the example of a lever. Do not begin by saying that a lever consists of a supported beam at the one end of which there is a force, and at the other end another force, as one so often finds in the Physics books. You should start from a pair of scales; let the child imagine that you are going to some shop where things are being weighed out, and from this pass on to equilibrium and balance, and to the conception of weight and gravity. Always develop your Physics from life itself, and your chemical phenomena also.

This is the essential thing, to begin with real life in considering the different phenomena of the physical and mineral world. If you do it the other way, beginning with an abstraction, then something very curious happens to the child; the lesson soon makes him tired. He does not get tired if you start from real life. He gets tired if you start from abstractions." (40 lecture 7)

He continued to speak about pupils feeling tired in lessons and even during breaks and then spoke about the importance of imagination in teaching during the last years of the middle school:

"In our work with children of elementary school we must see to it that we engage the rhythmic system only. The rhythmic system never tires, and is not over-exerted when we employ it in the right way, and for this rhythmic system we need not an intellectual but rather a pictorial method of presentation, something that comes out of imagination. Therefore it is imperative that imagination should hold sway in the school. This must still be so even in the last period of which we have spoken, from eleven and two thirds to fourteen years; we must still make the lifeless things

live through imagination and always connect them with real life, It is possible to connect all the phenomena of Physics with real life, but we ourselves must have imagination in order to do it. This is absolutely necessary." (40 lecture 7)

Physics and chemistry (together with mineralogy) belong to the same sphere of the inanimate world. The distinction between the two subjects is based on their historical development. If one accepts the view that lifeless matter becomes organised (formed through the "elements" and "the different ethers" [20 and 21]) this distinction between physics and chemistry becomes quite arbitrary and one should try to avoid it when teaching these subjects. Steiner expressed this view quite clearly when the curriculum for Class 12 was made (his words are quoted at the beginning of this chapter). If the teacher works towards this aim, he must begin already in Class 6 or 7, when introducing physics and chemistry. Therefore I have put this section before going into details of chemistry and physics teaching, because I wanted to bring together everything which the two subjects have in common.

For the time being it does not yet appear right to break away from the tradition of treating physics and chemistry as two separate subjects. Neither does Steiner introduce them simultaneously in his curriculum, viz. physics in Class 6 and chemistry in Class 7. He has told us why in physics one should deal with outer happenings in Class 6, e.g., with those of light, but not yet with the process of seeing, which necessitates following the light into the human organism. As far as I know, he has not given any reasons why chemistry should not be taken before Class 7. Though he asked us to teach all other branches of physics in Class 6, mechanics was to be introduced in Class 7. In history too, he has called for a different approach in Classes 6 and 7, namely from the descriptive history in Class 6 to one where one seeks reasons and explanations in Class 7.

Physics

Class 6:	4 weeks	
Class 7 and 8: each	3 weeks	Main lessons
Class 9 to 12: each	4 weeks	

In the eighth lecture of the Practical Course Steiner said after having spoken about the changes taking place in the twelfth year:

"You may talk to the child before this about the organization of the human eye as clearly as possible – but before he is twelve he will not be able to master its formation properly and with understanding. For what are you really doing when you teach the child about the formation of the human eye? You are drawing his attention to the way in which rays of light strike the eye, enter it, are taken up by the lens and refracted, how they then pass through the vitreous humour and form an image upon the back wall of the eye, etc. You must describe all these as physical processes. You describe a physical process which really occurs in man himself, namely in a human sense organ. If you want to do this you must have already developed the ideas in the child which enable him to respond. That is, you must have already shown the child the refraction of rays of light.

This is very easily explained by showing him a lens, explaining the focus, and showing how the rays of light are refracted. But you are then describing purely physical facts which take place outside the human being. This can be done between the turning-point of the child's ninth year and the turning-point of his twelfth year. Only at the end of the twelfth year should this physical description be applied to the organs of man himself, because only then does the child begin to estimate at its right value the action of the outer world upon man, the process by which the activity of the outside world is projected into the human being and prolonged within him. He cannot understand this before he is twelve. He can understand physical processes – but not the consummation of physical processes in the human being." (12 lecture 8)

This definitely fixes the time when physics should be introduced. This same lecture is full of valuable indications specially for lessons in elementary physics.

Curriculum indications

The following syllabus indications for the middle school are taken from the curriculum lectures:

Class 6

"We start with the teaching of physics in the 6th class in such a way that it is linked with what the child has acquired through the teaching of music. We start our teaching of physics by letting acoustics grow out of the musical. You bring acoustics into relation with musical science when you describe the human larynx physically and physiologically. You cannot describe the human eye (or the ear) at this age but the human larynx you can. Then you proceed to optics and the science of heat, taking the most important items. The principles of electricity and magnetism should be taught in the sixth class as well." (16 lecture 2)

Class 7

"In the seventh class you extend the teaching of acoustics, heat, optics, electricity and magnetism, and only from there do you proceed to the most important principles of mechanics, i.e., the lever, wheel and axle, roller, pulley, inclined plane, cylinder, screw, etc." (ibid)

Class 8

"In the eighth class you enlarge again, revise what you have fostered in the sixth class and then pass on to hydraulics, the theory of power working through water. You take everything belonging to the concepts of lateral pressure of the water, buoyancy, the Archimedean principle, etc. It would have been marvellous to deliver lectures on pedagogy here for three whole years and to have worked through with you for once, as a sort of model, all the details that will build up through your own discoveries. However, this cannot be, so we must rest content with what we have been able to do. Thus you bring the physics lessons to some sort of conclusion with aeromechanics in which everything concerning climatology, the barometer and meteorology is discussed." (16 ibid lecture 2)

It is surprising that Steiner expected all branches of physics to be introduced within the short period of four or even three weeks, i.e., in some forty-eight to fifty-six lessons (excepting mechanics and processes explained in terms of physics, which take place in the sense organs). Therefore teachers have tried time and again to take only one or another branch in order to continue with the uncovered branches of physics in Classes 7 and 8. However, there is no doubt that Steiner wanted this arrangement to be carried out since he pointed out twice what should be covered in Class 6. Evidently his intention was that the teacher should, already in Class 6, give a complete picture of what man can experience when observing the inanimate world, because before the great changes in the eleventh – twelfth year the child is still able to look outward more or less unhindered by his own soul life and thus is able to enlarge his experience of the world. At that time he is still completely immersed in this experience of the outer world and for the time being he does not want any more. To enable him to do this as fully as possible Steiner has arranged the introduction of physics in such an all embracing manner.

In Class 7 when the great changes have already taken place, the situation becomes quite different. The young people have built a bridge to the outer world, and now their own organism also becomes an object for them. They are now able to relate it to the outer processes and a new approach to physics is indicated. This need not be a monotonous repetition of the physics taught previously for surely there is plenty of subject matter and even if one were to take the same phenomena again, this new approach would open up new aspects. Mechanics should be introduced only in Class 7.

Steiner has spoken about it in the Oxford Course and his sentences were quoted in the section dealing with the general aspects of physics and chemistry. In Class 8 physical phenomena are treated on a higher level. At this time, as in all other subjects, single phenomena have to be treated as part of bigger processes.

A new approach to physics in Class 9 is characterised by the words from Steiner's Berne Course, even though these words do not specially refer to physics:

"We must strive to educate in such a way that the intellect, which awakens at puberty, can then find its nourishment in the child's own nature. If during his early school years he has stored up an inner treasury of riches through imitation, through his feeling for authority, and from the pictorial character of what he has been taught, then at puberty these inner riches can be transmuted into intellectual content. He will now be faced with the task of thinking what up till now he has willed and felt, and we must take the very greatest care that this intellectual thinking does not appear too early. For a human being can only come to an experience of freedom if his intellectuality awakens within him of itself, not if it is poured into him by his teachers. But it must not awaken in poverty of soul. If he has nothing within him that he has acquired through imitation and imagery (this probably means, what has been naturally accepted at the age of authority and then recreated in accordance with the example set by the teacher) and that can therefore rise up into his thinking out of the depths of his

soul, then, when his thinking should develop at puberty he will find nothing within himself to further his own growth, and his thinking can only reach out into emptiness. He will find no anchorage in life and just at the time when he ought really to have found a sort of security in himself he will be running after anything and everything. In these awkward years of adolescence he will be imitating all kinds of things which please him and usually they are just the things which do not please his elders, who have a more utilitarian point of view. He imitates these things now because as a young child he has not imitated rightly and in a living way. So it is that we see many young people after puberty seeking support in this or that and so deadening their inner experience of freedom." (38 lecture 5)

Syllabus for Classes 9-12

Class 9

"In physics you ought to teach first of all acoustics and electricity, including magnetism, so that the pupils can understand how the telephone works. Then you should take heat and mechanics to enable them to understand the working of a steam locomotive." (22.9.20)

Steiner's intention was obviously to give the pupils a practical understanding of the construction and usefulness of modern machines which are widely used by people who do not know anything about them at all. It therefore would be in keeping with his views, if one were to introduce later inventions which are already replacing the railway steam engine and the telephone. In the Stuttgart Waldorf School the internal combustion engine was therefore taught as well as the railway engine. On the other hand it appears right to wait till Class 11 before introducing engines of communication which are based upon electromagnetic waves.

Steiner's answer to a question by a teacher whose lessons he had visited, gives useful information about teaching electricity:

"Naturally in teaching electricity you should build upon the phenomena themselves in a rational way, avoiding theoretical speculations as much as possible. For in any case these would not leave lasting impressions, at least not from a practical point of view. I should think that in this subject it would be ideal to develop the necessary concepts out of the experiment itself. Do not draw anything on the blackboard unless you have to, but develop everything out of the experiment. Thereafter one can use the Socratic approach, as you have done. But if you develop the subject too theoretically, the Socratic method is useless. How should the children have the necessary pre-knowledge? You can hardly begin in this manner. As you have the facilities for making experiments, I should make full use of them. In this way you can save a great deal of time. If you introduce electricity in this way, you will succeed." (15.11.20)

The next quotation, which is taken from the pedagogical lectures given in Stuttgart in 1922, summarises what has been said about the adolescent stage after puberty, and covers the transition from Class 9 to Class 10.

"You see, these things must penetrate the teacher in full consciousness in the transition from the ninth to the tenth class. It is the complete change over that in this case is educational. When the children come to you at about 6 or 7 years old the break has already taken place through the fact of coming to school. So you do not have to transplant them into another situation in life. But when you lead the children from the ninth to the tenth class you have to transplant them into another situation; then the child must say to himself: Heavens! What has happened to our teacher? Up to now we have held him to be a shining light, a man who has had so much to tell. But now he is speaking more like an ordinary person. Yet the whole world seems to speak through him. If one can experience a really intense interest in each world problem and at the same time is in the fortunate situation of being able to discuss these problems with young people, then the world will speak through one. Then it is as if spirits were talking through one's mouth. However, when dealing with children of 14 or 15, and 20 and 21, such conversations have to be full of pulsating, vibrating life, life which stimulates above all the powers of imagination." (No. 28 'Stuttgart' 1922)

He then continues to speak about the importance of imagination just at this stage of life.

Class 10

After a remark by a teacher that mechanics was the subject that had been taught least during the past Class 9:

"Now is the right time to teach mechanics. You should have to start with mechanical forms (probably a mis-print, should read: start teaching mechanics from the beginning). The right time for introducing it would be after a period of mathematics. All you need to aim at is that the children thoroughly understand simple machines." (17.6.21)

Steiner supplemented the syllabus of Class 10 in the first "Conference" (*4) after the summer holidays 1921, when the physics teacher reported that mechanics had been taught comparatively little:

"Then you had better go through the simple machines again, with trigonometry. It is better to deal with projections by means of equations. Will the children understand the equation of a parabola? If you work that out in a concrete case, there is no need to discuss it. The whole treatment of projection and its essential nature has only an educational value when children have grasped the equation of the parabola and understand its law. To be able to express reality in terms of mathematical equations is what we should strive for. Philosophy is supposed to begin with wonder, but this is only partly true. When teaching, wonder should be experienced by the pupil at the end of a chapter. Children must be led towards wonder, and this wonder must be a deep experience. You should get them to grasp that here you are dealing with something before which a Novalis would have fallen on his knees." (11. 9.21)

Soon after, the physics of flying was introduced in the Stuttgart Waldorf School.

Class 11

"In physics – and this is something which I worked out

very thoroughly when I had to teach it myself – in physics it is an exceptionally good thing at this age to bring the more recent achievements, wireless telegraphy, the X-ray facts and certainly something of such things as α, β, λ, rays. These can indeed be used in a way that will awaken great interest in the children." (21.6.22)

For the transition to Class 12 the quotation given at the beginning of this section will be enlarged because its significance can be appreciated only now:

"In physics and chemistry we ought to find the means of working out a principle according to which the whole system of chemistry and physics is an organism, a unity, and not an aggregate as is accepted today. In Class 12 we come to a kind of conclusion, we must arrive at results in every branch of our work. Answer questions such as, Why are there five regular solid bodies? That we must do in crystallography and mineralogy." (25.4.23)

The following words which were spoken in 1923 when the first Class 12 was to be prepared for the forthcoming examination, indicate what could be done if one were freed from examination pressure. Compared with the aims of Class 12 in 1924 which did not have to work for an examination, they demand a great deal. More concrete indications for physics were not given at that time.

Class 12

"Beginning with Class 9 we cover telephone and steam engine, heat and acoustics. 10. Mechanics as such. 11. The modern theory of electricity. 12. Optics. Pictures instead of rays. We must deal with the qualitative element. Light fields and light spaces. Do not speak of refraction, but of the contraction of the light field. We must get rid of these expressions. When we speak of what a lens is, we must not draw the cross section of the lens, and then a fantastic cross-section of rays, but we must continue to conceive of the lens as the image contracting, condensing or coming asunder. Thus in fact keeping only to what is immediately seen in the field of vision. You must completely supplant the theory of rays. This must be done in optics. Elsewhere other points need to be considered. Above all, dwell on the qualitative aspect of phenomena. I am not talking about a colour theory but simply about facts relating to colour. I am not speaking about a hypothesis but merely about actual happenings. Take optics in its widest context. This would include first of all:

1 light as pure phenomenon, light and its power to radiate.

Then

2 light meeting matter, usually called refraction; enlargement and diminution of the image, displacements, then
3 the origin of colours,
4 phenomena of polarisation,
5 the nature of double refraction as it is called, the phenomena of incoherence in the spreading of light.

Mirrors belong to the first chapter, to light's nature of radiation. Optics is a very important subject because many of its individual features are directly connected with the life of the Spirit. First consider for a moment: why is there so little understanding for what is spiritual? For it could well exist. But it does not exist because of the lack of a real theory of knowledge, instead of which we find abstract speculations and mere hypotheses.

Why is there no real epistemology? Because since Berkeley wrote his book about seeing, no one has rightly connected seeing with cognising. If you see connections in this way you will no longer explain the mirror phenomena by saying: there is a mirror, a ray of light falls on it in a perpendicular direction. But you will say: here is the eye. And now you will have to explain why, if the eye sees in straight lines, nothing else happens than that the eye sees in straight lines. You must come to realise that fundamentally the mirror attracts the image of the object for your eye (?). You find subjective forces of attraction. You must start with the act of seeing. The entire field of optics will reveal itself to you in a new way. If you look in a straight line, you gain an undisturbed picture. If you look through a mirror, you do not see an undistorted image, but you really look in a one-sided way in the direction towards the object. The moment you use mirrors, polarisation takes place. One spatial dimension disappears when you see through a mirror. You can find further details in my lectures on optics." (29.4.24)

The lectures on optics referred to are the ones of the so–called Light Course of Christmas 1919. (20)

Chemistry

Class 7 to 9: each	3 weeks	
Class 10:	2 weeks	Main Lessons
Class 11 and 12: each	3 weeks	

It is certainly more difficult for a young person to understand chemical processes than those belonging to physics, because chemistry invades his own corporeality more directly than physics does. The chemical processes which we observe in our laboratories do not halt at man's corporeality; they would dissolve his own physical existence unless prevented from doing so. We cannot understand chemistry properly unless we learn to respect this refusal of chemical action to halt before our skin; unless we appreciate that chemical substances which have been brought into our organism are exposed to counterforces within our body which transform and assimilate them unless they prove too potent.

Experiencing the effect of chemical forces can make the observer feel as if he were losing firm ground from under his feet, because these chemical forces dissolve into a liquid what is solid and what he is wont to look upon as his solid physical foundations. Therefore a higher degree of objectivity is necessary for pupils to make a direct contact with chemistry than in the case of physics, which deals more with inanimate matter whereas the chemical element works directly into living substances. These thoughts may help us to understand why Steiner wanted chemistry to be introduced one year later than physics.

Dr. Eugen Kolisko was the first teacher and school doctor in the Waldorf School who carried out Steiner's ideas of teaching chemistry as part of a carefully planned syllabus. Steiner had this to say about his efforts:

"If you applied Kolisko's Chemistry in detail, you would find it incomprehensible to the present day chemist. The imaginative capacity needed for its understanding you can impart up to the 18th, 19th year, till the end of the moon cycle. After a period of 18-19 years the same constellation of the moon re-appears. That is the period which pupils should have reached in order to grasp certain concepts. A chemist with an ordinary education cannot understand Kolisko's Chemistry. He has not developed the necessary concepts for it. It would be good to aim at making this possible for our pupils. This we cannot accomplish if we are obliged to ruin their brains in the way that is prevalent to-day." (25.4.23)

The chapter dealing with the problem of examinations will make this quotation comprehensible.

Eugen Kolisko's attempts at working out the teaching of chemistry were published under the title "First Lessons of Chemistry". In 1930 there were violent arguments about this little book. One should value it as the first, very courageous attempt completely to reorganise the teaching of chemistry and to realise the demands made by Steiner for this subject.

In the curriculum indications for Class 11 we read the following sentence:

"We shall pay less attention to the historical side, namely to the distinction between organic and inorganic chemistry." (21.6.22)

This sentence, though spoken in connection with Class 11, is of importance for the entire chemistry teaching, for in its tendency can be recognised more or less clearly indications given regarding the teaching of chemistry.

Curriculum indications

Now follows the syllabus for each class:

Class 7 (after a course in physics)

"You make your start with a process such as burning and from such an ordinary process you try to achieve a transition to simple chemical concepts." (16 lecture 2)

Class 8

"You extend the simple chemical concepts so that the child learns to understand how industrial processes are connected with chemistry. Using chemical concepts you try to develop a link with substances which build up the human organism, such as starch, sugar, albumen and fat." (16 lecture 2)

Steiner here sets the chemistry teacher the difficult task of forming adequate pictures about the chemical processes taking place within the human organism, using only qualitative aspects.

Class 9

"What we have put down for Class 8, viz the elementary chemistry taking place in our organism, should be extended in Class 9 to include the understanding of substances such as alcohol and ether." (22.9.20)

It is probable that the curriculum for Class 8 was influenced by the thought that many children would be leaving school at the end of the year and that they should take away with them as many wholesome ideas as possible. If this were the case, it might be better to introduce the chemical processes taking place in an organism ("organic" chemistry) only in Class 9, unless many pupils are likely to leave before that time.

It is worth noting that the three main substances in chemistry, viz acids, salts and bases, have not been mentioned at all in connection with the two classes just dealt with. Apparently these classes are to be introduced to substances which are directly available and not to those whose existence is the result of chemical reactions, substances which in reality are nothing else but chemical processes artificially arrested. This is mainly the case with acids and bases, less so with the salts.

Class 10

(After the teacher had reported that the difference between acids and bases had been taught during the previous year.)

"Have the children a clear picture of the significance of a salt, an acid, a base? These things must be taken first. A great deal could be done this year simply by letting the pupils observe in a thorough and accurate way anything pertaining to the formation of bases, acids and salts. Then speak of alkali and acid reaction, and afterwards – in order to help them to come to an understanding – you could start (from something else) from the contrasting reactions of let us say food-sap and bee-blood, because in those two you find alkali and acid substances. Let your lesson culminate in the contrasting behaviour of bee-blood and food-sap. In this way you find your approach to physiological processes. You only need to work out the concepts: alkali, acid, base, salts. Then, because it is a characteristic example, introduce bee-blood and the food-sap of the bee which react in opposite ways. The reaction of food-sap is acid, and that of bee-blood is alkaline. There is this polarity of blood and food-sap which the bee has in its digestive organs. You find the same principle in man, but it cannot be substantiated in such a striking manner. You can re-create the process taking place in the bee quite easily on the laboratory bench." (17.6.21)

Here we see quite clearly that Steiner thought it essential to show via the concepts of acid, base and salt, processes governing the entire field of chemistry right into organic life, processes which by degrees, take different forms in minerals, plants, animals and man. The experiment with the food-sap and the blood of the bee illustrates the point of this distinction: acid and alkaline substances which become balanced in inanimate matter in any case, have become subject to a higher principle to which they have to attune themselves.

These fundamental ideas underlying the structure and general build-up of the material world are to be expanded also in Class 11.

Class 11

"In chemistry it would be necessary to explain the leading concepts, acid, salt, base, as fully as possible, so that they know what is an alcohol and what is an aldehyde. We will pay less attention to the traditional separation between organic and inorganic chemistry. It seems to me that this is the right moment to introduce a survey of

chemical elements. In my opinion it would not be right to introduce chemistry by beginning with its elements. It is better to explain the processes first and only afterwards to introduce chemical elements and the metals. Through your teaching you should evoke the feeling that when dealing with elements, you are only dealing with arrested processes. A picture should emerge of the elements as being processes which have been frozen. If I stand here and it rains tremendously I find myself directly involved in a process. If, however, I look at the cloud above me, this cloud appears as an outer object. If I consider certain processes, it is as though I were involved in them, as for instance, when I am standing in the rain. If I look at sulphur, I am in a similar situation as if I were looking at a cloud above me. Such instances appear like fixed and arrested processes." (21.6.22)

The typical process to which Steiner is referring in this instance is the process of salt formation with all its variations and transformations.

Class 12

A plan for teaching chemistry in the first Class 12 (1923/24) does not exist but there is a significant answer which Steiner gave when asked for advice about the use of chemical formulae (April 24th 1923). Up to this time the teachers had not yet felt it necessary to introduce the terminology of chemical formulae.

"You ought to find out what the examiners expect the pupils to know. The trouble is that we may be forced to make compromises because we must make sure that our pupils can pass examinations. It is really dreadful. If it were possible to apply at least structural formulae, there would be some meaning in it. Most formulae are written only in one plane and are senseless. The processes must be understood. (The usual way of using formulae) is quite senseless; it is sad, but we cannot ignore it." (24.4.23)

A little later, Steiner once more spoke about chemistry in Class 12, after a visit to the education authorities, where he had made enquiries about the conditions of entry for the official examination.

"Now since we know that only subjects taught in the top class are examined, it would be advisable to bring to a close everything else in order to concentrate on what is required by the authorities. To a certain extent we complete our chemistry teaching. Then we must try to pass on to subjects needed for the examination. Very little has been done in geology. Children are slow in getting hold of it. Before the end of this term you could at least awaken some understanding for what geological formations are, how there are different kinds of rocks and fossils. You could give some sort of outline before the holidays and let the children learn the details later. We shall be obliged to limit our subjects. As a preliminary you must try to bring chemistry to a conclusion. Before the holidays, give a summary of geology up to the Ice Age, and afterwards give them an understanding of alcohol, of the functions of alcohol, the concept of ether, the functions of etheric oils, the nature of organic poisons, of alkaloids, and also a concept of cyanic compounds in contrast to the hydrocarbon compounds. You need to bring qualitative relationships.

You can reach a complete understanding by studying the qualitative relationships." (12.7.23)

For the next Class 12 (1924/25) the chemistry syllabus was given on 30th April 1924:

Class 12

"Let us consider chemistry in its closest connection with the human being. The children who are with us already have an understanding of organic and inorganic processes. In Class 12 we must go on to the processes which are not only found in the animal but also in man; we must speak of the formation of ptyalin, pepsin, pancreatic juice, etc. The metal processes in man should be approached in such a way that something of the lead principle in man can be understood by the pupils. You must show that all matter and processes are transformed in man. With regard to the formation of pepsin, it is important to start once more from the formation of hydrochloric acid; consider it as a lifeless substance and the formation of pepsin as something which can only be accomplished within the etheric body, into which even the astral body must work.

There is thus a complete breaking up of the process which subsequently is built up again. Start with the inorganic process of hydrochloric acid, gained from cooking salt or by synthesis, and talk about the qualities of hydrochloric acid. Then try to emphasise the difference between such a process and one that takes place in an organic body. This should culminate in the difference between plant albumen, animal albumen, and human albumen, so that you impart a concept of an evolving albumen, founded in the different structure of the etheric body. Human albumen is somewhat different from animal albumen. You can start with the difference, say between the lion and the cow. In the lion you find a process which is connected more with the circulation than in the case of the cow, where the whole process is linked more to the digestion. The lion even brings about its digestive process with the aid of the breathing process, whilst in the cow the breathing process is geared to the digestion. In this way the processes themselves become alive. There ought to be an inorganic, organic, animal and human chemistry. Here are some examples for pupils. Hydrochloric and acid-pepsin, prunus-spinosa sap and ptyalin. In this way you can bring out what ought to be said. Or, the process of metamorphosis, formic acid – oxalic acid." (30.4.24)

It is surprising to find that in Class 12 one is supposed to distinguish between four different branches of chemistry, after having been told previously not to discriminate between organic and inorganic chemistry (see Class 11). This, however, could be explained by the following considerations:

The antiquated 'traditional' distinction between organic and inorganic chemistry still reminds us of the difference between chemical processes taking place in either inanimate mineral matter or in living substances, but it has been replaced by a purely arbitrary distinction between the chemistry of the carbohydrates and that of all other substances. After first refuting the use of this now senseless term "organic", Steiner gives it a new meaning by placing it next to "mineral", "animal" and "human" chemistry, so that for him the term "organic chemistry" refers to processes, especially the life-giving processes, which are taking place in an organism. The old distinction separated substances found outside an organism from those only found within an organism.

No different outlook is involved. The new distinction is based on the view that processes which occur in the mineral world and which follow a certain pattern, become modified quite specially according to whether they take place in plants, animals, or human organisms.

The curriculum of chemistry presents a very difficult problem. It asks for no less than a completely new revaluation of the present system right to the conceptual grasp of the facts. This becomes even more evident if one considers what Steiner said after having given the curriculum indications quoted above. He was asked whether one should also teach the quantitative side of chemical processes:

"It is indeed extraordinarily difficult to explain these things with the data we are at liberty to use. You would have to start from cosmic rhythms and explain the periodic system. You would have to take this round-about way, which, however, has no place in a school. It is on the whole nonsense to start from the weight of atoms. You would have to explain all the quantitative connections by means of vibrations. There is something like an octave in the relationship of oxygen and hydrogen. That, however, could lead too far. I believe you should develop these concepts which we have already mentioned.

That brings us to the end of the curriculum for Class 12." (30.4.24)

12 Gardening

Classes 6 to 10, each two lessons a week.

Steiner's words from lecture 10 of the Dornach Christmas Course 1921/22 show most clearly what his intentions were with regard to gardening, a subject which originally had not been catered for in the curriculum but which suggested itself through the large and magnificent grounds surrounding the school:

"Although it may seem absurd, it must be stated that a person who has not learned to distinguish an ear of rye from an ear of wheat is no complete human being. It can even be said that a person who has learned to distinguish between rye and wheat without having observed them growing in the fields, has not attained the ideal. As teachers we should avoid going on botanical expeditions to collect specimens to be shown in the classroom. The children themselves should be taken out and wherever possible, be brought to understand the plant world in its actual connection with the earth, with the rays of the sun, with life itself. Through this we can find the transition in a quite naive way to something else which is very important." (27)

After this passage he shows how the teacher can find the

transition from the study of plants to geography. Here we merely wish to point out that especially children living in towns can be led to a right experience of the life and cycle of the plant world through healthy gardening lessons. Therefore the sentences spoken immediately before the last quotation will be added:

"We must try to realise what it means for the evolution of humanity that for a long time past large numbers of people have been drawn into the towns, with the result that generation after generation of young people in the great towns has grown up in such a way that they can no longer distinguish rye from wheat." (27)

Steiner did not formulate a syllabus for gardening and some remarks and answers to questions which can be found in the "Conferences" (*4) do not give an adequate picture of how such a subject should be developed. The first remark, made on the 14th June 1920, was an answer given to the teacher of gardening after he had complained about the laziness and quarrelsomeness of some pupils. (14.6.20)

Then, soon after the opening of the first Class 12, Steiner said in one of the teachers' meetings:

"Gardening till Class 10. The children would like to learn the art of grafting. If they were introduced into the mystery of tree grafting, they would willingly do it." (25.5.23)

This can be looked upon as an indication of how far gardening should be taken and what Steiner expected children of sixteen to be able to do out of their devotion for tending plants. These words also remind us that he gave a similar task to children of the same age for their lessons in First Aid.

In the spring of 1924, during the first teachers' meeting which Steiner led after the Dornach Christmas Conference, school gardening was once more discussed and also the question of how the practical results of gardening lessons could be made use of in botany lessons. At that time the Agricultural Course of Koberwitz had not yet taken place, and this should be borne in mind when reading the next quotation:

"Cow manure! Horse manure is not good. The whole thing must be carried out prudently as far as finance is concerned. Unless there is a proper relationship between the number of cows in the field and the amount of plant growth, the necessary balance will not come about. If there are too many plants in comparison with the amount of cow manure available, conditions will become unhealthy.

You cannot make use of a late product such as peat, for this is unhealthy. Peat will not bring about an increase. Naturally, it depends on how you want to use the plants. In the case of flowers it does not matter so much, but if you use peat as manure for nutritive plants, you will only get an apparent increase, for the nutritive value is not enhanced in this way. Try to realise how you diminish the nutritive value by cultivating shoots in peat. You must try to make the soil suitable for cultivation by mixing a certain amount of humus with it. For this it is still better to use Meier's manures, horn refuse prepared by Alfred Meier. By this means the earth becomes somewhat softer. He makes use of horn refuse. That is really homoeopathic manure.

In the school garden you can plant to fit in with your botany lessons. You can teach the systematic grouping of plants into twelve parts." (5.2.24)

These sentences reveal the most important tasks in gardening viz. looking upon an agricultural centre as an individual and living organism; understanding the true function of manuring as an intrinsic part of nutrition; the application of the homoeopathic principle when dealing with the living earth. The above lines also confirm the rightness of using gardening lessons as part of practical botany. Steiner did not carry out his intention of working out a plant system consisting of twelve groups. This was done later by A. Usteri.

In 1920 Gertrud Michels undertook to work out a proper syllabus for gardening. She took part in the Koberwitz Course and then drafted a curriculum which is given below:

"Gardening should begin in Class 6 when the pupils are twelve years old, when handicrafts are introduced. These two subjects run parallel so that one half of the class can have gardening while the other half is occupied with handicrafts. During the first two years, in Classes 6 and 7, the pupils are mainly occupied with cultivating the ground, with looking after vegetables and flowers. Tasks for Class 8: planning and making a house garden (vegetables, fruit and flowers), tending annual and perennial plants. In Classes 9 and 10: fruit-growing; cultivation and tending of fruit trees and of fruit-bearing shrubs, different ways of grafting and finally improvement of the soil, study of soil and of manuring. This is the end of the gardening syllabus at the conclusion of Class 10." (From: Kolisko, Bilder von der Freien Waldorf Schule, Stuttgart 1926).

Hans Strauss, Gertrud Michel's successor, has also left a draft for a curriculum, which he kindly offered for this publication. He thought it important to use the time of year when children cannot be expected to work in the open air, for practical work under cover and for deepening the experiences gained while they had been working outside in the fields and gardens. With his cooperation the following syllabus was made during the year after the closing of the first Stuttgart Waldorf School in 1938.

Classes 6 to 8

The children are introduced to practical gardening in a simple way and they practise cultivating the soil, tending and harvesting plants. The repetition of this work throughout three years enables them to gain direct insight into the nature of the rotation of crops. When it becomes impossible to work outside during the winter months, work done during the summer is discussed to enable pupils to see how the different stages develop and also how through their own attention and care they have contributed towards a healthy growth and a good harvest. Apart from this, matting is made and other simple tasks are given.

Class 9

The pupils now concentrate on vegetable gardening, helping in the cultivation of shoots and making compost heaps. Tending flowers, fruit-bearing shrubs and trees is also practised. During the winter months the connections between plant growth and sub-soil, weather and astronomical conditions are studied, as well as the origin of the most important cultivated plants, the necessary conditions for their cultivation and the different methods of reproduction.

Class 10

Continuation of work done in Class 9: thinning out of trees and shrubs. During the winter the damaged gardening tools should be repaired and paths made. Finally the teacher should give a careful introduction of manuring which offers opportunities for discussions on the problems of agriculture and stock farming.

13 First Aid

In Class 10, two weeks, each of six lessons in the afternoons.

Steiner's words, spoken before the opening of the first Class 10 in summer 1921, are the only indications I could find on this subject:

"In hygiene, simple bandaging of the kind applied during first aid in accidents should be practised. Let the boys take part. Create a gentle and orderly atmosphere. What matters is not that they consider themselves proficient, but that they should get an idea of these things. One hour a week for six months. You must see that the girls watch the boys when they perform tasks for which they are more gifted by nature and vice versa. The boys should not always be the active ones. They should get into the habit – and this is quite a good thing – of taking an interest. Let them talk a little about which girl displays the greatest skill in her task." (17.6.21)

As may have been noticed, a different number of lessons in First Aid was finally allotted in the time table from what was suggested during this first plan of June 17th 1921. This was due to lack of available time, but the first allowance of lessons should be considered the ideal one.

14 Technology and Lessons Preparing for Life (*6)

| Class 10: | 9 weeks | 4 afternoon |
| Classes 11 and 12: | 3 weeks each | lessons each |

In the first of the three lectures about "Volkspädagogik" (*9) Steiner asks the question of what should be done with a person who has left school and who is about to go into life. He then continues:

"Today we must learn to let people participate in life; and if we organise education so that people are able to participate in life, at the same time setting to work on education economically, you will find that we are really able to help the human being to a living culture. This, too, will enable anyone with a bent towards

handicrafts to take advantage of the education for life that begins about the 14th year,

A possibility must be created for those who in early life show a bent towards handicraft or craftsmanship to be able to participate in what leads to a conception of life. In future, pupils who have not reached their 21st year should never be offered any knowledge that is only the result of scientific research and comes from scientific specialisation alone. In our days only what has been thoroughly worked out and has reached a stage of maturity should have a place in education." (9 lecture 1)

And after speaking about the necessity to work extremely economically, he continues to deal with the question asked at the beginning:

"Human judgment can be cultivated only from and after the 14th year when those things requiring judgment must be introduced into the curriculum. Then all that is related for example, to the grasping of reality through logic can be begun. When in future the carpenter or mechanic sits side by side in school or college with anyone studying to be a teacher, the result will certainly be a specialisation but at the same time one education for all; but included in this one education will be everything necessary for life. If this were not included matters would become socially worse than they are at present. All instruction must give knowledge that is necessary for life. During the ages from 15 to 20 everything to do with agriculture, trade, industry, commerce will have to be learnt. No one should go through these years without acquiring some idea of what takes place in farming, commerce and industry. These subjects will be given a place as branches of knowledge infinitely more necessary than much of the rubbish that constitutes the present curriculum. During these years all those subjects will be introduced which I would call world affairs, historical and geographical subjects, everything concerned with nature knowledge – but all this in relation to the human being, so that man will learn to know man from his knowledge of the world as a whole." (9 lecture 1)

Here is a picture being given of an ideal Waldorf School.

It is not related to the actual Waldorf School which at that time was in the process of becoming. This picture is ideal because it shows a Comprehensive Steiner School (*2) right up to university level, which caters in its upper classes for the future university student as well as for the apprentice, whereas in today's Steiner Schools we may find future university students in the upper classes but practically no apprentices. He continues:

"Now, among the young people who have been educated in this way, there will be those who, driven by the social conditions they meet, will choose to involve themselves in spiritual work, They will receive their training in the various subjects needed for this work in schools specially catering for such students." (9 lecture 1)

Here is a description of a comprehensive Steiner School (Einheitsschule (*2)) for the entire population, a school leading to all professions, especially in its upper part which has two aims: Knowledge of life (Lebenskunde (*6)) and subjects leading towards an individual world philosophy; the latter consisting mainly of subjects which have already been taught in the upper classes of the schools offering a higher education. Lessons preparing for life (Lebenskunde (*6)) have been added by Steiner as a new subject which united man in every way with the social life of modern times. If one added the artistic activities, one could show that with these words the entire range of teaching and pedagogy has been embraced. With this addition to modern schooling of lessons preparing for life (*6) Steiner has accomplished what is needed for the education of today.

In the third lecture we read the same thing:

"From the age of 14 or 15 upwards, when the sentient soul with its delicate vibrations is coming into life, the adolescent must be led directly to all that touches and moves him most vitally in the life of his time, instead of his being plunged back into the most ancient epochs of culture which were founded on quite different social conditions. He should learn to know what is happening in agriculture, what is going on in the world of trade, he should learn about commercial links in the business world. All this the young person should absorb. Imagine how in this way he could face life in quite a different manner and what an independent personality he would become. How he would refuse to have forced upon him what to-day is hailed as the highest achievement of civilisation, whereas in reality it is nothing but deadly decadence." (9 lecture 3).

We find the same attitude in the second lecture on Volkspädagogik (*9):

"I do not hesitate to maintain that anyone who has never worked with his hands, is unable to see truth in a right way and that such a person will never find his right relationship to spiritual life." (9 lecture 2)

In the Practical Course for Teachers Steiner tackled the problem of lessons preparing for life from quite a different angle. At the beginning of lecture 12, after having stressed the importance of the subconscious and the unconscious for the time shortly before puberty, he pointed out that today most people were unable to understand the machines used in their daily surroundings. Then he continued:

"We live in a world produced by human beings, moulded by human thought, of which we make use and which we do not understand in the least. This lack of comprehension for human creation, or for the results of human thought is of great significance for the entire complexion of the human soul and spirit. In fact, people must benumb themselves to escape the realisation of influences from this source. It must always remain a matter of great satisfaction to see people from the may we call them 'better classes' enter a factory and feel thoroughly ill at ease. This is because they experience, like a shaft from their subconsciousness, the realization that they make use of all that is produced in the factory, and yet, as individuals, have not the slightest intimacy with the processes taking place there. And there is at least some pleasure in seeing people who are completely ignorant of the workings of an electric railway, get in and out of it with a slight feeling of discomfort. For this feeling of discomfort is at least the first glimmering of an improvement in attitude. The worst thing is participating in a world made

by human heads and hands without bothering in the least about that world." (12 lecture 12)

A little further on:

"We can only fight against this attitude if we begin our fight as early as the last stage of the elementary school course, if we simply do not let the child of fifteen or sixteen leave school without at least a few elementary notions of the most important functions of the outside world. The child must leave with a craving to know, and insatiable curiosity about everything that goes on around him, and then convert this curiosity, and craving for knowledge into further knowledge. We ought therefore, to use the separate subjects of study towards the end of the school course as a social education of the individual in the most comprehensive sense, just as we employ geography on the lines already described as in a résumé." (ibid)

Through this comparison, geography and lessons preparing for life assume parallel tasks; both are to convey a complete picture of man, geography through the medium of space and lessons preparing for life through social concepts. Steiner then recommended:

"We should not neglect to introduce the child, on a basis of such physical, natural history concepts as we can command, to the workings of at least the factory systems in his neighbourhood. The child should have acquired some general idea at fifteen and sixteen of the way a soap-factory or a spinning mill is run." (ibid)

and after turning towards Herr Emil Molt:

"I think that Herr Molt will agree with me when I say that one could teach the child, in an economical fashion, the entire factory process for preparing cigarettes, from beginning to end, in a few short sentences. Such shortened instructions of certain branches of industry are of the very greatest benefit to children." (ibid)

"If everybody were to keep an exercise book in which to enter notes on soap or on cigarette manufacture, spinning, weaving, etc., it would be a good thing." (ibid)

He then developed this theme a little further, as can be read in the appropriate pages.

So far the lessons preparing for life (*6) as described in "Volkspädagogik" (*9) have been shown for the last classes of the middle school and for the upper school. This however brings us back to what was said in the curriculum lectures about nature study in Class 7:

"In the 7th class we go back to man and try to bring forward what should be taught in connection with food and health. They should try with the ideas you have been able to evoke in physics and chemistry, to build up a comprehensive survey of industrial and economic conditions, transport and the management of a business. All this should arise out of the study of nature in connection with the teaching of chemistry, physics and geography." (16 lecture 2)

and for Class 8:

"Now a comprehensive picture of the conditions of industry and transport related to physics and chemistry should be given." (ibid)

These two passages were quoted in the chapter dealing with geography, where they belong. However, it does seem important to point out how the different lines of development converge here, so that a picture of outer space and a picture of the social development are given just at the moment when the pupil is to leave school to enter into life. This line is being further developed. In Class 9 the physics syllabus is directed entirely towards this study and knowledge of life. In other subjects it remains more in the background but nevertheless one can find in the curriculum a trend towards looking upon the whole world as the stage of man's activity.

In Classes 7 and 8 this preparation for life is given through geography, in Class 9 mainly through physics, but in Class 10 it becomes a subject of its own. Steiner said in his Supplementary Course (lecture 5) after dealing with the development taking place in boys and girls just before the onset of puberty:

"Now it is important that at this stage the children should begin to have an understanding for the practical life that is going on all around them. And now that we are about to start a 10th class, we must make this a matter of our immediate concern. We have, you see, the task of leading the subjective to make its contact with the objective." (26 lecture 5)

A few lines further he continued:

"Now we must introduce into our curriculum subjects that will lead a boy to come to grips with practical life, subjects that will bring him into touch with the external world. This will not be forgotten when we are drawing up our time table for the 10th class; we shall have to approach the matter in the following way. In order to make right provision for the social factor in human life, we must have boys and girls together in class. We will, as we have seen, have to allow for some differentiation between them in their practical activities, but we must not separate them. The boys should see what the girls are doing, even though they do not take part in it; and the girls what the boys are doing. There should be constant social communication between them. But now we have also to take with these older children subjects where the thinking is led away from the head and carried down into the inner mobility of the hand. The action of the hand may however have to be simply learned here by heart as theoretical knowledge. For the children must also be able to acquire a theory of practice. We should accordingly do some mechanics with the boys – not the mere theoretical mechanics that we teach them in the physics lessons, but the first elements of technical mechanics that lead on to the construction of machines. We shall in this way be giving our boys something that is exactly suited to their years. And the girls should learn spinning and weaving. They must acquire skill, and also clear ideas of how spinning and weaving are done, of how a spun or woven substance has come about. If I say: 'This is a piece of material', they must know what that means. They must know that 'material' in this sense is something that has come about by mechanical means. Girls should be introduced to the technical origin of such things; they should find their relationship to the technical processes that lie behind them. This will be the right kind of instruction for a girl of

this age. The boy should also learn the elements of surveying and planning, if only just enough to acquire an elementary understanding of them, A boy ought to be able to draw a field or coppice to scale. And the girls will also need to be taught the first elements of hygiene – practical and theoretical; they should learn something of bandaging, etc.

Both sexes should share in all these lessons. The spinning and weaving, and also the hygiene, will be done by the girls; practical work in these will fall to the boys only later on. And when the boys are manipulating the spirit level, for instance, then it will be the turn of the girls to look on. For this can be done in our school; we can quite well teach the boys to measure differences of level and draw small plans to scale of a given area. In short, we want to awaken the children to an understanding of all that has to take place for life to go on as it does. If we fail to do this, they will be living all the time in surroundings that remain unknown to them." (26 lecture 5)

After speaking about this problem from the aspect expressed in his "Volkspädagogik" (*9) he continued:

"There is a further important point about this knowledge of practical affairs. When a young man takes up surveying as his profession, he begins to study it in his 19th or 20th year at the earliest. There is in our time hardly the opportunity for him to acquire at any younger age the most elementary knowledge of surveying and drawing to scale, or even the use of a measuring rod. But it makes a great difference in after life whether a man has learned something of these things as a boy when about fifteen years old, or only approaches them later when he is about nineteen or twenty. At this later age these subjects will give the impression of something that is quite outside him. When however a beginning is made in the study of them at about fifteen years old, they become entirely one with the human spirit so that they are then the boy's own personal possession, not merely something he has to acquire as part of his professional training. It is the same with the beginnings of mechanics, and also with the subjects I advised for girls." (26 lecture 5)

Curriculum indications

The words above were spoken on 16th June 1921. During the meeting (*4) on the following day the curriculum for Class 10 was made and the aims of the supplementary course were put into concrete terms:

Class 10

"It is essential to teach at least the fundamentals of technical mechanics. These lessons need not take up more time than the language lessons. For technical mechanics we only need one lesson per week, as also for surveying and topographical drawing. For mechanics you should start with the screw – though this is not the usual practice – because technical mechanics has an affinity to matter and density. Dynamics should be taken later. There is plenty of substance for six months, if you go far enough, even without teaching dynamics. Take everything which is connected with the screw. Of course, you must teach the children how to draw the screw, the drill and the worm gear." (17.6.21)

Then Steiner spoke about surveying:

"For surveying it is sufficient if you get as far as the treatment and fixing of the horizontal and if you show quite small distinctive features on the maps: vineyards, grazing land, orchards, so that they get an idea of how this is done."

About spinning he said:

"To begin with, speak of various implements, such as the spinning wheel, the loom, etc., and then introduce simple spinning and weaving. You can only give them a knowledge of the fundamentals, but they only need to know how to thread and on this depends the entire web. You can be content if you achieve any skill within a period of three years – you need to impart to them a thorough knowledge of materials and also the cultural-historical background in the form of stories which will make it palatable for them. Naturally you must become acquainted with the later more complicated methods since the simple elementary ones have gone out of use." (17.6.21)

Then first aid was discussed which, though a separate subject like surveying, also belongs to these lessons preparing for life; and finally applied mechanics:

"Whilst the boys are drawing, let the girls get into the habit of doing exercises on the theoretical side. The strange thing about technical mechanics is that you can do very little in a very long time. All sorts of things can be done in this context. It needs a great deal of time. Nothing has been done yet, but the lessons can be made thoroughly stimulating, otherwise you will not hold the boys. But lessons must be made still more interesting at this age." (17.6.21)

These passages about "Lebenskunde" (*6) for Class 10 give a picture of a social comprehensive school (Einheitsschule (*2)) which really caters for children from every walk of life. Thus two paths of education which previously led to different goals are now united without loss of these goals, because they are set by life itself.

This then gives us the direction towards which the Waldorf School, (i.e., all the Steiner Schools) should move. These thoughts occupied Steiner specially in the Dornach Christmas Course for teachers in 1921/22:

"Directly after the pupil has reached the age when school is no longer compulsory, he must enter into what will prepare him for this or that calling. Things must be brought to him now which no longer proceed entirely from human nature but which have become part of our civilization because they are adapted to this or that profession. Thus the individual must now learn to find his place within a specialised society. In our education we try to prepare for this going out into life by gradually introducing to the young people of 14 or 15 some practical crafts such as spinning and weaving. Having handled the processes of weaving and spinning is not only important for someone who is going to become a weaver or spinner, but of significance for every human being who wishes to have practical ability in life. But what really matters is to introduce the right things at the right time." (27)

This extract comes from lecture 12. In lecture 14 Steiner again speaks about this important matter, starting with a remark about Augustine and about his attitude towards the development of human consciousness:

"Augustine says that man makes himself acquainted with everything that wells up in the evolution of mankind as crafts and skills through the fundamental attributes of his astral body. When we build a house, put together a plough, construct a spinning machine, the relevant forces of the human being are bound up with the astral body. It is actually through his astral body that man learns to know everything in his surroundings which has been brought about by human beings themselves. It is therefore based entirely on a true knowledge of man when, in our teaching, we try to introduce in a practical way to pupils passing through puberty, those aspects of life which are the result of man's activity." (27)

After pointing out what was lacking in our present times in this respect, he again returned to the subjects preparing for life, taught in Waldorf Schools. (*10)

"To arrange the curriculum for just those pupils who are reaching the age of puberty in a way that is as economical as possible from the soul aspect, entails a great deal of care, but it can be done. It can be done by developing in oneself a sense for what matters most in the affairs of life and then bringing this to the boys and girls as economically as possible, so that they learn to know in the simplest way what they are really doing when they receive or make a telephone call, how the tramway with all its associated apparatus functions, and so on. It is only necessary to develop in oneself the faculty to reduce all these things to the simplest possible formulae; then at the appropriate age they can certainly be brought to the pupils in an intelligible way. For we must strive toward the pupils becoming thoroughly acquainted with the meaning of the conditions of life of our civilization. Our chemistry and physics teaching must be prepared in such a way that it has value for just that period of life which precedes puberty. Then when puberty is reached the really practical side of life can be built up on this basis in the most economical way." (27)

One can only fruitfully carry out these indications for the upper classes on the fundamentals already laid in the middle school. One can say that "Lebenskunde" (*6) really embraces the entire education.

After referring to the necessity to distinguish between pupils who intend to take up work of an intellectual nature as their profession and those who intend to go in for more practical types of work, he continued:

"Naturally those pupils whose individual gifts fit them for professions of a more intellectual kind must be educated and taught accordingly. Nevertheless that which in later life tends to evolve in people in a one-sided way must become balanced by development towards a kind of totality, by the development of something quite different. If we bring to the pupils a will impulse which leads in a more spiritual direction than the knowledge impulse this must be so developed that the person has a concrete insight into the practical domains of life for this will enable him to see life as a totality. The astral body demands that when its will impulse is developed in a certain direction, then the knowledge impulse lying within it should

be developed in the opposite direction of life." (27)

A little further:

" The educational problem presenting itself in this sphere is in fact the selection in an economical way of what has to be done at this age." (27)

Once more summarising the problem:

"Here the point is to make the pupil who is turning towards a more spiritual or intellectual profession acquainted as comprehensively as possible with the external, manual things of life; and, on the other hand, to bring to the pupil who is turning towards manual tasks – as far as his power of judgment allows and within certain limits – what is entailed in a spiritual or intellectual profession. It must be emphasized that it should at least be our endeavour to foster this practical side of life through the school itself. Manual aspects of life should not be fostered by placing young people among grown ups in a factory. There should be possibilities available within the sphere of the school for taking the practical side of life into account, so that what the young person has acquired in a short time from the model – figuratively speaking – may be transferred to practical life.

What is acquired from the model can in fact be so practical that the subject in question may readily be carried over into practical life. Nor am I in agreement with the view that, because in our prisons it has been successful to let the prisoners fabricate things which play some role in outside life, things should not be made in the school workshops which could be sold outside.

But so that the young person can remain as long as possible in the school environment, which must certainly be a sound one, we must see to it – for this corresponds with the inner being of man – that the pupil approaches life gradually and is not pushed out into it suddenly." (27)

After some further remarks:

"One does not need to be endowed with any particular ability to adorn a table with a beautiful bunch of flowers, for Nature is responsible for this. But one must possess a certain amount of practical ability to construct even the simplest machine. This ability is there only one does not notice it because one does not direct one's attention in the right way to oneself. And so ability of this kind (as in technical matters) is, for the unconscious kind of person, highly distasteful if the requisite understanding of objective things is not supplied. Through finding our way into the practical things of life we gradually learn to bear with the intellectual ability which is today poured out over the present age as an abstraction." (27)

Leading over to handwork teaching, he continued:

"It is a fact that one can only be brought to understand the tramway, to understand a steam engine, when at the right age one has acquired an understanding for a picture or plastic work of art." (27)

This is a hint of an important point which is elaborated in the chapter on art teaching and aesthetics.

In conclusion an answer of Steiner will be quoted which he gave two years after the introduction of these lessons preparing for life (*6), when he was informed that the pupils had asked for reasons why they should have to learn spinning:

> "It is admirably adapted to their soul life, and by this means they really learn to know practical life. People cannot really know it by merely looking at a thing, but by carrying it out as it is carried out in reality. The children should realise that they can learn how to make a pair of boots in a week, but that it is necessary to be a shoemaker's apprentice for three years." (14.2.23)

Class 11

In summer 1922 technology was further extended for the new Class 11 which at that time was the top class:

> "Then we must be clear that bookbinding and box making are part of the work of this class, as also a knowledge of water wheels and turbines. The manufacture of paper should also be included in lessons on technology. As a matter of fact, there is plenty of work to be found in the study of water wheels, turbines and in the manufacture of paper." (20.6.22)

Bookbinding and box-making (Kartonage) became part of handwork lessons.

On the following day these matters were discussed once more and the curriculum for Class 11 was fixed:

> "Water wheels, turbines and paper manufacture. In my opinion it is essential that the boys take part in all these activities. We cannot tolerate opposition, for this would defeat our purposes." (21.6.22)

When the teacher of technology asked whether he should include weaving after spinning, since he had been unable to teach it in Class 10 because of lack of space for the weaving frames, Steiner answered:

> "The children surely know the principles. It would indeed be good to introduce water turbines and the making of paper. We can come back to weaving later. I said before that this must be learnt by degrees. It will be of great value to the children if we show them how paper is made, how water wheels and turbines function. In this way we widen their outlook. Geography enters here because of the significance of river courses. You can lead over to an elementary study of national economics." (21.6.22)

Class 12

For Class 12 the curriculum had to be given twice:

In 1923:

> "We can only give one lesson on chemical technology as a new subject." (25.4.23)

And in 1924:

> "Technology was taught from Class 10 onward. In Class 10 we planned a course of weaving (which in fact was never given) in which cloths were to be woven in the most simple way possible. It is enough to do this with a model frame. In Class 11 steam-turbines (refer to turbines generally)."

This is Steiner's last passage about technology and "Lebenskunde" (*6). The word "steam turbine" must be looked upon as an error, though it could be possible that he wanted the introduction to the structure and function of the water turbine extended to a short description of the steam turbine. No theme for Class 12 is mentioned. Perhaps it was not taken down in shorthand.

Survey of Indications about "Lebenskunde" (*6)

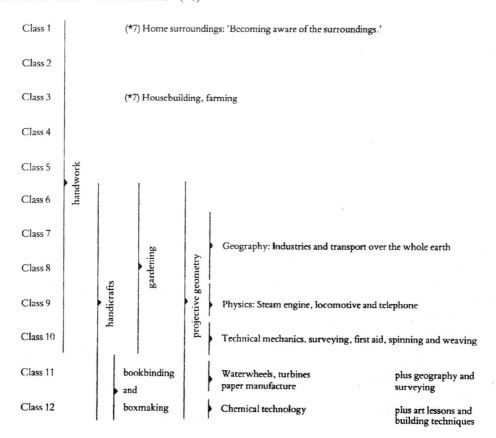

15 Music

Singing in all classes, one lesson per week.

Recorders (taught in classes) and Violins (if enough violinists are available in the class): from Class 1 to 4, each two lessons:

Ensemble playing of suitable children from Classes 5 to 8: 2 lessons a week.

School Orchestra consisting of suitable pupils from Classes 9 to 12: 2 lessons a week.

Mixed Choir of pupils from all classes.

In lecture 1 of the Practical Course, Steiner speaks about the musical forces working through the child before the first dentition. Later, in lecture 3, he gives the first outlines of music teaching for the Waldorf School, which was just about to be opened:

> "The musical element, which lives in the human being from birth onwards, and which – as I have already said –expresses itself particularly in the child's third and fourth years in a gift of dancing, is essentially an element of will, potent with life. But, extraordinary as it may sound, it is true that it contains as it plays its part in the child, an excessive life, a benumbing life, a life directed against consciousness. The child's development is very easily brought by a profoundly musical experience into a certain degree of reduced consciousness. One must say, therefore: The educational value of music must consist in a constant inter-harmonizing of the Dionysian element springing up in the human being, with the Apollonian. While the death-giving element must be vivified by the plastically formative element, a supremely living power in music must be partially subdued and toned down so that it does not affect the human being too profoundly. This is the feeling with which we should introduce music to children," (12 lecture 3)

Steiner wants the so-called unmusical children also to take part in music (class) lessons:

> "... that the unmusical child must be kept apart from all music and only the musical children must be given a musical education, is thoroughly false; even the most unmusical children should be included in any musical activity. It is right without a doubt, from the point of view of producing music more and more, only to encourage the really musical children to appear in public. But even the unmusical children should be there developing sensitiveness, for you will notice that even in the unmusical child there is a trace of the musical disposition which is only very deep down and which loving assistance brings to the surface." (ibid)

Steiner's suggestions for music teaching will be given in chronological order, so far as this appears necessary for the understanding of the curriculum.

In the Basle Course, after some remarks about "artificial" methods of singing instruction, Steiner speaks about the technique of teaching singing:

> "The important thing is that the child should learn to listen; the musical hearing must be trained. The child must above all grow accustomed to hearing rightly and then the tendency to imitate correctly what it has heard must be aroused. There again the best method for the teacher is to lead the singing with a certain love, and then go into the points which are at fault. In this way the pupil develops his natural need to imitate what he has heard and he learns from his teacher's corrections. But as regards singing itself, the child should adjust its organs instinctively." (23 lecture 10)

and after speaking once more about the "artificial" methods, he said:

> "At any rate these artificial methods must not enter the school room. Above all, the natural relation must prevail between the teacher and the learner, between the educator and the one who is educated. The loving devotion of the child to its teacher must replace artificial adjustments and methods. It is here that what is imponderable must be the basis of things. Nothing is more fatal than when these 'music uncles' and 'music aunts' gain entrance to schools, with their methods. In school the spirit must prevail and not the outward form. This spirit can only be there when one is right in the subject oneself, not when one brings it to the children by outward methods." (23 lecture 10)

In the fourth lecture of "Meditatively Acquired Knowledge of Man", which contains some puzzling sentences, the theme of the quotation from lecture 3 of the Practical Course – the harmonising of the Dionysian and Apollonian streams – is taken up again:

> "that an element of will expresses itself from within in opposition to an element of will coming from without."

> "These forces that are of a musical nature derive more from the outer world, the extra-human world, from the observations of processes in nature, particularly from the observations of their regularities and irregularities. For everything, after all, that takes place in nature is permeated by a mysterious music: the earthly projection of the music of the spheres. In every plant, in every animal, there is really incorporated a tone of the music of the spheres. That is also the case still with regard to the human body, but it no longer lives in what is human speech – that is, not any more in the expressions of the soul – but it does live in the body, in its forms and so forth. All this the child absorbs unconsciously, and that is why children are musical to such a high degree. They absorb all this into their organism. While that which the child experiences as the form of movements, lines and contours and sculptural elements in his surrounding works from within, from the head, all that is absorbed by the child as tone-formation, as speech-content, comes to him from without. And this again, i.e., what comes from without, is opposed – only somewhat later: around the 14th year – by the spiritual element of music and speech that is gradually developing from within. It is dammed up again now, in the woman in the whole organism and in the man more in the region of the larynx where it brings about the change of voice. The whole process, then, is brought about by the fact that here an element of will expresses itself from within in opposition to an element of will coming from

*without, and in this struggle there comes to expression
that which at puberty appears as the change of voice.
This is a struggle between both inner and outer forces
of music and speech." (25)*

However, these sentences only convey one principal theme
from the second of the four lectures. This lecture needs to
be read in its entirety, even though it does not merely deal
with music. The passage from the Practical Course (Lecture 3) also belongs to this wider aspect.

In the Supplementary Course 1921 the same problem is discussed but this time Steiner takes it beyond the realm of
music. Again he speaks about a struggle, about "defending
oneself", about "impressing" and "adapting oneself":

*"Looking at man in his totality, we find him an extraordinarily complicated being – this 'man' that we teachers set out to understand! Take the process I have just
been explaining. When you teach a child eurythmy, the
child's physical body is brought into movement, and the
movements are carried over into the ether body. Although, to begin with, astral body and ego put up a
resistance, they also have to receive an impress of the
activities that are taking place in the physical and ether
bodies. Then comes sleep. Astral body and ego go out
of the physical body and bring this impress into contact
with quite other – spiritual – forces. In the morning
they come back again and what they bring with them
bears evidence of a marvellous concord between what
has been received from the spiritual world during sleep,
and what was experienced the day before by physical
and ether bodies when the child was doing eurythmy.
We gave the child certain experiences – we might say,
in preparation. The way these experiences turn out to
harmonize with the spiritual experiences which he undergoes afterwards during sleep, can reveal to us what
eurythmy really does for the child. When we find the
result next morning, then – and not until then – are we
able to appreciate the wonderfully health-giving power
that is latent in eurythmy. If we give the child eurythmy
in the right way it is actually so that when he wakes up
next morning and enters his body, he carries down into
it spiritual substance. A similar process takes place with
singing. In this case the activity developed by the child
is essentially an activity of the ether body. The astral
body has then to do its best to adapt itself to receive
this activity. In spite of resisting at first, it does receive
it, and carries it over into the spiritual world. When the
astral body returns next morning, you have again clear
proof that a health-giving power has been at work. It
can furthermore be observed that the health-giving influence of eurythmy works directly upon the bodily
well-being of the child, whereas in singing we have an
influence that works rather on the whole system of movement in the child and only thence back upon the health
of the physical body." (26 lecture 3)*

These last three passages elucidate each other. In the same
Supplementary Course we find another remark, which indicates important possibilities for the further development
of Steiner Schools.

*"Then again in all the lessons that have to do with music
it will be good if there too you bring with you a clear*

*idea of the dispositions of the children in respect of
imagination – whether they have very little, or a great
deal, and how this works over into their memory. Where
a child is poor in imagination and finds great difficulty
in recalling his ideas, we should turn his attention more
especially to instrumental music; whereas a child who
is rich in imagination and who is easily tormented by
his ideas, perhaps even to an extreme degree, such a
child we should rather occupy with singing. The ideal
plan would be, if only we had the necessary space, to
have music lessons and singing lessons going on at the
same time.*

*A wonderfully harmonising effect is also produced in
the children by the interworking of the two experiences
of listening to music and making music; and it would
perhaps even be possible to arrange for the children to
have the two experiences in turn, one after the other.
We could for instance, let one half of the class sing while
the other listened, and then the other way round. It would
be well worth while if a lesson could sometime be arranged in that way. For the listening to the singing has
a specifically healing influence upon the part that the
head has to take in the organism; whilst the singing
itself has a corresponding healing influence upon what
the body has to do for the head. Really, you know, we
would have a far healthier humanity if we could do all
that we should in education!" (26 lecture 4)*

The Dornach Christmas Course of 1921/22 shows how the
experience of the musical forces changes with the different
stages of the child's development and how what at first is
done quite instinctively gradually moves into the sphere of
consciousness:

*"A baby is an entirely unconscious sense organ. He
forms himself by inwardly imitating what he takes in
from the people in his environment. But these inner pictures are not pictures only, they are at the same time
forces which inwardly work upon the organisation of
the child in a material, plastic way. Then, with the
change of teeth, these imitative forces pass over into
the system of movement, into the rhythmic system; here
only do they wish to enter. Certainly some of the plastic
moulding element still remains behind, but added to it
is the other element which previously was not present
to the same degree. The whole way in which a child is
related particularly to rhythm and beat is different before and after the change of teeth. Previously rhythm
and beat were also something which the child imitated,
but which became transformed into a plastic moulding.
Afterwards it became transformed into an inner musical element.*

*Only between his ninth and twelfth year does the child
acquire an understanding for rhythm and beat as such,
for melody as such. Now he is no longer so strongly
impelled to form himself inwardly in accordance with
rhythm and beat; he grasps these as such, as actualities existing outside himself. Previously the child experienced rhythm and beat; afterwards he begins to develop the understanding, the faculty to comprehend what
they are. This phase which is affected not only by the
musical sphere but by everything in the world, lasts until*

towards twelve years old. At this age, even somewhat earlier, the child first begins to develop the faculty of leading over the fantasy-imbued experience of what is musical – rhythm, beat – into what is purely of the nature of thought.

In everything that is perceived with the eye of the soul, the interworking of the bodily-physical can also be beheld. I have already spoken of how the child, informing his muscles and bones, copies what is inwardly present within him. Now, towards the twelfth year, the child no longer wishes to live only in rhythm and beat but rather to let the feeling of rhythm and beat flow over into what is of the nature of abstract thought just as at this time he gradually strengthens ever more and more that part of the muscles which passes over into mere sinew. Before this time all movement is directed towards the muscles as such, now it is directed into what flows over from the muscles into the sinews. Everything which takes its course in the soul-spiritual is to be found again in the bodily-physical. And this concentration into the life of the sinews in their connecting of muscles and bones is the external physical expression of the passing over of the purely feeling-experience of rhythm and beat into what is now logical and no longer rhythm and beat. The knowledge thus won from the study of man must now be brought together with the art of education and teaching." (27)

In the two lectures about music, held in 1923, Steiner goes into details about the tasks of the music teacher, after having given an historical account of the development of music:

"All these facts are of the utmost importance when we face the task of directing human development in regard to music.

For just observe that the child, up to about the ninth year, even though we are able to bring to it the major and minor modes, has not yet any proper apprehension of major and minor. When a child enters school it can be prepared for a subsequent perception of the major and minor modes; but the child has in the beginning neither the one nor the other; it actually lives, little as one may desire to concede the fact, in the feeling of the 5th interval. Pieces containing 3rds can naturally be used for teaching purposes. But if we wish to touch the essential child nature, we must cultivate its musical understanding by starting with the relations of the 5th interval. This is the important point; you will always confer a great benefit upon the child by helping it to appreciate the major and minor modes and especially to experience the relation of the 3rds, at the age which has been elsewhere indicated as occurring after the ninth year, a time when the child begins to ask serious questions. One of the serious problems is the urge to go through the experience of the major and minor 3rds. That is an event which occurs around the ninth and tenth years and which should receive special attention. As far as possible, in view of existing musical conditions, we must endeavour, about the twelfth year to cultivate the octave understanding. Thus again, what will be suitable for this age must be brought to the child from this side of education." (31 lecture 1)

In his second lecture about music, Steiner once more speaks about the development of mankind's musical experience and then he looks at music from the point of view of man's threefoldness.

Again he returns to pedagogy:

"At this point you will find it understandable in the first place when dealing with a child who is going to school, that you are more apt to find in the child a comprehension of melody than a comprehension of harmony. Naturally this must not be taken pedantically. Pedantry is not allowed to play a part in matters of art. It is of course possible to bring all sorts of things to a child's attention. But just as a child during its first school years should only comprehend 5ths, possibly 4ths, but not 3rds (these it only begins to understand inwardly from the ninth year of its life onward) so it should grasp the element of melody readily; it only begins to grasp the element of harmony from the ninth year on. Of course the child understands tone already, but the harmony connected with it can only he cultivated from that age on. But rhythm assumes the most varied forms. The child will comprehend a certain inner rhythm while it is still very young, but apart from the kind of rhythm thus experienced instinctively, a child should not be bothered with rhythm as it appears for instance in instrumental music until it is nine years old. That is the age to draw a child's attention to these things. In musical matters also it is quite possible to gather from the child's age what should be done. Approximately the same life-stages will be discovered there as are to be found in the theory and practice of teaching of the Waldorf School." (31 lecture 2)

The Dornach Easter Course of 1923 deals with the great change between the ninth and tenth year and how this becomes manifest especially in the musical experience and will-life of the child. In lecture 3 we read:

"All the child's forces, now that he has passed through the change of teeth, strive towards what is inwardly plastic and pictorial. And we support this picture-forming element, when we ourselves, in everything we impart to the child, approach him in a pictorial way. For between the 9th and 10th years something remarkable happens. Now, much more than formerly, the child feels the need to be gripped by what is musical, to be gripped by rhythms. When we observe how the child takes in music up to this stage of life between the 9th and 10th years – how what is musical also lives in the child as something essentially plastic, and how this plasticity naturally becomes an inner formative force of the body, passing over extraordinarily easily into what is dance-like, into movement – then we must recognise how the inner grasping of music as such comes into being only between the 9th and 10th year. This will be quite clearly apparent. Of course, these things are not clearly separated from each other; and those who have insight into them will also foster the musical element before the 9th year, but in the right way – tending more in the direction which I have just characterized. For the child between 9 and 10 would get a shock if the musical element were suddenly to take hold of him, before he was inwardly ready and accustomed to being gripped in this strong way." (34)

In the eleventh lecture of the Ilkley Course of 1923 we read about the importance of music teaching as a means of educating the child's will:

"By beginning musical instruction with song, but leading on more and more to instrumental playing, we develop the element of will in the human being. This musical instruction is not only a means of unfolding his artistic qualities, but also his purely human qualities, especially those of the heart and will. We must of course start with song but pass on as soon as possible to an understanding of instrumental music, in order that the child may learn to distinguish the pure elements of music – rhythm, measure, melody – from everything else, from imitative or pictorial qualities of music and the like. More and more he must begin to realise and experience the purely musical element. By leading the child into the sphere of art, by building a bridge from play to life through art, we can begin, between the eleventh and twelfth year – and that is the proper time – to teach him to understand art. In the principles of education which it is the aim of the Waldorf School to fulfil, it is of vital importance for the child to acquire some understanding of art at the right age." (35 lecture 11)

He then speaks about the tasks of art lessons (in Germany music belongs to the art subjects) during the time in which the natural sciences and technical knowledge with their logical and causal structure have to be taught:

"At the age when the child must realize that nature is ruled by abstract law to be grasped by the reason, when he must learn in physics the link between cause and effect in given cases, we must promote an understanding of art as a necessary counterbalance. The child must realize how the several arts have developed in the different epochs of human history, how this or that motif in art plays its part in a particular epoch. Only so will those elements which a human being needs for an all-round unfolding of his being be truly stimulated. In this way, too, we can unfold the qualities which are essential in moral instruction." (ibid)

In the Arnheim Course of 1924, after having dealt with music in the world and in man, Steiner spoke about the importance of instrumental music in education:

"And just as man experiences what belong to the realm of music, so the forms of his body are plastically shaped out of music itself. Therefore if the teacher wishes to be a good music teacher he will make a point of taking singing with the children at the very beginning of their school life. This is essential; he must understand as an actual matter of fact that singing induces emancipation, for the astral body has previously sung and has brought forth the forms of the human body, Now, between the change of teeth and puberty the astral body frees itself, becomes emancipated. And out of the very essence of music there emerges what forms the human being and makes him independent. It is therefore in no way surprising if a teacher who understands these things introduces as a matter of course into the singing lessons and also into the teaching of instrumental music what by its very nature is human through and through. This is why we try not only to introduce singing as early as possible in the education of the child, but also we let those children with sufficient aptitude learn to play a musical instrument, so that the child has the possibility of actually grasping and entering into the musical element which lives in his form as it frees and emancipates itself." (39)

In the Torquay Course, Steiner gave details about the first singing and instrumental lessons:

"Our nerves are really a kind of lyre, a musical instrument, an inner musical instrument, that resounds up into the head. This process begins of course before the change of teeth, but at the time the astral body is only loosely connected with the physical body. It is between the change of teeth and puberty that the astral body really begins to play upon the single nerve fibres with the in-breathed air, like a violin bow on the strings. You will be fostering all this if you give the child plenty of singing. You must have a feeling that the child is a musical instrument while he is singing, you must stand before your class to whom you are teaching singing or music with a clear feeling: every child is a musical instrument and inwardly feels a kind of well-being in the sound. For you see sound is brought about by the particular way the breath is circulated. That is inner music. To begin with, in the first seven years of life, the child learns everything by imitation, but now he should learn to sing out of the inward joy he experiences in building up melodies and rhythms. To show you the kind of inner picture you should have in your mind when you stand before your class in a singing lesson, I should like to use a comparison which may seem a little crude but which will make clear to you what I mean." (40 lecture 6)

... now follows the comparison with a herd of cows which are digesting and with what they are inwardly experiencing...

"... but I want to show that there is something that should really be present in the child at a higher stage, this feeling of well-being at the inward flow of sound. Imagine what would happen if the violin could feel what is going on within it! We only listen to the violin, it is outside us, we are ignorant of the whole origin of the sound and only hear the outward sense picture of it. But if the violin could feel how each string vibrates with the next one it would have the most blissful experiences, provided of course that the music is good. So you must let the child have these little experiences of ecstasy, so that you really call forth a feeling for music in his whole organism, and you must yourself find joy in it.

Of course one must understand something of music. But an essential part of teaching is this artistic element of which I have just spoken. On this account it is essential, for the inner processes of life between the change of teeth and puberty demand it, to give the children lessons in music right from the very beginning, and at first, as far as possible to accustom them to sing little songs quite empirically without any kind of theory: nothing more than simply singing little songs, but they must be well sung! Then you can use simpler songs from which the children can gradually learn what melody, rhythm and beat are, and so on; but first you must accustom the children to sing little songs as a whole, and to play a little, too, as far as that is possible. Unless there is clearly no bent at all in this direction every Waldorf child begins to learn some instrument on entering school; as I say as far as circumstances allow, each child should learn to play an instrument. As early as possible the children should come to feel what it means for their own musical being to flow over into the objective instrument, for which purpose the piano, which should really only be a kind of memorising instrument, is of course, the worst possible thing for a child.

Another kind of instrument should be chosen, and if possible one that can be blown upon. Here one must of course have a great deal of artistic tact, and I was going to say, a great deal of authority too. If you can, you should choose a wind instrument, as the children will learn most from this and will thereby gradually come to understand music. Admittedly, it can be a hair-raising experience when the children begin to blow. But on the other hand it is a wonderful thing in a child's life when this whole configuration of the air, which otherwise he encloses and holds within him along the nerve fibres, can now be extended and guided. The human being feels how this whole organism is being enlarged. Processes which are otherwise only within the organism are carried over into the outside world. A similar thing happens when the child learns the violin, when the actual processes, the music that is within him, is directly carried over and he feels how the music in him passes over into the strings through his bow.

But remember, you should begin giving these Music and Singing lessons as early as possible. For it is of very great importance that you not only make all your teaching artistic, but that you also begin teaching the more specifically artistic subjects, Painting, Modelling and Music, as soon as the child comes to school, and that you see to it that he really comes to possess all these things as an inward treasure." (ibid)

After these general remarks about man's relationship to music and after a broad outline of music teaching, we now come to Steiner's indications for each individual class.

First a remark found in the first curriculum lecture of 1919 about the place of music teaching within the entire school, especially with regard to speech in Class 1. After speaking about language teaching he continued:

"This would be supported by what we are going to discuss; elasticity and flexibility for his speech organs will be gained in the singing lessons, and a finer sensibility for long and short sounds will arise by itself. It is not necessary to plan to bring this about through music, provided the child is introduced to the music given out by the instrument in a way that stimulates his 'hearing understanding'. To begin with this must be a simple 'super-hearing' way, if I may coin such an expression, since one cannot say, 'lucid clear' (übersichtlich). What I mean will be understood: super hearing (überhörlich) is what is inwardly experienced as one amid the many; not taking things into us pell-mell." (16 lecture 1)

The next quotation also mainly concerns the music teacher of Class 1:

"We must above all realise how music must first be taken from what is most elementary and simple in the first class, making a transition to what is more complicated somewhere about the third year, so that the child acquires, little by little, by the study of an instrument (more particularly by instrumental playing but also by singing) just that which is formative, just what forms his capacities. Gymnastics and eurythmy will be brought out of all the rest: these must be developed from music and all the other artistic activities." (16 lecture 2)

Curriculum indications

The actual music syllabus for the first eight years is found at the beginning of the third lecture. It is headed by a remark, which will be quoted first, of how these ideas are to be considered:

"In the same way as it is only possible to give general indications for the plastic arts, so one can only give general indications for the musical. The details naturally must be left to the freedom of the teacher. Therefore I would beg you to regard these general indications as linking up all that is essential for the teaching of music." (16 lecture 3)

Classes 1-3

"In the first, second and third classes, you are dealing essentially with simple musical measures, and here the aim should be so to utilise the musical material that it acts formatively on the growing human being. Therefore everything musical should be directed in such a way that it brings about in the human being a proper development of all that is connected with the voice, tone, ear training." (16 lecture 3)

Classes 4-6

"Then come the 4th, 5th and 6th classes. By this time you will have got on well with explanations of the signs and the notes and will be able to make comprehensive exercises with scales. In the 5th and 6th class the different keys can be introduced – you can bring in D major etc.

You wait as long as possible with the minor but it can be introduced somewhere about now. But all that is really essential is this: that you begin to work in the opposite direction. Now the child's attention will he directed to the claims of music, therefore the lesson will be directed more towards the aesthetic aspect. Previously 'the child' was the chief thing, and everything was done to get him to learn to sing and hear. Now that the child has passed through the first three classes where he himself was the first consideration, he must conform to the demands of music as an art. That is the main consideration from the educational point of view." (ibid)

Classes 7-8

"And in the last two years, the 7th and 8th, I ask you to note that the child should no longer feel 'drilled' but should already have the feeling that he studies music because it gives him pleasure, because he likes to enjoy

it as an end in itself. It is towards this that the so-called music lesson should work; thus in these two years the forming of musical judgment can be practised.

The particular nature of different musical works of art can be brought out and the different style of a piece by Beethoven or of Brahms can be brought to exercise musical consciousness. Through simple forms the child should be brought to exercise musical judgment. Before this all musical discrimination should be kept back, but now it may be fostered.

It will now be quite especially important that a certain understanding is evolved. You know I gave just the same indications this morning for the plastic arts. I said, first we use drawing in such a way that writing proceeds from it, then later develop drawing for its own sake. The whole point is that it becomes an art at the moment when the child makes the transition from utility forms in painting and drawing to free artistic forms. At that moment (between the 3rd and 4th school year) the transition must also be made in music, as I have shown. First work so that it bears on the psychological development of the child, then work so that the child must adapt itself to the musical art. These transitions should correspond to each other in drawing, painting and music." (16)

It is remarkable that Steiner encouraged musical judgment before the time of puberty, whereas in all other subjects he asked us not to let pupils make judgments until after puberty. This exception should be seen together with another specific feature of music which is described in the second lecture on music:

"The element which occupies the middle position in music today... is harmony. Harmony stirs human feeling directly... Feeling itself is that which occupies the middle position in the sum-total of human experience. On the one side feeling flows out into will and on the other it flows out into the world of ideas. Thus, observing the human being we can say that in the middle we have feeling; on the one side we have feeling flowing out into ideation; on the other side we have feeling flowing out into willing. Harmony affects feeling directly. Harmony is experienced by the feelings. But our feeling nature as a whole is twofold. We have one kind of feeling which tends more towards the world of ideas; for example, in as far as we feel our thoughts, our feeling tends towards ideas. And we have a feeling that tends towards willing. In respect of a deed we feel whether it pleases or displeases us just as in respect of an idea we feel whether it pleases or displeases us. Feeling really falls apart into two fields in the middle. The peculiarity of musical experience is such that it is neither allowed to ascend, on the one hand, completely into ideation – for a musical experience that might be grasped by means of ideas, by the brain, would instantly cease to be something musical – nor on the other hand to descend utterly into the realm of willing... It must be arrested in both directions. The experience of music must start in the realm lying between ideation and will; it must entirely take place in that part of the human being which actually does not belong to his ordinary consciousness,

but which has something to do with that which comes down from spiritual worlds, embodies itself and again undergoes death." (31 lecture 2)

He then showed that melody guides the musical element out of the realm of feeling into that of imagining (vorstellen) without itself becoming part of imagery (Vorstellung); and that rhythm carries the musical element into man's willing which does not spread outward into the surroundings.

Seen in this context, music lives in a realm of unearthly happenings, in which the forming of judgments also occupies a different position from the other "down to earth" happenings.

The upper classes (9-12)

Suggestions for the upper classes will now be given. However, since we are dealing with a somewhat exceptional subject, it appears better not to split up the actual syllabus items contained in Steiner's remarks, in order to retain a chronological account of how the musical life was developed in the school. This account is taken from the "Conferences" (*4) shorthand notes.

On September 25th 1919, a few weeks after the opening of the school, the music teacher, Paul Baumann wished to teach musically gifted children in special choir practices, where more complicated pieces could be rehearsed. Steiner replied:

"It would not be at variance with the whole constitution of our school if choirs were put together gradually out of the four upper classes (5-8) and out of the four lower classes (1-4), perhaps for Sunday choirs. Through a thing of this kind you can weld the children together better than by other means. But on no account encourage false ambitions, for this must be excluded from our methods of teaching. Ambitions should exist only in relation to subjects, but not to persons. Keep the singers from the four upper classes separate from those of the four lower classes because their voices are different. Otherwise this subject need not be taught in separate classes. Treat the groups, composed from different classes, as one class. However, in music, too, we must strictly adhere to what has been pointed out regarding the different ages. This ought to be strictly observed. But in our choirs, which we might possibly use for our school activities on Sundays, we can put together the four older and the four younger classes. We must strictly observe the period round the 9th year and the period round the 12th year according to their special positions." (25.9.19)

When the curriculum of the first Class 9 was made Steiner said, after the necessity for a large room for music making had been pointed out:

"The music teaching cannot be as it should be, until we have the large room. We are concerned with two things that matter. We must give as perfect a form as possible to our music teaching. If we want to give our children a preparatory musical education, our instruments cannot be good enough for our pupils. Their ear will be spoilt if they hear bad instruments. These are important aspects of your work. We could well develop further the singing of old 'church songs'." (22.9.20)

The "two things that matter" obviously refer to a suitable room for the lessons and to excellent instruments.

The music teacher:

"I wished to draw attention to the major and minor modes and to their quality of tone (timbre) only from the point of view of sound."

Class 9

"This should be the very subject for Class 9. You should endeavour to bring it at all costs. You can treat this theme a little theoretically but you must also appeal to the musical experience of major and minor through the feeling." (22.9.20)

The music teacher continued:

"In lessons of social behaviour (Anstandsunterricht) (which had been given to him as a special task), I have related this polarity to the male and female element. Then the children appeared to be interested."

Steiner:

"I think it would be a good thing to link this polarity to singing, to relate it to male and female voices. Little has been tried out in this direction, and it is certain that such teaching, calling attention to the varying compass of the male and female voices would at this age be an exceptionally good counteraction to the false feeling of sex which is appearing too strongly today. That would have a beneficial effect. It grieves me that we cannot make any progress with regard to the handling of instruments. That is irreparable. Private instrumental lessons are private lessons. Here we should see to it that, as we have already explained, instrumental lessons are part of the whole education. A private lesson makes no contribution towards this. It is indeed a pity that we cannot change it. I fear it will be a very long time before we can alter the circumstances." (22.9.20)

On January 16th 1921, when the different teachers gave reports of their work to Steiner, he said to the music teacher:

"The use of two-part songs for little children can hardly be recommended. That should not be begun until the fifth class. I should keep to unison principally with children up to ten years old. Is there a possibility of letting the children sing alone what they have sung in chorus?" (16.1.21)

When the music teacher agreed:

"That is also something we must consider. I mean that you must not omit letting the children sing solos apart from their singing in chorus. Especially when they speak in chorus you will find that the Group soul makes itself felt. Some speak very well in chorus but when you call them out individually you get nothing. They should be able to do individually what they can do in chorus, especially in speech. What happens in the class in this way during singing lessons depends on what you consider right." (16.1.21)

During a teacher's meeting in May 1921, towards the end of the second year, the question was asked whether pupils who intended to go in for a full musical training should be excused from lessons which might affect their manual skill. Steiner said:

"We could individualize the time-table with this in view. That certainly could be done. We should also have to think of having special rooms for practising. They would have to attend the lessons which belong to general education. Otherwise we can specialize." (26.5.21)

Class 10

When the curriculum for Class 10 was made in the first meeting of the school's third year Steiner said:

"Continue with instrumental music in Class 10."

The music teacher: *"We ought to do this earlier."*

Steiner: *"Above all in Class 10."*

The music teacher informed the meeting of his intention to organise a little class-orchestra with the pupils who could play an instrument, mentioning that most of them could be included. Steiner said:

"Those who are unable to join should nevertheless take part in the lessons. One should make sure that they get some kind of understanding for what is going on." (17.6.21)

The music teacher then developed his further plans to take Classes 8, 9 and 10 together in singing and only to teach theory of music, (which begins in Class 9) to separate classes. Steiner said:

"We should do some harmony. With the 10th class harmony referring to counterpoint, so that they have a longing to write something themselves. Do not force anything, let it come out of themselves, but do not force it." (17.6.21)

Class 11

On June 20th 1922 the curriculum was fixed for the first Class 11. Steiner said about music:

"In Class 11 solo singing. Lead over to music appreciation." (22.6.22)

The same thought was expressed, though in other words, on the following day:

"In eurythmy and music lessons it is obvious that you must consider at this age how to lead over to the cultivation of taste. This can be done by making use of what has already been learnt. You do not need to take much that is new in content, but develop good musical judgment and taste." (21.6.22)

Class 12

"The main task for this class is to enable the pupils to become aware, out of their own musical experience, what distinguishes Bach's style from that of other composers." (25.4.23)

In 1924 music for Class 12 was not discussed.

A conversation held on September 18th 1923 and quoted below rounds off this chapter about the place of music in the Steiner Schools. The music teacher asked Steiner to show him how to handle rhythms which were used differently in music and eurythmy. He asked whether only the 2-, 3-, and 4-beat rhythms were important or whether other rhythms,

tory subject from the day of the school's foundation.

In the first of a series of lectures given only a few months before the opening of the Waldorf School, when speaking about physical culture, Steiner said:

"What is taught the growing human being as mere physical gymnastics we want to replace by an ensouled physical culture." (9 lecture 1)

On the subject of will training he said:

"Even in these early years it will be a question of cultivating the will. For this purpose we must bring into play exercises of a bodily nature and artistic activity. In this respect a quite new approach will have to be made. A beginning has been made in the type of movement we call eurythmy.

You can see much cultivation of bodily movement which is in a state of decadence: but many people like it. In this situation we want to introduce something which, if given to the growing human being instead of what has been customary hitherto as bodily exercise, is an ensouled physical (body) culture.

Now this is capable of cultivating the kind of will power which will stay with a person throughout life, whilst all other ways of cultivating the will have a peculiarity of being weakened by the various events and experiences of life." (9 lecture 1)

When the Waldorf School was opened in the autumn of 1919, for quite external reasons only the eurythmy lessons could be introduced; gymnastics were added several years later.

On account of the close relationship between both forms of movement, it was necessary for Steiner again and again to speak about the differences between them and their mutual relationship. He did this for the first time in the Practical Course for Teachers which contains an important reference to the significance of eurythmy for the child before the change of teeth.

"It is a fact that the individual is born into the world with the desire to bring his own body into a musical rhythm, into a musical relationship with the world, and this inner musical capacity is most active in children in their third and fourth years. Parents can do an enormous amount if they only take care to build less on externally induced music than on the inducement of the whole body, the dancing element. And precisely in this third and fourth year infinite results could be achieved by the permeation of the child's body with an elementary eurythmy. If parents would learn to engage in eurythmy with the child, children would be quite different from what they are. They would overcome a certain heaviness which weighs down their limbs." (12 lecture 1)

In the fourth lecture of the same course the following quotation occurs on the quality of listening:

"Our listening, particularly to verbs, is in reality always a participation. The most spiritual part of man, in fact, participates, but merely as 'tendency'. But only in eurythmy is it fully expressed. Eurythmy gives, besides all else, a form of listening. When someone tells a tale, the listener all the time participates with his ego in the
physical life behind the sounds, but suppresses it. The ego performs a constant eurythmy, and the eurythmy expressed in the physical body is only listening made visible. So you are always engaged in eurythmy when you listen, and when you are actually performing eurythmy you are only making visible what you leave invisible when you listen. The manifestation of the activity of the listener is, in fact, eurythmy. People will learn from eurythmy to listen rightly... A kind of healing or restoration of the soul's being must take place again. Consequently, it will be particularly important to add the hygiene of the soul to all the materialistic hygienic tendencies of gymnastic training and to all that is exclusively concerned with the physiology and the functions of the body. This can be achieved by having alternate gymnastics and eurythmy. Then, even if eurythmy in the first place is art, the hygienic element in it will be of particular benefit, for people will not only learn something artistic in eurythmy, but they will learn for the soul what they learn for the body in gymnastics, and, moreover, there will result a very beautiful interplay of these two forms of expression." (12 lecture 4)

In the "Study of Man" in connection with the threefold nature of man, considering the apparent stillness of a person riding in a train, Steiner says:

"Thus the head brings to rest in you what the limbs perform in the world by way of movements. And the breast system stands betwixt them. It mediates between the movement of the outer world and what the head brings into rest.

Now, as men, our purpose is to imitate, to absorb the movement of the world into ourselves through our limbs. What do we do then? We dance. This is true dancing. Other dancing is only fragmentary dancing. All true dancing has arisen from imitating in the limbs the movement carried out by the planets, by other heavenly bodies or by the earth itself.

But now, what part do our head and breast play in this dancing, this imitation of cosmic movement in the movement of our limbs? The movements we perform in the world are stemmed or stopped, as it were, in the head and in the breast. The movements cannot continue through the breast into the head, for the head, lazy fellow, rests on the shoulders and does not let the movements reach the soul. The soul must participate in the movements while at rest, because the head rests on the shoulders. What then does the soul do? It begins to reflect from within itself the dancing movements of the limbs. When the limbs execute irregular movements it begins to whisper; when the limbs carry out the harmonious cosmic movements of the universe, it even begins to sing. Thus the outward dancing movement is changed into song and into music within." (11 lecture 10)

The text says "outward" and "within"; this quite confuses the meaning. It is a question of transforming outer dancing into an inner activity, a singing and making music within the soul. This is made clear in the following sentences:

"...man's external movements are brought to rest in the soul, and through this begin to pass over into tones. The same is also true with regard to all other sense

expressions. As the organs of the head do not take part in the outer movements, they ray these outer movements back into the breast, and make them into sounds and into the other sense impressions." (11 lecture 10)

An important remark on movements which either have meaning or are meaningless, is made in lecture 13 of the Study of Man:

"Thus it is not a question of whether man is active or not, for a lazy man too is active, but the question is how far man's actions have a purpose in them. To be active with a purpose – these words must sink into our minds if we would be teachers. Now when is a man active without purpose? He is active without purpose, senselessly active, when he acts only in accordance with the demands of his body. He acts with purpose when he acts in accordance with the demands of his environment and not merely in accordance with those of his own body. We must pay heed to this where the child is concerned. It is possible, on the one hand, to direct the child's outer bodily movements more and more to what is purely physical, that is, to physiological gymnastics, where we simply enquire of the body what movements shall be carried out. But we can also guide the child's outer movements so that they become purposeful movements, movements penetrated with meaning, so that the child does not merely splash about in the spirit in his movements, but follows the spirit in his aims. So we develop the bodily movements into eurythmy. The more we make the child do purely physical gymnastics the more he will be at the mercy of excessive desire for sleep; and of an excessive tendency to fat. We must not entirely neglect the bodily side, for man must live in rhythm, but having swung over to this side we must swing back again to a kind of movement which is permeated with purpose – as in eurythmy, where every movement expresses a sound and has a meaning. The more we can alternate gymnastics with eurythmy the more we shall bring harmony into the need for sleeping and waking; the more, too, shall we maintain normal life in the child's will, in his relations to the outer world. That gymnastics, moreover, has become void of all sense or meaning, that we have made it into an activity that follows the body entirely, is a characteristic phenomenon of the age of materialism and the fact that we seek to 'raise' this activity to the level of sport, where the movements to be performed are derived solely from the body, and not only lack all sense and meaning – this fact is typical of the endeavour to drag man down even beyond the level of materialistic thinking to that of brute feeling. The excessive pursuit of sport is Darwinism in practice. Theoretical Darwinism is to assert that man comes from the animals. Sport is practical Darwinism, it proclaims an ethic which leads man back again to the animal." (11 lecture 13)

In the Stuttgart lecture of 1919 stress is laid mainly on eurythmy.

In the 6th lecture of the Basle course of 1920 there are extensive passages on eurythmy in comparison with gymnastics. In this lecture eurythmy is called "ensouled" gymnastics as against "physiological" gymnastics which takes its starting point from a study of the human body.

"Eurythmy distinguishes itself from this through the fact that every movement is ensouled... that every movement is at the same time the expression of the soul, just as the sounds of speech are an expression of the soul." (23 lecture 6)

At that time Steiner referred briefly to eurythmy as such, contrasting it with dreaming.

"In dreaming man is half asleep, in eurythmy he is more awake than he is in ordinary life." (23)

The consideration, which I cannot quote fully here, ends with the following sentences:

"Current gymnastics do not strengthen the initiative of will. The initiative of will is strengthened when a child executes movements of a kind where each one is at the same time expressive of a movement of the soul, where the soul pours itself into each single movement." (23)

This quotation should of course be considered in its totality. In lecture 13 of the same course (23) there is a significant passage on child play to which the reader's attention is directed.

In the first year of the Waldorf School the necessity to introduce gymnastics was already discussed.

In connection with a remark made in July 1920 on the teaching of music Steiner said spontaneously:

"We can consider adding some gymnastics as soon as possible. We could include it at once so that we can say – in the statement of our aims and in the curriculum – 'gymnastics and eurythmy'. That would be quite a good thing. They only need to go side by side, so that we do physiological gymnastics with psychological eurythmy. As soon as the question is asked it can be said that we have not excluded it, that it is included." (24.7.20)

And on the same day after variously discussing the possibility of letting boys and girls do gymnastics in the same room and at the same time:

"Gymnastics lessons need not be given in the 3 lowest classes. Eurythmy will be sufficient for the 1st and 2nd classes. But after that we must have gymnastics in order not not-to-have it. It will also be quite a good thing if it is done. It would be a good thing if, as far as possible, it could follow eurythmy, that the children first do eurythmy and then some gymnastics... That would be enough – one hour for eurythmy and then gymnastics at the end. One hour eurythmy, half an hour gymnastics." (24.7.20)

In 1920 gymnastics was referred to as an unavoidable necessity.

Steiner made an important remark on the use of eurythmy in school festivals in the conference of March 23, 1921:

"The principle of showing the eurythmy of the school is overthrown by forming a special class. That should not be done. If it is a real principle of the school it will not be done. We do not prepare a special group. It would be taken out of the ordinary course of school lessons. The school education will be disturbed if you make an aristocracy of pupils... There must be some among the

ordinary pupils who can be used. It is uneducational to prepare some especially in a group by themselves." (23.3.21)

The same problem was dealt with on May 26, 1921 and also on November 16 of the same year, but there in reference to tone eurythmy. The reader is advised to look it up.

On May 26, 1921 gymnastics could still not be given. Steiner said:

"There are many boys in Class 5 who could do with gymnastics. One lesson a week would properly belong to our curriculum. We shall spiritualise (according to Stockmeyer, Steiner used the word "spiritualise" = vergeistigen, not "realise" = verwirklichen, only on the basis of the former can the next passage be understood) this as soon as we can." (26.5.21)

Steiner is therefore announcing a reorganisation of gymnastic teaching. And a few weeks later in the Supplementary Course (26) he speaks about gymnastics; how it could or rather should be and how then it would come into "direct contact" with eurythmy. What he intended to say by this statement becomes clear. Eurythmy was ready made, as far as one can say that of a living thing; it had been taken up immediately at the founding of the Waldorf School. Gymnastics also had to be part of the curriculum because parents and children alike wanted it – and it was a recognised subject at that time. But it could not be introduced if it remained unaltered.

Steiner undertook the task of remodelling it, so that here too the principle was put into practice that the person doing gymnastics would accompany each movement with the experience of its meaning. How this new aim takes on a more concrete form at each step is discernible in what he further has to say. In the Supplementary Course (26) of 1921 we still see disparaging remarks made about the gymnastics in vogue until then, but also a clear indication of the new aim.

In the first lecture of this course Steiner speaks of the physiological processes which take place in the child's organism as a consequence of a more contemplative teaching on the one hand, as against a teaching that is carried on more by activity:

"For the very same phenomenon is produced in his organism, to a less intense degree, as is produced in sleep. All the time that we are teaching subjects that appeal almost exclusively to thought and contemplation a certain ascent of organic activity is taking place in the children. They are developing in their organism the same activity that is developed in sleep: the products of metabolism are rising up into the brain. We must understand that, as long as we are awake, whatever is ill in our organism is kept back from the higher organs, is not allowed to rise up. When we go to sleep, however, a definite ascent of the illness takes place; it rises up into the higher organs. And so, if we are getting a child to study and observe and consider, then whatever is not quite its order in his organism, is rising up the whole time. On the other hand, suppose we are teaching the child eurythmy, getting him to sing or play music, giving him gymnastics or some kind of

handwork, or even if we are letting him write – in all these cases we have in the child an enhanced waking. When therefore you teach singing or eurythmy, there is no doubt about it, you set going in the child a hygienic – yes, even a therapeutic activity... The activity is perhaps all the healthier if you do not go about it in the spirit of amateur doctors, but simply leave it to your own natural healthy feelings and outlook. Nevertheless, as teachers working together, it is good that we should know how we do really work for one another. We should know, for example, that the children owe the healthy ascent of organic fluids – of which we are seeing the good results in our history lessons – that they owe this to the singing or eurythmy that they had the day before." (26 lecture 1)

Here for the first time gymnastics are shown to be part of the kind of teaching referred to above, i.e., "carried on more by activity."

In the second lecture of the same course eurythmy is again talked about, and also gymnastics, but after a good deal of negative characterization of the ordinary kind of gymnastics we hear once more the demand made in 1906 in the lecture 'The Education of the Child", that the person doing gymnastics should participate with his soul in what he is doing with his body.

Only now by taking up this impulse expressed in the "Education of the Child" does it become possible to take gymnastics in Waldorf education as a really educative instrument. This incisively important passage runs as follows:

"Man has no place in these gymnastics. Natural science has already excluded him in theory, but here, in gymnastics and drill, he is excluded in actual practice. Because man as man has no place there, these gymnastics, deeply rooted as they have become in our so-called civilization, are most reprehensible, we could even say impious. They make the children into mimics of a model. That is no goal for education! The true educator will see that the child assumes a position, a posture, that he also experiences inwardly. The same with the movements we require him to make. They should be movements that he experiences inwardly. Take, for example, breathing. We ought to know that in breathing in, the child can be brought to feel a faint suggestion of some nice-tasting food, which is slipping down under his palate. The experience should not get as far with him as an actual perception of taste; there should only be the faintest suggestion of it, just enough for the child to be able to feel, as he breathes in, that he is sensing something of the freshness of the world. Try to get him to feel this, and then to ask himself: What colour is my breathing in? If the child can come to a right sensation of his breathing in, he will tell you that he feels it greenish in colour, something like a natural green. You will know that you have achieved something if you have been able to bring the child to feel that his breathing in has a greenish colour. And you will find that his body will then take up, of its own accord, the right position for breathing in, The child's inner experience will lead him, unfailingly, to hold his body correctly. Then you can go on to exercises.

Similarly, you can bring the child to a corresponding experience with out-breathing. The moment he begins to feel, in breathing out: I do think I'm really a splendid fellow! – the moment he has this feeling of his own strength and of wanting to send it out into the world, he will also experience rightly (as something absolutely in harmony with himself) the corresponding movement of the abdomen in breathing out, the movements of the limbs, the carriage of the head, the position of the arms, When the child has once entered fully into the feeling of breathing out, he will experience within him the right movements to correspond.

I have taken breathing as an example. We could start with some other activity that the child can feel – movements of the arms or legs, running, etc., or even the actual carriage of the child, how he holds himself. Each time, it is the inner soul experience that we have to find and develop, for that will of itself lead to a right bodily expression, And here we have come to the point where we can bring gymnastics into immediate connection with eurythmy. And this is just what we need to do.

Eurythmy brings an element of soul and spirit to immediate appearance, it fills all that moves in man with soul and spirit. It takes as its starting point what man has developed as regards soul and spirit in the course of human evolution. But the bodily-physical can also be experienced in a spiritual way. One can, if one takes matters far enough in this direction, experience the breathing and the metabolism. In this respect man can develop himself far enough to have a sensation of himself, to feel 'with' his corporeal-bodily nature. And then I should like to say what comes to the child on a higher level as eurythmy can finally arrive at gymnastics. Certainly a bridge can be built between eurythmy and gymnastics. But the gymnastics should be done in no other way than the child fetching the movements it does in gymnastics out of the experience of the bodily-corporeal, out of the experience of soul and spirit, and letting the bodily-physical movements be attuned to these experiences." (26)

Just as this passage is important for an understanding of the alternating effect of sleeping and waking and their relation to contemplative and – shall we say – "active" teaching (i.e., teaching via activity), so there is a further passage in lecture 3 of the "Supplementary Course" which in its main part has already appeared in the chapter on music.

"Looking at man in his totality, we find him an extraordinarily complicated being, – this 'man' that we teachers set out to understand! Take the process I have just been explaining. When you teach a child eurythmy, the child's physical body is brought into movement, and the movements are carried over into the ether body. Although, to begin with, astral body and ego put up a resistance, they also have to receive an impress of the activities that are taking place in the physical and ether bodies. Then comes sleep. Astral body and ego go out of the physical body, and bring this impress into contact with quite other – spiritual – forces. In the morning they come back again and what they bring with them bears evidence of a marvellous concord between what has been received from the spiritual world during sleep,

and what was experienced the day before by physical and ether bodies when the child was doing eurythmy. We gave the child certain experiences – we might say, in preparation. The way these experiences turn out to harmonize with the spiritual experiences which he undergoes afterwards during sleep, can reveal to us what eurythmy really does for the child. When we find the result next morning, then – and not until then – are we able to appreciate the wonderfully health-giving power that is latent in eurythmy. If we give the child eurythmy in the right way, it is actually so that when he wakes up next morning and enters his body, he carries down into it spiritual substance." (26 lecture 3)

This shows how the school should take into account the sleep of the child as an effective measure for the way in which the work is built up.

The following sentences which are also taken from the Supplementary Course (26) lecture 4, indicate a very important measure derived from the knowledge of man and directly affecting the practice of teaching where bodily activity is concerned.

"When the child does eurythmy, he comes into movement; and the spiritual which is in the limbs streams upwards on the path of the child's movements. We set the spiritual free when we give the child eurythmy. (And it is the same with singing.) The spiritual with which the limbs are full to overflowing is released. This is a real process that takes place in the child. We draw away the spiritual, we call it forth. And then, when the child stops doing the exercises, the spiritual that we have called forth is, so to speak, waiting to be used. (I spoke of this situation yesterday in another connection.) The spiritual is also waiting to be established, to be secured. We must meet this need.

We have, you see, spiritualised the child. Through doing gymnastics or eurythmy or singing he has become a different being, he has in him much more of the spiritual than he had before. This spiritual element in him wants to be established, wants to remain with him; and it is for us to see that it is not diverted. There is a very simple way of doing this. After the lesson is finished, let the children remain quiet for a little, Give the whole class a rest, and make sure that during this time – it need only be a very few minutes – they are quiet and undisturbed. The older the children the greater the need for this pause. We must never forget to provide for it; if we do, then on the following day we shall not fail to find in the children what we need." (26 lecture 4)

After having talked about the transition in the life of the child at the time of the change of teeth from imitation to "beautiful copying" there follows a remark in the last lecture of the Supplementary Course (26) which runs as follows:

"For when a child does eurythmy, or sings, what is he really doing? He is breaking loose from the habit of imitation, and yet in the very act of freeing himself from it, he is in a way carrying it a stage further. He is making movements. When he is singing and even when he is listening to music he is a-move (inwardly) in the same way as he is when he is imitating, When we let a child

do eurythmy, then instead of putting a slate-pencil or a pen into his hand and getting him to write an A or an E, to which he can have no possible relation other than one of learning by rote – instead of this, we are getting him to write, with his own human form, the content of language; he is learning to inscribe into the world what he can inscribe into it by means of his own organism. This means, the child is continuing in another way the activity in which he was engaged in his pre-existence. And if we then go on to teach him writing and reading, giving him not the abstract symbol but the picture, we shall not be alienating him from his real being, On the contrary, he will have to rouse his being into activity; we shall be calling upon him to exert himself with his whole being." (26 lecture 8)

A specially important turn of events as far as gymnastics are concerned occurs in the "Christmas Course" 1921/22. Of this course Steiner said: *"this is the course which will give information on these matters"*. In the third lecture he reveals an unexpected and startling aspect of sport related as it is to gymnastics.

"Religion has lost the inner force to strengthen the physical in man. Because this is so the instinct has arisen of wanting to acquire the same force in an external way. And as everything in life works polarically we are confronted with the fact that what man has lost in the sphere of religion he instinctively wants to acquire externally. Well I am certainly not going to indulge in tirades against sport as such and I am convinced that it will even develop further in a healthy manner. But it will play a different part in future from what it does today when it has become a substitute for religion. Such things appear to be paradoxical when they are brought forward nowadays. But it is just the truth that appears paradoxical nowadays because we have got ourselves into so many situations in this modern civilization of ours." (27)

The seventh lecture of the same course contains a consideration on gymnastics following on a lengthy exposition on the subconscious processes between child and educator and also about the supersensible wisdom in the child and the earthly understanding of the educator.

"If it is necessary for us for the purpose of teaching or educative measure to have the child sitting quietly in class, even on hygienically constructed benches we are in any case causing the child to sit still so that the activity is not in the metabolic-limb system, on the contrary all that is working has to be called forth from the head. This is a one-sidedness into which we place the child.

We balance this out again later on, and it is right that it should be later on, by unburdening the head of its activity and getting the metabolic-limb system to stir, by letting the child do gymnastics.

When one is conscious how polarically opposed the processes in the head organism and in the metabolic-limb system are, one will readily understand how important it is to alternate properly in this sphere also.

But then when we let the children do gymnastic exercises, jump and so on, and then take them back into the

classroom and continue to teach them in class – well, what happens then?

You see whilst man has his metabolic limb system stirring, those thoughts that are artificially induced into the head between birth and death are not in the head but outside. The child runs around, moves, brings its metabolic limb organism into movement. The thoughts implanted during earthly life recede.

But that which at other times is playing into dreams, this supersensible wisdom, is now present in the head unconsciously, makes itself felt in the head.

If therefore we take the child back into the classroom after the gymnastic lesson, we put something that is subconsciously inferior for the child in front of it, in place of what it thought previously during the gymnastic exercises.

For during the gymnastic exercises it is not only the sensible but also the supersensible which is given a particular opportunity to work on the child.

For this reason the child inwardly becomes unwilling. And we spoil it, we inculcate a tendency to sickness, by allowing ordinary teaching to follow the gymnastic lesson.

Were it not for the fact that we older people had already become stiff in our organisation, that which we bring into our heads as external wisdom, acquired by intellectual means, rays back properly into our memory pictures, it would stream down later into the rest of the organism. And however paradoxical this may sound, that which should remain in the head according to the normal organisation of man, if it does stream down into the metabolic limb organism, makes man ill, it acts like poison.

Rational wisdom is indeed a kind of poison if it gets to the wrong place, at least if it gets into the metabolic organism. We can only live with this rational wisdom, if the poison (I say this in quite a technical sense, not as a moral judgment) does not penetrate down into our metabolic-limb organism. There it works terribly destructively. But this stiffness does not exist in the child's case, If we come along with our mature (this might have been stiff = steif, not reif, according to Stockmeyer) wisdom, this poison penetrates downwards and in fact poisons our metabolic-limb organism. If you want to make the child specially clever according to the life-wisdom of today, in other words if you sit it down and stuff it as much as possible while it is sitting, then something else happens, then one prevents the unconscious wisdom in the child from working.

For this unconscious wisdom works exactly when the child is actively moving about, when it makes more or less rhythmic movements. For the rhythm promotes the uniting of the organism with the unconscious wisdom by virtue of the peculiar intermediary position which this rhythmic organisation assumes between the head organisation and limbs and metabolism." (27)

And in the 15th lecture of the same course (Christmas Course 1921/22) Steiner again speaks about the free play of children and of gymnastics:

"In an education which is based on a knowledge of man we must see to it that we learn to understand in what manner the child wants to be freely active in its play. Everything we bring to the child by way of stereotyped thought-out (ausgetuftelt) forms of play harnesses the child into something that is foreign to it, it represses what should be inwardly stirring in it. As regards its own inner activity the child becomes indolent and because an outer activity is foisted on to it the child itself tends to be engaged in this outer activity without interest. One can acquire specially good insight into these matters if one notices that one is letting the child's play merge into gymnastic occupation too much rather than remaining in the sphere of play where one is much more prone to take the intentions of the child into account...

Generally speaking it must be said that gymnastic exercises are formed in such a way that they approach the child in a more external manner. So that if one has real knowledge of man one will prefer to see the children occupying themselves with parallel bars, horizontal bars and rope ladders, rather than that the gymnastic teacher should direct the movements with which the child has to comply as something external, something observed and not having arisen out of the child itself. This free play is something which must be studied. One must get to know the child, then one will find the possibility to stimulate it to this free play. In this free play girls and boys should participate alike. The girls should do in a slightly modified form what the boys are doing in their free play." (27)

The training of movement is considered from three completely different aspects in this course, firstly as sport in its connection with religion, then moving freely in its alternation with intellectual learning, and finally as free play from the hygienic point of view. (Anaemia in girls).

The Waldorf School still had no gymnastics teacher. The boys were missing gymnastics very much. Steiner expressed himself as follows in the conference of January 16th 1922:

"I think that in teaching gymnastics we must be very careful with regard to the personality. It may be that we shall have to put our gymnastics lessons on a broader basis, so that they may be carried out in a reasonable way. We must find someone who is interested in this. I have shown how the whole organism must gradually be claimed by the soul. That must be introduced in gymnastics. I should like this course to be printed as quickly as possible, for it can give information about things of this sort. I have not had the opportunity before of explaining these things precisely enough for the gymnastics teacher to be able to enter into the matter. I will go into this question." (16.1.22) (27)

"This course" is the one from which the last quotations were taken; it was given in Dornach at Christmas 1921/ 22. In it only gymnastics in the wider sense were spoken of – but not eurythmy. It is the one "which will give information on such matters."

In the lectures of this course gymnastics are taken into the positive practice of education in a new form and in a new style.

It was about the summer of 1922 that Count Fritz von Bothmer came as the first gymnastics teacher. He was prepared to undertake the difficult task of translating Steiner's fundamental demands into the concrete practice of teaching. Some short remarks that Steiner made in the conferences during this time still exist:

"In gymnastics you must work with the whole teaching staff. Here judgment in taste must come into the other things." (21.6.22)

On August 24th 1922 (in Oxford) Steiner spoke about the eurythmy figures in detail. The reader is referred to the relevant passage.

"I was glad about the gymnastics lesson. In addition to this the whole gymnastics work must be definitely strengthened. The boys grow really slack." (15.10.22)

"Side by side with eurythmy it is very good to have gymnastics, especially for boys, when it is not carried out in the usual pedantic way but aims at having a body forming force. It must not be done too early. Younger classes must only see it." (15.10.22)

And in the course of making a new ruling on the timetable in the Autumn of 1922:

"Gymnastics as far as possible in the afternoon. The gymnastics lesson is not in the nature of recreation. It is not good to put the gymnastics lesson amongst other subjects. There can be two classes at the same time. I must discuss the method with the gymnastics teachers. I have only given indications. But in gymnastics it is always possible to arrange your exercises in such a way that you make use of two large classes. Not long ago it was still quite good to have gymnastics in the open air. It was very clearly to be seen that the lads have not got their bodies in control by the way they lounge in every direction. The boys are very lacking in the management of their bodies owing to the fact that they have had no gymnastics for three years. That cannot be denied." (28.10.22)

Once when the children had wanted to have the gymnastics lessons from 7.30 to 8.30 am:

"The children come to main lesson thoroughly tired. They will not be more tired, but just as if they had had a regular lesson before it." (9. 12.22)

The building up of the gymnastics teaching was now inaugurated step by step as apart from free play:

"With regard to what concerns the first two classes, we cannot do much at the moment, but in the future we will make the following plan. In the first two classes it is too early to give real gymnastics, but on the other hand systematic games should be carried on. This we ought to introduce as soon as we have time to breathe so that in Class 3 a transition can be made from playing to gymnastics. The children must have movement, right movement." (17.1.23)

Because of the new character that Steiner had given to gymnastics, especially in the Christmas Course, Dornach 1921/ 22, and also because of the separation in the first classes of child play from gymnastics proper, new demands were made on the style of gymnastics teaching. These Steiner gave expression to in the following sentences from the conference on January 17th 1923:

"The following must be taken into consideration: in a school such as this the gymnastics lesson can only gradually be built up. It is more than likely that even next year we shall be able to pay special attention to the development of gymnastics in Class 12. Up till now it has been treated as though by a step-mother – we still have to work together in our gymnastics instruction. I believe that in the future growth of our Waldorf School gymnastics lessons will bring many difficult tasks – above all from a particular class onwards quite a definite conscious exercise will be done for the strengthening of the human organism, a kind of hygienic general massage of the human organism. I think you ought now to direct your attention more towards this, more towards the upper classes. With regard to the lower classes, I thought of developing games more with the women teachers – Also the gymnastics teachers should not suffer the loss of their authority by first playing with the children. You should have your authority through what can only come through gymnastics. Not that the children should have the feeling that now their games teacher is teaching them gymnastics. This does not mean that I am speaking slightingly of games. If the teacher of games is in Classes 1 and 2 she will not change to gymnastics. Through the change a feeling of dissatisfaction would be aroused in the children. (By games I understand games with movement.)" (17.1.23)

March 1st 1923 is an important date in the development of the work for the teaching of gymnastics and eurythmy. On this occasion the gymnastics teacher gave an account of the aim he had in view after a short period of working his way in, and Steiner developed his own ideas in response to these comments. The words of the gymnastics teacher are not quoted here as they appear in metamorphosed form later. Steiner said:

"About the relationship of gymnastics to eurythmy – there can really be no collision between gymnastics and eurythmy. Generally speaking, the gymnastics exercises in the way they are shaped, will look, of course only in a general way, like a continuation of eurythmy exercises. That is to say: take an arm movement in eurythmy and a corresponding arm movement in gymnastics; you will certainly notice that the form produced in eurythmy lies nearer the centre of the body than is the case in gymnastics. But there can be no collision.

That will be best seen if I point out that eurythmy has essentially to do with what in the human organism plays its part in immediate connection with the inner breathing process: thus, what an arm, or a leg, or a finger or toe carries out in eurythmy is in immediate contact with what takes place inwardly as the process of breathing, as an inner process which happens when air passes into the blood. Whilst gymnastics is essentially that process in the human organism which lies at the root of the passing of blood into the muscle. This is the essential thing physiologically; at the same time it sheds a flood of light over what should be accomplished. As soon as we come to an understanding – and that must be instinctively, intuitively – as to what has to be done in each gymnastic

movement with regard to becoming strong, growing, to the increased elasticity of the muscle through the shooting of the blood into the muscle, the more will it be possible to discover free exercises in ourselves.

Now, the same thing can be said from another angle. Eurythmy is essentially a plastic formation of the organism, or, rather, eurythmy lives in the plastic formation of the organism; gymnastics in the statics and dynamics of the organism. You felt that inasmuch as you said that in gymnastics, space is really felt. You see this best if you add the further conception of how an arm or leg is placed in the direction of space or in the conditions of gravity in space. You will see that there will be no collision with eurythmy if attention is also paid to its character. This happens far too little, because it does not come so much into consideration in the artistic performances, whereas in education it is particularly important. When you have seen the figures you will have noticed that we distinguish between movement, feeling and character. Movement and feeling are quite satisfactory, whereas what constitutes character in the eurythmy movement has not yet penetrated. This is quite natural, because it is not of great significance in the carrying out of artistic eurythmy when it is looked at by others. On the other hand, the character of a movement must form an essential element in teaching. The one who is doing eurythmy must feel the return of any movement or position into his own perceptive faculty. Thus for instance in the E (pronounced 'ay') movement he must feel the pressure of one limb on the other, and the streaming back of the pressure into the centre of the body. There are colours laid on in the figures in order that this should be clear. You see everywhere three colours in the eurythmy figures, one for movement, another for the feeling – that passes over to the veil – and the third for the character, i.e., for that definite part of the body where the eurythmist must particularly stretch his muscles and must feel the direction of his stretching. That belongs to the life of eurythmy in the inner, plastic element of the body.

... Since it is also important for a more psychological physiology, the Waldorf teachers in general should study these figures; they should study them in order to acquire knowledge of the human organism. What can be learnt from these figures is at the same time a foundation for general artistic perception, for a knowledge of the inner human organism.

Thus it must be said that the essential thing for the gymnastics teacher is that he should have spiritually before him the statics and dynamics of the human organism, who has a clear-cut picture of what it means to raise a leg, lower or raise an arm, in relation to gravity, whilst the eurythmy teacher must have a strong feeling: it is thus that the body wishes to form its limbs plastically. It is not right to say that the gymnastics teacher stands like a sculptor before his sculpture. That is true for the eurythmy teacher. The gymnastics teacher has the task of having before him an ideal man, consisting of lines, forms, movement formations, into which he must shape this really slovenly, overstrained, distorted human being standing before him. That was a right expression when you pointed out that the children should carry their bodies. Whilst the eurythmist must strive for the muscle to feel itself, to feel in its condensation the character of the movement, the gymnastics teacher must feel whether the pupil senses truly the heaviness or lightness of a limb. The child, not intellectually, but instinctively, must sense, from the point of view of gravity, each raising of the arm, each raising of the leg, must, for instance, acquire the power of sensing how a foot becomes heavy when he stands on one leg and raises the other.

Thus the gymnastics teacher has the dynamically ideal man in his soul, and wants to transform the pupil before him into such a one. Of course, the artistic element must take part in this work insomuch as human dynamics can only be drawn out by means of an artistic sense. Whilst the artistic sense plays a large part in eurythmic plastic work, in the case of the drill teacher it must precede the formations which he calls forth in statics and dynamics.

With regard to the question of breathing, the point is that eurythmy lies nearer breathing whilst gymnastics is nearer the blood process. What is essential for gymnastics is that, with the exception of the acceleration of breathing in the course of doing gymnastics, which is a physiological process, the method of doing gymnastics should be so arranged that the breathing process is not affected by it. Where the deportment is as it should be, a gymnastic exercise cannot take place if it is injurious to the breathing process...

It is true that in gymnastics the will comes into consideration, and just for that reason the gymnastics teacher must have an instinctive, intuitive experience of the connection between a bodily movement and an expression of will. He must be able to feel how a movement is connected with the will. In eurythmy the will is also cultivated, but by way of inner feeling, on a different plane; how will expresses itself through the feeling. Just that which I have described as character is the experience of the feeling of an act of will. The gymnastics teacher has to do directly with the act of will; the eurythmy teacher with the experience of the feeling in an act of will. In all this there can be a sharp division. And we must take it into account when we work out the curriculum... Perhaps we shall not be able to do it at once in a way that will realise the highest ideals. Then we shall observe both these things, that of course the eurythmic element will enter into gymnastics more easily with girls than with boys, With boys, these things are differentiated. For this reason we shall have to let the boys and girls do gymnastics in the same room, but in different groups, so that the girls form a group to themselves, and the free exercises re-establish the give and take between them. Their joy is enhanced if they have exercises with variations for boys and girls.

I think this will only be clear when we are able to discuss the curriculum in detail. It is also variable according to age.

With regard to apparatus, I should like to remark that the form of the apparatus could be modified and perfected, but that on the whole, approximately at least, the customary apparatus is not so fearfully bad that we can do nothing with it. Although I do not wish to insist fanatically on our having climbing poles, I should still not abuse them too much..."

And after a reference to the climbing trees in village church fetes: (These climbing trees were trunks of fir or pine trees stripped of their bark and decorated with ribbons and a wreath at the top. Youths climbed them in a similar way to which sailors climb ship masts):

"That is something which works very strongly on the effect of the will on the bodily nature. That is something which can be exercised artistically on climbing poles. Of course, there is some advantage if the children have to climb a rope. The pole, I must say, is an apparatus of limited importance. But I do not wish to exclude it completely. Parallel bars, the horizontal bar, horse, if used properly – something can be made out of them.

I agree with diversifying the exercises to a certain extent by combining them, because in this way, presence of mind comes more into consideration, and that must be brought into play in apparatus work. That has a retroactive effect and strengthens the muscles. They get in this way the right strength and elasticity.

I agree, but I still believe that even horizontal bars gain greater importance if you lay more value on quick and judicious observation, not with the eyes, but with the feeling of the body. Surely this one thing is useful; you let the child swing so that he must catch the bar. He must hold himself in the air. This exercise is only given to indicate its purpose. It can be done with the hands, but also with the whole arm. The movement has no significance until it is done with the arm.

It can be begun with the hands. These are things which must really lead the child to feel the apparatus with his whole body; this brings about more sympathy with the apparatus than there was in the beginning. The first thing to be considered is that the child learns to work on the horizontal bar with his legs. Then you can also combine the exercise by letting him move along the bar with his legs, with his legs hanging.

That should only indicate the spirit and the aim. I do not think that it is absolutely necessary to speak of dead apparatus and of a mere routine. It has become so. It does not need to be routine if you call out this experience of the apparatus. The legs can be employed in a really wonderful way on the bars." (1.3.23)

Here I should like to report on a remark made by Steiner which I remember and which can possibly throw light on what he said about exercises on the horizontal and parallel bars. It was probably on this occasion that he recommended arm movements to be done, not with the arms outstretched but bent at the elbows, so to speak with a shortened arm. I should imagine that he was thinking particularly, or at least in passing, of exercises on the horizontal bar as suggested above. It is also possible, however, that he was thinking of exercises without apparatus. It would be useful to read up a passage in the Ilkley lectures which will be quoted later in this connection, to see whether a reference can be found in it to the bending of the lower arm. One should also remember that the activity which expresses itself in the outstretched arms without restraint in an outward radiation, comes to an experience of itself again in this bending, thus leading the human being back to himself. Something takes place on another level, as happens in the sense experience and in its transition to representation (Vorstellung) – in reflection.

But one is first of all surprised in the lecture of the Ilkley course of August 6th by the significant consideration of the ancient Greek ideals of education and of what happened in those centres of education of long ago. There we read as follows:

> *"What we behold when we turn our attention to one of these places in Greece where the young were educated from the seventh year of life onwards, can, if it is rightly permeated with modern impulses, afford us a true basis for understanding what is necessary for education and instruction to-day." (35 lecture 2)*

The considerations which then follow are too long to reproduce here in full, important as they are both for the eurythmy and the gymnastics teacher.

In the choice of quotations from Steiner's lectures, the method in any case had to be that, as far as possible, passages were chosen which gather a truth that has been under consideration, into a few sentences, and where possible to illuminate significantly their connections with other matter. One cannot of course expect a step by step building up of knowledge in these passages, and that is why it is assumed that the reader will not be satisfied with just reading the quotations but will himself turn to the works, lectures and conferences listed, in order again to experience the short sentences in the context out of which Steiner has written or spoken them.

A last reference of Steiner's from the Ilkley Course in the lecture of August 17, 1923 in the morning, once again characterizes the relationship between gymnastics and eurythmy – gymnastics now being spoken of as it had been inaugurated by Steiner in the Waldorf School:

> *"Let me only say now that we have introduced eurythmy into our Waldorf School because it affords such a wonderful contrast to ordinary gymnastics. As already indicated, bodily exercises are adequately carried out in the Waldorf School, but as regards ordinary, external gymnastics, we elaborate them in such a way that with every exercise the child is first given a sense of space, of the directions of space which are there, of course, as the primary thing. The child feels the direction of space and then his arms follow it. In his gymnastics he gives himself to space. This is the only healthy basis for gymnastic exercises.*
>
> *Space is conditioned in all directions. To our abstract conception of space, there are three directions which we can in no way distinguish. They are only there in geometry. In reality, however, the head is above, the legs below – there we have the above and below. Then we have right and left. We live in this direction of space when we stretch out our arms. The point is not to ask: where is the absolute direction? Of course we can turn*

this way or that. Then we have our forward and backward direction, front and behind. All other directions of space are oriented with respect to these. If we understand space in this way, we can discover really healthy movements for gymnastics, where the human being gives himself up, as it were, to the laws of space.

> *In the eurythmy, the character of the movement is determined by the human organism, and then the question is: what is the soul experiencing in this movement or that? This indeed underlies the eurythmic movements for the different sounds. What is happening when the forces of your being flow into the limbs? In the ordinary gymnastic exercises the human being lends himself to space; in eurythmy he carries out movements that express his being and are in accordance with the laws of his organism. To allow what is inner to express itself outwardly in movement – that is the essence of eurythmy. To fill the outer with the human being so that the human being unites himself with the outer world – that is the essence of gymnastics." (35 lectures 12)*

Now follows an illuminating passage on the use of eurythmy figures in reply to a question put to Steiner in a conference regarding the way the figures should be set up:

> *"Until a child has learnt the gesture in question he cannot connect a concept with the figure. The moment he has learnt the gesture he is bound to relate it to the figure. Besides that he will understand the movement, not the character and feeling. The feeling is expressed in the veil. 'You are still too young for a veil'. From the moment when the children learn to live themselves into the sound in their inner being you can gradually convey to them the nature of character. When they grasp the principle involved in making these figures it will have a favourable effect on the eurythmy lessons. An artistic feeling develops in the course of time. If it is possible to develop this feeling, it should be done." (18.9.23)*

A more detailed discourse on these figures is to be found in the Oxford Course but this passage I cannot quote here on account of its length. The reader should read it up at this point. (29 lecture 8)

In the last course that Steiner gave to the Waldorf School teachers exclusively, he adds the following words to his description of the historic ideals of gymnast, rhetorician and doctor:

> *"But to-day, we are just at the point when we must cultivate the synthesis of these three elements in man (for Gymnast, Rhetorician and Professor also represent three sides of human nature) and the cultivation of this synthesis is more necessary in education than in any other sphere. For this reason if everything could be conducted according to an ideal, the ideal would be for a body of teachers to be able to cultivate all three elements continuously; on the other hand they should also separately cultivate gymnastics and rhetoric with all that belongs to them according to the older conception, and the element of professor, all in the noblest sense, but these three elements should be united. I shrink almost with horror from characterising so dryly what you must know and take into consideration in*

this connection; for I fear that it will degenerate, as do many things which must be said. It ought not to degenerate. It ought to be seen already that the teacher needs for his art of education and teaching, the unity of outer movement, of the specialised gymnast, of the thoroughly ensouled rhetorician, and thirdly of the spiritual which has become living, not the spiritual grown dead and abstract.

Thus the whole body of teachers should really take part in what affects us in the noblest sense in gymnastics, in what we have in drill and in eurythmy; they should make all these things their own. And if you really succeed in entering so deeply into eurythmy that you experience it yourselves, you will see that in every eurythmy movement there lives an element which affects soul and spirit. Every eurythmic movement calls a soul-element out of the deepest foundations of human nature; and every gymnastic movement, if only it is used in the right way, calls forth to a certain extent in the human being a spiritual atmosphere, into which the spiritual can enter, not as something abstractly dead, but as something living." (36 lecture 1)

There is a very clear statement on eurythmy and its position between visual and sounding art in the Arnheim Course of 1924. Gymnastics are only spoken of in their traditional form:

"And in bringing to the child that which is formative in the artistic (what is meant is 'the formative-artistic') we bring to it something that is in the deepest sense akin to the ether body, if as I indicated yesterday we occupy ourselves with the child as it models freely. This is what enables the child, as it inwardly takes hold of its own being, to place itself rightly into the world as human being. And in bringing the musical element to the child, it forms the astral body. And if both these are joined together – if one does the sculptural work in such a way that it passes over into movement and one made this movement sculptural – then we get eurythmy which follows directly out of the relationship of the etheric to the astral body in the child.

It is for this reason that the child now learns to do eurythmy, the language which manifests in articulated gesture, just as in former years it had learnt to speak by itself.

One will never meet with obstacles as regards the learning of eurythmy so long as the child is healthy for in eurythmy it is simply expressing its own being – it wants to realize its own being...

So you see eurythmy has arisen out of the whole man, out of the physical, etheric and astral body; one can only study it with anthroposophical knowledge of man. Gymnastics of today only addresses itself physiologically, in a one-sided way, to the physical body; and because physiology can't help it a few laws about vitality are brought into it.

But one does not educate total human beings through gymnastics but only partial human beings.

This is not saying anything against gymnastics, but

nowadays it is over-rated. For this reason eurythmy must be put side by side with gymnastics." (39 lecture 4)

The reader should take the trouble to read the three sentences of the above quotation beginning with "and" (underlined by Stockmeyer) and seeing in them a repetition in abbreviated form of the train of thought expressed at the beginning of the Supplementary Course (26) which treats of the three struggles that go on in the development of the child.

A final summary on eurythmy and gymnastics as newly conceived by Steiner is to be found in the Torquay Course.

"Gymnastics as taught today and all kinds of sport are something quite different from eurythmy. You can quite well have both together. For the conception of space is very often considered in quite an abstract way, and people do not take into account that space is something concrete." (40 lecture 6)

Then follow remarks on the above and below at different points of the earth. Some fifteen lines later it continues as follows:

"Space is something concrete of which man is sensible. He feels himself within space and he feels the necessity of finding his place in it; when he thus finds his way into the balance of space, into the different conditions of space, then sport and gymnastics arise. In these man is trying to find his own relationship to space.

If you do this gymnastic movement (arms outstretched) you have the feeling that you are bringing your two arms into a horizontal direction. If you jump you have the feeling that you are moving your body upwards by its own force. These are gymnastic exercises. But if you feel you are holding within you something which you are experiencing inwardly – the sound EE – and you reflect upon it, then you may make perhaps a similar movement, but in this case, the inner soul quality is expressed in the movement. Man reveals his inward self. That is what he does in eurythmy, which is thus the revelation of the inner self. In eurythmy there is expressed what man can experience in breathing and in the circulation of the blood, when they come into the realm of soul. In gymnastics and in sport man feels as though space were a framework filled with all sorts of lines and directions into which he springs and which he follows, and makes his apparatus accordingly...

That is the difference between gymnastics and eurythmy. Eurythmy lets the soul life flow outwards and thereby becomes a real expression of the human being, like language eurythmy is visible speech.

By means of gymnastics and sport man fits himself into external space, adapts himself to the world, experiments to see whether he fits in with the world in this way or that. That is not language, that is not a revelation of man, but rather a demand the world makes upon him that he should be fit for the world and be able to find his way into it." (40 lecture 6)

When reading Steiner's often very spirited remarks on gymnastics, one is again and again faced with the question of deciding whether he is speaking about gymnastics of the traditional kind or of the gymnastics he himself inaugurated in the Waldorf School.

To follow these quotations as they occurred during the years of development of the Waldorf School can awaken an impression of the many phases of the struggle Steiner had on behalf of the gymnastics in order to raise them to a truly human level and so win them for an education bearing the seeds of the future.

This seems to bring to a conclusion a path of development by which something entirely new, bearing seed for the future, has come about out of a bodily training belonging to the past.

The new bodily training is on the one side eurythmy, on the other gymnastics, both of which can be looked upon as fully justified vis a vis the true aims of humanity.

Curriculum indications

Here follow the indications for the curriculum, first for eurythmy and then for gymnastics as far as they are available.

Eurythmy

| 1st-4th school years: | 1 lesson a week |
| 5th-12th school years: | 2 lessons a week |

The following are indications by Steiner which were given in the teachers' meeting of June 21st 1922 for a eurythmy curriculum.

For the school years 1-8 (3rd curriculum lecture)

"Now there is one thing that is very much to our advantage in the official curriculum. That is that no gymnastics of any kind were provided for in the first three years. So we begin with eurythmy.

It would be good if:

In the first school year eurythmy were done in conjunction with music so that actually an integration of eurythmy into geometry is practised.

In the 2nd school year we would begin with forming the sounds, and this is continued into the...

3rd school year always relating eurythmy to music, geometry and drawing. And then...

in the 4th, 5th and 6th school years, forms concrete, abstract, etc., things which are possible for the children now because they have meanwhile got this far in grammar. Then we continue...

in the 7th and 8th school years with more complicated forms." (16)

9th school year, 'continuation in eurythmy of all that belongs to grammar.' (22.9.20)

10th school year, 'In the eurythmy teaching one would have to work towards a reasonable kind of ensemble. By now the children have grown into young men and young ladies; they can produce finished ensemble forms. In tone eurythmy it is a question of bringing items that

have so far only been in the nature of a sketch to an artistic conclusion. It is better to restrict oneself to three or four items in the whole year, than start too many things, bringing the few to a proper perfection. One can get over the obstacle of boredom.' (17.6.21)

11th school year, 'There should be a certain concordance in eurythmy with other subjects. In aesthetics style will be considered in relation to certain works of poetry. If these were done simultaneously in eurythmy it would be a great help. You may find that this or that poem is particularly appropriate and then you will usually find that it contains quite special points of stylistic refinement. The teacher of aesthetics will want to make use of the poem to show a sonnet. Among the forms I have indicated you will find some for sonnets by Shakespeare and Hebbel. You will find that these forms vary greatly because they are completely adapted to the style'." (21.6.22)

There are no indications for the 12th school year.

In the years 1938/1939, when the Stuttgart Waldorf School had already been dissolved by the Hitler regime, the eurythmy teachers collaborated in putting down on paper what had become the custom in the eurythmy teaching. The result was the following list:

1st school year: Taking one's departure from elementary geometrical forms (viz. introduction to writing) and from simple musical exercises, the children are introduced to the simplest eurythmic movements and forms.

2nd and 3rd school years: Continuation of geometrical and musical exercises. Children should now firmly commit to memory the forms relating to the sounds.

4th-6th years: Forms for grammatical concepts are now added to the exercises practised up to now. In addition, more complicated geometrical forms.

7th and 8th school years: More complicated forms are dealt with, especially group forms for poems and music.

9th school year: We now begin with a systematic introduction to the laws of eurythmy forms and movements.

10th-12th school years: In speech eurythmy reasonable ensembles are practised in connection with poetic works of larger scope. In tone eurythmy we take musical pieces in several voices as a basis of group exercises. At this point close cooperation with the teachers of other subjects is desirable, particularly with the teacher(s) of aesthetics.

Gymnastics and apparatus work

From the 1st to 4th school years, 1 hour a week, and from the 5th school year, 2 hours a week.

At all levels boys and girls practise together by classes, though the tasks may partly be differentiated.

During Steiner's life-time the forming of a concrete curriculum was not arrived at. The principles however are laid down. What could be developed out of these up to the dissolution of the Waldorf School in 1938 was developed and put together by one of the gymnastic teachers who had been working till then, Count Fritz von Bothmer.

The urge for bodily movement arising from the disciplined, artistically directed work of the children in other subjects, should be taken up in gymnastics and brought to life. Children should so be able to move in conformity with the impulses working in them as a result of the teaching that has gone before, that they may really enjoy every movement. Therefore for younger children it will be especially important that the teacher is capable of stimulating truly free play. This would also apply to the apparatus exercises which of course are done by girls and boys alike.

By means of an activity stirred up from within the functions of the organs come into play in the healthiest manner and the children experience healthy sleep. Stereotyped movements on the contrary, which are imposed on the children from outside, paralyse their own activity and the participation of their soul. At the same time such movements paralyse the functions of the organs and make them diseased.

As the children grow older, say from the 4th and 5th school years, activity calling for courage is stimulated, ability to decide and steadfastness. Running, jumping, climbing, moving along when hanging from a bar, the beginnings of wrestling, throwing and games of a similar type, can then be the main content of the gymnastic lessons. Here too the children should participate in the activities with their whole being.

From about the 8th school year one can count on the fact that the boys and girls will enjoy regular practice in all domains of gymnastics, athletics and apparatus work, and can consciously experience a strengthening of their health. Gymnastics with or without apparatus will then become a consciously experienced activation of the whole body which can develop into an abiding habit for the whole of life as a result of the joy that young people feel through this activity.

Swimming is taught as in common practice.

17 Painting, Modelling, Drawing

Classes 1 to 8: as part of main lessons and, if possible, two extra lessons a week. (There were six main lessons a week in Germany, as Saturday was an ordinary school day.)

Classes 9 to 12: as part of the handicraft periods (lasting six weeks of three double lessons).

Steiner's indications for the three activities are given in chronological order. As painting, modelling and drawing form a unity, a different order would be impractical.

"In teaching children reading and writing we are teaching in the domain of the most exclusively physical. Our teaching is already less physical in arithmetic, and we are really teaching the soul and the spirit when we teach the child music, drawing, or anything of that kind." (12 lecture 1)

After speaking about the introduction of writing through drawing suitable objects (e.g., a fish for the letter "f") he continued:

"Consequently, we proceed by letting every child cultivate something to do with drawing and painting. Thus we begin with drawing, the drawing-painting, in the simplest way. But we begin, too, with the musical element, so that the child is accustomed from the first to handle an instrument." (ibid)

After a remark about the working together of thinking, feeling and willing, we read in the same lecture about the importance of artistic activities just in the early years:

"The point is never to pervert the willing by false means into the wrong direction, but to secure the strengthening of the will by artistic means. To this end from the first, teaching in painting, artistic instruction, and musical training too, should be employed. We shall notice incidentally that particularly in the first stage of the second period of his life, the child is most susceptible to authoritative teaching in the form of art and that we then can achieve the most for him with art. He will grow as if of himself into what we desire to pass on to him, and his greatest imaginable joy will be when he puts something down on paper in drawing or even in painting, which, however, must not be confused with any merely superficial imitation. Here, too, we must remember in teaching that we must transport the child, in a sense, into earlier cultural epochs, but that we cannot proceed as though we were still in these epochs. People were different then. You will transport the child into earlier cultural epochs now with quite a different disposition of soul and spirit. So, in drawing, we shall not be bent on saying: You must copy this or that, but we show him original forms in drawing; we show him how to make one angle like this, another like that; we try to show him what a circle is, what a spiral is. We then start with self-contained form, not with whether the form imitates this or that, but we try to awaken his interest in the form itself." (12 lecture 1)

After mentioning the legend of the acanthus leaf he continued:

"Then at last there will be an end of the fearful error which devastates human minds so sadly. When people meet with something formed by man, they say: It is natural – it is unnatural. But a mere correct imitation is of secondary importance. Resemblance to the external world should only appear as something secondary. Rather in man should live an impulse of becoming one with growing forces of the form itself. One must have, even when drawing a nose, some inner relation with the nose-form itself, and only later does the resemblance to the nose result. The inner feeling for form one would never be able to awaken between the age of seven and fourteen by merely copying the forms outside. But one must realize the inner creative element which can be developed between seven and fourteen. If one misses this inner creative element at such a time, it never can be retrieved." (12 lecture 1)

Steiner then mentioned exceptions, where what was missed at the right time, could still be done later though in rather an imperfect way. As these exceptions do not belong to class teaching they are not quoted here.

The following quotation from lecture 1 of the Practical

Course speaks about how through an artistic experience the whole human being can be involved in an activity:

"You elevate feeling into an intellectual experience in utilizing either the musical element or the element of drawing or modelling. That must be done in the right way. Everything today is in confusion, particularly where the artistic element is being cultivated. We draw with the hands, and we model with the hands – and yet the two things are completely different. This is most striking when we introduce children to art. When we introduce children to plastic art, we must pay as much attention as possible to seeing that they follow the plastic forms with the hands. When the child feels his own forming, when he moves his hand and makes something in drawing, we can help him to follow the forms with his eye – but with the will acting through the eye. It is in no way a violation of the naivete in the child to instruct him to feel this, to feel over the form of the body with the hollow of his hand. When, for instance, he is tracing the curves of a circle, we draw his attention to the eye. This is absolutely in no sense a violation of the child's naivete, but it engages the interest of the whole being. Consequently, we must realize that we are transporting the lower being, into the higher being, into the nerve-sense-being." (12 lecture 1)

In order to understand Steiner's ideas about teaching drawing, it is helpful to follow a certain line, beginning with the second lecture of his "Study of Man", then touching on several of his other lecture courses and finally to end with the Torquay Course. In this way the same problems can be looked at from different angles. I can only quote the most significant sentences from the Study of Man and must leave it to the reader to deepen his knowledge by returning to the actual lectures:

"You must then further represent to yourself that mental picturing is continually playing in from the other side of birth and is reflected by the human being himself. And it is because the activity which you accomplish in the spiritual world before birth or conception is reflected by your bodily nature that you experience mental picturing." (11 lecture 2)

Three pages further on we read:

"When you use this faculty today as physical man you do not do it with a force which is in you, but with a force which comes from a time before birth, and which still works on in you. You might suppose it ceased with conception, but it remains active, and we make our mental pictures with this force which continues to ray into us. You have it in you, continually living on from pre-natal times, only you have the force in you to ray it back. You have this force in your antipathy. When in your present life you make mental pictures, each such process meets antipathy, and if the antipathy is sufficiently strong a memory image arises." (ibid)

Actually this does not refer to drawing, painting and modelling but an appropriate place in lecture 2 of the course of 1920 will supply the necessary link.

After an illuminating remark about the deeper meaning of Goethe's colour theory Steiner said in lecture 3 of the Practical Course:

"Begin as early as possible to bring the child into touch with colours, and in so doing it is a good idea to apply different colours to a coloured background from those you apply to a white surface; and try to awaken such experiences in the child as can only arise from a spiritual scientific understanding of the world of colour." (12)

After characterising such an approach, he continued:

"In an elementary fashion we can invite children to understand this living inwardness of colours.

Then we ourselves must be very profoundly convinced that mere drawing is something untrue. The truest thing is the experience of colour; less true is the experience of light and shade, and the least true is drawing. Drawing as such already approaches that abstract element present in nature as a process of dying. We ought really only to draw with the consciousness that we are essentially drawing dead substance. With colours we should paint with the consciousness that we are evoking the living element from what is dead." (12 lecture 3)

After a few more sentences about the "line" of the horizon:

"In this way you will gradually realize that the form of nature really arises from colour, that therefore the function of drawing is an abstraction. We ought already to produce in the growing child a proper feeling for these things, because they vivify his whole soul's being and bring it into a right relation with the outside world." (12 lecture 3)

This remark about the quality of "untruth" in drawing which is akin to "that abstract element existing in nature as a dying process and which mainly belongs to what is dead", has often been interpreted as a wholesale condemnation of drawing. Remarks such as this one from the third lecture of the Practical Course led to teachers discouraging pupils from drawing lines altogether. It actually happened that line drawings done by Steiner himself were changed to the shaded-drawing technique in order to avoid a continuous line of a circle. It therefore is good to know that Steiner spoke very positively about drawing lines on the very same day during which he had made the negative observations mentioned above, namely on August 23rd 1919. He expressed the same views again on the following day when he spoke about elementary drawing with special reference to the children's temperaments. These positive statements are backed by others made in three lecture courses held abroad. In these he aimed at awakening a concrete space consciousness in children through appropriate tasks in drawing and at letting children experience spatial relationships between figures and free shapes, such as symmetry, diametry, movement and countermovement, repetition and intensification, etc. The following list indicates lectures which will explain the meaning of the above statement and which show how an artistic plan for elementary and geometrical drawing can be made by the teacher. Apart from the discussions already mentioned, there is the Dornach Christmas Course of 1921/22, the Ilkley Course and the Torquay Course. In the Dornach Course exercises are given which can lead the children towards a sense of beauty. (Please note that the copy of Steiner's drawing – the symmetry of an oak leaf – which was printed in shaded drawing technique misrepresents Steiner's artistic intentions. It stands to reason that the shaded drawing technique can only be used for filling in areas and not for drawing lines.) (27) The Second Course (Ilkley) shows similar tasks for drawing which awaken the sense of symmetry and, in this way, the child's concrete space experience of its own body. After having explained that during sleep the etheric body continues to evolve geometrical exercises done during the day, Steiner continued:

"In geometry, therefore, we must not take as our starting point the abstractions and intellectual constructions that are usually considered the right ground work. We must begin with inner, not outer, perception by stimulating in the child a strong sense of symmetry for instance. Even in the case of the very youngest children we can begin to do this." (35 "Ilkley" lecture 9)

In the Torquay Course tasks are given which are similar to those of the Ilkley Course:

"One will be able to do exercises of the following kind with children of approximately eight years old, even if they are a little clumsy at first." (40)

Here we find typical linear drawing exercises, not given to the youngest children (Ilkley) but to eight year olds, who nevertheless, belong to the youngest group – the first three school years.

It appeared necessary to interrupt the chronological sequence in order to correct a possible misunderstanding of Steiner's views caused by his words "dead", "abstract", "untrue" in connection with the drawing of lines. We therefore quoted his positive remarks about line drawings. Now we will continue chronologically:

In lecture 4 of the Practical Course Steiner described the first school lessons of pupils in Class 1 and after making several recommendations for this great event, he showed how one can guide the little ones in drawing during this very first lesson:

"When you have talked with the child for a time about hands and about working with hands, go on to let him make something or other requiring manual skill. This can sometimes be done in the first lesson. You can say to him: 'Watch me do this' (you draw a straight line). 'Now do it with your own hand.' Now you can let the children do the same, as slowly as possible, for it will naturally be a slow process if you are going to call the children out one by one and let them do it on the board and then go back to their places. The right assimilation of teaching in this case is of the greatest importance." (12 lecture 4).

Then followed the passage about a straight and a curved line. He also showed how painting can be introduced to the children:

"On a white surface that you have previously pinned on the board with drawing pins, you apply a small yellow patch. When you have made this small yellow patch, again let every child make his own yellow patch like it." (ibid)

He then placed blue areas between yellow areas and also between beautifully arranged green ones, in order to lead the children to the experience of yellow-blue on the one hand, and yellow-green on the other. This elementary exercise in drawing original shapes and painting original colour "intervals" is given right at the beginning of school life. I mention in passing that this should also be done in music by appropriate exercises. The next lecture, the fifth, once more illustrates the very first steps which the child takes upon entering school:

"Let us now suppose that you have pursued such exercises with pencil and with colour for some time. It is absolutely a condition of well-founded teaching that a certain intimacy with drawing should precede the learning to write, so that, in a sense, writing is derived from drawing. And a further condition is that the reading of printed characters should only be developed from the reading of handwriting. We shall then try to find the transition from drawing to handwriting, from writing to the reading of handwriting, and from the reading of handwriting to the reading of print. I assume for this purpose that you have succeeded, through the element of drawing, in giving the child a certain mastery of the round and the straight-lined forms which he will need for writing." (ibid lecture 5)

He then dealt with writing lessons and it is interesting to find that writing is a part of drawing lessons, part of linear drawing. On the afternoon of the 4th, discussion after a member of the group had spoken about stereometry, Steiner made a remark which is of general interest:

"Why should you want to go from solids to plane surfaces with a child? You see three-dimensional space is never an easy thing to picture and for a child least of all. You will not be able to impart to a child anything but a very hazy idea of space. And indeed his imagination will suffer if you expect a child to be able to imagine solid bodies. You are going on the assumption that the solid is the concrete thing, the line the abstract; that is not the case. If a child is to apply his imagination to a solid, then he must first have within him the necessary elements for building up this imaginative picture. For instance, he must really have a clear picture of a line and a triangle before he can understand a tetrahedron. It is better for him first to have a real mental picture of a triangle; the triangle is an actuality, it is not merely an abstraction taken from the solid. I should recommend you to teach Geometry, not in the first place as Solid Geometry but as Plane Geometry, giving figures with plane surfaces lying between them. This is very desirable, for the child likes to use powers of understanding for these things, and to start with Plane Geometry will be a support to him. You can add still further to the effect by connecting it with your drawing lessons. A child will be able to draw a triangle comparatively early on and you ought not to wait too long before you let him make copies of what he sees." (13, 4th discussion)

This point has been added to show how limited the young child is in its spatial consciousness, at least when entering school in Class 1. The last sentence, however, shows that children should be guided even at that age to grasp shapes and to copy what they have been looking at. Steiner does not mean the copying of different objects. This he wants avoided until a later age when he demands a strictly aesthetic and artistic attitude. He wants the children to copy what the teacher as the authority has drawn, so that in this way they can imitate what the teacher has created for them. Patterns or shapes of pedagogical value only are to be copied, not outer fixed objects.

The following passages from the Conferences (*4) show how difficult it was for the teacher to realise the pedagogical tasks given for painting and drawing.

After a report about work done in class:

"It is better to use water colour than coloured pencils. Crayons (Oelkreide) are possible." (22.12.19)

For a difficult boy:

"One should let 'X' draw some intricate pattern, a line which interlaces and which finds itself again. Start with drawing." (1.1.20)

About modelling:

"Don't encourage the child to make a slavish copy of the original object – force him to observe." (1.1.20)

When asked about left-handed writing:

"On the whole it will be found that children with a natural inclination to the spiritual are ambidextrous. But children with a materialistic bent would be driven crazy if they were made to write with both right and left hands. There is indeed a reason for right-handedness. It is quite true that in this materialistic age children would become idiotic through (an enforced) left-handedness. It would be harmful to make children use their right and left hands alternately as long as they are engaged in work of an intellectual or reasoning kind. Drawing is quite a different matter. They could well be asked to draw with both hands." (14.6.20)

In the Stuttgart Course of 1920 these puzzling sentences are found:

"There you have a case of actual co-operation between soul and body when you realize how the soul emancipates itself in the seventh year and begins to function – no longer in the body but independently. Now those forces which in the body itself come newly into being as soul-forces begin to be active in the seventh year; and from then on they operate through into the next incarnation. Now that which is radiated forth from the body is repulsed, whereas the forces that shoot downwards from the head are checked. Thus at this time of the change of teeth the hardest battle is fought between the forces tending downward from above and those shooting upward from below. The physical change of teeth is the physical expression of this conflict between those two kinds of forces: the forces that later appear in the child as the reasoning and intellectual powers, and those that must be employed particularly in drawing, painting and writing. All these forces that shoot up, we employ when we develop writing out of drawing." (25 lecture 2)

What was said here about the forces working through drawing, painting and writing, forces which Steiner usually called plastic forces, has a counterpole in what he said about the musical forces. When a teacher complained that the children found it very difficult to achieve forms with water colours Steiner gave the significant answer:

"Chalks should not be encouraged. The important thing would be – only we have not reached this stage yet (we have not yet made the relevant syllabus) – to decide (what each class should do). In the lower classes it would at first be a more orderly, a cleaner type of syllabus. In the lower classes – the others (the older ones) will have to do almost the same (because they have not been shown these things, as they have joined us only recently) but we must adapt it to their ages – the principle thing (in the lower classes) is that an inner feeling for the building up of colour is awakened in the children, that you awaken in them a feeling for a living world of colour through their experience of fairy tales." (15.11.20)

The teacher found this answer unclear and thought that one ought to give the children forms, definite motifs, whereupon Steiner gave the surprising answer which apparently seems to turn upside-down all previous ideas about painting.

"You will get your forms, if you allow their fantasy to work. You must let these forms grow out of the colours. You can talk to the children directly in a colour-language. Just think how stimulating it would be to enable them to understand you when you say: Here is this coquettish mauve, and on his neck a cheeky little red fellow is sitting. In the background there is a meek and humble blue. If colours become as concrete as objects, they will help to develop the soul. Let colours activate the soul. Everything which arises out of colour itself can be applied in fifty different ways." (15.11.20)

During this first stage, which has to be modified according to the age of the pupils, Steiner did not want outer objects or scenes to be copied naturalistically in paintings, but suggested themes born out of the feeling life, such as the one of "the cheeky little red." He also wanted children to experience right from the beginning how colours create space, how blue appears far distant, whereas red seems to move towards the observer, etc. When seeing the paintings of other children in this class, the pupils can experience that one theme may be painted in many different ways ("in fifty different ways..."). Thus a picture originating from the realm of feeling becomes "objective", in as far as it is put outside into space.

Steiner continued:

"You must let the children live in the experience of colour by saying, for instance, 'Here the red is peeping through the blue', and then really get the children to bring this about on paper, You should try to bring a great deal of life into this. By stimulating them in this way, you free them from a kind of lumpishness, sluggishness. Speaking generally, it is important for our time that living in the experience of colour is cultivated and deepened. This in turn will stimulate the musical element." (15.11.20)

So much about the first stage of painting. The second stage will give some answer to the above-mentioned problem of themes in painting, if understood rightly. This second stage would entail the children's knowing beforehand what effect pure and mixed colours will have with regard to space and form ('objective' painting, in the above sense). Only then will the third stage be reached, consisting of a given theme taken from the outside world, which can now be painted because the pupil knows how to build it up entirely out of the element of colour.

Steiner's sentences about linear drawing are just as instructive as these sentences about painting with young children. When a teacher asked whether one should practise drawing in a similar way Steiner answered:

> *"Do not practise line-drawing as such, except in geometrical constructions. The other kind of drawing is important, namely working with light and dark areas. In this respect Class 9 has not yet shown much progress. One must make use of anything which will help."* (15.11.20)

After a discussion about physics in Class 10, Steiner said quite spontaneously on September 11th 1921:

> *"I should like to stress the importance of Baravelle's work for any teacher who has to deal with drawing. I have mentioned this on several occasions. These matters are of great importance also in aesthetics. All teachers ought to occupy themselves with his dissertation. Handwork especially could greatly benefit from such a study. There is much that would throw light on how to make a collar, a girdle or a garter. A treatise like Baravalle's is of fundamental importance for any Waldorf teacher, because it shows the transition from mathematical thinking to mental imagery. This could be applied in a much wider sense. What he has worked out for the various forms and shapes could also be applied to colour and even to the world of sound. Regarding sound you will find many a hint in Goethe's outlines of a theory of sound, published in my last volume of the Kurschner and Weimar edition. This index is full of content. The theory of colour can also be treated in the same manner."* (11. 9.21)

Baravalle's book about drawing of shapes should be studied carefully, for it can lead to fundamental ideas in kindred subjects. His concrete division of areas and space by means of curves which, by their aesthetic appeal, can bring about a real understanding of space, is the underlying principle of the book.

The Dornach Course of 1921/22 also deals with first painting lessons in Class 1:

> *"And added to this the child brings with him potentialities. He is inwardly a sculptor and we can draw out this potential faculty from his general aptitudes. But he brings other potentialities with him, so, however troublesome this may be, we should let him do all kinds of things on the paper in colour, for by this means he can be led into the secrets of the world of colour. It is, for instance, extremely interesting to see how the children find their way into the nature of colour, if to begin with they are allowed simply to cover a white surface with bright colours. They cover the white surface with colours in which, through the inborn potentialities of the child, a certain colour harmony will already exist. What they spread over the paper is not without meaning; it has a certain colour harmony. One must only be careful not to let the children use the colours which are found in so-called 'children's paint-boxes', from which the*

> *colours are painted on to the paper direct from the tablets. This is always detrimental even in painting as an art. The paint should be used from jars in which the colours are dissolved either in water or in some similar substance. One must develop an inner, intimate relation to colour. The child must have this, too. There is no intimate relation to colour when one simply paints directly from the palette; this only develops when one uses colours dissolved in a jar.*

> *If one says to the child: Look now, what you have done there is beautiful. In the middle you have painted a patch of red, and this showed you what to do next. Everything you painted after that went together with the patch of red. Now do it in just the opposite way. Exactly where you painted the red patch, now put a blue one. And now you must arrange everything to go, not with the red in the middle, but with the blue. In the first place the child is tremendously stimulated by such an exercise; secondly when the child is given something of this kind to do (perhaps with a little guidance from the teacher) he will certainly work out this transposition into another fundamental colour sequence in such a way that he gains an immense amount in his inner connection with the world. Further, whatever inconvenience this may entail, the child should be allowed to model little plastic objects... well, out of material which somewhere or another you are able to find. It is very important, however, to prevent the children from making themselves into a mess. This is certainly troublesome but the gain to the children is infinitely greater than if they were allowed to get themselves into a mess."* (27)

In the Spiritual Ground of Education, Steiner spoke about painting with children whose mental images remain stuck in their heads:

> *"Everything depends upon the contact between teacher and child being permeated by an artistic element. This will bring it about that much that a teacher has to do at any moment with an individual child comes to him intuitively, almost instinctively. Let us take a concrete illustration for the sake of clarity. Suppose we find difficulty in educating a certain child because all the images we bring to him, the impressions we seek to arouse, the ideas we would impart, set up so strong a circulation in his head system and cause such a disturbance to his nervous system that what we give him cannot escape into the rest of his organism. The physical organism of his head becomes in a way partially melancholic. The child finds it difficult to lead over what he sees, feels or otherwise experiences, from his head to the rest of his organism. What he learns gets stuck, as it were, in the head. It cannot penetrate down into the rest of the organism. An artist in educating will instinctively keep such a thing in view in all his specifically artistic work with the child. If I have such a child I shall use colours and paint with him in quite a different way from how I would paint with other children. Because it is of such importance, special attention is given to the element of colour in the Waldorf School from the very beginning. I have already explained the principle of the painting; but within the painting lesson one can treat each child individually.*

We have an opportunity of working individually with the child because he has to do everything himself."
(29 lecture 6)

The following pages of the same lecture give a complete background to the last quotation. The next passage contains Steiner's words spoken during the Oxford Course, when a geographical map was shown to him:

"You see here (maps) how fully children enter into life when the principle from which they start is full of life. You can see this very well in the case of these maps: first they have an experience of colour and this is an experience of the soul. A colour experience gives them a soul experience. Here you see Greece experienced in soul. When the child is at home in the element of colour, he grows to feel in geography: I must paint the island of Crete, the island of Candia, in a particular colour, and I must paint the coast of Asia Minor so, and the Peloponnesus so. The child learns to speak through colour, and thus a map can actually be a production from the innermost depths of the soul. Think what an experience of the earth the child will have when this is how he has seen it inwardly, when this is how he has painted Candia or Crete or the Peloponnesus or Northern Greece, when he has had the feelings which go with such colours as these. Then Greece itself can come alive in his soul, the child can awaken Greece anew from his own soul. In this way the living reality of the world becomes part of a man's being. And when you later confront the children with the dry reality of everyday life they will meet it in quite a different way because they have had an artistic, living experience of the elements of colour in their simple paintings, and have learned to use its language." (ibid)

The principle to which Steiner refers is that the children are allowed to experience colours inwardly first, so that the resulting forms are a direct consequence of their colour experience. To a question about the treatment of colours in art lessons (apparently in Class 9) Steiner answered in a teachers' meeting:

"Can you not carry out what I said yesterday to the boys and girls – what I said directly about the treatment of colour? This would have to be the subject of many lessons. Perhaps someone could get Dornach to send us what I have said about this subject there. I think that with this class you must pass on directly to the practical treatment of colours, so that they become conscious of what they do in the lower classes. They must become conscious of this.

For of course much will have to be developed regarding the method of teaching and this should be linked to what you have already begun in corresponding lessons and to what you have let them draw hitherto. I do not refer merely to curve drawing. You can use the same method when using colours. For instance, you can contrast, just as you would be doing it with curves, a round and well-defined blue patch with a yellow patch trailing on without boundary. From there you can pass over to comparative anatomy. Contrast the front and hind extremities. You can contrast certain animals' capacity of sense-perception and feeling with the wagging of a

dog's tail. There you find the same criterion. In this way you enter life and reality. These methods ought to be introduced into all branches of teaching." (15.10.22)

I have not been able to find out whether these words about the practical treatment of colour were addressed to the teachers of the art lessons or to the teachers of handicrafts. The second part of the passage refers undoubtedly to all the teachers of the upper school. Again one is faced with the puzzle of the course of 1920.

In the Dornach Course of 1923 we find a revealing passage about colour perspective and linear perspective:

"Yes, when one has once accustomed oneself to having a sense for such aspects of life, we are led on to other matters. You see, all the different things which are introduced to the child must be brought into connection with each other. As I said to you, we let the child paint something or other out of his own picture-forming forces – naturally not with pencils but with actual colours. Then I notice that the child lives with the colours. Gradually (one must only have the feeling oneself that this is how things are) the child will notice that blue is something which goes away from us, which recedes into the distance, whereas it is the nature of yellow and red to approach. This is something that appears very strongly even in a child of 7 or 8, if only he is not tormented at this age by any kind of formal training in drawing or painting. If one merely lets the child paint houses or trees naturalistically, this method will not work. But if the child follows the teacher's intentions, so that it can feel, 'Wherever I move my fingers, colour will follow – the material of the colour is of minor importance – colour will come to life in my fingers.' Here it wants to continue to flow. If we achieve this we arouse in the child's soul something of deep meaning: colour perspective; the child gets the feeling that the yellows and reds approach nearer, that the blues and violets go further and further away.

Thus working out of inner experience, we develop a sense for what will later have to be worked out with the child, the perspective which is carried out in lines. It is extremely harmful to a child to introduce perspective at a later age without having previously brought to him a kind of inner colour perspective, it has a terribly externalizing effect when he has to accustom himself to acquiring quantitative perspective without having previously experienced the inner, qualitative perspective which lies in the perspective of colour. And something further is inherent in this connection: If you prevent the child from living intensively in this colour perspective, he will never learn to read as quickly as he should, but always with the limitations which I spoke of yesterday - though here it is in no way meant that at the beginning reading should be brought to the child as quickly as possible. But from this colour perspective the child acquires pliant ideas, pliant feelings and perceptions, pliant impulses of will. Everything in the soul becomes more mobile, Maybe, because of all that is required here – the development of reading out of painting-drawing, out of drawing-painting – you will have to take somewhat longer in teaching the child to read. But then, at the appropriate age it will certainly be possible to bring reading to the child in the right way, so that it does not enter in a too superficial way into the body, into the whole being of the child – which can also happen – nor yet inducing it too deeply into the child by imparting the form of each separate letter in a way which makes a tear in the social being of man." (34)

Quite spontaneously on 25th April 1923, after speaking about astronomy, Steiner said:

"The pupils in the school in Dornach have done brilliantly in their painting. I have shown how to distinguish between sunrise and sunset, and some have caught the idea excellently. Things of this kind can be given. Rainy atmosphere in a wood is an exercise for 14-15 year olds." (25.4.23)

After a visit to a Class 8 he said:

"I had a look at their work. Here I should like to say that it is essential for the children to stretch their paper, if they are to paint with water colours. Otherwise you encourage slovenliness. They must learn how to stretch their paper.

The work in their exercise books could not possibly stimulate ideas in the children. They ought to learn to stretch their paper properly, using paste. Let them use liquid colour only on stretched paper. They set about their tasks far too haphazardly." (3.7.23)

Steiner gave a report on his visit to the Ministry of Education:

"I told him that when we have gone far enough and have built up our curriculum, I shall try to develop the whole of the freehand drawing from Dürer's picture, Melancholy. In it there is every shade of light and dark and it can also be transposed into colours. If you can help the pupils to come to an understanding of the whole picture, they should be able to do anything." (12.7.23)

On the 12th July 1923 Steiner said:

"There is one question which I have very much at heart. That is how we ought to solve this problem of exercise books, into which they have been painting, seeing this can only rightly be done on stretched paper. It is indeed true that in this way great slovenliness is being developed, Drawing boards we cannot have because they are much too expensive. A board evenly planed, would also be a solution. Could not such boards, on which paper can be stretched, be made in the handicraft lessons? This method of allowing children to paint in an ordinary exercise book does not prove satisfactory. As soon as you begin to use water colours, you must also begin to stretch the paper." (12.7.23)

Another aspect of painting and drawing lessons is found in the fourth lecture of the Ilkley Course:

"And so we look at the human being; we see his head. In the head the growth-forces of the teeth free themselves and become the force of thinking. Then, pressed down, as it were, into speech, we have all the processes for which the teeth are no longer directly responsible, because the etheric body now takes over the responsibility. The teeth become the helpers of speech. In this, their relationship to thought is still apparent. When we understand how

the dental sounds find their way into the whole process of thinking, how man takes the teeth to his aid when through sounds like d or t, he brings the definite thought-element into speech, we again see in the dental sounds the particular task performed by the teeth." (35)

In the lecture of August 16th 1923 Steiner pointed out the important connection between modelling and the physical ability to see:

"Thus, according to the Waldorf School principle, we begin to give painting and drawing lessons at a very tender age of childhood. Modelling too is cultivated as much as possible, albeit only from the ninth or tenth year and in a primitive way. It has a wonderfully vitalizing effect on the child's physical sight and on the inner quality of soul in his sight, if, at the right age, he begins to model plastic forms and figures. So many people go through life without even noticing what is most significant in the objects and events of their environment. As a matter of fact, we have to learn how to do it before we can see and observe in the way that gives us our true position in the world. And if the child is to learn to observe aright, it is a very good thin for him to begin, as early as possible, to occupy himself with modelling, to guide what he has seen from his head and eyes into the movement of fingers and hand. In this way we shall not only awaken the child's taste for the artistic around him – in the arrangement of a room, perhaps – and distaste for the inartistic, but he will begin to observe those things in the world which ought to flow into the heart and soul of man." (35)

After a remark about music lessons he continued:

"The mineral kingdom can be understood in the light of cause and effect. The physical can be grasped in this way. When we come to the plant world, however, it is impossible to grasp everything through logic, reason and intellect. The plastic faculties of man's being must here come into play, for concepts and ideas have to pass into pictures. Any plastic skill that we develop in the child helps him to understand the formations contained in the plants." (ibid)

On February 5th 1924 a long discussion followed a remark of the handicraft teacher about painting lessons in the upper school, which unfortunately could not be given as regularly as lessons in the lower classes. The question referred to the technique of painting in the lower classes and Steiner's answer touched upon all aspects of the child's painting:

"It does not matter if the painting lessons are interrupted for a few years and replaced by modelling. The facts are that regular painting lessons in the younger years have an after-effect in the subconscious, and it is important that a resumption of painting lessons is carried out with vigour and skill on the part of the pupils. It is always the case that if an activity has been brought to a halt, a very marked progress will show itself on resumption, just because of the previous interruption.

I believe that in the lower classes there is still need of improvement in the teaching of painting. Some teachers have not paid enough attention to the technical aspects. Materials have not been used rightly. You should not let the children paint on paper which does not retain a smooth and even surface, but you should make them stretch their paper before painting. Then you should insist on the children finishing their paintings right to the end, so that the picture represents a stage of completion. Most of their paintings are mere beginnings.

What you aim to achieve will depend on your discussing the technical problems, the handling of the materials, etc., with your colleagues, since you, as a trained painter, have the necessary experience. There is no other practical solution.

In the two top classes (at that time Classes 11 and 12) you could let the gifted pupils paint again. Enough time is available. You would have to let them begin again with very simple tasks. If you let them be guided entirely by artistic principles, you will not encounter difficulties. For younger children it is right to create out of their feeling life, but in the case of older pupils you need to consider more objective artistic aspects. For instance, you should draw their attention to the fact that light, when it falls on an object, immediately creates an artistic effect, etc. Take everything from a practical point of view. After the tenth year you should not encourage children to paint outer objects, for this practice would have harmful effects." (5.2.24)

Steiner began to draw on a blackboard with coloured chalks:
"The older the children are, the more you should concentrate on the painter's power of observation. Show them: Here is the sun. The sunlight falls upon the tree. Now do not start by drawing the tree with its shape, but by putting down the dark and light surfaces, so that the tree begins to appear out of the meeting of light and dark areas, out of the light and darkness of colours resulting from the falling sunlight. Do not begin with the abstract concept: the tree is green. Do not let them paint green leaves. Leaves should not be painted at all, only areas of light with its different shades. This should be carried through: Then, if I were obliged to begin only with 13 and 14 year olds, I should make use of Dürer's 'Melancholy', should call attention to the wonderful distribution of light and shade. The light in the window, the distribution of light in the polyhedron and the globe. Then take Jerome in his study, etc. Starting with Dürer's 'Melancholy' is quite wonderful, this transposing of a black and white picture by means of colour imagination.

You cannot expect all teachers to be skilful painters. There may be some who do not wish to paint because of their poor resources. It must be possible for a teacher to give painting lessons, even if he cannot paint adequately himself. It is hardly possible for us to train all our pupils to perfection in every branch of the arts and sciences." (5.2.24)

This is probably the most important passage regarding painting. In it Steiner does not mention painting with the lower classes but this he has done often enough on other occasions, especially in a "Conference" on November 15th 1920. There he spoke about beginning with the sense-impressions of colour, with arranging colours side by side in

space without copying outer shapes. This introduction to painting in the first class again is based on the principle of not letting children paint outer objects. This point may have been the cause of Steiner's reprimand given to teachers who "had not bothered to try hard enough" and naturally it was made also because the children painted on paper which had not been stretched.

Free painting out of the child's imagination is right for the younger ages, even if this means painting scenes, figures or objects, for these are not copied from the outside but are pictures of an inner "soul-space". This, however, is only advisable after an initial introduction into the "Language of the Colours". With older pupils one needs to show the painter's point of view. The meaning of this phrase becomes clear if one thinks of the example of a tree lit up by the sun. There only areas of light and shadow (darkness) should be painted and out of this the tree begins to grow on paper. This is the 'painter's point of view', which is different from merely painting the "object tree". We therefore get the two stages:

Children under 10

The "language of colours", painting out of feeling for colour which allows illustrations of scenes experienced inwardly but not copied from outside.

After the 10th year

A return to painting lessons, if these have been temporarily discontinued; painting from "the painter's point of view". No themes of outer objects should be given, but the world of colour outside should be approached via light and shadow (darkness).

This shows a development from an inner experiencing of colour, which has to be awakened in younger children, to an experience of colour outside in nature where objects are lit up. If one has to introduce painting to 13 to 14 year old pupils who have not had any previous training, one can make a beginning with the exercise of Dürer's 'Melancholy'. For at this age it is no longer feasible to appeal to an inner 'space-creating' experience of colour. On the other hand, pupils are not yet ready to paint entirely out of the observation of light and dark shades in lit-up objects of the surroundings. Therefore Dürer's 'Melancholy' is given as an example which may well stimulate all kinds of questions including those of perspective.

When talking about ways of nurturing the gift of fantasy in children, Steiner had this to say in Arnheim about introducing the element of drawing into painting and vice versa. ("painting-drawing, drawing-painting")

"Quite apart from the fact that in no circumstances do we begin by teaching the children to write but we let them paint as they draw, and draw as they paint. Perhaps we might even say that we let them daub (patzen), which involves the possibly tiresome job of cleaning up the classroom afterwards.

We guide the child as far as possible into the realm of the artistic by letting him practise modelling in his own little way, but without suggesting that he should make anything beyond what he himself wants to fashion out of his own inner being. The results are quite remarkable. I will mention one example which shows how something wonderful takes place in the case of rather older children." (39 Arnheim lecture 3).

Steiner described how the study of anthropology stimulates the wish in the children to model forms. This is a most interesting point which should be followed up by reading lecture 3.

In the Torquay Course Steiner showed how children can be led to the experience of colour-harmony already in their eighth year:

"Suppose we do an exercise with the child by first of all painting something in red (red patch). Now we show him, by arousing his feelings for it, that next to this red surface (inside) a green surface (around it) would be very harmonious. Now you can try to explain to the child that you are going to reverse the process. 'I am going to put the green in here inside; what will you put round it?' Then he will put red round it. By doing such things you will gradually lead to a feeling for the harmony of colours. The child comes to see that first I have a red surface here in the middle and green round it, but if the red becomes green, then the green must become red. It is of enormous importance just at this age, towards the eighth year, to let this correspondence of colour and form work upon the children." (40 lecture 4)

This exercise of elementary colour harmony shows what Steiner meant when he suggested that the way of looking at geometrical forms as shown in Baravalle's book should also be applied to colours and different hues. In the same Torquay Course Steiner showed why the pupil has such a strong desire to form plastic shapes:

"We must be clear in our minds that the independent activity of the etheric body of man only really begins at the change of teeth. The etheric body in the first seven years has to put forward all the independent activity of which it is capable in order to build up the second physical body. So that this etheric body is pre-eminently an inward artist in the child in the first seven years; it is a modeller, a sculptor. And this modelling force, which is applied to the physical body by the etheric body, becomes free, emancipates itself with the change of teeth at the seventh year. Then it can work as an activity of soul.

This is why the child has an impulse to model forms or to paint them. For the first seven years of life the etheric body has been carrying out modelling and painting within the physical body. Now that it has nothing further to do as regards the physical body, or at least not as much as before, it wants to carry its activity outside. If therefore, you as teachers have a wide knowledge of the forms that occur in the human organism, and consequently know what kind of forms the child likes to mould out of plastic material or to paint in colour, then you will be able to give him the right guidance. But you yourselves must have a kind of artistic conception of the human organism." (ibid)

Finally Steiner spoke in this same course about the true value of drawing, pointing out that this activity tended to be grossly overrated in our times because of a wrong approach to optics:

"An artistic feeling will prompt you to work out what is really there out of black and white or colour. Lines will then appear of themselves. Only when one traces the boundaries which arise in the light and shade or in the colour do the 'drawing lines' appear.

Therefore instruction in drawing must, in any case, not start from drawing itself but from paintings, working in colour or in light and shade. And the teaching of drawing as such is only of real value when it is carried out in full awareness that it gives us nothing real. A terrible amount of mischief has been wrought in our whole method of thinking by the importance attached to drawing. From this has arisen all that we find in optics, for example, where people are eternally drawing lines which are supposed to be rays of light. Where can we really find these rays of light? They are nowhere to be found. What you have in reality is pictures. You make a hole in a wall; the sun shines through it and on a screen an image is formed. The rays can perhaps be seen, if at all, in the particles of dust in the room – and the dustier the room, the more you can see of them. But what is usually drawn as lines in this connection is only imagined. Everything, really, that is drawn, has been thought out. And it is only when you begin to teach the child something like perspective, in which you already have to do with the abstract method of explanation that you can begin to represent aligning and sighting by lines." (40 Questions and Answers)

Thus the Torquay Courses gives us important guidelines for painting, modelling and drawing.

Curriculum indications

Now follows a summary of Steiner's indications for the first eight classes, taken from the curriculum lectures:

"Now I should like to draw your attention to the fact that up to the 6th year we have taken geometrical forms – circle, triangle – out of drawing. We were doing drawing in the first school year in order to teach writing. Then gradually we made the transition from employing drawing for the sake of writing, to the development of more complicated forms for their own sake, drawing them for drawings sake, and also painting for painting's sake. We guide the drawing and painting lessons into this sphere in the 4th class. In drawing we teach what a circle is, an ellipse, etc. This is learnt through drawing. This we take further, always leading to practical forms, using Plasticine for modelling, in order to bring about a fine feeling for form.

In the early classes as we have seen, we conduct the drawing lessons in such a way that the child acquires a certain feeling for round and angular forms, etc. Out of these forms we develop writing. During these elementary drawing lessons we avoid any copying whatsoever of outer objects. Do avoid as much as possible letting the child copy a flower or other objects; instead encourage him as much as possible to draw lines and forms, round, pointed, semi-circular, elliptical, straight, etc. Arouse in the child a feeling for the difference between the curve of a circle and of an ellipse; in short awaken the feeling for form before the urge to imitate outer objects awakens. Only later, when he copies objects, let him apply what he has learnt from his first drawing exercises. Let the child draw an angle so that he grasps it through its form, then show him a chair and say to him: You see, here is an angle and there is another. Do not let the child copy until you have cultivated in him, out of his inner feeling, the form as self-creative activity. And you keep to this when you start treating drawing and painting and modelling in a more independent way." (16 lecture 2)

"Then you bring forward in the 6th class a teaching of simple projection and the study of shadows, drawn freehand but also with ruler and compass and similar instruments. See that the child gets a good grasp of the following and can draw it: Here is a cylinder and there a globe, and the globe is shone upon by a light, how will the shadow of the globe look when it falls on to the cylinder? Simple projection and shadow drawing must be taken in the 6th school year. The child must get an idea and be able to copy how shadows fall on a flat and on a bent surface, and from other surfaces more or less flat, and from solid objects. The child must also discover in the 6th class how the technical can be combined with the beautiful, how a chair can be technically adapted to its purpose and at the same time have a beautiful shape. This idea of combining the technical with the beautiful must enter into the child." (ibid)

For a better understanding of the above quotations, a remark made by Steiner in the meeting of January 16th 1921 will be quoted. A teacher had asked whether it would be preferable to introduce projections artistically or through geometry:

"Where possible, it is best to teach in such a way as to build a bridge between something that is purely geometrical, something that does lead over into art. I do not believe that you can treat this artistically. What is meant is the conical projection. I certainly think that the children really ought to know what the shadow of a cone is like on a plane – they ought to have an inner picture of it." (16.1.21)

This remark brought the question: "Should teachers use technical terms such as rays of light, rays of shadow.

Steiner answered:

"This is a more general question. It is not advisable to introduce things into projective geometry which do not exist at all. There is no such thing as light rays, still less are there shadow rays. There is no need to use such concepts when dealing with projective geometry. Rather think in terms of space being filled with varied content. Light rays and shadow rays do not exist, but cylinders and cones exist. A body of shadow exists which is caused by a solid cone, standing oblique, and being lit up by a point of light, if the shadow falls on an inclined plane. In such an instance a 'shadow body' does exist, and the child ought to be able to grasp this fact. A child ought to be able to understand the curved border line of the shadow-body. Just as later on it will have to understand in projective geometry what happens when one cylinder interpenetrates another cylinder of a smaller diameter. It is of real importance to teach this to the

children. You need not fear that such a thing will undermine an artistic sense, for you are remaining within the artistic element. You are training flexibility in ideation. Your powers of imagination will become pliant if you know as a matter of course what kind of curve will arise when cylinders intersect each other. It is of great importance to introduce such matters, but do not teach abstractions." (16.1.21)

"In the seventh school year everything connected with interpenetration of solids should be practised. Taking a simple example you could say: 'Here is a cylinder with a post going through it. The post has to be pushed right through the cylinder. You have to show what kind of a surface line arises where the post enters and where it leaves the cylinder.' The child has to learn what happens when solids or planes intersect each other so that he knows the difference between the aperture made by a stovepipe piercing the ceiling vertically, thus causing a circular aperture, and one made by a slanting pipe, in which case an elliptical aperture ensues. In addition, during the same year, the child should gain a clear grasp of perspective, of simple perspective drawing with lines becoming shorter in the distance and longer in the foreground, etc.; also overlaps should be explained and drawn.

Then you should show how an architectural problem can be solved in a way which may either satisfy our sense of beauty or not, so that the child will get an idea whether, let us say, a projection covering the wall of a house would improve or spoil its appearance. Such considerations make a particularly strong impact upon a child of thirteen plus if they are introduced in class seven.

Towards class eight all these considerations should reach a kind of artistic climax." (16 lecture 2)

Up to this time art lessons were given by the class teacher. From Class 9 onwards painting, modelling and drawing become part of handicrafts. In these lessons pupils practise modelling, they produce all kinds of handmade articles, they learn black and white drawing, furthermore they are taught simple carpentry and they should practise water colour painting. Further details can be found in the section on handicrafts.

Steiner expected a great deal from the teachers of painting, modelling and drawing. Painting with liquid paints on carefully stretched paper, at first mainly a technique, should lead to an experiencing of colours and their subtle harmony. Colour harmony represents only the first stage, and movement of colour with its inherent colour space or colour perspective, the second stage.

The children's elementary painting leads at first to chance results because they do not yet know how to build up a picture entirely from the colour aspect. In these chance results we can discover the unconscious nature of the children.

The children's paintings in this first stage remain within a soul space created entirely through colour perspective, if a leaning on outer objects has been avoided.

The second stage is reached when the children have experienced the space-creating quality of colour, so that they know already before dipping the brush into the paint pot, which movement and thereby which form will result. At this stage the teacher should give themes out of the sphere of feeling and not themes representing the outside world.

A third stage, which can be aimed at already in Classes 4 and 5, is reached if one adds lit-up surfaces found outside to the inner colour experience. With this step the painting from imagination of, let us say, a fairy-tale picture, becomes transferred through an inner awakening to the solid objects found in outer space.

In all paintings we find these two elements:

a) the outer objects appear as lit up or shadowed areas perceived quite unconsciously, or:

b) there is movement of colour experienced inwardly.

Much has been achieved if during the painting in the middle school these aims have been carried out methodically so that they have become a capacity, however small. After an interval lasting two years, all that has been learnt previously is now lifted into the sphere of consciousness and learnt anew (see section dealing with handicrafts).

Only very few hints and indications exist for modelling. The children should begin modelling in the ninth or tenth year. They should be guided to make plastic forms out of the hollow of their hands and then forms for forms' sake can be made out of the previous results. A similarity to outer objects should be discovered only when the form is completed. We have been told that a real knowledge of the forms of human organs awakens a desire for modelling in the child which, however, will not result in his copying outer forms. Drawing penetrates other subjects again and again. First the drawing of simple shapes leads to writing (Class 1). Then the symmetry and kindred exercises help to develop a spatial consciousness, which leads to geometry, starting in Class 4 with accurate drawing of geometrical shapes. Beginning with Class 6 geometrical drawing leads to geometrical proofs and finally to projective geometry up to the end of the middle school. In Class 9 this branch of drawing is developed into a strictly mathematical drawing which is continued throughout the upper school.

In Class 10 map drawing in the surveying course and in Class 11 map projections as part of geography represent the last branches of this subject.

Survey of the aims in painting, modelling, drawing

		Painting	Modelling	Drawing
1	*Feeling for the inner laws of form fostered, but never through mere imitation.*	Colours and shapes as aids for learning writing. Outer objects are not to be copies, but shapes are to be recreated.		
2		Inner feeling for the building up of colour (colour harmony) for the movement of colours for colour space and colour perspective. "Colours become concrete" "No object-motives" Creating out of the soul" creating in soul-space		Simple pattern drawing as aid for learning writing. Symmetry and other spatial relationships – copying what has already been drawn – triangles comparatively soon
3				
4			Modelling from 9 to 10 years old within the framework of main lesson. Experience of form with the hollow of the hand, with the will working through the eye	gradual transition to geometry ("describing")
5		From now on awaken a feeling for fundamental laws of painting. Warning: no outer objects are to be copied, but only what arises out of colour-areas should lead to the picture.

Up to Class 8

Special task:
Dürer's "Melancholy" transposed into colour. St Jerome in his Study | | |
6				Projective geometry and shadow drawing. The bridge between pure geometry and art. Combining what is functional with what is aesthetic
7				Interpretation, perspective again combining what is functional with what is aesthetic
8				All this (from Class 6) to be artistically deepened
9		Black and white drawing in handicraft lessons. (No painting)	Modelling in free forms in handicraft lessons	Descriptive geometry in mathematics period
10				Map drawing in the surveying period
11		Take up painting again in handicraft lessons. "Begin again with the simplest things but from the aspect of painting" i.e., colour perspective and the creating of space through colour patches		Map projection in the mathematics period
12				

18 Handwork and Bookbinding

Class 1 to 4	each 2 lessons (double period)
Class 5 to 7	each 1 lesson
Class 8	2 lessons
Class 9 and 10	each 1 lesson a week
Class 11 and 12	each 6 weeks of 4 lessons

On his first school day the pupil of the Steiner school already gets a taste of "handwork". Steiner thought it very important that "the child knows that it has hands to work with." In the 4th lecture of the Practical Course, which deals with the first school lessons, he describes how the teacher tells his new pupils why they are coming to school, in order to make them realise the significance of the human hands:

> "Look at yourself, now. You have two hands, a left hand and a right hand. You have these hands to work with; you can do all kinds of things with these hands. In such a way one can try to awaken the child's consciousness regarding the nature of man. The child must not only know that he has two hands, but he must be conscious that he has hands. Of course, you will probably say here: 'Obviously he is conscious of having hands'. But there is a difference if while knowing he has hands to work with this thought has never crossed his soul. When you have talked with the child for a time about hands and about working with hands, go on to something or other requiring manual skill. This can sometimes be done in the first lesson." (12 lecture 4)

Steiner showed how one can introduce drawing exercises which later will lead over to writing.

Steiner's first remark about handwork was made on July 30th 1920:

> "I have attended only a few handwork lessons, but in one of them I had to ask myself, 'Why has the child no thimble?' I have always said that we must accustom the children to using a thimble for their sewing. A child cannot sew without a thimble. That can hardly be done. They were sewing without a thimble and this won't do." (30.7.20)

Here the thimble represents orderliness and efficiency which should be taken for granted and which Steiner wanted in handwork lessons engrained in the young children.

On January 16th 1921, during the third year of the Waldorf School, Steiner gave the first guide-lines for handwork lessons:

> "When choosing the different kinds of tasks, you must consider how to fit them to their purpose. It is not possible to apply an artistic touch to every article made. Though you should not neglect to foster an artistic feeling, you can hardly make use of it when knitting a stocking. But you can always let the child make something pretty when he has completed his stocking. Beware of sliding into Froebel methods! One can always make useful articles artistically and in good taste." (16.1.21)

When the syllabus of the first Class 10 was made Steiner said only these few words about handwork lessons:

> "Handwork in Class 10 must become more and more artistic." (16.6.21)

Again a reminder to the teachers to endeavour to reach artistic standards with their pupils.

On June 17th 1921 handwork teachers were recommended to teach knitting to newcomers to a higher class, but then to let them join the main work done in the class.

In September 1921 Steiner spoke enthusiastically about Hermann von Baravalle's dissertation. He had joined the staff only recently. He compared the importance of this work with the introduction of projective geometry by the Frenchman Monge. What mattered in Steiner's opinion was not so much the mathematical aspect, but the influence of this book upon the non-mathematical, to space:

> "I should especially like to recommend anyone who teaches drawing, to study Baravalle's thesis. I have taken trouble to refer to it in various ways. These things in Baravalle's thesis are also extremely important for aesthetics. Each of you should make it your business to study it. Handwork teaching above all can receive a great deal from it. There is certainly much that can be gained from it if you work out the form of a collar, a garter, according to the principles indicated here, collar, girdle and garter.

> A work like that of Baravalle – however, he must not become arrogant – is of fundamental importance for the Waldorf teacher, because it shows the transition from mathematical thinking to that of mental imagery. This could be applied in a much wider sense. What he has achieved with regard to form could also be applied to colour and even to the world of sound. Regarding sound, you will find many a hint in Goethe's outlines of a theory of sound, published in my last volume of the Kürschner and Weimar edition. This index is full of content. The theory of colour can also be treated in the same manner." (11. 9.2 1)

On November 16th it was agreed to give handicraft lessons in block periods. The effect of such an arrangement on other subjects was also discussed. A handwork teacher pointed out that she preferred to teach her pupils once a week. Steiner answered:

> "If we are not aiming at a training in arts and crafts, such intervals of time do not matter. If we are aiming at the latter, then it is desirable to get the children to work in a concentrated manner. If you let them do book binding, you must get them to work with concentration; also when they make cardboard boxes. This will also be introduced. In Class 10 we already have practical lessons. In such a class one ought not to take any other handicraft." (16.11.21)

In the Dornach Christmas Course for teachers Steiner said this about handwork lessons:

> "The handwork teaching is arranged according to the Waldorf School principle that boys and girls shall be together in one class, and also that they shall be engaged on the same work. It is a real joy to see boys and girls in the handwork lessons working together at knitting, crochet, and the like. From practical school experience one can give an assurance that, although

a boy gets something different out of knitting from what a girl does, he nevertheless gains a great deal from it; first and foremost, perhaps, the delight he takes in doing it. The significant part which this working together can play in a person's whole development – I shall discuss this later in detail – has already shown itself. Again, in the handicraft lessons, the girls must do exactly the same work as the boys, heavier types of work, so that the pupil's skilfulness, the development of his skilfulness, can everywhere be kept in view." (27)

In lecture 14 of the same course, which deals with the aesthetic aspect of education, Steiner said:

"Beauty must be regarded as an integral part of life. Everywhere a sense must be developed for the fact that beauty is not something enclosed in itself, but that it is something which has been woven into life. And in this respect, particularly in regard to its teaching and educational aims, our present civilization has much to learn." (27)

This is followed by advice on how clothes and objects of utility can be made to look beautiful.

During a meeting on April 28th 1922 when the syllabus for Class 11 was discussed, Steiner said:

"We should consider teaching bookbinding in handwork lessons, The main thing is that the children learn how to bind a book, that they gain the skills involved." (28.4.22)

On June 20th of the same year, Steiner remarked.

"Then the question arises how to provide for handwork lessons in this class. It must be possible for that to play a part... Then we must be clear that bookbinding and box-making is part of the work of this class." (20.6.22)

In the Oxford Course Steiner showed how good painting lessons led to good results in handwork lessons:

"You will observe that the aim is to build up the handwork lessons in connection with what is learned in the painting lessons. Do not let the children draw first and then embroider, but really let them deal freely with the element of colour itself. Thus it is immensely important that children should come to a right experience of colour... (after rejecting work from the palette).

"It is necessary that children should learn to live with colours, they must not paint from a palette or block but from a jar or mug with liquid colour in it, colour dissolved in water. Then a child will come to feel how one colour goes with another, he will feel the inner harmony of colours, he will experience them inwardly. And even if this is difficult and inconvenient,... yet enormous progress can be made when children get a direct relation to colour in this way, and learn to paint from the living nature of colour itself, not by trying to copy something in a naturalistic way. Then colour mass and colour form come seemingly of their own accord upon the paper... It is a matter of putting one colour beside another colour, or of enclosing one colour within other colours, In this way the child enters right into colour and, little by little, of his own accord he comes to produce form out of colour. Here, what

is attempted, is not to paint something, but to paint experience of colour. The painting of outer objects or scenes can come later on. If this is begun too early, a sense for a living reality is lost and a sense for what is dead is allowed to enter."

"If you proceed in this way, when you come to the treatment of any particular object in the world it will be far livelier than it would be without such a foundation... In this way (through his experience of colour), the living reality of the world becomes part of a man's being. And when you later confront the children with the dry reality of everyday life they will meet it in quite a different way, because they have had an artistic living experience of the elements of colour in their simple paintings, and have learned to use its language."

On October 28th 1922 the number of handwork lessons was fixed:

"In future we will give one double period per week to Classes 1 to 4; for all other classes one single period per week." (28.10.22)

When the girls of the upper classes complained that the boys were interfering with their handwork, the teacher suggested making handwork a voluntary subject for boys. Steiner replied:

"How could we do that? We have fitted this handwork lesson into our timetable in a way that gives no reason for making a change. It cannot be left optional. How should that be done? Then we should have to make it a principle that the children only come to what suits them.

It is possible to have variety in the lesson. In the handwork lesson, the children are fully occupied and this offers good opportunities of giving them different tasks. There is no need for all of them to do the same kind of work. From Class 8, 9 onwards, you can, as far as I am concerned, occupy the children in a variety of ways; giving the boys one kind of work and the girls another. If we make it optional, we should destroy our curriculum." (9.12.22)

From the Dornach Easter Course 1923:

"Just for that period which makes its appearance in human life with puberty, the transition to the external actualities of life must also be found; so that now to an even greater degree there must play into the school what, in a higher sense and in accordance with body, soul and spirit, will make of the pupils, people useful in life. In these matters we have not nearly enough psychological insight. For the finer spiritual relationships inherent in the human organization of spirit, soul and body are at present not even surmised. These are only divined today by those who make it their task to learn to know the life of the soul. And out of a certain self-knowledge I can tell you in all modesty that there are matters in the domains of spiritual science, which to-day perhaps – indeed certainly – appear to many as the reverse of useful, which could not have been put forward as I put them forward, if for instance at a certain age (not through Waldorf School education but through destiny) I had not learned the craft of book-binding. The particular human activity involved

in book-binding provides something quite special for the most intimate aspects of spirit and soul, especially when introduced at the right age. This is the case just with the practical activities! And I should regard it as a sin against the being of man if with us in the Waldorf School, just at a particular age which can be read from human nature itself, the handwork lessons were not to include book-binding and the making of boxes, the working with cardboard. These things must play their part if one is to become a complete human being. It is not the fact of having made this or that box, or bound this or that book, which is the essential matter; but that one should have carried out the processes which are involved, should have experienced the particular feelings and thoughts." (34)

In his lecture, entitled "Education towards Inner Freedom" held at Ilkley on August 17th 1923 Steiner said:

"The art of education originating from Waldorf Pedagogy also reckons with the modern striving towards improving the social life. Much that would otherwise remain remote from the one sex to the other can be developed when boys and girls are educated together... During the handwork lessons in the Waldorf School, you will find boys and girls sitting together all engaged in knitting and crochet. That this is not unnatural but absolutely natural activity, is proved by the fact that our boys learn to knit and even dam stockings with a certain pleasure. It never occurs to them that such work is unworthy of their manhood! We do not include these things so much for the sake of giving the boys a knowledge of them, as for the sake of an all-round understanding of life. One of the chief faults of our present social conditions is that man has so little understanding of what his fellow men are doing. We must really cease existing as isolated individuals and groups and face each other with full and complete understanding, and the main point is that this kind of handwork gives the human being practical skill in many different directions. Incongruous though it may appear, my opinion is that nobody can be a real philosopher who is not also able, in an emergency, to darn his stockings or mend his clothes!" (35 lecture. 12)

On September 18th 1923 the question was asked whether sewing cards, i.e., cards with imprinted patterns for sewing, would be suitable for children aged twelve, because of their geometrical patterns. Steiner replied:

"Yes, that is right. After the 12th year it would be too much like play. Only I should never want to introduce things into the school which are not met with in life, as these could be alienated from life. Froebel things are specially invented for school. Only things drawn from external culture, from real life, should be brought in a suitable way into the school." (18.9.23)

Steiner also spoke about handwork and bookbinding in the Torquay course on August 19th:

"I should dearly like to have a shoemaker as a teacher in the Waldorf School, if this had been possible. It could not be done, but for example, in order that the children might really learn to make shoes and to know, not theoretically but through their own work, what this

entails, I should have dearly liked from the very beginning to have a shoemaker on the staff of the school. It is just the very thing that would have been in accordance with real life. Nevertheless we do try to make the children into practical workers." (40 lecture 7)

He then spoke about embroidering useful articles in a similar way, though with less detail, as in the Dornach Course of 1921/22.

This is all that can be found about handwork. Steiner did not give a definite syllabus for each class and he left it to the co-operation of the handwork teachers and the teachers of painting and aesthetics to work out details. In this way a proper curriculum was made, mainly through the initiative of Fraulein Hedwig Hauck. It was as follows:

Class 1   The children learn knitting with two needles by knitting small face flannels. Every double period ends with little artistic tasks, such as drawing on the blackboard.

Class 2   Work started in Class 1 is completed. Then crochet work is introduced and small articles are made. The children also design and make some smaller artistic articles.

Class 3   The children make some larger useful articles in crochet, such as caps, jumpers, tea-cosies, etc. They continue with the smaller subsidiary tasks begun in Class 2.

Class 4   The children learn exact sewing by making little bags in handwork, which they embroider with their own designs.

Class 5   The children now learn how to make different parts of their own clothing. One begins in Class 5 with knitting socks and gloves. Apart from that, the children make toys such as animals, dolls and dolls' houses. For this work the children also make their own designs.

Class 6   Now eurythmy shoes and slippers are sewn and sensibly embroidered. Toy-making is continued.

Class 7   The children sew a shirt or other article of clothing and learn how to embroider it after their own designs. The boys learn how to make their own gym-shorts or shirts.

Class 8   Work begun in Class 7 is continued and working with sewing machines is introduced. The different cloths and materials are explained and mending, ironing and mangling practised.

Class 9 and Class 10   The pupils are guided in designing and making articles such as cushions, cases, covers, which are to serve a definite purpose. Basketry and raffia work are introduced and hammocks, hats, dresses, etc., made. Painting posters and designing book covers with water colours are also practised.

Class 11 and Class 12   The pupils learn book-binding and box making. (Kartonagen).

19 Handicrafts

Arts and Crafts (manual skills)

From Class 6 to Class 8, two periods a week. From Class 9 to Class 12, six afternoon periods for six weeks a year.

Steiner mentioned handicrafts for the first time in the 11th lecture of the Practical Course, after speaking about geography teaching:

> *"Do not omit, even at the beginning, when showing the child the connection between agriculture and human life, to give him a clear idea of the plough, of the harrow, etc., in connection with this geographical idea. And try especially to make the child imitate the shapes of some of these implements even if only in the form of a little plaything or piece of handiwork. It will give him skill and will fit him for taking his place properly in life later on. And if you could even make little ploughs and let the children cultivate the school garden, if they could be allowed to cut with little sickles, or mow with little scythes, this would establish a good contact with life. Far more important than skill is the psychic intimacy of the child's life with the life of the world. For the actual fact is: a child who has cut grass with a sickle, mown grass with a scythe, drawn a furrow with a little plough, will be a different person from a child who has not done these things. The soul undergoes a change from doing things. Abstract teaching of manual skill is really no substitute." (12 lecture 11)*

So much for the first task of handicraft which most likely has not yet been put into practice by any Steiner School.

When summarising the work done in the first year of the Waldorf School, Steiner said:

> *"One must try to teach out of Anthroposophy, so that all our teaching is imbued by it, without however teaching any Anthroposophy in a theoretical way. Anthroposophy will live in your teaching if you try, as your ideal, to use rhythm in your class work. Try for instance to link what has been done in music and singing lessons to handicraft lessons. I recommend Karl Bücher's 'Work and Rhythm' in this context. Such an approach has an extraordinarily beneficial effect on children. All manual work was based on musical rhythm. To-day this is hardly noticeable any longer. However, if you went into the country and listened to people threshing, you would realise how the flail was handled rhythmically. I think we could recapture such a way of working. What I really mean is, we must bring spirit back into our activities. This underlying principle, however sophisticated and pedantic it may appear in the book, you will find in Bücher's 'Work and Rhythm'. (23.6.20)*

At the beginning of the second year of the Waldorf School, when the curriculum of the first Class 9 was planned, Steiner gave the following instructions:

> *"I should have thought that in handicraft lessons one could quite unobtrusively cultivate in whatever one is doing, an artistic element, a feeling for what is truly artistic. Let the children make all kinds of things which, however, they must finish properly. I should not let them make only utilitarian things but also toys, sensible toys. For instance I think it would be a nice idea if they made out of wood two smiths facing each other and moving together when the wooden handles are being manipulated. Such toys make the children develop manual skill. You can also let them make presents for other people. This, too, offers many possibilities.*
>
> *And if you can let them gather moss – and this is something which will introduce a festive mood into the children's lives – and, at Christmas time, ask them to make little cribs entirely by themselves, if you let them paint their little sheep, etc., then something of great inner value and benefit can develop. – Do not neglect the making of the more utilitarian articles. The children will have great fun in making rattles, which are like a practical joke.*
>
> *We rattle, we rattle, all twelve together,*
> *The bells they come from Rome," (22.9.20)*

These indications, given for the benefit of the then new handicrafts teacher, Max Wolffhügel, are the first general directions. The specific instructions for each class are taken from conversations of Max Wolffhügel with Steiner.

On January 16th 1921 Steiner said to the handicrafts teacher:

> *"There is no objection to the children making cooking spoons. Don't let them make far-fetched articles and, if possible, no fancy articles." (16.1.21)*

At the beginning of the third year of the Waldorf School the syllabus for handicrafts was made for the first Class 10:

> *"Handicrafts lessons must be guided into the really artistic element, as you have already done with your modelling. This you can alternate with painting; those who are clever at it can paint with you. We can regard those who have just come into the 10th class as though they were at the Gymnasium, (*3) and so we can treat our art work and handicrafts in a really artistic way. I mean that we still need something in the nature of aesthetics, and there Dr. Schwebsch will be of value by showing the aesthetic connection between the sculptural-painting and the musical element. He has occupied himself a great deal with the musical side. With regard to the aesthetics of music – whose fundamentals should be introduced – you should form a sub-committee of the college to work out how arts and crafts can be developed from manual skills, and how this leads over into the musical element, so that the aesthetic rather than the theoretical aspect can be nurtured. I think that you should open the children's eyes as early as possible to what is beautiful, say in the construction of a chair or a table. Do it in such a way that you get rid of the nonsensical idea that a chair should look beautiful to the eye. You should appreciate the chair's beauty when sitting on it. I pointed out a similar thing yesterday in the handwork lesson, when I said that the children should express in the manner of their embroidery where the opening side is of an article (e.g., in a tea-cosy). I believe that such an awareness will become more general. Handwork, handicrafts and artistic feeling, they will all flow together. Of course this must be done properly and not as in the 'Gymnasium' (*3) where all this has been done, or is still being done in quite a dreadful*

way, Herman Grimm always complained when people came to him and he showed them pictures, that they could not discover whether a person in the pictures was standing in the front or at the back of the picture. They had no idea. The pupils from the Gymnasium (*3) had no idea whether a person was standing in the front or at the back of the picture." (17.6.21)

On November 16th 1921 the handicrafts teacher expressed the wish to teach his subject in block periods in the upper school:

"Every day for one week with one group of pupils." (16.11.21)

On June 22nd, 1922, the same question was discussed once more. Steiner said:

"We ought to consider whether we could not gain a period by dropping a language for a limited time. This would also relieve the teachers to a certain extent without letting the teaching suffer. Such a break in language lessons would not be harmful, in the languages such an interval is quite feasible." (22.6.22)

When asked how long such a break should be he replied:

"One can begin in Class 9, in periods lasting a fortnight. This could be done every six weeks and distributed over the year." (22.6.22)

In the Oxford Course the artistic aspect in handicrafts was stressed:

"The instruction and education can appeal better to the child's whole nature because it is conceived as a whole in the heart of the teachers' meetings, as I have described. This is particularly noticeable when the education passes over from the more psychic domain into that of physical and practical life. Particular attention is paid in the Waldorf School to this transition into physical and practical life.

Thus we endeavour that the children shall learn to use their hands more and more. Taking as a start, the handling little children do in their toys and games, we develop this into more artistic crafts but still such as come naturally from a child.

This is the sort of thing we produce (showing the toys, etc.). This is about the standard reached by the 6th school year. Many of these things belong properly to junior classes, but, as I have said, we have to make compromises and shall only he able to reach our ideal later on – and then what a child of eleven or twelve now does, a child of nine will be able to do. The characteristic of this practical work is that it is both spontaneous and artistic. The child works with a will on something of his own choosing, not at a set task. This leads on to handwork or woodwork classes in which the child has to carve and make all kinds of objects of his own planning." (29 lecture 7)

Steiner continued to speak about carving, especially carving moveable toys, and then he made the following statement:

"The children do this between the eleventh and fifteenth years and nowadays even later, but gradually we shall have to bring it down into the younger classes,

where the forms have to be simple." (29)

It is interesting to see that tasks which are set in Class 6 and later, are supposed to be given to younger classes. "Then a nine year old child will be able to make what now an eleven to twelve year old child is making with regard to practical tasks." Such statements should be thought about again and again.

A further discussion about arranging handicraft lessons in afternoon periods can be found under 28.10.22.

When a pupil asked to be excused from taking part in handicrafts because of his music lessons, Steiner said in a teacher meeting:

"If this occurred often we should be obliged to arrange a special group of pupils who want changes of this kind, and the parents would have to agree that their children should miss much of what we are aiming at in our teaching. Each case would have to be dealt with individually for the pupil to receive such exceptional treatment." (14.2.23)

In his lecture given on August 17th 1923 at Ilkley Steiner also spoke about handicrafts:

"At the proper age – indeed comparatively early – we let our children make toys and playthings for themselves. They carve toys from wood and in this way too we bring the element of art into their play.

To lead play gradually over to the creation of artistic forms and then to the practical work of which I have just spoken, is to act in complete harmony with the demands of man's nature. And it is absorbingly interesting to find that the children's plastic, artistic activity turns quite naturally to the making of playthings and toys. Here again we lead over from art per se to art as a factor in industrial life. The children are shown how to make simple implements, simple thing for use in the house and at the same time learn how to use saws, knives and other tools in joinery and carpentry. Boys and girls alike love to be in our workrooms, working with knife and saw and other tools, in addition to their ordinary lessons, and are delighted when they succeed in making something really useful. In this way we stimulate all their instincts for the practical side of life. On the one hand then, we unfold a sense for the practical side of life and on the other, for art." (35 lecture 12)

Here we find a significant keynote: the child's play is to be guided towards an artistic activity and this activity leads to a practical way of working.

Though Steiner gave general outlines for this subject, he hardly set any detailed tasks for the various classes. Some of these details were worked out by the teacher of handicrafts, Max Wolffhügel, and they are listed below:

Class 6 The children are introduced to woodwork and they make simple practical objects.

Class 7 The experience gained so far is applied to the and making of moveable toys. After this, simple Class 8 artistic objects with regular shapes are made.

Class 9 Free modelling is introduced. Useful objects and with free shapes are made, and black and white Class 10 drawing is practised.

Class 11 Continue with last year's work. Elementary furniture making is introduced.

Class 12 Black and white drawing is continued and led over to painting with water colours. Carpentry is continued.

20 Free Religion Lessons

Two lessons a week for all classes.

The unique character of religion teaching in the Steiner schools has prompted me to introduce Steiner's quotations in chronological order.

The cultural situation in Germany in 1919 which led to the founding of the Waldorf School and which also influenced the position of religion lessons, was characterised by Steiner at the end of his first curriculum lecture:

"Now I need hardly tell you that with the teaching material of which we have spoken up to now, very many things will be developed through the child's consciousness – that spirit permeates everything in the world; that spirit lives in speech; that spirit lives in what as geography covers the earth; that spirit lives in history. When we attempt to feel the living spirit in everything we shall find the right enthusiasm for bringing this living spirit to our pupils. And then in the future we shall learn to make good what has been sinned against by Religious Confessions since the beginning of modern times. These Religious Confessions which have never provided for free human development have furthered materialism from many sides. When one may not use the collective world-material to show man that spirit works, then religion lessons become a breeding ground for materialism. Religious knowledge has taken upon itself the task of forbidding spirit and soul being spoken of in other lessons as it wished to preserve this as a privilege. Therefore religious knowledge has dried up the reality more and more, and what is brought forward in the religion lessons has as substance (?) mere sentimental turns of speech and phrase. And what as mere phrase dominates the whole world today is in reality more closely connected with ecclesiastic than with worldly culture. For the emptiest phrases are made use of in religious instruction to-day, and these phrases, working in man's instinct, are carried over to everyday life. Certainly external life also gives birth to much that is mere empty phrase, but religious knowledge sins most in this direction.

We shall see, my dear friends, how the first subject on the syllabus, religion (in Rudolf Steiner's days religious instruction headed the list of subjects in the official syllabus) – which I do not touch upon at all in these talks as that will be the task of the Church communities – will influence the other subjects in our Waldorf School teaching. This subject must be left entirely alone. The religion lesson will be handed over to the religion teachers. Here they will be free men. Here they do not listen to us... We shall do our duty in this respect, but we shall also do it by charming spirit into all the other subjects taken with the children." (16 lecture 1)

In the 12th lecture of his Practical Course Steiner spoke about the position of the religion lessons:

"We shall have to make compromises as you know, with regard to religious instruction, which will have the disadvantage that the religious element will not come in close connection with the other subjects. But even to-day, if the religious parties would make the same compromises from their side, much might be achieved by the close association of religious instruction with other subjects. If, for example, the teacher in religious instruction condescended now and then to take up some other aspect of study; if for instance, he were to explain to the child, as an incidental part of his religious teaching, and connected with it, the steam engine or something of a quite worldly nature, something having to do with astronomy, etc., the simple fact that the teacher of religion is doing this would make an extraordinary impression on the consciousness of the growing children." (12 lecture 12)

In the last two quotations, which belong to the time of the founding of the Waldorf School, Steiner only referred to religious instruction given by visiting priests of different denominations. The words from his opening speech of September 7th also refer to this arrangement:

"But we shall honour our promise: the priests of the different religious denominations who are to give religion lessons in this school, will be free to bring into this school the principles of their world outlook. We shall wait and see whether what they will introduce to the school, without any hindrance on our part, will affect adversely what we wish to bring into the school with all modesty as a new art. For we know: Mankind must first understand that an art of education can be evolved out of a spiritual outlook upon the world, before it can achieve real insight into the problems of the different religious backgrounds and their reciprocal relationships. This means that we are not founding an ideological school, but we shall endeavour to create a school in which the art of education can be practised." (17 end part of the speech)

During the following two weeks Steiner was in Berlin and in Dresden and only returned to Stuttgart on September 24th. During this interval members of the Anthroposophical Society, who also were parents of children at the Waldorf School, asked Steiner to initiate religious instruction for their children which was based on anthroposophy.

Thereupon he founded a non-sectarian, or "free" religious teaching which was to be offered side by side with the other denominational instruction. In other words, these dogma-free religion lessons were not instituted by the school for the school, but in response to a request made by the anthroposophical parents that their children should also receive religion lessons in the school as the children of parents of the various denominations did. Many pupils whose parents worked at the Waldorf-Astoria cigarette factory and who most likely would not have had any religion lessons, now enrolled for these newly opened religion lessons. Steiner spoke about this development in his 8th lecture of the Dornach Christmas Course of 1921/22:

"Because it is in no way our intention to create a school standing for a particular world conception – as might easily be supposed – but rather to carry Anthroposophy into educational practice, it was also a matter of comparative indifference to me if we simply left the very core of people's world conception – namely their religious outlook – in the hands of the representatives of the traditional religious denominations; and so it came about that the Catholic religion teaching was placed at the disposal of the Catholic priest and the Evangelical religion teaching in the hands of the Evangelical pastor. But things turned out in such a way that, when our friend Emil Molt founded the Waldorf School, the main proportion of the children were those of the proletarian workers of his factory. For the most part these people were dissenters, whose children, had they gone to another school, would have taken part in no religious teaching at all, who would have grown up without religion. In their case matters turned out in such a way that we became aware just through the children themselves in the way things can become apparent through children, that their parents felt the need for their children too to have something of a similar kind. So to fill this need we had to arrange our own religion teaching. Just as the Evangelical teaching was given over to the Evangelical pastor and the Catholic religion teaching to the Catholic priest, these lessons now became an accepted part of the time-table, and were given over to certain of our own teachers who were then regarded as the teachers of religion.

In this way anthroposophical religion lessons are being given. And today things have already reached the stage where this anthroposophical religion teaching means a great deal for the children of the proletariat, but also for the other children. Here a particular difficulty appears. We have an Anthroposophy for adults, but to-day the teacher, if he is to succeed in his anthroposophical religion teaching, must wrestle with the task of creating real content in what he is to take through with the children. This means that he must first cast the anthroposophical world-conception into a form in which it can be brought to the child, and we are engaged in various ways on working through to an anthroposophical world-conception suitable for children and which is in keeping with the human spirit. Here for instance, it is necessary to enter deeply into the degree in which symbols, which must be used, affect the child, and how what is imponderable comes into consideration." (27)

Steiner discussed this situation, which had already developed in the Autumn of 1919, during the first teachers' meeting (*4) which he led after his return from Dresden:

"You must tell the children that whoever wishes to have free religion lessons must decide definitely, and then this lesson must take its place as a third beside the other two (denominational religion lessons). There must be absolutely no doubt that the children cannot attend other

religion lessons as well. Nevertheless you can arrange these free religion lessons according to classes. Let us say the four upper and the four lower classes can be grouped together. Someone of us can give these lessons." (25.9.19)

On the same day Steiner remarked:

"We will not mix the denominational and the free religion lessons. Neither will we try to win over pupils. We will only act in accordance with what is desired. We would rather advise pupils to attend the denominational lessons. Those pupils who do not want to attend religion lessons, we will leave alone, but at the same time it might be good to try to find out why they do not want to have religion lessons. We should have to find this out in each individual case. Some might wish to take up denominational religion lessons again or they may prefer to attend our anthroposophical religion lessons. Something should be done about it. We do not want the children to grow up without any religious teaching." (25.9.19)

When asked whether the class teacher was to give these religion lessons, Steiner answered:

"One of us could take on this task, but it need not be the class teacher. It is not desirable that someone unknown to us should be chosen. We should remain within our own teaching body. If there were sixty children, we should divide them into two groups of thirty each. Perhaps we could put together pupils from the four upper and the four lower classes. I shall give you a syllabus for these lessons. This subject must be taught with the greatest care." (25.9.19)

On the same day Steiner drafted the first syllabus for these two groups composed of pupils from classes one to four and five to eight.

"In the first group everything that has to do with reincarnation and karma must be omitted. These themes must only be talked of with the second group. But there they must be introduced. From the 10th year onwards these things must be taken. When speaking about these themes, it is particularly necessary that right from the beginning you should have the pupils' own participation in mind. Reincarnation and karma should not be spoken of just theoretically but practically.

Children, when they approach their 7th year, still have something like a memory of all kinds of conditions which were present before birth. Sometimes they relate the most curious things, which are a picture of these earlier conditions – this is not an isolated example, but typical – children come and say: I came into the world through a funnel which stretched further and further. They describe how they came into the world. Yet let them describe these things, you let them co-operate, and you foster this, so that it is drawn out of the (sub)-consciousness. That is very good, but do avoid talking at the children. You must elicit what they themselves have to say. But that you are doing, that belongs to our way of teaching. The subject could be enlivened in this way, as shown in yesterday's public lecture. It could be the most beautiful thing if one's teaching were to put new life into every minute of one's pedagogical efforts, simply because it is based on a true knowledge of man; if there were no tendency on the part of the teacher at indoctrinating pupils in a one-sided world conception. This was the underlying theme of my last article in the Waldorf magazine, covering the educational basis of the Waldorf School (19). What I indicated in this article is in effect a summary of what we studied in our course, only written for public consumption. I should like to ask you to look upon the content of this article as an expression of our teaching ideals.

One and a half hours religion teaching a week is sufficient for each group: three quarters of an hour twice a week. It would be specially good if it could be on Sundays, but this would be difficult to arrange. In these lessons you could also make the children familiar with the verses of the 'Calendar of the Soul'." (25.9.19)

When a teacher wondered whether these verses would not be too difficult for the children, Steiner said:

"There must be nothing which is too difficult for the children. What matters is not how they take in thought-content, but the way the thoughts develop. I should like to know what could be more difficult for the children than the Lord's Prayer. People only imagine that it is easier than the verses in the Calendar of the Soul. This is true also of the Creed, and therefore they oppose it. Otherwise they would not do so. It contains only what is really obvious, but up to their 27th year people have not developed far enough to be able to understand it, and after that they learn nothing more from life. The treatises on the Creed are childish. There is nothing in it about which it is possible to come to any decision from out of oneself. You can also recite the verses from the Calendar of the Soul with the children before the lesson." (25.9.19)

On the next day, 26th September 1919, Steiner gave the teachers the detailed syllabus for the two stages:

"These lessons must be given in two stages. If you are prepared to teach Anthroposophy in religious terms, you will have to take the concept of religion far more seriously than this is usually done. Usually the concept of religion is distorted because all kinds of extraneous things are brought into it, things which really belong to world conceptions. Because of this, religious traditions have carried over from one age to the next, ideas and concepts which have not changed with the times.

Thus old world-conceptions remain side by side with those evolving along new lines. You find grotesque examples of this situation at the time of Galileo and Giordano Bruno. The way such things are still being justified to-day in Apologias is almost funny. The Catholic Church used as an excuse the fact that the Copernican system was not yet recognised at that time although the church itself had suppressed it. This was the reason why Galileo was not allowed to talk freely about the Copernican picture of the universe. I do not wish to go into details here, I merely mention it in order to point out that religious teaching must be taken seriously as soon as we are dealing with anthroposophical matters.

Anthroposophical knowledge stems from a world conception which, as such, we definitely do not wish to disseminate through our teaching. On the other hand, we must develop the religious feelings which are the result of an anthroposophical world outlook for the sake of those pupils whose parents have asked for such religion lessons. However, we must be careful not to allow anything false, above all nothing premature to enter into our work. We shall therefore divide our pupils into two groups. First we shall put together the children of the four lower classes and then those of the upper four classes. In the four lower classes we shall talk about matters and processes belonging to the human realm in our surroundings in such a way that the children begin to feel that spirit dwells in nature. We can use the examples already given: For instance you might wish to bring to the children the concept of the human soul. To do this, it is essential to speak first of all about the meaning of life itself. This you can do by drawing their attention to the fact that human beings are born very small, that they grow up, become old, get grey hair and wrinkles in their face, etc. With other words you make them aware of the serious nature of man's life and of man's death; for sooner or later the children are bound to come across the meaning of death.

Then it becomes by no means unnecessary to draw comparisons between what goes on in the human soul during sleep and during waking life. Such things you can discuss even with the youngest children. Describe the characteristic features of waking and sleeping, point out how the soul is at rest, how the sleeping person lies still, etc. Then you talk about the way the soul permeates the body on awakening, and how a force of will shows itself in the movement of the limbs; how the body gives to the soul the senses by means of which men can see, hear, etc. Such things can prove to the child that spirit works through the physical realm. These matters you should discuss with the children.

What you must avoid at all costs is any kind of superficial teaching of functional purposes in nature. Anthroposophical religion teaching must hold itself entirely aloof from the doctrine of functionalism which would answer the question: 'Why do we find cork in the bark of a tree?' by saying, 'So that we can manufacture stoppers for champagne bottles. The good God has arranged it wisely so that we can use cork for bottle stoppers.' The inherent idea that everything has its purpose in nature which is useful for man is veritable poison for the mind and must be avoided altogether. Whatever you do, do not introduce such trite utilitarian ideas into your teaching.

Just as little must you encourage the idea which so many people cherish, that the unknown is a proof for the existence of the spirit. Some people are given to say, 'Oh, this we cannot fathom, for there the spiritual reveals itself.' Instead of gaining the conviction that they can learn to recognise the spirit which reveals itself in matter, people so often are tempted to look upon anything which lies beyond human explanation as proof for the existence of the divine.

Those two tendencies must be excluded from our religious teaching, that of a false and superficial idea of the purposefulness of natural phenomena and the other which equates unfathomable miracles with the proof of the existence of the spirit.

On the other hand our real task is to evoke an awareness of how the supersensible is living behind the tapestry of outer nature. To quote an old example: We talk to the children about the chrysalis and how the butterfly emerges from the chrysalis, in this way giving them a picture of the immortality of the human soul. We can say, 'Yes, man must die and his immortal soul rises out of his corpse like an invisible butterfly out of the chrysalis.' But such a picture has value only if you yourself are convinced of its truth, if to you the picture of the butterfly emerging from the chrysalis is a symbol of the soul's immortality placed before your eyes into nature by Divine Powers. If you yourself are not sure of this, your words will not carry any weight at all.

Ideas of this kind should stimulate the children and they will become specially powerful if you can show how a being, an archetypal form can live in many different guises. In religion lessons it is important to nurture what belongs to the feeling realm and not what is part of a world philosophy. Poems about the metamorphosis of plants and animals are quite suitable in this respect as long as you appeal to the feeling content of each line. You can speak about nature in a similar way up to the end of class four. You also must arouse in the children time and again the picture of man with his whole thinking and willing as belonging to the entire universe. Furthermore you should awaken again and again the idea that God lives in all that lives in us. Come back again and again to the following imaginations: The Divine lives in every leaf, the Divine lives in the sun, in each cloud and river does the Divine live. But the Divine also lives in our flowing blood, it lives in the beating heart, in all we feel, in all we think. Always engender the idea that man is permeated by the Divine.

A further task for the religion teacher at this stage would be to convey to the children the feeling that man, as the representative of God, has the moral duty to be good, and that man does an injury to God if he fails in this. From a religious point of view man has not been placed into the world for his own sake, but as a revelation of the Divine. This has often been expressed with the words: Man does not exist for his own sake but 'for the glory of God'. But in reality 'for the glory of God' signifies in this case 'for the revealing of God'. Just as the words 'Glory to God in the highest' really mean 'The Gods reveal themselves in the heights'. In a similar way, the sentence: 'Man exists for the glory of God' should read 'Man lives on earth in order that he may express the Divine through his deeds and through his feelings'. And if Man does something bad, if he is irreligious and worthless, then he commits an offence against God which distorts God, through which even God becomes something that is not beautiful.

This picture of God indwelling in Man is a very important one, which should be created already at this first stage. On the other hand I should leave out Christology at this age and only awaken the feeling of the Divine Father living in nature and in natural processes. I should try to link to this subject conversations about the Old Testament themes in particular the Psalms of David as far as they are suitable, and this they are, provided they are treated in the right way. The Psalms of David, the Song of Solomon, etc. This then would be the first stage.

When reaching the second stage in the four upper classes, destiny, human destiny would become the main theme. You must try to give the children a concrete idea of the meaning of destiny so that they can really feel that each person has his own destiny. It is important for them to be able to appreciate the difference between what may happen to a person quite accidentally and what happens by destiny. You have to deal with the question of destiny at this stage. You cannot explain by way of definition whether an occurrence happens as a result of destiny or merely accidentally. But you can illustrate this problem by giving examples. Supposing that I can feel when some event befalls me, that I had been looking for it, waiting for it, then I have an example of the working of destiny. On the other hand, if I cannot experience such an awareness, however dimly, if I feel completely caught by surprise, if I can also feel that I will learn from the happening a great deal for the future, then I am faced with a chance happening which will become destiny. Such examples will eventually enable the children to experience a feeling for the difference between 'fulfilled karma' and 'growing, becoming karma". The problem of destiny has to be treated step by step from the point of view of karma.

In the newest edition of my 'Theosophy' you will find these differences of feeling described in greater detail in the chapter 'Reincarnation and Karma', which has been entirely revised. In this chapter I tried to work out how such differences of feelings are experienced, and how there are really two kinds of happenings: In the first case you can inwardly perceive that you have really sought them out. For example, if you meet another person for the first time, you usually feel that you have been seeking him.

If, however, you are overtaken by a natural catastrophe in which you are involved, you may sense that you can learn a great deal from your experience for the future. If something happens to us through the activities of other people, we usually have a case of fulfilled karma. Even the fact that we find ourselves sitting together here in the Waldorf School as a college of teachers is a case of fulfilled karma. We have found each other because we have been seeking each other. This you cannot explain by definition, you can only experience it as an inner feeling. You must tell the children a great deal about all kinds of particular destinies, clothed in the form of stories. Especially in history you can choose examples of how destiny becomes fulfilled through the deeds of historical personages. Destiny is the right theme which will point to the depth of life.

Then I should like to make clear to you what is meant by the word 'religious' in an anthroposophical sense. This word describes our inner feelings, resulting from our world outlook, from our attitude towards the world, the spirit and life itself. One's world-conception belongs to the head, whereas the religious element springs from the entire human being. Hence a religion which depends on dogma is not truly religious at all. What matters is that the whole human being, and particularly man's feeling and willing are active in his religious life. The part which a world conception plays in any religion is there only to exemplify, to support and to deepen the feelings and the will. What should flow from a man's religion should enable him to develop his soul and to strengthen his will without dependence on transitory and earthly things.

After dealing with the question of destiny you talk to the children about the difference between what we inherit from our parents and what we bring with us from earlier earth lives. During the second stage you talk about previous earth incarnations and you collect suitable material to enable the children to grasp both with their reasoning and with their feeling that man lives on earth in repeated incarnations.

Then you should show how man can raise himself to divine realms in three stages. To sum up: After having introduced the children to the concept of destiny, slowly and with the aid of suitable stories, and also to the concept of heredity, and that of repeated earth lives, you lead over to the three spheres of the heavenly worlds: (1) The first sphere leads to the realm of the angel beings. Every individual human being has a guardian Angel. Here you speak about how each single person is guided from one incarnation to the next by his personal genius. You first deal with man's personal link to the divine worlds through the angel who is his guide. (2) You now try to explain that there are higher divine powers, the archangels, and that it is their task to direct groups of people, such as nations, etc. Here you enter by degrees into the realm of history and geography. You have to approach it in such a way that the child learns to distinguish clearly between the God of whom for instance Protestantism speaks, who in reality is only an Angel, and between the Archangel who is more sublime than the divinity which is spoken of by evangelical religious teaching.

(3) The Spirit of Time would represent the third sphere, a divine being who rules for a period of time. Here you find the link between history and religion. And only when you have introduced such matters to the children should you lead over, roughly during their twelfth year, to actual Christology. At the present we are not yet able to carry this out in our school and therefore we shall have to do it in two stages. It does not matter if the children hear at an earlier time what they will be able to understand only later on. We lead over to Christology by dividing the entire world evolution into two parts: into pre-Christian times which were a period of preparation and into the Christian era which is a time of fulfilment. What is important here is the children's recognition that the divine worlds revealed themselves through Christ in the fullness of time. Only now do you pass on to the Gospels.

Until now you have chosen stories from the Old Testament in order to elucidate the meaning of Angel, Archangel and Time Spirit. You can take the story of Moses as an example to show the children the emergence of a new Time Spirit, in contrast to the previous Time Spirit, who was the guide before the revelations of Moses. You then proceed by showing how in the sixth century BC again a new Time Spirit took over. Take the Old Testament as the basis for this period.

And when you have passed on to Christian times, after having looked upon preceding times as a period of preparation, you lead over to the Gospels, choosing various themes. However, always make it clear that the fourfoldness of the Gospels represents four points of view. Just as a tree needs to be photographed from four different sides so that a complete picture of it can be gained, so should the four Gospels of St. Matthew, at another time the Gospel of St. Mark, then again the Gospel of St. Luke and that of St. John and realise how important it is for the pupils to experience this fourfold point of view. You must look upon this difference of quality as being of greatest importance.

This then could constitute the content of the second stage. Everything which we can recognise as divine powers working through nature, revealing themselves through wisdom, should belong to the first stage. In the second stage a great change must come about: Man perceives the divine not only through wisdom but through the force of love.

These are the two leading themes for the two stages in our religion teaching." (26.9.19)

After this detailed description of the curriculum for the middle school Steiner answered questions:

Should pupils memorise passages?
"Yes, preferably from the Old Testament and later on from the New Testament. But not the kind of verses which you often find in books of prayers, for these are usually quite trivial. Take verses from the Bible and also verses from anthroposophical sources. There you can find all kinds of verses suitable for anthroposophical religious teaching." (26.9.19)

Should the Ten Commandments be learnt?
"The Ten Commandments belong to the Old Testament. You must always make the children feel the depth and gravity of such matters. I have always emphasised as do the Commandments, that the name of God should not be uttered in vain. This commandment is broken by almost every preacher in his pulpit who tends to use the name of Christ in vain on so many occasions. All this must grow in depth, matured by the right kind of feelings. Altogether religion lessons should not appeal to the head but to the heart. What matters is not the content of the Creed but the feelings which it evokes. The belief in God the Father, the Son, the Spirit is not as important as our deepest feelings of reverence towards the Father, the Son and the Spirit. This will make us feel in the depths of our soul: Not to recognise God is an illness, not to recognise the Christ is destiny or a grave misfortune, not to recognise the Spirit is a most serious limitation of the soul." (26.9.19)

A further question: Should one teach the historical development of the Zarathustra individuality up to the revelation of Christianity and the story of the two Jesus boys?

"One should conclude religion lessons with a complete account, but naturally one has to speak about these matters very carefully. The first stage represents more an aspect of nature-religion and the second stage represents more the historical side of religion." (26.9.19)

This is the first outline of the religion lessons, whose two stages cover Classes 1 to 4 and 5 to 8. However, the passage dealing with the introduction of Christology clearly shows that Christology really belongs to a third stage which should not be begun until the pupils are ready for it.

Steiner led the teachers' meetings again shortly before Christmas, on December 22nd and 23rd, but only little is known about the content of these meetings. After hearing a report by the religion teacher Steiner gave an answer of which only the following lines remain:

"Express your story content in mythical and pictorial style. Pictorial accounts should be in the foreground; try to elaborate them. Use cult-pictures (Kultbilder)." (23.12.19)

At this time the children's service was introduced for pupils taking part in the new religion lessons, for their parents and for the teachers. Only a short remark from an incomplete shorthand account remains:

"The Sunday service is given only for those pupils who take part in the non-denominational religion lessons. It is to replace the ritual of a church service for the children and their parents. End it with music." (6.3.20)

When told that a pupil who had taken part in the non-denominational religion lessons had again gone over to the Catholic religion lessons, Steiner said:

"Such withdrawals from the non-denominational religion lessons are to be avoided. Withdrawals of the ministering priests have to be accepted." (6.3.20)

During Easter 1920 Steiner gave his first pedagogical course abroad, the Basle Course for Teachers. At the end of lecture eleven there is an outline of the sectarian and the non-denominational religious instruction in the Waldorf School. (23)

On June 14th 1920 the curriculum of the religion lessons was subdivided into three stages for Classes 1 to 3, 4 to 6, 7 to 9. On the same day it was decided who would take part in the Sunday services. The curriculum for the new third stage (Classes 7 to 9) was announced on September 22nd of the same year:

"To this group composed of pupils from the seventh, eighth and ninth classes, you could explain theoretically, but in quite a free way, subjects such as pre-existence and life after death. Give them examples. Show the pupils how the great civilisations are linked together. Speak about man's mission to earth. You only need to look at Goethe's or at Jean Paul's life from this point of view. You can see, you can point out, how their gifts stem from life before birth.

Furthermore the body of Laocoon offers a very good picture which can be raised into the religious sphere and which you can explain. What really happens in the case of Laocoon is that his etheric body is withdrawing and consequently his physical body appears so distorted. There is much that can be demonstrated in this breaking up of Laocoon's physical body. One should have a group (the whole group). But you must lift up into religious feeling this awe in the presence of the dissolving human body." (22.9.20)

A class teacher reported that he had been attending a religion lesson given to his class, in order to keep discipline and that he felt like a watch dog:

"In this situation it is right to make an exception (in having a second teacher present in a lesson). By doing this we are not departing from our general principles. We must accept the fact that classes and their teachers belong together. But since these religion lessons are given to combined classes, I think it quite feasible that the class teacher concerned should be present while the subject teacher gives his lesson. The only way of solving the difficulties would be to aim at having smaller classes." (26.5.21)

Quite spontaneously Steiner made the following remarks which refer to the third stage (Classes 8, 9 and 10)

"Make this the central point of all your deliberations to which you can return again and again. Christ's life on earth is the central pivot. We must guard the personal relationship to Christ, also in the lower classes, so that it may become a kind of inward cult. Guard the children's personal relationship to the Christ! An ideal mood of worship must pervade the lessons. Symbolism and picture-forming must play their part so that the feelings will be engaged very intensively." (26.5.2 1)

During a timetable meeting for Classes 8, 9 and 10, Steiner, in speaking about the non-denominational religion lesson said:

"I have looked and looked and found no one. It is essential that the children should be divided according to classes. I want to avoid the impression that religion lessons have been added as an extra to the syllabus." (16.6.21)

During a discussion about the curriculum for Class 10, Steiner said about the religion lessons:

"We have not yet reached the point where we could study psalms in religion lessons. The ten year olds should be able to understand psalms. Have a conversation about the psalm you have chosen, a kind of inner contemplation of its content and crown it by singing it." (17.6.21)

When asked what a teacher should use after his pupils had outgrown the fairy-tale stage:

"Symbolism from themes that are taken; the significance of the festivals of the year. You will find much material in the lectures about Christmas, Easter and Whitsun. You can use most of what is said in these lectures provided you adapt their content to suit the children. Such conversations are very helpful for this particular age. It is possible to start these themes even at an earlier age and to go on with them to a later stage. Speak about the Christmas festival for a period of four weeks." (17.6.21)

(It is not clear for which class this suggestion was made.)

When asked, Steiner agreed that the teacher should use Michelangelo's pictures of the prophets. (ibid) After a question about the continuation of the religion lessons:

> "One must not believe that one can omit Christ. This must not happen."

A teacher of a different group: "I took the history of the Old Testament."

Steiner:

> "Do not take exclusively the history of the Old Testament."

When the same teacher wanted to know how he should begin Steiner gave a general survey of the themes for the two original stages:

> "We have always tried to let the phenomena of nature be the starting point of our lessons. This was a definite theme at the lower stage (comprising Classes 1 to 4) and then we went on to stories. After that we took the gospels and gradually introduced stories composed by the teachers. We then took scenes from the Gospel of St. John in greater detail. We took our beginning with a kind of nature religion. Your task will be to lead the children over in a natural way to a religious experience when discussing all kinds of other themes." (17.6.21)

On November 16th of the same year it was reported in a teachers' meeting that some teachers had arranged special times for free discussions with individual pupils, during which they could talk about problems of life. Steiner said:

> "It is not surprising that the pupils taking part in the denominational religion lessons do not avail themselves of this opportunity. Nevertheless such conversations are a good thing. You can hardly avoid that such talks have an anthroposophical flavour. You might avoid it in your religion lessons, but scarcely even there. In these discussions with individual pupils you cannot hide your anthroposophical background, neither should it be necessary to try." (16.11.21)

I should like to draw the reader's attention once more to the Dornach Christmas Course for Teachers of 1921 (27) in which in the sixteenth and last lecture a general characterisation of the religion lessons is given.

Class 11. A teacher thought that religion lessons lasting only forty-five minutes were too short. Steiner said:

> "It would do the children good to have this lesson more often. I cannot see why a lesson lasting three quarters of an hour should be too short. In my opinion it would be better if the children were reminded of religion twice a week. I would even prefer shorter but more frequent religion lessons." (28.4.22)

About the relationship of the art lessons to the religion lessons in Class 11:

> "The religion lessons ought to have quite a different quality. In art lessons everything should be directed towards an artistic appreciation, towards an understanding of the artistic element, whereas in religion lessons the chief aim in my opinion should be the creation of a truly religious mood. It is this mood which represents the pedagogical value. Formerly a great deal of effort used to be devoted to the more intellectual aspect of religion." (10. 5.22)

When the curriculum for Class 11 was given on June 21st 1922 Steiner had this to say about the free religion lessons:

> "In the presentation of your subject matter you now appeal more to the pupils' power of judgment. Encourage them to enter discussions. In earlier years the important thing was a 'picture language' but now the time has come to aim at a more conceptual understanding. You should speak about destiny from the religious point of view: about the problem of guilt and atonement: about the Father, the Son and the Holy Spirit. You progress from pictures to concepts, and this introduces into your teaching something of the nature of cause and effect." (21.6.22)

He continued:

> Classes 8 and 9 – what did we do?

A teacher: "We spoke about the statue of the Laocoon group."

Steiner:

> "It is not necessary to cover the whole of it. You have taken parts of the Gospel of St. John. It is terribly difficult to teach the children the story of creation, unless one has occupied oneself with this subject a great deal. You need not take any other chapter from the Old Testament. In doing this you can refer to St. Luke's Gospel." (21.6.22)

On June 22nd 1922 the task of the religion lessons was discussed at length. (See 22.6.22)

On December 5th 1922 the conditions were discussed under which a teacher should become eligible to give religion lessons and also to hold the children's services. (See 5.12.22)

Asked about the treatment of Parsifal in Class 11, Steiner answered:

> "In religion lessons and in history lessons the way of dealing with the subject is what matters..." (9.12.22)

Then followed a detailed description of how the Parsifal theme changed in the history of literature.

On January 17th 1923 Steiner spoke about pupils arguing for arguing's sake in religion lessons, and about the school's relationship to Anthroposophy as a world-outlook and finally about symbolism in the treatment of Parsifal.

On March 8th 1923, the Youth service and confirmation in the Christian Community were discussed.

Class 12. On April 25th 1923 the curriculum for the first Class 12 was fixed:

> "Take the historical aspect of religion. A survey of the religious evolution of humanity could be given. Start with ethnographical religions, then speak about national religions and finally about universal religions.
>
> Begin with ethnographical religions, i.e., those which are linked to a particular race, e.g., the Egyptian religions of local gods. Also in Greece local deities could be found everywhere. One has to take the theme step by step. First there are the religions in which the cult is

fixed to a definite place, the sanctuary. Then there are those, as in the case of nomadic tribes, where the tent substitutes the holy place, where the celebration of the cult becomes mobile. Here national religions emerge. And finally there are the universal religions, Buddhism and Christianity. No other religion can be called a universal religion." (25.4.23)

For Class 9:
"For Class 9 Luke's story of the apostles, the outpouring of the Holy Spirit." (ibid)

After a question about the Apocrypha:
"The children are not yet sufficiently mature for the Apocryphal Books. These contain much that is more correct than what is found in the gospels. We have always used as a supplement for the gospels what can be substantiated from the Apocryphal Books. However, great contradictions appear. When reading in one of the gospels, the children must always be ready to consult the other three. It is not at all easy to explain away the contradictions. If the children are given the Apocryphal Books as well, then nothing seems to agree any more. I should take the Acts of the Apostles." (25.4.23)

After a further question about religion in Class 10:
"Take the Gospel of St. John again. There are several possibilities; choose either Mark or Augustine. Choose the 'Confessions', where he speaks about the religious element." (25.4.23)

After a visit of outsiders Steiner said on July 12th 1923:
"The other danger is that you become much too anthroposophical. I was sitting on thorns yesterday lest these visitors should think that the history lesson has become too religious. It is not right that a history lesson should appear to be a religion lesson. For this reason we have separate religion lessons. Our guests seem to have been well-disposed towards our school. Nevertheless it could easily happen that we gain the reputation of teaching our subject matter far too much from an anthroposophical point of view." (12.7.23)

When asked what the teacher should choose as an example of folk-religion:
"Old Testament, the Hebrews." (31.7.23)

A short excerpt from the lecture held on August 15th at Ilkley:
"He who would educate in the sense of true Christianity must realise that before the age of 9 or 10 it is not possible to convey to the child's soul an understanding of what the Mystery of Golgotha brought into the world, or of all that is connected with the personality and divinity of Jesus Christ. The child is exposed to great dangers if we have failed to introduce the principle of universal divinity before this age, and by universal divinity I mean the divine Father-Principle. We must show the child how divinity is in all nature, in all human evolution, how it lives and moves not only in the stones but in the hearts of other men, in their very acts. The child must be taught, by the natural authority of the teacher, to feel gratitude and love for this universal divinity. In this way, the basis for a right attitude to the Mystery of Golgotha just between the 9th and 10th years is laid down.

You see now why it is of such infinite importance to understand the being of man from the aspect of his development in time. Try for a moment to realise what a difference there is if we teach a 7 or 8 year old child about the New Testament, or – having first stimulated a consciousness of universal divinity in the whole of nature – wait until he has reached the age of 9 $\frac{1}{2}$ or 10 before we pass to the New Testament as such. In the latter case, right preparation has been made and the Gospels will live in all their supersensible greatness. If we teach the younger child about the New Testament it will not lay hold of his whole being, but will remain mere phraseology, just so many rigid, prosaic concepts. The consequent danger is that religious feeling will harden in the child and continue through life in a rigid form, instead of in a living form which through and through pervades his feeling for the world. We prepare the child most beautifully to take into himself from the 9th and 10th years onwards, the glory of Christ Jesus if, before this age, he has been introduced to the principle of universal divinity imminent in the world." (35 lecture 10)

Steiner clarified the relationship of the free religion lessons to the Anthroposophical Society on February 5th 1924.

He declined to add anything to the children's services which would relate the ritual to the seasons.
"In this way one would preoccupy the children with an artificially induced mood."

He did not want to make the service depend on the calendar.

Asked for subject matter in religion lessons for Class 9 he answered'
"Augustine, Thomas à Kempis." (5.2.24)

In answer to a question put by a member of the audience at the Berne Course, Steiner gave a short summary of the free religion lessons which were given to children of parents who had asked for them and which were taking place side by side with the denominational religion lessons in the Waldorf School:
"First of all we had to work out a suitable curriculum for the religion lessons for these children. In the case of the Catholic and Evangelical religion lessons the responsibility lay entirely with the respective visiting teachers. The educational principles we bring to the children in these lessons are the same as underlie all the other subjects we teach as far as these are based upon a spiritual conception of man. To begin with we aim at allowing the child in his second period of life (roughly from 7 to 14) to develop in soul and spirit what quite naturally pervades his body during the first seven years. I have shown how, in the first period of life the relationship of the child's body to its surroundings is based on an attitude of nature-religion. This attitude withdraws later into the child's soul-life and as the body becomes emancipated from it, it is the task of the religion teacher to reawaken this devotion to his surroundings in the child's life of soul and spirit. This can best be achieved by trying to develop in the child a feeling for the world of the fairy-tale or the legend. Above all,

try to awaken in him a feeling of gratitude for existence itself and for the manifold beauty of the world. If such a feeling of gratitude can be engendered, one may trust that this gratitude will gradually turn into love. Out of the child's experience the moral element in him can be developed." (38)

For the new Class 12, which was to be prepared for the leaving examination in Class 13, the religion syllabus was made on April 30th 1924:

"Generally speaking, we have already outlined the character of the religion lessons. There is really nothing in what you have given me which I need to alter. We are discussing the upper classes. The climax of the religion lessons in Class 12 ought to be a survey of the world's religions, but this survey must not convey the impression that none of them are genuine. On the contrary, you ought to show their relative authenticity by choosing significant examples. So much for the ninth stage. The eight previous stages should be devoted to Christianity, but in such a way that in the ninth Christianity appears as the synthesis of all religions. Christianity itself should be studied in detail during the eighth stage, and in the ninth the world religions should be taken in such a way that they culminate once more in Christianity. For the seventh stage one ought to aim at a harmonising of the four gospels. The true nature of Christianity and its outward form should be presented. By that time the pupils will be familiar with the gospels. Briefly, seventh stage: harmonising of the gospels; eighth stage: Christianity; ninth stage: religions of the world." (30.4.24)

The following arrangement was made for the free religion lessons:

Stage 1:	Classes 1 and 2
Stage 2:	Classes 3 and 4
Stage 3:	Class 5
Stage 4:	Class 6
Stage 5:	Class 7
Stage 6:	Class 8
Stage 7:	Class 9
Stage 8:	Class 10
Stage 9:	Classes 11 and 12

When asked which selection of Bible stories should be chosen for Class 3 Steiner recommended the Bible of Schuster saying:

"It is better to give a free rendering of the stories to the children rather than to stick to the original text. One should tell these stories freely. The book merely serves as an aid to memory." (2.6.24)

When asked what the difference was between Bible stories in religion lessons and in main lessons, Steiner answered:

"You will learn a great deal if you ponder about the fact that we have to teach Bible stories in two different rent places in our curriculum. When we teach Bible stories in main lessons, we treat them as something belonging to mankind's general history. There we simply make the content of the Bible known to the children without giving it any particularly religious colouring. We treat it as a secular subject, as classical literature

amongst other classical literature, which doubtlessly it is. However, when teaching the Bible in our free religion lessons, we look upon it from a religious point of view and make it serve the development of a truly religious element. If we succeed in distinguishing tactfully between these two methods, if we can avoid giving shallow explanations in the main lessons then we should be able to learn a great deal for our own pedagogy. What matters is the 'how' and what an extraordinary difference there can be in this 'how'! – The Bible stories which have been told in class should be read again so that their knowledge becomes consolidated. I do not think that this Schuster Bible is a bad reader." (2.6.24)

On June 19th 1924 Steiner spoke in detail about the relationship of the free religion lessons to those given by the Christian Community.

In August 1924 in Torquay Steiner gave his last pedagogical lecture course. During question time he gave the following answer about the free religion lessons:

"We have a 'Method-School', we do not interfere with social life as it is at present, but through Anthroposophy we find the best method of teaching, and the school is purely a 'Method School'.

Therefore I arranged from the outset that religious instruction should not be included in our school syllabus, but that Catholic religious teaching should be delegated to the Catholic priest, and the Protestant teaching to the pastor and so on.

In the first few years most of our scholars came from a factory (The Waldorf-Astoria cigarette factory), and amongst them we had many dissenting children, children whose parents were of no religion. But our educational conscience of course demanded that a certain kind of religious instruction should be given them also. We therefore arranged a 'free religious teaching' for these children, and for this we have a special method. In these free religion lessons we first of all teach gratitude in the contemplation of everything in Nature. Whereas in the telling of legends and myths we simply relate what things do – stones, plants and so on – here in the Religion lessons we lead the child to perceive the Divine in all things. So we begin with a kind of 'religious naturalism', shall I say, in a form suited to the children.

Again, the child cannot be brought to an understanding of the Gospels before the time between the ninth and tenth years of which I have spoken. Only then can we proceed to a consideration of the Gospels in the religion lessons, going on later to the Old Testament. Up to this time we can only introduce to the children a kind of nature-religion in its general aspect, and for this we have our own methods.

Then we should go on to the Gospels but not before the ninth or tenth year, and only much later, between the twelfth and thirteenth years, we should proceed to the Old Testament.

This then is how you should think of the free religion lessons. We are not concerned with the Catholic and

Protestant instruction: we must leave that to the Catholic and Protestant pastors. Also every Sunday we have a special form of service for those who attend the free religion lessons. A service is performed and forms of worship are provided for children of different ages. What is done at these services has shown its results in practical life during the course of the years; it contributes in a very special way to the deepening of religious feeling, and awakens a mood of great devotion in the hearts of the children.

We allow the parents to attend these services, and it has become evident that this free religious teaching truly brings new life to Christianity. And there is real Christianity in the Waldorf School, because through this naturalistic religion during the early years the children are gradually led to an understanding of the Christ Mystery when they reach the higher classes." (40 Questions and Answers)

Unfortunately Steiner's outlines for religion teaching have remained incomplete. Neither did he give a list of themes for the different stages mentioned. The syllabus for the upper school was not given. However, the general outlines are clear. There only remains one difficulty: The indications given at Stuttgart put the Old Testament stories into the first stage, which is in accordance with the plan to let the Father God, the divine principle working in nature, speak to the child at the youngest stage. Most of the lecture courses held abroad agree with this plan although in the Ilkley Course the transition to Christology is put earlier than the Stuttgart courses, namely between the ninth and tenth year instead of the twelfth year. The same difference is found in the Torquay Course. However, in the Torquay Course the teaching of the Old Testament is suggested in the twelfth or thirteenth year, whereas all the other lectures dealing with this point recommend these stories to be told in the youngest classes.

SECTION 3 – OTHER ASPECTS

Quotations Relating to the Different Age Groups

The child after the change of teeth

"Up to the time of puberty the child should be laying up in his memory the treasures of thought on which mankind has pondered; afterwards is the time to penetrate with intellectual understanding what has already in earlier years been firmly impressed upon the memory. Indeed it is necessary for man, not only to remember what he already understands, but to come to understand what he already knows, in a similar way in which the child assimilates his mother tongue. This fact has a wide application." (6)

"These are the three golden rules for the development of memory:

Concepts burden the memory.

An artistic and imaginative presentation build up the memory.

Active involvement anchors the memory." (35 lecture 11)

"What the child has absorbed in a dreamlike manner through his senses out of the activities going on around him, this becomes transformed into inner pictures during his second period of life between the change of teeth and puberty. Now the child begins to experience what I should like to call dream pictures of the activities of his surroundings, whereas in his first period of life he reacted by imitating them quite directly and spontaneously. Now, however, he begins to spin dreams about the activities of his surroundings." (34 lecture 3)

"If we recognise how the child is intrinsically an imitative being, how he is a kind of ensouled sense organ which is given over to its surroundings in a bodily-religious way, then we shall aim at directing the influences which work upon him from his surroundings in such a way that he can absorb and inwardly digest them. Above all we shall have to pay heed that the child will imbibe the moral soul-spiritual background of whatever he makes his own through his senses, so that when he approaches the time of dentition we have already laid the foundations for the most important impulses of later life.

When the child enters school, approximately at the time of second dentition, he is in no way a blank sheet of paper, but rather one which already is deeply imprinted by his previous imitations. We shall have to realise during our practical pedagogical considerations here that we can put nothing new or original into the child during the time between his change of teeth and puberty, but that we must learn to recognise the impulses in him which have already been formed during his first seven years and that we must give them the direction which later life will demand. It is therefore so important for the teacher to make himself sensitive in perceiving the tender stirrings in the young, for when they enter school already a whole web of trends has been formed which he must guide and direct. He should not have somewhat-fixed opinions of what is right or wrong, or of what he ought or ought not to do, but he must learn to discriminate what lives in the child in order to guide his pupil's impulses." (34 lecture 4)

"At this stage, what matters is not that knowledge is instilled into the child, step by step, but that at certain decisive moments in his life, one brings him to undergo definite and appropriate experiences – that one helps him over what one might call certain high mountain passes in the life of man which happen to fall into the age of childhood. Such experiences can have lasting beneficial consequences for the rest of his life." (ibid lecture 5)

"From the time of the second dentition to the age of adolescence, the development of the rhythmic system – i.e., the breathing and the circulation of the blood, together with all that belongs to the regular rhythm of the digestive functions, is all-important. Whereas the teacher finds the need for pictorial imagery in the soul of the child, he has to deal with the rhythmic system as an organic bodily thing. For this reason, a pictorial, imaginative element must prevail in all that the child is given to do; a musical quality, I might even say, must pervade the relationship between teacher and pupil. Rhythm, measure, even melody must be there as the basic principle of the teaching, and this demands that the teacher have this musical quality himself, in his whole life.

It is the rhythmic system that predominates in the child's organic nature during this first period of school life, and the entire teaching must follow a certain rhythm. The teacher must have this musical element so deeply in him, that true rhythm may prevail in the classroom." (35 lecture 7)

"Only from the 9th to approximately the 12th year, i.e., during the second life-period, do we begin to train the pupil's self-consciousness. And this we do by introducing grammar, for at this stage, after having undergone the changes which I have just characterised, the child is in a position to bring to his self-consciousness what grammar can reveal to him. We begin with the parts of speech, and after that we take animal study, as I have illustrated it with the examples of cuttle fish, mouse and man. Only later do we take the study of plants, as you will demonstrate it this afternoon.

"Further at this stage in the life of the human being we can go on to geometry, whereas we have hitherto restricted the elements of geometry to drawing. In drawing, of course, we can evolve for him the triangle, the square, the circle, the line. That is, we evolve the actual forms in drawing, by drawing them and then saying: This is a triangle, this is a square. But what geometry adds to these, with its search for the relations between the forms, is only introduced at about nine years old. At the same time, of course, the foreign language is continued and becomes part of the grammar teaching. Last of all we introduce the child to physics." (12 lecture 10)

"When the child reaches his ninth or tenth year he begins to differentiate himself from his environment. For the first time there is a difference between subject and object; subject is what belongs to oneself, object is what belongs to the other person or other thing; and now we can begin to speak of external things as such, whereas before this time we must treat them as though these external objects formed one whole together with the child's own body." (40 lecture 3)

"At this stage, between the 9th and 12th years, the child is ready to meet the outside world if it is brought to him in a pictorial form. Until approximately his 9th year, he wants actively to participate in the picture; at that stage he does not let the picture approach him from without. But now the teacher must always work in such a living way that what he and the child do together makes a harmonious picture. In fact, this working together of teacher and pupil must in itself be a picture. This does not necessarily mean working at actual pictures or at something else. The working together, the lessons themselves, must form a picture. So between the 9th and 10th year the child develops a special sense for the pictorial element. This pictorial element needs to be made use of and it gives the teacher the possibility to introduce the children in a suitable way to the world of the plants and animals. And the more the teacher is able to represent in a truly imaginative manner what is usually found to be completely devoid of any pictorial element in our botanical text books, the better for the child aged from 9 to 12. To succeed in transforming one's subject matter into true pictures, this is what can bring a sense of achievement and satisfaction. For if one tries to translate the plant world with its manifold forms into pictures, one has to be creatively working together with the powers of creation." (34 lecture 5)

"Until about the twelfth year the child has no understanding whatsoever of the concept of causality. He perceives what is mobile, ideas which have movement. He is open to the pictorial, musical element; this he perceives. But the concept of causality means nothing to him until about the twelfth year. In all that we bring to the child up to this age therefore, we must leave the concept of causality entirely out of account. Only then can we begin to reckon on the child having some comprehension of the general connections between causes and effects.

Only then does he begin to form thoughts, for up to this

time he has mental pictures. Now however, there begins to light up what at the age of puberty appears in its completeness, the life of thought and of the judgment which, in a narrower sense, is bound up with thought. The life of the child between the change of teeth and puberty, is bound up with feeling; and the life before the change of teeth with an inwardly unfolding willing, which at this age is not influenced by thoughts, but by the imitation of what comes to meet him. But together with what approaches the child in a bodily sense, the moral, the spiritual element within the physical, also takes firm hold of him. This is why in the tenth to eleventh year and usually in the eleventh to twelfth years too, it is impossible to bring to the child what must depend upon the concept of causality." (34 lecture 5)

"After puberty, when the child has reached his fifteenth or sixteenth year, a change takes place in his inner nature, leading him from dependence upon authority to his own sense of freedom and hence to the faculty of independent judgment and insight. Here is something that must claim our most watchful attention in education and teaching. If, before puberty, we have awakened the child's feeling for good and evil, for what is and is not divine, these feelings will arise from his own inner being afterwards. His understanding, intellect, insight and power of judgment are uninfluenced, he can now form independent judgments from out of his own being.

If we start by telling the child that he ought to do this and ought to do that, it all remains with him through his later years and then he will always be thinking that such and such a thing is wrong. Convention will colour everything. Now in true education today, the human being should not stand within the conventional but have his own judgment even about morality and religion, and this will unfold naturally if it has not been prematurely engaged.

At the Waldorf School we allow the child of fourteen or fifteen to find his own feet in life. We put him really on a par with ourselves. He unfolds his judgment but he still looks back to the authority which we represented and retains the affection he had for us when we were his teachers. His power of judgment has not been fettered if we have merely worked upon his life of feeling. And so, when the child has reached the age of fourteen or fifteen, we leave his nature of soul and spirit in freedom and, in the higher classes, appeal to his own power of judgment and insight. This freedom in life cannot be achieved by inculcating morality and religion in a dogmatic, canonical fashion but by working simply and solely on the child's powers of feeling and perception at the right age – the period between the change of teeth and puberty – The great thing is to enable the human being to find his place in the world with due confidence in his own power of judgment. He will then feel and sense his complete manhood because his education has been truly and completely human...

Children of fourteen or fifteen, educated according to modern methods, begin to be aware of a sense of mutilation if they are not permeated with the qualities of moral judgment and religious feeling. Something seems lacking in their manhood. There is no better heritage in the moral and religious sense than to bring children up to regard the elements of morality and religion as such an integral part of their being, that they do not feel themselves wholly man if they are not permeated with morality, warmed through and through by religion." (35 lecture 12)

"At the right age they will awaken their own free sense of religion and morality which will then become part of their very being. And they feel that only this can make them fully man. The great aim at the Waldorf School is to bring up free human beings who know how to direct their own lives." (35 lecture 12)

2 The Decoration of Classrooms

"How it is to be deplored, my dear friends, that the schoolrooms for our children are a veritably barbaric environment for their young hearts and minds. Imagine every school room, not decorated in the way often thought artistic today, but shaped by an artist in such a way that each single form is in harmony with what his eye should fall upon when the child is learning his tables.

Thoughts that are to be socially effective cannot work socially unless, while they are being formed, there flows into the soul as a side-stream of the spiritual life what comes from a really living environment. For this however, art needs to take a quite different course during the children's growing years from what is now accorded it... As I have already said, just as a reasonable school system, thinking more of concentration than of a wretched timetable, would give the human being an

independent power of understanding and reason, so real permeation by social art of our community throug education would give us a true culture of the will. Fo no-one can have will who has not had it drawn out by genuinely artistic education." (9 lecture 3)

More details of Steiner's suggestions for classroom colour and pictures can be found in Hedwig Hauck's book "Hand work and Handicrafts, Rudolf Steiner's Indications".

When the school was opened in the old house on "Uhlandshöhe" in 1919, the walls were plastered red and pictures were not available. When in the summer of 1920 the first part of the barracks could be used, Rudolf Steiner suggested a lilac colour with a blue tinge for the first four classrooms and indigo for the provisional singing-room. The colours were to be shaded lighter upwards towards the ceiling in three steps. As it was likely that the classrooms had to be changed year by year, it was not possible to give a definite colour for each class. This situation changed in the Spring of 1922 when part of the big school building was completed. Rudolf Steiner inspected the finished classrooms with me. The three lowest classes were to remain in the big barrack and the classrooms there were to keep the old lilac shades. All other classes were to move into the new building. This is the reason why the column headed: New building 1922 only begins with class 4. (See list on page 145).

Steiner made new suggestions for the two other schools which had newly opened in Hamburg-Wandsbeck and in London. Although these indications differ from the ones made for the Stuttgart school, they do have in common the fact that all first classes were to be painted in colours representing the red end of the spectrum whereas the upper classes were to be painted in violet or lilac shades. On 29th July 1920 a light bluish lilac colour was suggested for the classroom desks. This was done at first but proved impracticable because of the necessity of exchanging classroom furniture. (See list on page 145).

3 Steiner's Indications for Classroom Colours

	Hut	Waldorf School New Building	New School (Michael Hall)	Hamburg
Class 1			5-6 years: red-yellow, orange	red: progressively lighter
Class 2			7-8 years: green	
Class 3				
Class 4	bluish-	light green	9 years: darker green	orange progressively lighter
Class 5	lilac	green towards blue	10-11 years: blue	
Class 6	colours	blue		
Class 7		indigo		yellow
Class 8		violet		green: lighter in 9 than in 8
Class 9		violet		
Class 10 –		lilac		blue: approaching violet in 11
Class 11 –		lilac, lighter than gymnasium		
Class 12 –				violet
Eurythmy Room –		mauve	light violet	
Physics Room –		blue		green
Passages	yellow	reddish lilac	yellow	
Choir Practice Room	indigo			lilac
Gymnasium –		reddish lilac		
School Doctor's Room –		reddish		

4 Classroom Pictures

Steiner's suggestions of 31.1.23

Class 1		Fairy tale pictures
Class 2		Pictures of legends
Class 3		Still life, i.e., plants
Class 4		Animals
Class 5		Groups of people of different ages (choose pictures which help to stimulate an awareness of what passes between one person and another)
Class 6		The individual man, heads, figures, man in nature
Classes 7 and 8		Raphael and Leonardo
Class 9	a)	Giotto or similar styles
	b)	Technical plans of situations or sky maps
Class 10	a)	Holbein, Dürer
	b)	The interior of the seas
Class 11	a)	Holbein, Dürer or older painters, Rembrandt
	b)	Geological cross–sections, relief-maps
Class 12	a)	Holbein, Dürer, Rembrandt
	b)	Physiological-anatomical diagrams
Music Room		Sculptures
		Paintings: only pure colour effects
Eurythmy Room		Dynamic of man's soul
Gym Hall		Man's relationship to the world from the aspect of balance and movement
Handwork		Pictures of interiors, with a suitable soul atmosphere
Handicrafts, Spinning		Artistic themes from practical life and from handicrafts
Frames		Make frames to suit the pictures. Use colours for the frames which are also found in the pictures.